MY FAVORITE RECIPES

Staff Home Economists
CULINARY ARTS INSTITUTE

Melanie De Proft
Director

JERRINE LEICHHARDT

MARIE ABDISHO • YVONNE NEHLS • PATRICIA TURNER

SHIRLEY KOPECKY • RUTH RUST

LOUISE BABITZKE • ELAINE BECHTEL

KATHRYN CLIFFORD • SHERRILL CORLEY • MARY NELSON

MITZI OKAMOTO • CARMEN TOWNER

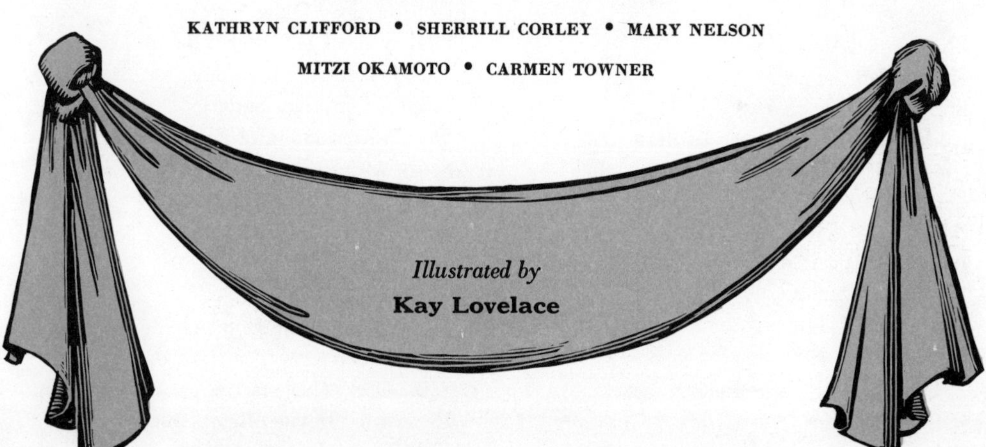

SPENCER PRESS • Chicago, Illinois

1974 Edition

International Standard Book Number: 0-8326-0537-9

Manufactured in the United States of America

Acknowledgments

For the beautiful and valuable photographs which illustrate the recipes in this cookbook, we gratefully acknowledge the generous cooperation of:

Ac′ cent
American Can Company
American Dairy Association
American Honey Institute
American Meat Institute
The Apple Kitchen
Ball Brothers Company
Blueberry Institute
Blue Bonnet Margarine
The Borden Company
Brer Rabbit Molasses
California Foods Research Institute
Campbell Soup Company
Corning Glass Works
Corn Products Refining Company
Delaware State Poultry Commission
Evaporated Milk Association
General Mills, Inc.
Idle Wild Farm's
Rock Cornish Game Hens
Kellogg Company
Kraft Foods Company
Kretschmer Wheat Germ
Minute Rice
Minute Tapioca
Nancy Haven's Beet Sugar Kitchen
National Biscuit Company
National Dairy Council
National Fisheries Institute
National Live Stock and Meat Board
Pan-American Coffee Bureau
Poultry and Egg National Board
The Quaker Oats Company
Sealtest Consumer Service
Shrimp Association of the Americas
South African Rock Lobster Association
Sugar Information, Inc.
Sunkist Growers
Swans Down Cake Flour
Swift and Company
Tea Council of the U. S. A., Inc.
Tru-Blu Berries—
Blueberry Cooperative Association
Underwood Deviled Ham
United Fruit Company
Wheat Flour Institute

Contents

There's No Substitute for Accuracy

Read recipe carefully.

Assemble all ingredients and utensils.

Select pans of proper kind and size. Measure pans inside, from rim to rim.

Use standard measuring cups and spoons. Use liquid measuring cups (rim above 1-cup line) for liquids. Use nested or dry measuring cups (1-cup line even with top) for dry ingredients.

Check liquid measurements at eye level.

Level dry measurements with straight-edged knife or spatula.

Sift all flour except whole-grain types before measuring. Spoon lightly into measuring cup. Do not jar cup.

Preheat oven 12 to 20 minutes at required temperature. Leave oven door open first 2 minutes.

Beat whole eggs until thick and piled softly when recipe calls for well-beaten eggs.

Beat egg whites as follows: *Frothy*—entire mass forms bubbles; *Rounded peaks*—peaks turn over slightly when beater is slowly lifted upright; *Stiff peaks*—peaks remain standing when beater is slowly lifted upright.

Beat egg yolks until thick and lemon-colored when recipe calls for well-beaten egg yolks.

Place oven rack so top of product will be almost at center of oven. Stagger pans so no pan is directly over another and they do not touch each other or walls of oven. Place single pan so that center of product is near center of oven.

Covering foods to be stored in the refrigerator will depend upon the type of refrigerator used.

For These Recipes—What To Use

AC'CENT—the brand of monosodium glutamate which is available everywhere through retail grocery stores. It is a basic seasoning, produced solely from natural sources, which is popularly used because of its unique property of improving natural food flavors without adding flavor of its own. Ac'cent is the registered trademark of International Minerals & Chemical Corporation.

BAKING POWDER—double-action type.

BREAD CRUMBS—one slice fresh bread equals about 1 cup soft crumbs or cubes. One slice dry or toasted bread equals about ¾ cup dry cubes or ⅓ cup fine, dry crumbs.

BUTTERED CRUMBS—soft or dry bread or cracker crumbs tossed in melted butter or margarine.

Use 1 to 2 tablespoons butter or margarine for 1 cup soft crumbs and 2 to 4 tablespoons butter or margarine for 1 cup dry crumbs.

CHOCOLATE—unsweetened chocolate.

CORNSTARCH—thickening agent. One tablespoon has the thickening power of 2 tablespoons flour.

CREAM—light, table or coffee cream, containing not less than 18% butter fat.

HEAVY or WHIPPING CREAM—containing not less than 36% butter fat.

FLOUR—all-purpose (hard wheat) flour. (In some southern areas where a blend of soft wheat is used, better products may result when minor adjustments are made in recipes. A little less liquid or more flour may be needed.) If cake flour is required, recipe will so state.

GRATED PEEL—whole citrus fruit peel finely grated through colored part only; white is bitter.

CROUTONS—slices or cubes of toasted bread, plain or browned in melted butter.

HERBS and SPICES—ground unless specified.

HERB BOUQUET—a bunch of aromatic herbs (such as a piece of celery with leaves, a sprig of thyme and 3 or 4 sprigs of parsley) tied neatly together and used to flavor soups, stews, braised dishes and sauces. Enclose fine, dry herbs in cheesecloth bag.

JULIENNE STRIPS—vegetables, meat or poultry cut into narrow strips.

LEEK—long bulb with flavor like that of an onion but milder and sweeter. Used mainly in soups. In light soups use white part only.

PEPPERCORNS—the dried berries of the pepper plant; used in pepper grinder or whole.

OIL—salad, cooking. Use olive oil only when recipe states.

ROTARY BEATER—hand-operated (Dover type) beater or electric mixer.

SCALLION—young green or "stick" onion.

SHALLOT—a member of the onion family; the small pear-shaped bulb of the shallot is milder in flavor than onions.

SHORTENING—a hydrogenated vegetable shortening, all-purpose shortening, butter or margarine. Use lard or oil when specified.

SOUR MILK—sweet milk added to 1 tablespoon vinegar or lemon juice in measuring cup up to 1-cup line and stirred well; or use buttermilk.

SUGAR—granulated (beet or cane).

VINEGAR—cider vinegar or use type of vinegar specified in recipe.

(See section introductions for information about specific types of food preparation.)

How To Do It

BASTE—spoon liquid (or use baster) over cooking food to add moisture and flavor.

BLANCH NUTS—the flavor of nuts is best maintained when nuts are allowed to remain in water the shortest possible time during blanching. Therefore, blanch only about ½ cup at a time; repeat as many times as necessary for larger amounts.

Bring to rapid boiling enough water to well cover shelled nuts. Drop in nuts. Turn off heat and allow nuts to remain in the water about 1 min.; drain or remove with fork or slotted spoon. Place between folds of absorbent paper; pat dry. Gently squeeze nuts with fingers to remove skins; or peel. Place on dry absorbent paper. To dry thoroughly, frequently shift nuts to dry spots on paper.

GRATE NUTS—use a rotary-type grater with hand-operating crank. Follow manufacturer's directions. Grated nuts should be fine and light.

GRIND NUTS—put nuts through medium blade of food chopper. Or use electric blender, grinding enough nuts at one time to cover blades. Cover blender container. (Turning motor off and on helps to throw nuts back onto blades.) Grind nuts until particles are still dry enough to remain separate—not oily and compact. Empty container and grind next batch.

TOAST NUTS—place nuts in a shallow baking dish or pie pan and brush lightly with cooking oil. Heat in oven at 350°F until delicately browned. Move and turn nuts occasionally. Or add blanched nuts to a heavy skillet in which butter (about 1 tablespoon per cup of nuts) has been melted; or use oil. Brown lightly over medium heat, constantly turning and moving nuts with a spoon.

SALT NUTS—toast nuts; drain on absorbent paper and sprinkle with salt.

BOIL—cook in liquid in which bubbles rise continually and break on the surface. Boiling temperature of water at sea level is 212°F.

BOILING WATER BATH—set a deep pan on oven rack and place the filled baking dish in pan. Pour boiling water into pan to level of mixture in baking dish. Prevent further boiling by using given oven temperature.

CHILL GELATIN MIXTURES—set dissolved gelatin mixture in refrigerator or in pan of ice and water. If mixture is placed over ice and water, stir frequently; if placed in refrigerator, stir occasionally. Chill gelatin mixtures until slightly thicker than consistency of thick, unbeaten egg white. Then add the remainder of ingredients, such as chopped or whole foods which would sink to the bottom of the mold if the gelatin were not sufficiently thickened. When gelatin mixture is already thick because of ingredients or is not a clear mixture, chill mixture until it begins to gel (gets slightly thicker) before adding chopped or whole foods.

UNMOLD GELATIN—run tip of knife around top edge of mold to loosen. Invert mold onto chilled serving plate. If necessary, wet a clean towel in hot water and wring it almost dry. Wrap hot towel around mold for a few seconds only. If mold does not loosen, repeat.

CLEAN CELERY—trim roots and cut off leaves. Leaves may be used for added flavor in soups and stuffings; leaves may be left on inner stalks when serving as relish. Separate stalks, remove blemishes and wash. Then proceed as directed in recipe.

CLEAN GARLIC—separate into cloves and remove outer (thin, papery) skin.

CLEAN GREEN or RED PEPPERS—rinse and cut into quarters. Remove stem, all white fiber and seeds with spoon or knife; rinse. Prepare as directed in recipe.

CLEAN and SLICE MUSHROOMS—wipe with a clean, damp cloth and cut off tips of stems; slice lengthwise through stems and caps.

CLEAN ONIONS (dry)—cut off root end and a thin slice from stem end; peel and rinse. Prepare as directed in recipe.

CRUSH CRUMBS—place cookies, crackers, zweiback or the like on a long length of heavy waxed paper. Loosely fold paper around material to be crushed, tucking under open ends. With a rolling pin, gently crush to make fine crumbs. Or place crackers or cookies in a plastic bag and crush.

If using electric blender, break 5 or 6 crackers, cookies or the like into blender container. Cover container. Blend on low speed, flicking motor on and off until crumbs are medium fine. Empty container and repeat blending until desired amount of crumbs is obtained.

CINNAMON SUGAR—mix thoroughly ¼ cup sugar and 2 teaspoons cinnamon. Use to sugar doughnuts, cookies or toast.

CUT MARSHMALLOWS or DRIED FRUITS (uncooked)—with scissors dipped frequently in water to avoid stickiness.

DICE—cut into small cubes.

FLAKE FISH—with a fork separate cooked fresh or canned fish into flakes (thin, layer-like pieces). Remove bony tissue from crab meat; salmon bones are edible.

FLUTE EDGE of PASTRY—press index finger on edge of pastry, then pinch pastry with thumb and index finger of other hand. Lift fingers and repeat procedure to flute around entire edge.

FOLD—use flexible spatula and slip it down side of bowl to bottom. Turn bowl quarter turn. Lift spatula through mixture along side of bowl with blade parallel to surface. Turn spatula over to fold lifted mixture across material on surface. Cut down and under; turn bowl and repeat process until material seems blended. With every fourth stroke, bring spatula up through center.

GRATE CHOCOLATE—use a rotary-type grater with hand-operating crank. Follow manufacturer's directions. Grated chocolate should be fine and light. Grated chocolate melts more rapidly.

MELT CHOCOLATE—melt over simmering water to avoid scorching.

MARINATE—allow food to stand in liquid (usually a seasoned oil and acid mixture) to impart additional flavor.

MEASURE BROWN SUGAR—pack firmly into measuring cup so that sugar will hold shape of cup when turned out.

MINCE—cut or chop into small, fine pieces.

POUND MEAT—to increase tenderness in less tender cuts of meat, place meat on flat working surface and repeatedly pound meat on one side with meat hammer; turn meat and repeat process. Meat may also be pounded with the edge of a heavy saucer or plate.

PREPARE DOUBLE-STRENGTH COFFEE BEVERAGE—prepare coffee in usual manner (method and grind of coffee depending upon type of coffee maker), using 4 measuring tablespoons coffee per standard measuring cup water. Use 6 measuring tablespoonsful for **triple-strength coffee.**

PREPARE QUICK BROTH—dissolve in 1 cup hot water, 1 chicken bouillon cube for **quick chicken broth** or 1 beef bouillon cube or ½ teaspoon concentrated meat extract for **quick meat broth.**

PREPARE QUICK-COOKING RICE—carefully follow directions on package for amount and timing when using packaged precooked rice.

REDUCE LIQUID—continue cooking the liquid until the amount is sufficiently decreased, thus concentrating flavor and sometimes thickening the original liquid. Simmer when wine is used; boil rapidly for other liquids.

RICE—force food through ricer, sieve or food mill.

SIEVE—force through coarse sieve or food mill.

SCALD MILK—heat in top of double boiler over simmering water just until a thin film appears.

SIMMER—cook in a liquid just below boiling point; bubbles form slowly and break below surface.

WHIP CREAM—(for use as topping or filling or as an ingredient in a cake) chill bowl, beater and whipping cream. Pour chilled cream into chilled bowl. Using chilled beater, beat (on high speed if using electric mixer) until soft peaks are formed when beater is slowly lifted upright. If whipped cream is to be incorporated into a frozen or refrigerator dessert or salad, beat only until of medium consistency (piles softly).

The maximum amount of cream that should be whipped at one time is 1½ cups. If recipe calls for more than 1½ cups whip 1 cup at a time. Whipping cream doubles in volume when whipped.

OVEN TEMPERATURES—Use a portable oven thermometer for greater accuracy of oven temperatures.

Very slow	250°F to 275°F
Slow	300°F to 325°F
Moderate	350°F to 375°F
Hot	400°F to 425°F
Very Hot	450°F to 475°F
Extremely Hot	500°F to 525°F

WHEN YOU BROIL—Set temperature control of range at Broil (500°F or higher). Distance from top of food to source of heat determines the intensity of heat upon food.

WHEN YOU DEEP-FRY—About 20 min. before ready to deep-fry, fill a deep saucepan one-half to two-thirds full with hydrogenated vegetable shortening, all-purpose shortening, lard or cooking oil for deep-frying. Heat fat slowly to temperature given in recipe. A deep-frying thermometer is an accurate guide for deep-frying temperatures.

If thermometer is not available, the following bread cube method may be used: A 1-in. cube of bread browns in 60 seconds at 350°F to 375°F.

If using automatic deep-fryer, follow manufacturer's directions for amount of fat and timing.

WHEN USING THE ELECTRIC BLENDER—Cover blender container before starting and stopping motor to avoid splashing. To aid even mixing, frequently scrape down sides of container with a rubber spatula, first stopping motor.

To grind, put in blender container enough food at one time to cover blades. Cover; turn on motor and grind until very fine. Turning motor off and on helps to throw food back on blades. Empty container and grind next batch of food.

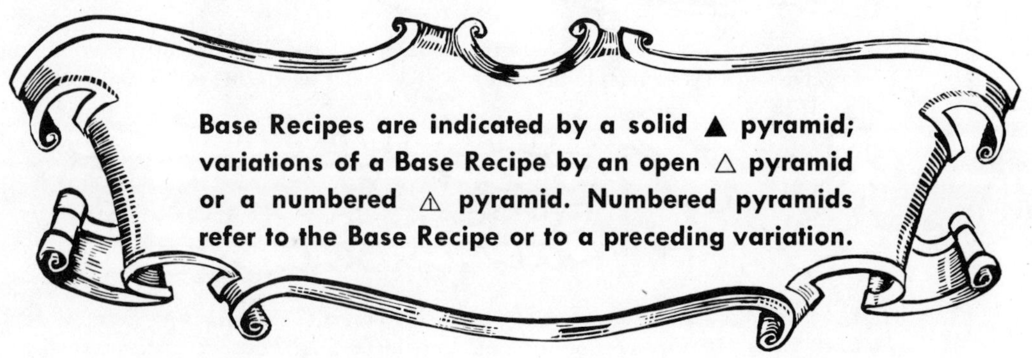

How to Make and Use a Pastry Bag

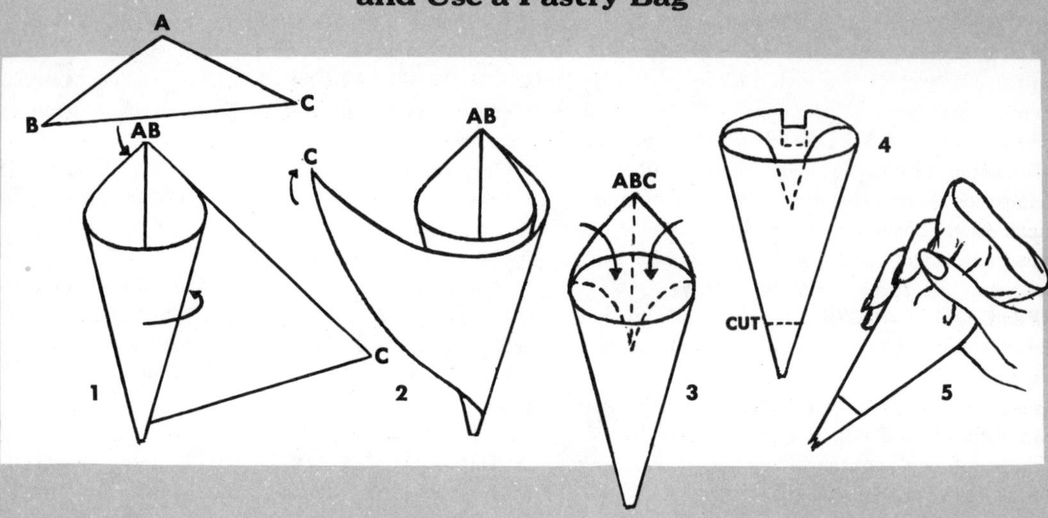

To Make a Pastry Bag: Cut a 24x17x17-inch triangle from parchment paper. Bring points A and B together (1). Bring C around cone so that A, B and C meet (2). Fold point ABC into cone (3) and cut a tab in rim; fold tab outward. Trim ½ to ¾ inch from tip (4). Insert tube indicated in recipe into tip; fill bag half-full; hold bag as in (5) and press. Practice with lard on the back of a cake pan.

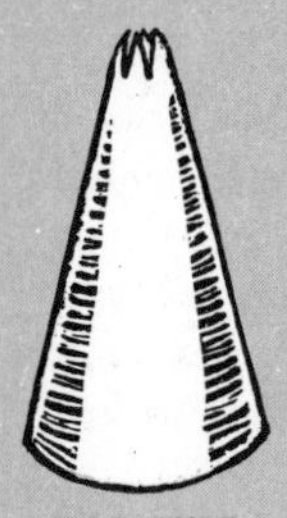

STAR TUBE

Use star tubes for rosettes (1,2,3), border (4) or writing (5). Use small decorating star tubes (No. 27) for small decorations; plain star tubes (Nos. 1-3) for larger ones.

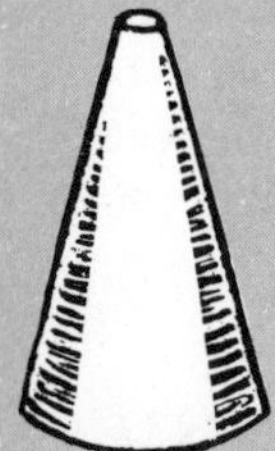

WRITING TUBE

Use decorating tubes Nos. 1, 2 or 3 to form forget-me-nots (1) or lilies-of-the-valley (2) with dots and lines. Or use for writing (3); sketch words first with wooden pick.

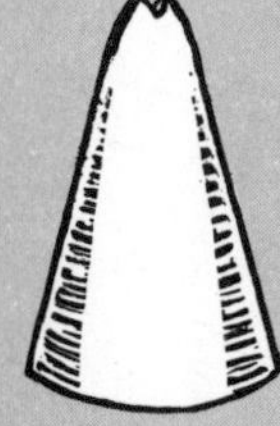

LEAF TUBE

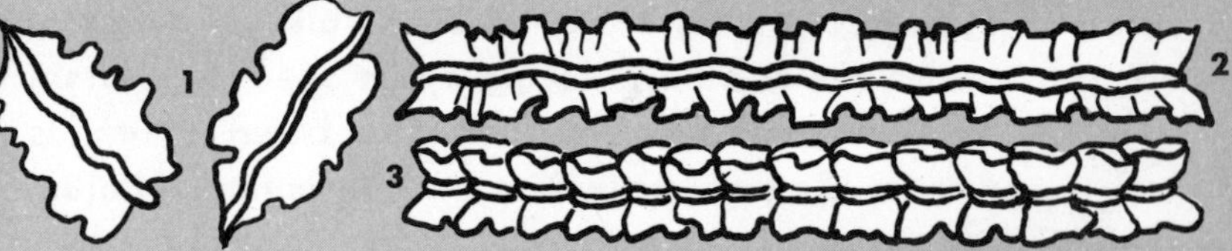

Use leaf tubes such as 65, 66 and 67 to taper leaves (1); vary pressure on bag. For border (2) use steady pressure; hold at angle. For (3) use overlapping motion.

Freezing Baked Products

One of the greatest conveniences of owning a freezer is to have on hand a variety of baked products—ready to be baked or baked.

Remember that freezer space is at a premium, so make efficient use of each inch of storage space. Freezing does not generally improve the quality of a product; therefore, for freezing choose only foods and ingredients of *high quality*.

A rapid turnover of frozen food indicates good management of freezer storage space. Date on label insures proper rotation of food. Keep an up-to-date record of freezer contents.

Thawed frozen foods should not be refrozen.

The best efforts in freezing will be in vain if the food is not protected by proper packaging. And a tight seal is of utmost importance for a successful frozen product.

There are many excellent products on the market—bags, cartons, jars and wrapping materials. In choosing, some important factors to be considered are: proper size, shape and material for the specific food to be frozen, ease of handling and economy of price and space. The packaging material should also be waterproof, moisture-vapor-proof and, when necessary, greaseproof.

The food package should be clearly labeled to indicate contents and date of freezing.

Quick Breads—These may be frozen before or after baking. In general, freezing after baking gives a more desirable product and a longer freezer storage time. Wrap the cooled, baked product in freezer material; seal, label and freeze. If it is to be served hot, place wrapped frozen product in oven until thoroughly heated; if not, thaw in wrapping material at room temperature.

Yeast Breads and Rolls—These may be frozen before or after baking. However, the volume of the product is usually greater if frozen after baking. Cool the baked product on a cooling rack, wrap in freezer material, seal, label and freeze. Place wrapped frozen bread or rolls in oven until thoroughly heated.

Cookies—Most types of cookies freeze satisfactorily whether frozen before or after baking. Meringue-type cookies do not freeze well. Cool baked cookies; then wrap, seal, label and freeze. Thaw in wrapping material at room temperature. Form cookie dough into rolls; wrap tightly in freezer material, seal, label and freeze. Thaw dough slightly in refrigerator, cut into slices and bake.

Butter-type Cakes—These cakes may be frozen in the batter state or after baking. Pour batter into freezer containers; seal, label and freeze. To bake: Place in refrigerator or at room temperature until just soft; turn into prepared pans and let stand at room temperature 10 to 20 min. longer and bake as directed for the individual cake. Cool baked cakes before freezing; wrap, seal, label and freeze. Thaw in wrapping material at room temperature or in a slow oven.

Angel Food and Sponge Cakes—These cakes are very successful if baked and then frozen. Wrap the cooled cake and seal, being careful not to crush the cake. Place in a sturdy box; label and freeze. Thaw the frozen cake in wrapping material in a slow oven for 20 to 30 min. (if manufacturer advises). Cool to room temperature and serve immediately. Or thaw cake at room temperature.

Pies—Chiffon pies are high on the list of pies suitable for freezing. They keep very well when frozen in baked shells. Cream pies may be frozen in baked shells, but without the meringue. Custard-type pies do not freeze successfully. Freeze chiffon and cream pies before wrapping; place in protective container, seal, label and return to freezer. Serve chiffon pies chilled rather than at room temperature. Pile meringue on frozen cream pies and bake until meringue is lightly browned.

In fruit fillings increase the flour or cornstarch, depending upon juiciness of the fruit. If fruit pies are frozen before baking, the top crusts should not be slit or pricked until after 10 min. of baking time. To freeze a two-crust pie, invert a pie pan of identical size over the prepared pie. Wrap in cellophane; heat-seal by using a warm iron, curling iron or a piece of equipment made especially for this purpose. Wrap in heavy paper to avoid damage to cellophane, label and freeze. Remove wrapping paper, cellophane and the inverted pie pan and bake as directed for specific pie.

Cool baked pie before freezing; place in protective container, seal, label and freeze.

Outdoor Cooking

Cooking outdoors is one of the most ancient and romantically satisfying ways of cooking; it is an adventure that never palls. All that is needed to become an expert in this increasingly popular kind of cooking is knowledge of a few rules.

EQUIPMENT—Basic equipment is a grill. This may be a small, inexpensive one or a more elaborate one with a motorized rotary spit and other accessories. The hooded grill intensifies the heat, shortens the cooking time and is the most practical grill for spit-roasting. Remember to remove the spit from the grill when preparing the fire and to fasten the meat or poultry securely to the spit.

Additional equipment should include useful items such as: long-handled tools with heat resistant handles (forks, spoons, turners, tongs), asbestos or well-padded mitts, a baster (which doubles as a douser if fat flares in the fire), a wooden cutting board, a sharp knife, a pot for marinades or sauces, a basting brush and paper towels. Skewers, a skillet (with a long handle), a steak broiler and a spit attachment are pieces of equipment that expand outdoor culinary skills

FUEL AND FIRE—Charcoal lumps or briquets or hard woods are fuels preferred by experts. Never use soft woods because they give food a tarry soot coating and do not give a satisfactory bed of coals. Start with a good bed of charcoal, 2 to 3 inches deep or enough to last the entire cooking period. Wait for the coals to burn to a gray color with a ruddy glow underneath (at least 30 minutes). A handful of dampened hickory chips tossed onto a charcoal fire just before grilling will give a superb flavor to anything you grill. The distance from the top of the coals to the foods helps determine the degree of heat. *Timing of cooking period will vary with the size of the firebox, degree of heat, amount and direction of wind and the type of grill used.* Timing and distances suggested are only guides.

GRILLING AND SPIT-ROASTING—Many foods that can be broiled in the kitchen can be grilled outside. Meat and poultry that can be roasted in the kitchen oven will adapt well to spit roasting.

Steak—Sirloin, porterhouse, T-bone or rib, cut 1½ in. thick. Grill 3 in. from coals on greased grill about 6 min. on each side. To test doneness slit meat near bone and note color of meat.

Hamburgers—Grill patties in greased steak broiler or on greased grill 5 in. from coals 4 to 6 min. on each side, depending upon thickness of burger.

Frankfurters—On the grill, in a roaster, in a skillet, in aluminum foil or on a skewer; turn frequently until lightly browned and heated through.

Roast Beef—Boned, rolled rib roast of beef with good layer of fat around outside or an additional layer of suet tied around it. Use motorized rotary spit. Roast 12 in. from coals, allowing 25 min. per pound for medium doneness; brush frequently with barbecue sauce. Test for doneness by cutting slit in meat and noting color of meat.

Chicken—Broiling chicken, about 1½ lbs. ready-to-cook weight, split into halves. Grill, cut side down, on grill 3 in. from coals 10 min. on each side, brushing frequently with Lemon Butter Sauce (*page 185*) or seasoned melted butter, or until chicken tests done—meat on thickest part of drumstick cuts easily and shows no pink color.

Trout—Small, about 10 oz. each. Wrap in bacon and grill in basket steak broiler 3 in. from coals, turning once, until bacon is very crisp (about 7 min.). Trout will then be cooked.

Rock-Lobster Tails—Thaw and prepare as for Broiled Rock-Lobster Tails, *page 123.* Grill, shell-side down, 4 in. from coals, brushing frequently with Lemon Butter Sauce, 10 min., or until shell is charred. Turn and continue grilling 6 min., or until meat is completely white and opaque.

Vegetables—Wet Spanish or Bermuda *onions* thoroughly and place on grill. Roll onions around occasionally. They are done when black on outside and soft and creamy on inside (about 50 min.).

Loosen husks only enough to remove silk and blemishes from ears of *corn;* dip ears in water. Shake well; rewrap husks around corn. Let ears stand in water until husks are soaked (about 1 hr.). Roast, turning often, on grill until corn is tender (about 15 min.).

Wash, scrub and wipe dry *potatoes;* rub entire surface with fat. Loosely wrap each potato in heavy aluminum foil; seal open ends with double fold. Bake on grill 1 hr., or until potatoes are soft when pressed with fingers (protected from heat by mitt). Turn several times.

Measurements and Equivalents

Dash	Less than ⅛ teaspoon (about 6 drops)
A few grains	Less than ⅛ teaspoon
60 drops	1 teaspoon
3 teaspoons	1 tablespoon
¼ cup	4 tablespoons
⅓ cup	5 tablespoons plus 1 teaspoon
½ cup	8 tablespoons
⅔ cup	10 tablespoons plus 2 teaspoons
¾ cup	12 tablespoons
1 cup	16 tablespoons
1 cup	8 fluid ounces
2 cups	1 pint
4 cups	1 quart
4 quarts	1 gallon
8 quarts	1 peck
4 pecks	1 bushel
16 ounces (*dry measure*)	1 pound
16 fluid ounces	1 pint
1 fluid ounce	2 tablespoons
1 wine glass	¼ cup
1 ounce	28.35 grams
1 pound	453.59 grams

2 tablespoons butter or margarine	1 ounce
½ cup butter or margarine	¼ pound or 1 stick
2 tablespoons sugar or salt	1 ounce
2¼ cups granulated sugar	1 pound
2¼ cups firmly packed brown sugar	1 pound
3½ cups sifted confectioners' sugar	1 pound
4 cups sifted all-purpose flour	1 pound
1 cup sifted all-purpose flour	1 cup plus 2 tablespoons sifted cake flour
1 cup sifted cake flour	1 cup minus 2 tablespoons sifted all-purpose flour
1 tablespoon cornstarch	2 tablespoons flour
1 square chocolate	1 ounce
1 square chocolate	3 tablespoons cocoa plus 1 tablespoon shortening
1 cup chopped nuts	about ¼ pound
1 pound Cheddar cheese	4 cups, grated
1 pound coffee	40 to 50 servings

Baking powder	1 teaspoon double-action baking powder will leaven 1 cup flour
Baking soda	½ teaspoon baking soda with 1 cup fully soured milk will neutralize the acid in that amount of milk and leaven 1 cup flour

Hors d'Oeuvres, Canapés and Cocktails

Small, dainty, tempting to the eye and teasing to the palate, appetizers are artful little contrivances for putting company in a company mood. Such at least is their purpose. But they are so delicious and charming in their almost infinite variety that it is sometimes difficult to remember that it is the obligation of hostess and guest alike to maintain a sensible restraint where appetizers are concerned.

Appetizers are found all over the world. In this country they are grouped into three main types: hors d'oeuvres, canapés and cocktails.

PLANNING APPETIZERS—There is no limit to the kinds of meat, poultry, fish, cheese, vegetables and fruits that can be used. Though imagination and ingenuity are the only limiting factors in selecting appetizers, there is one rule that should be followed—*Do not repeat any food in the main part of the meal that has been used in the appetizers.* Remember they are a part of the whole menu; select them to harmonize with the rest of the meal. Choose them for complementary flavors, for contrast in texture and color and variety of shape. Picture the serving dishes, trays and other appointments as you plan the menu.

Avoid a last-minute rush by wise selection (do not include too many appetizers that require last-minute doing), by careful buying and beforehand preparation.

Take cues from assembly-line production techniques for organizing your work. For example, use large sandwich loaves, cut in lengthwise slices, for canapé bases and finger sandwiches; stack several slices together and cut several identical shapes at one time; spread canapé bases all at one time.

HORS D'OEUVRES—Cold or hot, simple or elaborate, hors d'oeuvres are savory tidbits about one bite in size and are eaten with the fingers or from wooden or plastic picks. They are usually passed in the living room or on the terrace to a gathering of people at a cocktail party or before dinner. A Continental custom is to serve the hors d'oeuvres at the table as the first course of a luncheon or dinner. Here the use of a fork is acceptable.

For successful hors d'oeuvres remember and practice the general suggestions and the rule given in PLANNING. The **Taste Teasers** (*page 14*) will give a helpful start. Look also at **Raw Vegetable Relishes** (*page 166*) for the pick-ups. Don't forget about the many dips and dunks and the snacks such as nuts and potato chips.

Fill miniature shells made from puff paste or choux paste, or spread waffle squares, thin griddlecakes or crêpes with piquant mixtures—delectable hors d'oeuvres!

Holders for pick-type hors d'oeuvres are available in housewares departments or can be made from a molded cheese (such as Edam), grapefruit, oranges, apples, a small head of red or green cabbage, a melon, eggplant, cucumbers or a cauliflower. If necessary, level base by removing a thin slice from the underside. Put hors d'oeuvres on wooden or plastic picks and insert into the holder.

CANAPÉS—Finger foods too, canapés are small bits of well-seasoned food spread on a thin base such as a slice of fancy-cut toast or bread or a cracker. They should have a fresh appearance and be easy to handle.

Take time to arrange canapés in an attractive design on the serving tray—the effect will be gratifying. Prepare enough to replenish the tray, recreating the original arrangement.

Bases for canapés are the many breads (plain, toasted or deep-fried), crackers and the packaged commercial products such as melba toast and potato chips. Brown bread, nut breads, rye, wheat, white and pumpernickel bread give variety to canapés. The bread slices, never more than ¼ in. thick, can be cut into many shapes—rounds, squares, diamonds, ovals, rectangles or crescents.

Spread canapé bases with any one of the **Seasoned Butters** (*page 19*), then with the filling or spread, and finally top with a garnish. Garnishes should be scaled to the dainty size of canapés and should be as good to eat as they are to behold.

Garnishes for Canapés

Anchovies—Fillets or rolled
Bacon (crisp, cooked)—Crumbled or small pieces
Carrots—Thin notched rounds
Caviar—Black or red
Cheese (sharp)—Grated
Cream cheese—Softened, plain or tinted and forced through pastry bag and No. 27 star decorating tube to form rosettes or border; a No. 2 or 3 decorating tube for designs or borders
Chives—Minced or chopped
Cucumbers—Notched slices, half slices or thin unpared slices
Eggs (hard-cooked)—Rings, slices, sieved egg yolk or egg-white cutouts
Green pepper—Cutouts or narrow strips
Lobster—Small pieces of claw meat
Mint—Sprigs or chopped
Mushrooms (slices)—Cooked in butter
Nuts (plain, toasted or salted)—Chopped, ground or whole
Olives (green or ripe)—Slivered, chopped, rings of pitted olives or pimiento-stuffed olives
Parsley—Sprigs, chopped or minced
Paprika
Pickles—Chopped or slices
Pimiento—Strips or chopped
Radishes—Thin slices
Shrimp (cooked, fresh)—Whole
Tomato—Cutouts
Water cress—Sprigs

Garnishes for the Canapé Tray

Carved vegetable flowers
Fresh flowers
Frosted grapes
Kumquats—With peel drawn back in petal shapes
Parsley bouquets
Radish Roses (*page 166*)
Water cress

COCKTAILS—The sea food or fruit (one or more kinds of fruit) cocktail is served as the first course of a meal at the table. Vegetable or fruit juices are served either at the table or in the living room before the meal.

Sea-food cocktails usually are served with peppy sauce that has ketchup, chili sauce, French dressing or mayonnaise as a base.

Fruit cocktails should be tart, though sometimes made with sweetened fruits. Frequently they are sprinkled with rum, kirsch or a liqueur that harmonizes in flavor with the fruit.

Add seasonings such as Worcestershire sauce, tabasco sauce or lemon juice to spark the flavor of vegetable juices.

Float a small scoop of fruit-flavored ice or sherbet on small servings of fruit juice—a refreshing shrub.

All cocktails should be fresh, colorful and appetizing in appearance and tantalizing in flavor. Thoroughly chill all ingredients and the serving dishes. Fruit and sea-food cocktails often are kept cold in beds of crushed ice. Sea-food and fruit cocktails are served in stemmed or footed cocktail glasses while the juices and shrubs are served in small glasses or punch cups. Some juice cocktails are served hot; be sure they are steaming hot and served in cups or glasses that are comfortable for your guests to hold.

Taste Teasers

Select an attractive array of Taste Teasers from these recipes. All are delightful bits of finger food, though some may be easier to serve if they have stems of wooden or plastic picks.

Meat 'n' Cheese Wedges—With a round cutter, cut 2½- to 3-in. rounds from slices of **ham,** canned **luncheon meat, ready-to-serve meat, bologna,** or other **sausage.** Repeat the process with thin slices of **Swiss** or **Cheddar cheese.** Alternately stack the meat and cheese rounds, using five in all. Wrap in waxed paper and chill in refrigerator until time to serve. Cut stacks into small wedges. Insert picks.

Bacon-Wrapped Olives—Wrap **pimiento-** or **almond-stuffed olives** in pieces of **bacon.** Fasten with picks. Put in shallow baking dish. Bake or broil until bacon is done.

Biscuit Bites—Dot toasted bite-size **shredded wheat biscuits** with **peanut butter.** Thread on picks alternately with thin slices of **sweet pickle.**

Pecan Sandwiches—Lightly brush large **pecan halves** with **butter** and spread one layer deep on baking sheet. Toast at 350°F about 20 min., or until delicately browned. Grate **Swiss cheese;** blend in **cream** to spreading consistency. Spread one side of one pecan half with cheese mixture and top with a second half. Press gently together.

Pineapple Delights—Wrap drained **pineapple chunks** each in one third of a slice of **bacon;** secure with a whole **clove** or wooden pick. Arrange in shallow baking dish and bake or broil until bacon is done.

Smoked Cheese Blossoms—Soften **smoked cheese** and mix with chopped **pimiento, sweet pickle** and crisp crumbled **bacon.** Roll into small balls and chill in refrigerator. Or pack mixture into a small pan, chill and cut into squares. Insert picks.

Caviar with Egg—Cut **hard-cooked eggs** into halves lengthwise or cut forming sawtooth edges (see photo, *page 54*). Remove yolks and set aside for use in other food preparation. Fill whites with chilled **caviar,** black or red. Garnish with small piece of **lemon.**

Cheese Popcorn—Sprinkle **salt** and ½ cup (2 oz.) grated sharp **Cheddar** or **Parmesan cheese** over 1 qt. hot buttered **popped corn.**

Dried Beef Tasters—Flavor **cream cheese** with a small amount of **prepared horse-radish.** Roll into small balls. Then roll and press balls in minced **dried beef.** Insert picks.

Olive Teasers—Coat large **stuffed olives** with softened **cream cheese.** Roll in finely chopped **nuts.** Chill in refrigerator; insert picks.

Stuffed Celery Spears—Blend together softened **cream cheese** and **milk.** Mix in few grains **celery salt,** few drops **Worcestershire sauce** and very finely chopped **radish** and **green pepper** or **pimiento** and **parsley.** Stuff cleaned **celery** with the cheese mixture.

Apple Sandwiches—Wash and core but do not pare small **apples.** Cut crosswise into thin slices, forming rings. Dip in **lemon, orange** or **pineapple juice** to prevent darkening. Spread **peanut butter** or a **cheese spread** on one ring; top with a second ring. Cut into thirds.

Fruit and Ham "Kabobs"—Alternate cubes of cooked **ham** or canned **luncheon meat** on picks with seedless **grapes** or cubes of **melon** or **pineapple.**

Stuffed Prunes or Dates—Pit and dry plump soaked **prunes** and pit **dates.** Stuff with a tangy **cheese spread.** If desired, add chopped **nuts,** drained **crushed pineapple** or chopped **maraschino cherries** to cheese.

Olive-Ham Appetizers and Tomato Cocktail (page 301)

Olive-Ham Appetizers

Set out a baking sheet.

Grind (*page 63*) enough cooked ham to yield
¾ cup ground cooked ham
Combine with the ham and mix thoroughly
½ cup chopped ripe olives
1 tablespoon thick sour cream
1 teaspoon prepared mustard
1 teaspoon Worcestershire sauce
Set aside.

Set out
1 tablespoon caraway seeds
Prepare and shape into a ball
Pastry for 1-Crust Pie (*page 242*)
Divide dough into 6 equal portions; roll each portion into a 5x3-in. rectangle. Sprinkle about ½ teaspoon of the caraway seeds over each rectangle. Spread ham mixture evenly over each rectangle almost to edges. Starting with long edge of each rectangle, roll up and pinch long edge to seal (do not pinch ends). Place on baking sheet, sealed edges down.

Bake at 450°F 10 to 12 min., or until appetizers are lightly browned.

Slice rolls; serve with **Radish Roses** (*page 166*) and ripe olives threaded with carrot sticks.

About 2½ doz. appetizers

Nippy Sausage Rounds

Baking sheets will be needed.

Drain contents of
1 4-oz. can Vienna-style sausages
Cut each sausage into 4 crosswise slices and set aside.

Prepare and roll ⅛ in. thick
Cheese Pastry for 1-Crust Pie (*page 243*)
Using a lightly floured 2¼-in. cookie cutter, cut pastry into rounds. Put a sausage slice in the center of one half of the pastry rounds. Spread top of each sausage slice with
Prepared mustard
Moisten edges of sausage-topped pastry rounds with water. Cover with remaining pastry rounds. Using a floured fork, gently press edges to seal.

Place rounds on the baking sheets and bake at 450°F about 10 min., or until lightly browned.

About 2½ doz. appetizers

Note: If desired, spread the top of each sausage slice with **prepared horse-radish** or **chili sauce** instead of mustard.

Veal-on-a-Pick

Grind (*page 63*)
¼ lb. veal loaf (about 1 cup ground)
Mix until well blended
3 oz. (1 pkg.) cream cheese, softened
1 teaspoon Worcestershire sauce
¼ teaspoon paprika
Blend in the ground veal loaf. Shape mixture into ¾-in. balls. Roll each ball in
Minced parsley
Chill thoroughly before serving. Insert a wooden pick into each ball to serve.

About 1 doz. appetizers

Chili Dip

Thoroughly mix together in a small bowl
¾ cup Mayonnaise (*page 177*)
3 tablespoons chopped sweet pickle
1 tablespoon chopped stuffed olives
1 hard-cooked egg, chopped
1½ teaspoons grated onion
1 tablespoon chili powder
¼ teaspoon seasoned salt
Cover and set aside in refrigerator 1 to 2 hrs. to chill and to allow flavors to blend.
About 1 cup dip

Fabulous Cheese Mousse

Lightly oil with salad or cooking oil (not olive oil) a fancy 1-pt. mold. Set aside to drain. Put a small bowl and rotary beater into refrigerator to chill.

Pour into a small cup or custard cup
¼ cup cold water
Sprinkle evenly over cold water
1 tablespoon (1 env.) unflavored gelatin
Let stand 5 min. to soften. Dissolve completely by placing gelatin over very hot water.

Force through a fine sieve
3¾ oz. (3 1¼-oz. pkgs.) Roquefort cheese
2⅔ oz. (2 1⅓-oz. pkgs.) Camembert cheese
Blend in until mixture is smooth
1 egg yolk, slightly beaten
1 tablespoon sherry
1 teaspoon Worcestershire sauce
Stir dissolved gelatin and add to cheese mixture, blending thoroughly.

Beat until rounded peaks are formed
1 egg white
Beat, using chilled bowl and beater, until cream is of medium consistency (piles softly)
½ cup chilled whipping cream
Fold (*page 6*) whipped cream and egg white into the cheese mixture. Turn into the mold. Chill in refrigerator until firm.

Unmold (*page 6*) onto a chilled serving plate.

Garnish with
Stuffed olive slices
Serve with crackers.
One 1-pt. mold

Avocado-Cottage-Cheese Dip

Force through a sieve or food mill and set aside
1 cup (8 oz.) cream-style cottage cheese
Rinse, cut into halves, and remove pit from
1 large ripe avocado
Carefully scoop out fruit, reserving the shells to use as containers for serving the dip. Put avocado into a bowl and mash well with a fork.

Blend in
2 teaspoons lemon juice
Mix in the sieved cottage cheese and
3 tablespoons minced parsley
2 teaspoons grated onion
½ teaspoon salt
½ teaspoon Accent
¼ teaspoon pepper
1 clove garlic (*page 6*), minced; or crushed in a garlic press
Blend until ingredients are thoroughly mixed. Spoon the dip into the avocado shells. Place in refrigerator to chill.

Before serving, sprinkle with
Paprika
Accompany with potato chips or small crackers.
About 2 cups of dip

Fabulous Cheese Mousse

Tuna Sensation

Drain and flake (*page 6*) contents of
1 7-oz. can tuna (about 1 cup, flaked)
Set aside.

Beat until very soft
8 oz. cream cheese
Add and beat until smooth
½ cup thick sour cream
1 tablespoon prepared horse-radish
1 teaspoon Worcestershire sauce
Blend in the flaked tuna and
2 tablespoons minced onion
1 clove garlic (*page 6*), minced; or crushed in a garlic press
and a mixture of
1 teaspoon crushed chervil
½ teaspoon salt
¼ teaspoon Accent
Few grains pepper
Cover and put into refrigerator for 2 to 3 hrs. to allow flavors to blend. One half hour before serving, remove from refrigerator and let stand at room temperature so that the mixture will be of dipping consistency.

Serve as a dip with crackers or potato chips.
About 1⅔ cups dip

▲ Buffet Cheese Spreads

For a big party, arrange cheese balls on a large serving dish or tray. For a smaller party, one of the three may be served as an appetizer. A variety of crisp crackers should accompany the cheeses.

For Cheese Base—Set out to soften at room temperature
½ lb. Roquefort cheese
8 oz. cream cheese
5 oz. (1 jar) sharp process cheese spread
Blend the cheeses together until well mixed. Divide the mixture into thirds (about 1 cup each) and combine each third with one of the following cheese spread variations.
3 cheese balls

△1 Parsley Cheese Spread

MRS. G. R. ENGEMAN
MOUNTAIN LAKE, MINN.

Mix together ½ cup (about 2 oz.) finely chopped **pecans** and ½ cup minced **parsley.** Mix ⅓ of Cheese Base ▲ with one half of the pecans and parsley, 1 tablespoon minced **onion** and ½ teaspoon **Worcestershire sauce.** Shape into a ball and roll in the remaining pecans and parsley. Chill in refrigerator. Let stand at room temperature before serving.

△2 Nippy Cheese Spread

MRS. R. D. BOWER, BREMERTON, WASH.

Mix together ½ cup (about 2 oz.) finely chopped **pecans** and ½ cup minced **parsley.** Mix ⅓ of Cheese Base ▲ with one half of the pecans and parsley and 1 tablespoon grated **onion,** 2 teaspoons **prepared horse-radish,** 2 teaspoons **prepared mustard,** ½ teaspoon **Worcestershire sauce** and ⅛ teaspoon **salt.** Shape into a ball and roll in the remaining pecans and parsley. Chill in refrigerator. Let stand at room temperature before serving.

△3 Rosy Cheese Spread

MRS. RAY GARRISON, BOWLING GREEN, KY.

Chop very finely ⅔ cup (about 4 oz.) blanched **almonds** (*page 5*). Mix ⅓ of Cheese Base ▲ with one half of the almonds and 1 tablespoon minced **pimiento,** 1½ teaspoons grated **onion,** 1 teaspoon **lemon juice** and ½ teaspoon **Worcestershire sauce.** Shape into a ball and roll in the remaining almonds. Sprinkle generously with **paprika.** Chill in refrigerator. Let stand at room temperature before serving.

Assorted Appetizers

Canapés

Savory canapés are the prologue to the meal, whetting the appetite. Plan a selection to harmonize with your menu.

Anchovy Canapés—Mix together thoroughly 1 finely chopped **hard-cooked egg,** 1 medium-size peeled, chopped **tomato,** 2 tablespoons flaked **tuna,** 2 tablespoons chopped **green pepper** and a mixture of 2 tablespoons **mayonnaise** and 6 mashed **anchovy fillets.** Spread **Lemon Butter** (*page 19*) on **bread crescents.** Spread anchovy mixture on each crescent. Sprinkle 1 or 2 drops **Worcestershire sauce** on each canapé. Garnish each with a sprig of **parsley.**

Dried Beef 'n' Cheese Squares—Blend together 4½ oz. softened **cream cheese** (1½ 3-oz. pkgs.) and 2 tablespoons **orange marmalade.** Spread part of the cream cheese mixture onto 3 slices white **bread.** Cut each bread slice into quarters. Place a slice of **dried beef** over each canapé. Top each with a small amount of remaining cream cheese. (For a special touch, force cream cheese through a pastry bag and No. 27 star tube.)

Bologna Diamonds—Blend thoroughly ½ cup ground **bologna,** 3 sieved **hard-cooked egg yolks,** 2 tablespoons **mayonnaise** and ⅛ teaspoon **garlic salt** and a few grains **pepper.** Spread small **bread diamonds** with **Mustard Butter** (*page 19*). Top with the bologna mixture. Garnish each with a strip of **pimiento.**

Clam and Cheese Canapés—Drain contents of 1 7-oz. can **minced clams.** Blend together 3 oz. softened **cream cheese,** 2 teaspoons **lemon juice,** few drops **tabasco sauce** and a mixture of ¼ teaspoon **salt,** ¼ teaspoon **Accent** and ⅛ teaspoon **pepper.** Blend in the minced clams. Spread on **toast fingers.** Garnish with sieved **hard-cooked egg yolk.**

Crab Nippies—Drain, remove and discard bony tissue and flake contents of 6- to 7-oz. can **crab meat.** Spoon crab meat onto **buttered toast rounds** and sprinkle **Accent** over tops; cover generously with grated sharp **Cheddar cheese.** Set temperature control of range at Broil. Arrange canapés on broiler rack and place rack in broiler with top of canapés 3 in. from source of heat. Broil 3 to 5 min., or until cheese is bubbly. Serve piping hot.

Anchovy and Egg Canapés—Spread **toast rounds** with **Parsley Butter** (*on this page*). Blend together 3 oz. softened **cream cheese,** ¼ cup **anchovy paste** and 1 teaspoon minced **parsley.** Set aside. Mix together 2 **hard-cooked egg yolks,** 2 tablespoons **mayonnaise,** ¼ teaspoon **dry mustard,** ⅛ teaspoon **salt,** a few grains **pepper** and ⅛ teaspoon **Accent.** Place a thin ring of **hard-cooked egg white** on each toast round. Fill centers with anchovy mixture. Top with a slice of **ripe olive.** Place a small amount of the egg-yolk mixture on each olive.

Shrimp Canapés—Marinate 12 cooked **shrimp** in **Garlic French Dressing** (*page 176*). Meanwhile, finely chop 6 more cooked **shrimp** and blend thoroughly with 2 tablespoons **butter** or **margarine.** Spread the Shrimp Butter onto 12 crisp **crackers.** Place 1 shrimp on each. Top with sieved **hard-cooked egg yolk.**

Cream Cheese Bits—Spread onto crispy **crackers** a mixture of 3 oz. softened **cream cheese,** 1 tablespoon minced fresh **mint leaves,** 1 tablespoon **brandy** and ¼ teaspoon **salt.** Garnish each with a tiny sprig of **parsley.**

Crispy Ham Bites—Mix together until well blended ½ cup ground, cooked **ham,** ¼ cup grated **Cheddar cheese,** ¼ cup **condensed tomato soup,** 1 tablespoon minced **onion,** ¼ teaspoon **prepared horse-radish,** ¼ teaspoon **prepared mustard,** and ⅛ teaspoon **Accent.** Spread mixture on small **bread diamonds.** Set temperature control of range at Broil. Arrange canapés on broiler rack and place rack in broiler with top of canapés 3 in. from source of heat. Broil 3 to 5 min., or until lightly browned. Serve piping hot.

Liver Sausage Rounds—Blend together 3 oz. softened **cream cheese** and ¼ teaspoon **prepared mustard.** Spread mixture on **bread rounds.** Place 1 thin slice of **tomato** on each round and season with **salt** and **pepper.** Place 1 thin slice of **Braunschweiger liver sausage** on top of each tomato slice. Sprinkle minced **parsley** around the edges and place a slice of **stuffed olive** in center.

Pastry Canapés—Prepare ½ recipe **Pastry for 1-Crust Pie** (*page 242*). Roll ⅛ in. thick. Cut into small strips or shapes. Sprinkle with grated sharp **Cheddar cheese** and **Accent.** If desired, sprinkle **poppy** or **caraway seeds** over cheese. Place on baking sheet; bake at 425°F about 10 min., or until lightly browned.

Cheese Pastry Sticks—Prepare ½ recipe **Cheese Pastry for 1-Crust Pie** (*page 243*). Roll ⅛ in. thick. Cut into small strips. If desired, sprinkle **caraway** or **poppy seeds** over pastry. Place on baking sheet; bake at 425°F about 10 min., or until lightly browned.

Seasoned Butters

Butters can be prepared hours ahead of time and refrigerated in a tightly covered container. Before using, cream to a spreading consistency.

FRESH HERB BUTTER—Cream ½ cup **butter** or **margarine** until softened. Gradually cream in 1 teaspoon **lemon** or **lime juice.** Blend 1 tablespoon fresh minced herbs, such as **chives, dill, parsley** or **mint** into the creamed mixture. *About ½ cup butter*

PERKY BUTTERS—Follow recipe for Fresh Herb Butter; omit fresh herbs. Blend in one of the following:

Anchovy Butter—1 tablespoon **anchovy paste** and ¼ teaspoon **paprika**

Horse-radish Butter—2 tablespoons **prepared horse-radish**

Lemon Butter—Increase the lemon juice to 1½ teaspoons

Mustard Butter—1 tablespoon **prepared mustard**

Parsley Butter—¼ cup minced **parsley**

Pimiento Butter—2 tablespoons minced **pimiento**

Water Cress Butter—4 tablespoons minced **water cress**

Hot Sardine Canapés

MRS. ED JENSEN, SIOUX CITY, IOWA

Set aside to drain the contents of

2 3¼ oz. cans sardines

For Sauce—Melt in top of a double boiler over simmering water

2 tablespoons butter or margarine

Blend in

1 tablespoon flour

Add gradually, stirring constantly until smooth, a mixture of

½ cup milk
⅓ cup mayonnaise
½ teaspoon vinegar

Continue to cook over simmering water until mixture thickens. Remove from heat and stir in

1 tablespoon chopped stuffed olives
1 tablespoon chopped sweet pickle
1 teaspoon chopped onion
2 teaspoons capers

Keep warm over simmering water.

For Canapés—Trim crusts from

6 slices white bread

Toast the bread on one side only.

Spread the untoasted sides with

Butter or margarine

Cut each slice into thirds. Arrange one drained sardine on each piece of bread. Spoon hot sauce over the sardine; sprinkle with

Paprika

Set temperature control of range at Broil.

Arrange canapés on broiler rack and place rack in broiler with top of canapés 3 in. from source of heat; broil about 5 min., or until canapés are slightly browned.

Serve piping hot. *1½ doz. canapés*

Cheese-Asparagus Canapés

Cook

1 pkg. (10 oz.) frozen asparagus spears

Drain if necessary. Set 8 spears aside for use in canapés. (Reserve remaining asparagus for use in other food preparation.)

Grate and set aside

2 oz. Cheddar cheese (½ cup, grated)

Prepare and set aside

Mustard Butter (*page 19*)

Trim crusts from

4 slices white bread

Toast the bread on one side only. Cut each slice into halves and spread the untoasted sides with the butter. Arrange one drained asparagus spear on each bread slice. If necessary, trim spears to fit. Sprinkle about one tablespoon of the grated cheese over each. Cut into halves and sprinkle with

Paprika

Set temperature control of range at Broil. Arrange canapés on broiler rack and place rack in broiler with top of canapés 3 in. from source of heat; broil 5 min., or until cheese bubbles.

Serve piping hot. *16 canapés*

▲ Summertime Melon Bowl

Set out

1 medium-size ripe cantaloupe or honeydew melon

To cut melon, use narrow, sharp-pointed knife. Mark points in a saw-toothed line at 1-in. intervals around center of melon.

Carefully cut down through marked line to center of melon. Pull halves apart. Remove and discard seedy center. Wrap one half in waxed paper and place in refrigerator for use in other food preparation. With a melon-ball cutter, scoop out balls from remaining half of melon. Wrap shell in waxed paper and place in refrigerator to chill with melon balls.

Prepare and chill in refrigerator

Watermelon balls or chunks, pitted cherries, strawberries, pineapple wedges, or any available fresh fruit

To serve, partially fill melon "bowl" with chipped ice. Impale the chilled fruit on wooden picks. Heap fruit, picks upright, on top of ice. Sprinkle over fruit

2 or 3 tablespoons lime juice

△ Pineapple Bowl

Follow ▲ Recipe; substitute a **fresh pineapple** for the melon. To prepare, cut whole pineapple into halves lengthwise through crown (spiny top). Wrap one of the halves in waxed paper and place in refrigerator, reserving for use in other food preparation. Cut out and discard core from remaining half. With a grapefruit knife or sharp paring knife, remove pineapple from its shell. Cut pineapple into chunks and use with other fresh fruit pieces. Chill fruit in refrigerator. To serve, fill the pineapple shell with the chilled fruits.

Fresh Fruit Cocktail

MRS. VIRGIL L. YOUTZ, CANTON, OHIO

The cooling fragrance of mint leaves tinges the flavor of this perfect-for-warm-weather cocktail of chilled fresh fruits.

For Mint Sirup—Measure into a small saucepan having a tight-fitting cover

1 cup water
½ cup sugar
2 tablespoons chopped fresh mint leaves
4 teaspoons lemon juice
1 teaspoon grated orange peel (*page 5*)
1 teaspoon grated lemon peel

Put saucepan over medium heat and stir mixture until sugar is dissolved. Bring mixture to boiling. Reduce heat, cover and simmer for 5 min. Uncover; cook 10 min. longer. Remove saucepan from heat and strain the mixture. Set aside to cool.

When sirup is cool, add

1 tablespoon chopped mint leaves

Cover and put into refrigerator for several hours or overnight. Strain before using.

For Preparing Fruit—Set out

2 slices fresh pineapple, cut 1 in. thick

Cut away rind and "eyes" and remove core. Cut the slices into small wedges. (Reserve remaining pineapple for use in other food preparation.)

Rinse, drain and set aside

1 cup fresh blueberries

With a sharp knife, remove peel and white membrane from

1 large orange

Remove sections by cutting on either side of dividing membranes; remove section by section over a bowl to save the juice. Put fruit into refrigerator to chill.

When ready to serve, carefully mix the fruit and strained mint sirup. Serve in chilled sherbet glasses garnished with **mint leaves.**

4 servings

▲ Herring Bits in Sour Cream

Drain and put into a bowl contents of

1 16-oz. jar herring fillets

Mix together and pour over herring

1 cup thick sour cream
3 tablespoons lemon juice
1 large onion (*page 6*), thinly sliced
1 tablespoon peppercorns
1 teaspoon salt
¼ teaspoon Accent

Carefully turn with fork to coat all pieces evenly. Let stand in refrigerator at least 2 hrs. before serving.

Serve garnished with

Lemon slices
Paprika

About 3 cups

△ Herring and Apples in Sour Cream

Follow ▲ Recipe. Whip chilled sour cream until it piles softly before blending in remaining ingredients. Omit peppercorns. Wash, quarter, core and dice ½ lb. (about 2 small) **apples.** Mix into herring mixture; chill.

Pickled Tuna and Sour Cream Appetizer

MRS. ED JENSEN, SIOUX CITY, IOWA

Set out a small saucepan.

Tie together in a spice bag (*page 305*)

2 bay leaves
2 teaspoons whole mixed pickling spices

Measure into the saucepan

⅓ cup wine vinegar
¼ cup water

Add the spice bag and put saucepan over medium heat. Bring to boiling. Reduce heat and simmer for 10 min. Remove spice bag and set liquid aside to cool.

Drain and separate into small chunks contents of

2 7-oz. cans tuna (about 2 cups)

Rinse, cut off ends and slice thinly (discarding seeds)

1 lemon

Cut into thin slices

2 medium-size onions (*page 6*)

Gently toss the onion, lemon and tuna chunks together with the cooled liquid and

½ teaspoon salt

Spread over mixture and gently mix in

1 cup thick sour cream

Chill in refrigerator.

Serve as a dinner appetizer. Arrange chilled **lettuce** on small plates. Spoon tuna mixture onto lettuce and garnish with **parsley.**

About 8 servings

Oysters on the Half Shell

To Open Oysters—Wash thoroughly in cold water

2 doz. shell oysters

Place flat side up and carefully open by inserting knife between edges of shell opposite hinges. (If necessary, break off the thin edges of the shell before inserting tip of knife.) Cut

Oysters on the Half Shell

the muscle from the top shell and remove top shell. Cut the lower part of the same muscle from the deep half of the shell, leaving oysters in the shell. Discard the top shells.

To Serve—Arrange oysters-in-the-shell on individual plates. Garnish with sprigs of **parsley** and **lemon wedges.** Serve with

Peppy Cocktail Sauce (*on this page;* omit onion juice and add 1 teaspoon chopped parsley and ¼ teaspoon dried tarragon)
Crackers

4 servings

Shrimp with Peppy Cocktail Sauce

For Shrimp—Prepare

1½ lbs. fresh shrimp with shells (see Cooked Shrimp, *page 126*)

Chill in refrigerator until ready to serve.

For Peppy Cocktail Sauce—To make about 1 cup sauce, mix thoroughly in a small bowl

1 cup ketchup
1 tablespoon lemon juice
1 teaspoon onion juice
¼ teaspoon Worcestershire sauce
Few drops tabasco sauce
1 tablespoon sugar
1 tablespoon prepared horse-radish
½ teaspoon salt
¼ teaspoon Accent

Chill in refrigerator.

For Completing Cocktail—Arrange in 6 chilled sherbet glasses

Lettuce or curly endive

Arrange about 5 shrimp in each glass. Top each serving with the Peppy Cocktail Sauce.

6 servings

Clams Casino

Clams Casino

Set out a 15½x10½x1-in. baking dish and fill ¼ in. deep with coarse salt.

Open (see Oysters on the Half Shell, *page 22*)

2 doz. clams

Remove clams from the half shell and drain juice from shells.

Blend together thoroughly

¼ cup butter or margarine
1 teaspoon anchovy paste

Spoon a small amount of the mixture into each shell. Cover with the clams. Sprinkle with

Lemon juice

Spoon over the clams a mixture of

¼ cup finely minced green pepper
¼ cup finely chopped onion

Season with

Salt
Pepper
Accent

Cut into small pieces

3 slices bacon

Top each clam with a few pieces of bacon. Place shells in the pan, pushing them down into the salt to keep shells from tipping.

Bake at 450°F 15 to 20 min., or until bacon is thoroughly cooked.

Serve immediately. *4 to 6 servings*

Soup Lore

Gone is the soup pot of yesteryear—the heavy iron kettle that bubbled on the cook stove the livelong day. The fire-blackened pot has gone, but its legacy remains, and soup—thick or clear and all the varieties in between—is still a national favorite. Soup making is a fine test of a homemaker's skill in striking a harmonious balance of flavors. Much of the satisfaction and special pleasure of making soup come perhaps from the simple fact that nothing is more gratifying than good soup.

ENDLESS VARIETY—Soups, usually served as a first course, are main-dish fare too. Thin, clear soups (such as broths, bouillons and consommés), fruit soups, delicate cream soups, thick hearty soups (such as chowders and bisques), winter hot or summer cold—there is no end to the variety.

REMINDERS—Always add hot, thickened tomatoes to cold milk to avoid curdling.

Thorough blending of fat and flour and cooking with the milk or cream help prevent a film of fat on cream soups. There will be a film of fat if soup is too thin.

Cream soups should be the consistency of a thin sauce. The vegetable used will determine the amount of flour needed to thicken the soup. At least ¼ cup chopped or ⅓ cup sieved vegetable per cup of thin white sauce will give a most satisfactory soup; 2 to 3 tablespoons sieved spinach per cup is a desirable proportion for cream of spinach soup. Add a little hot milk or cream if the soup is too thick or thicken with a flour-water mixture if the soup is too thin.

Clear soups such as broth and consommé may be clarified as for **Chicken Broth** *(page 28)*.

The electric blender is the modern soup pot—blending everything and anything into savory soups. Remember—add liquid first, usually ½ to 1 cup, then add the other ingredients.

Cool soups to lukewarm before storing in covered container in refrigerator; keep several days only.

SOUP GARNISHES—Garnishes are to soup as jewels are to the costume—a glamorous accent. They need not be elaborate. The normally stocked refrigerator will usually yield the wherewithal for garnishes that furnish a touch of enticement.

Bacon—Diced and panbroiled, supplies a touch of crispness, color and flavor.

Croutons—Provide texture contrast (see *page 51*).

Grated Cheese—Parmesan is the classic accompaniment for onion soups, but other sharp cheeses enhance flavor of chowders and other soups.

Herbs—Chervil, chives, tarragon, parsley—fresh, minced or chopped—add a flash of color.

Lemon Slices—Notched or cut in fancy shapes and set afloat in clear bouillon or consommé.

Sour Cream—Connoisseur's preference for borsch.

Vegetables—Thin, small raw pieces floating on clear soups give appealing color and flavor.

Whipped Cream—Salted or plain; perfect with cream of tomato soup.

Toasted Almonds—Sliver; garnish cream soups.

▲ Potato Soup

Every country has its own way with potato soup. In this delicious recipe the addition of sour cream reveals the touch of central Europe.

Set out a heavy 8-in. skillet.

Bring to boiling in a 3-qt. saucepan having a tight-fitting cover
1½ qts. water
Meanwhile, wash, pare and cut into 1-in. cubes
3 large (about 1½ lbs.) potatoes
Add the potatoes to boiling water with
1½ teaspoons salt
½ teaspoon Accent
Cover saucepan and cook 15 min., or until potatoes are tender when pierced with a fork.

Meanwhile, prepare, reserving fat
4 slices Panbroiled Bacon (*page 87*)
Crumble cooled bacon; set aside for garnish.

Heat in the skillet
2 tablespoons reserved bacon fat
Add and cook over medium heat, occasionally moving and turning with a spoon, until the onion is transparent
2 tablespoons finely chopped onion
Blend in with the onion and fat
2 tablespoons flour
Heat until mixture bubbles and is lightly browned, stirring constantly. Remove from heat and add gradually, stirring constantly
¼ cup water
Add onion mixture to contents of saucepan and bring rapidly to boiling, stirring constantly; cook 1 to 2 min. longer.

Just before serving, vigorously stir about one cup of the hot soup, adding it gradually, into
1 cup thick sour cream
Immediately blend into hot soup. Heat thoroughly; do not boil. Garnish with crumbled bacon. *6 servings*

△ Sweet Cream Potato Soup

Follow ▲ Recipe. Substitute **sweet cream** for sour cream, adding it directly to soup.

Split Pea Soup

Set out a large sauce pot or kettle having a tight-fitting cover.

Wash, pare or scrape and cut into ¼-in. slices
6 medium-size carrots (about 1½ cups, sliced)
Finely chop
1 medium-size (about ½ cup, chopped) onion (*page 6*)
Set vegetables aside.

Wipe with a clean, damp cloth
1 ham bone, cracked
Put bone into sauce pot with
1½ qts. water
Cover sauce pot and bring water slowly to boiling.

Meanwhile, wash thoroughly and sort
1 cup (about ½ lb.) split peas
Set peas aside.

Skim foam off the water in sauce pot. Put the carrots and onion into sauce pot and again bring water to boiling. Add peas gradually so that boiling will not stop. Add
1 teaspoon salt
½ teaspoon Accent
⅛ teaspoon pepper
Cover sauce pot and simmer about 3 hrs.

Meanwhile, prepare and set aside
Croutons (double recipe, *page 51*)
Remove and discard ham bone from kettle.

Vigorously stir about 3 tablespoons hot soup into a mixture of
2 egg yolks, slightly beaten
1 tablespoon sugar
Immediately blend into hot soup. Stirring constantly, cook over low heat 2 to 3 min. (Do not overcook or allow soup to boil.)

Set out about
1 cup milk
Blend into soup enough of the milk for consistency desired. Heat thoroughly, but do not boil. Serve immediately with the Croutons.
About 8 servings

Creamy Tomato Soup, picture-puzzle sandwich and milk

Creamy Tomato Soup

Always a favorite of the small fry, tomato soup tempts young appetites by giving eye-appeal to the entire lunch.

Put into a 2-qt. saucepan and mix thoroughly
2½ cups (No. 2 can) tomatoes
⅓ cup finely chopped onion
3 to 4 tablespoons sugar
1 teaspoon salt
½ teaspoon Accent
½ bay leaf (optional)
Simmer for 5 min. Remove bay leaf; force mixture through sieve or food mill. Set aside.

Wash the saucepan; melt in it over low heat
2 tablespoons butter
Blend in
3 tablespoons flour
½ teaspoon salt
Increase heat to medium and cook, stirring constantly, until mixture bubbles. Remove from heat and gradually add hot tomato mixture while stirring constantly. Return mixture to heat and bring rapidly to boiling, stirring constantly. Cook 1 to 2 min. longer. Stirring constantly, gradually add the hot tomato mixture to
2 cups cold milk
Return soup to saucepan. Heat rapidly, stirring occasionally; do not boil. Serve hot with **popcorn.** *About 1½ pints soup*

Lobster Bisque

Prepare and set aside
5 cups quick chicken broth (*page 7*)
Melt in a large sauce pot or kettle over low heat
¼ cup butter or margarine
Blend in
¼ cup flour
1 teaspoon salt
½ teaspoon Accent
⅛ teaspoon pepper
Heat until mixture bubbles. Remove from heat. Add gradually, stirring constantly, 2 cups of the broth. Return the sauce pot to heat and bring rapidly to boiling, stirring constantly. Cook 1 to 2 min. longer. Remove from heat; gently stir in the remaining broth.

Add to the sauce pot
½ cup (1 medium-size) minced onion (*page 6*)
⅓ cup (about 2 medium-size) minced carrots
1 leek, white part only, minced
1 bay leaf
Cover and simmer over low heat about 10 min.

Meanwhile, drain and mince, reserving a few large pieces of lobster for garnish
2¼ cups (three 5-oz. cans, drained) lobster meat
Stir the minced lobster into simmering soup. Cover and simmer about 10 min. longer. Remove from heat and remove the bay leaf.

Place a food mill over a large bowl and pour soup mixture through the food mill, forcing through as much lobster as possible. Return soup to saucepan and reheat.

Beat slightly
2 egg yolks
Quickly stir about 3 tablespoons hot soup into the egg yolks. Immediately return egg-yolk

mixture to soup, stirring vigorously. Cook until well blended, about 5 min., stirring constantly. Do not boil. Add gradually, stirring in

1 cup cream

Add lobster remaining in food mill and reserved large pieces of lobster to soup. Stirring constantly, heat soup thoroughly.

6 servings

▲ Mushroom Soup

Set out a heavy 10-in. skillet and a large sauce pot or kettle having a tight-fitting cover.

Wipe with a clean, damp cloth

1 veal soup bone, cracked

Put soup bone into the sauce pot with

1½ qts. water
1½ teaspoons salt
½ teaspoon Accent
3 or 4 sprigs parsley
2 or 3 peppercorns

Bring water slowly to boiling. Skim off foam. Cover sauce pot and simmer soup about 1 hr., skimming as necessary.

Shortly before end of cooking period, cut off and discard tops, wash, pare or scrape and cut into ¼-in. slices

4 medium-size carrots (about 1 cup, sliced)

Add carrots to sauce pot, cover and simmer 15 to 20 min., or until carrots are tender.

Meanwhile, clean and slice (*page 6*)

1 lb. mushrooms

Heat in the skillet

½ cup butter or margarine

Add mushrooms with

1 small onion (*page 6*), chopped
2 tablespoons chopped parsley
1 teaspoon paprika
½ teaspoon salt

Cook slowly, occasionally moving and turning with a spoon, 5 to 8 min., or until mushrooms are lightly browned and tender; set aside.

Prepare and set aside

Croutons (1½ times recipe, *page 51*)

Remove kettle from heat. Remove and discard bone, peppercorns and parsley sprigs. Blend contents of skillet into soup. Vigorously stir ⅓ cup of the hot soup gradually into

4 egg yolks, slightly beaten

Immediately blend into hot soup. Stirring constantly, cook over low heat 2 to 3 min. (Do not overcook or allow soup to boil.) Remove immediately from heat and cover.

Combine in a bowl

1 cup thick sour cream
1 teaspoon lemon juice

Add gradually, stirring vigorously, about 1 cup hot soup to sour cream mixture. Immediately blend into the remaining hot soup. Heat thoroughly; do not boil. Serve with Croutons.

6 or 7 servings

△ Sweet Cream Mushroom Soup

Follow ▲ Recipe; substitute 1 cup **heavy** or **light cream** for the thick sour cream. Omit lemon juice. Add cream directly to the soup.

Oyster Stew

Set out a saucepan.

Scald (*page 7*)

2 cups milk
2 cups cream

Meanwhile drain, reserving liquid

1 pt. oysters

Pick over oysters to remove any shell particles.

Heat in the saucepan

¼ cup butter

Add oysters with reserved liquid. Simmer 3 min., or until oysters are plump and edges begin to curl.

Stir oyster mixture into scalded milk with

2 teaspoons salt
¼ teaspoon Accent
⅛ teaspoon pepper

Serve at once with **oyster crackers.**

6 servings

▲ Chicken Broth

Set out a 4-qt. sauce pot or kettle having a tight-fitting cover.

Clean, rinse and disjoint

1 stewing chicken, 4 to 5 lbs., ready-to-cook weight

(If chicken is frozen, thaw according to directions on package.)

Put chicken into the sauce pot and cover with

2 qts. cold water

Cover sauce pot and bring water slowly to boiling. Skim off foam as necessary.

Add

2 or 3 stalks celery (*page 6*) with leaves
2 carrots, washed and pared or scraped
1 medium-size onion (*page 6*)
2 teaspoons salt
1½ teaspoons Accent
2 or 3 peppercorns
1 bay leaf
3 parsley sprigs

Cover and simmer 3 hrs., or until thickest pieces of chicken are tender when pierced with a fork.

Remove chicken for use in other food preparation. Strain liquid through a fine sieve and set aside to cool. When cool, put into refrigerator to chill. Remove the hardened layer of fat from the chilled broth.

To clarify broth, stir into the cold stock

1 egg white, slightly beaten
Crushed shell of the egg
1 tablespoon cold water

Heat slowly to boiling, stirring constantly. Boil gently, stirring constantly, 7 to 10 min. Remove from heat and let stand 25 min. Strain through 2 thicknesses of cheesecloth. Reheat broth and serve very hot. Garnish with **parsley.**

About 1 qt. Chicken Broth

△ Chicken Broth with Rice

Omit clarifying broth. Bring broth slowly to boiling. Add ½ cup uncooked **rice** to broth, reduce heat and simmer 20 min., stirring occasionally, until a kernel is entirely soft when pressed between fingers. Serve hot.

△ Greek Chicken Soup

MRS. RAY POWELL, ROGUE RIVER, ORE.

Prepare △ Recipe. When the rice is almost cooked, beat 1 **egg yolk** until thick and lemon-colored. Beat 1 **egg white** until rounded peaks are formed. Add the beaten yolk to the beaten white, and beat until well blended.

Add and beat in 1 teaspoon **lemon juice.** Add about one cup of the hot broth to the egg mixture, while stirring vigorously. Immediately blend into the hot broth and cook over low heat for 1 min. Serve immediately.

French Onion Soup with Cheese

Originated by a king, French Onion is, in the opinion of many, the king of soups. The inspiration for this noble dish came to Louis XV one night when he returned to his hunting lodge and found only onions, butter and champagne in the royal cupboard. With imperious disregard for tradition and spurred on by the pangs of hunger, Louis simply combined all ingredients and created a new masterpiece.

Set out a heavy 3-qt. saucepan having a cover.

Cut into thin slices

5 medium-size (about 1 lb.) onions (*page 6*)

Heat in the saucepan over low heat

3 tablespoons butter

Add the onions and cook over medium heat,

occasionally moving and turning with a spoon, until the onions are just golden in color (about 10 min.).

Blend in gradually

1½ qts. bouillon or quick meat broth (*page 7*)

Season with

½ teaspoon salt
½ teaspoon Accent
⅛ teaspoon pepper

Bring to boiling. Reduce heat, cover saucepan and simmer about 15 min.

Meanwhile, measure

1 to 2 tablespoons butter

Grate

¼ cup (1 oz.) Gruyère or Cheddar cheese

Set aside.

Set temperature control of range at Broil.

Arrange on broiler rack

6 slices French bread

Place in broiler with top of bread 3 in. from source of heat. Toast one side only. Remove and spread untoasted side of each slice with ½ to 1 teaspoon of the butter. Cut slices into halves if desired. Place slices, buttered side up, on broiler rack.

Sprinkle about 2 teaspoons of the grated cheese onto each slice. Place in broiler with top of bread about 3 in. from source of heat. Toast until cheese is melted.

Pour soup into tureen, hot soup plates or earthenware bowls. Float a toast slice on top of each serving.

Bread may be toasted lightly, floated on top of soup, and grated cheese sprinkled over toast. Serve additional grated cheese in a bowl. Accompany with

Bread sticks

6 servings

French Onion Soup with Cheese

Chilled Cucumber Soup

MRS. MARY HUGHES, PHILADELPHIA, PA.

Wash, pare and finely chop

1 medium-size cucumber

Peel, rinse, trim tops to within 3 in. of white part and finely chop

6 green onions or scallions

Finely chop

¼ cup (1 oz.) walnuts
1 sprig parsley

Mix the vegetables and nuts together.

Blend together thoroughly

1 pt. yogurt
1 cup water
½ teaspoon salt
½ teaspoon Accent

Blend the vegetable mixture into the yogurt mixture. Serve in chilled bowls. If desired garnish with thin **cucumber slices.**

4 servings

Note: To make extra-smooth soup, put water into an electric blender container. Add vegetables, nuts and seasonings. Cover container, turn on motor and blend until thoroughly mixed. Add contents of blender container to the yogurt and mix thoroughly.

Philadelphia Pepper Pot

MRS. L. S. HEEBNER, NORRISTOWN, PA.

Set out a large sauce pot or kettle.

Wipe with a clean, damp cloth
1 lb. tripe
1 veal knuckle, cracked
Cut the tripe into small pieces (about ¼-in.) and put knuckle and tripe into the sauce pot.

Add to the sauce pot
3 qts. cold water
2 tablespoons salt
1 teaspoon Accent
½ teaspoon peppercorns
½ teaspoon pepper
¼ teaspoon thyme
Cover sauce pot and bring water slowly to boiling. Skim. Cover and simmer about 4 hrs., or until tripe is tender when pierced with a fork. Skim off foam as necessary.

Remove veal knuckle at end of cooking period.

Strain liquid through fine sieve; discard peppercorns and set tripe aside. Cool stock.

When stock is almost cooled, heat in sauce pot
⅓ cup butter
Add and cook over medium heat, occasionally moving and turning mixture with a spoon, until onion is transparent
3 carrots, washed, pared or scraped and chopped
2 stalks celery (*page 6*), chopped
1 medium-size onion (*page 6*), sliced
1 green pepper (*page 6*), chopped
When onion is transparent, carefully remove vegetables from sauce pot with a slotted spoon, allowing butter or margarine to drain back into sauce pot; set vegetables aside to keep warm.

Skim the fat from the cooled soup stock.

Stir into the sauce pot, blending thoroughly with the butter
2 tablespoons flour
Heat until mixture bubbles. Remove from heat. Add gradually, stirring constantly, one cup of the soup stock. Return to heat and bring mixture rapidly to boiling, stirring constantly. Cook 1 to 2 min. longer. Stir in the remaining soup stock and the vegetables. Cover and simmer about 20 min., or until vegetables are tender.

Meanwhile, remove meat from the veal knuckle. Add to sauce pot the tripe, meat and
1½ cups (12-oz. can) tomatoes, cut into pieces
½ cup (about 1 oz.) uncooked noodles
3 tablespoons chopped parsley
Bring to boiling over moderate heat; reduce heat, cover and simmer about 10 min., or until noodles are tender. *About 3 qts. soup*

▲ Square-Meal Vegetable-Beef Soup

Set out a 6-qt. sauce pot or kettle having a tight-fitting cover.

Wipe with a clean, damp cloth and cut into 1-in. pieces
1 lb. lean beef (chuck or plate)
Coat meat evenly by shaking 2 or 3 pieces at a time in a plastic bag containing a mixture of
½ cup flour
1 teaspoon Accent
½ teaspoon salt
⅛ teaspoon pepper
Heat in the sauce pot
2 to 3 tablespoons fat
Add meat to the sauce pot, and move and turn meat occasionally with a fork or spoon until browned on all sides.

Wipe with a clean, damp cloth
1 large soup bone, cracked
Put into the sauce pot with
½ cup (about 1 medium-size) chopped onion (*page 6*)
2 qts. boiling water
Cover the sauce pot and over high heat bring water again to boiling. Reduce heat and simmer 2 to 3 hrs., or until meat is almost tender.

Remove soup bone from sauce pot.

Square-Meal Vegetable-Beef Soup

Vegetable Cream Soup and Crackers

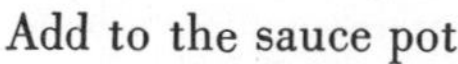

Add to the sauce pot
- **2 cups diced raw potato**
- **1 cup sliced raw carrots**
- **1 cup sliced celery (*page 6*)**
- **¼ teaspoon Accent**

Cover and simmer 30 min. Remove from heat; set aside to cool. Skim fat from cooled soup.

Meanwhile, force through a sieve or food mill
- **2½ cups (No. 2 can) tomatoes**

Stir the sieved tomatoes and their liquid into the skimmed soup with
- **¼ cup chopped parsley**

Reheat soup and serve hot. If desired, float **celery leaves** in the soup for garnish.

10 to 12 servings

△ Vegetable-Noodle Soup

Follow ▲ Recipe. After vegetables have cooked for 20 min. add ½ cup (about 1 oz.) uncooked **noodles.** Cook 10 min., or until vegetables and noodles are tender. Cool and add tomatoes and parsley as in ▲ Recipe.

△ Vegetable-Rice Soup

Follow ▲ Recipe. After vegetables have cooked 10 to 15 min. add ⅔ cup uncooked **rice.** Continue cooking 15 to 20 min., stirring occasionally, until vegetables and rice are tender. Cool and add tomatoes and parsley as in ▲ Recipe.

Vegetable Cream Soup

(Blender Method)

PHINA W. NORMAN, PORTLAND, ORE.

(See *page* 7 before using electric blender.) Set out a 1½-qt. saucepan having a cover.

Put into a blender container
- **1 cup water**
- **1 cup cooked peas**
- **½ cup cooked carrot pieces**
- **2 stalks celery with leaves (*page 6*), cut in several pieces**
- **1 medium-size cooked potato, cut in pieces**
- **1 beef bouillon cube**
- **1½ teaspoons salt**
- **⅛ teaspoon white pepper**
- **½ teaspoon Accent**

Cover and blend until almost smooth.

Add contents of blender container to the saucepan and blend in
- **1 cup milk**

Bring to boiling, stirring constantly. Reduce heat, cover and simmer about 5 min.

Garnish with **parsley.** *About 4 servings*

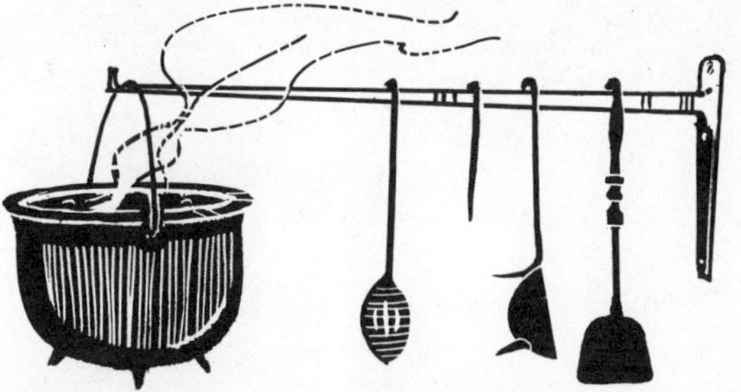

Bread and life, home, and hospitality are inextricably associated in the human imagination and experience. Old as history, breadmaking was one of the first culinary arts practiced—and at a time when home itself was little more than a few flat stones arranged round a fire. Now most of the peoples of the earth have breads characteristically their own. In our own country we have no single traditional bread. We have, instead, welcomed the traditions of all the peoples that have come here and made them our own. Made with or without leavening, bread appears in a hundred different, delightful guises—as soft loaves and crusty loaves, holiday breads and coffee cakes, waffles, griddlecakes, popovers, muffins and doughnuts, and in other forms too numerous to mention.

YEAST grows in the presence of a given amount of moisture and sugar at a temperature of about 80°F, producing in the process tiny bubbles of carbon dioxide gas which leaven the bread dough. A dough must be leavened to rise and become light.

Compressed Yeast (*moist cake*)—Grayish tan though may be slightly browned at edges; breaks with a clean edge and crumbles easily between the fingers when fresh; must be kept in refrigerator and used within a week for best results; soften in lukewarm liquid (80°F to 85°F).

Active Dry Yeast—May be kept without refrigeration; to obtain best results use before date on package expires; one package when softened has the leavening power of one cake compressed yeast; soften in warm water (110°F to 115°F) only.

FLOUR—All-purpose flour is used for breadmaking in the home. The moisture content of flour varies with changes in humidity and also from one flour to another. To allow for this difference and to obtain the desired consistency of the dough, indefinite amounts of flour are given in recipes.

A small amount of flour (about 1 cup) is added to the fat-liquid mixture before the softened yeast is added to prevent the yeast from becoming coated with fat. Fat tends to retard the growth of yeast.

LIQUID—Water and milk are the liquids most commonly used in bread doughs. Fluid milk must be scalded before using in breadmaking. Evaporated milk does not need to be scalded because it has been preheated. The liquid must be hot enough to

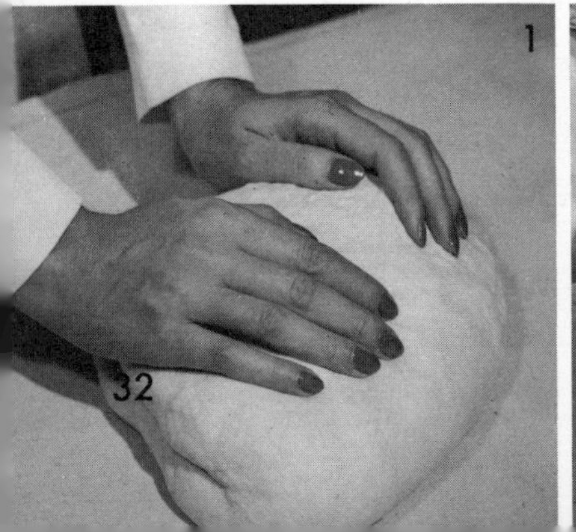

melt the shortening when added to shortening-sugar-salt mixture. For optimum yeast growth, this mixture, plus a small amount of flour, must be *lukewarm* (80°F) when softened yeast is added.

REFRIGERATOR DOUGHS are richer and sweeter than plain bread dough and can be successfully kept in the refrigerator (45°F to 50°F) three to four days. Place dough in the refrigerator immediately after mixing and kneading or after the first rising period (be sure it does not rise too much). Dough must be punched down occasionally if it rises during refrigeration. The dough is greased and well covered to keep the surface of the dough moist and elastic. When ready to bake, remove dough from refrigerator, shape, allow to rise until light and doubled before baking.

KNEAD DOUGH by folding opposite side over toward you. Using heels of hands, gently push dough away (see photo 1). Give it a one-quarter turn. Repeat process rhythmically until the dough is smooth and elastic, 5 to 8 min., using as little additional flour as possible. Always turn the dough in the same direction.

RISING—When dough looks double its original size, test by gently pressing two fingers into the dough; if dent remains, dough has doubled and is light (see photo 2). Punch down doubled dough with fist (see photo 3); pull edges in to center and turn dough completely over in bowl. Dough is either allowed to rise again or it is shaped.

SHAPING LOAVES—Form dough into a smooth round ball and with a sharp knife, cut dough into halves. With fingers flatten one half of the dough (see photo 4) and form it into a 9x7x1-in. oblong. The width should be about the same as the length of bread pan (see photo 5). Fold narrow ends to center of oblong, overlapping slightly (see photo 6). Press each end down firmly; shape evenly. Seal dough into shape by pinching center fold and ends. Round top of loaf and place sealed edge down, in prepared pan. Repeat for other half of dough. Cover loaves and let rise until doubled.

A Check-List for Making Successful Yeast Breads

(See For These Recipes—What To Use, How To Do It and Oven Temperatures on *pages 4-7*.)

√ **Read again** "It's Smart To Be Careful—There's No Substitute for Accuracy" (*page 4*).

√ **Prepare pan**—grease only bottom of pan or lightly grease baking sheet. If recipe directs, "Set out pan or baking sheet," do not grease. Some rich yeast doughs should be baked in lightly greased pans.

√ **Test** for lukewarm liquid (80°F to 85°F): a drop placed on wrist will feel neither hot nor cold.

√ **Apply baking tests** when minimum baking time is up. Yeast breads are done when they are golden brown and sound hollow when tapped lightly (see photo on *page 38*).

√ **Remove rolls and loaves** from pans as they come from the oven, unless otherwise directed. Set on cooling racks to cool.

√ **Keep tops** of yeast loaves and rolls soft by immediately brushing with butter or margarine as they come from the oven. For a crisp crust, brush loaves and rolls before baking with milk or a mixture of egg yolk and water.

√ **Store bread** when completely cooled—Wrap in moisture-vapor-proof material and store in freezer (it will remain fresh for several weeks) or wrap in waxed paper, aluminum foil or moisture-vapor-proof material and store at room temperature.

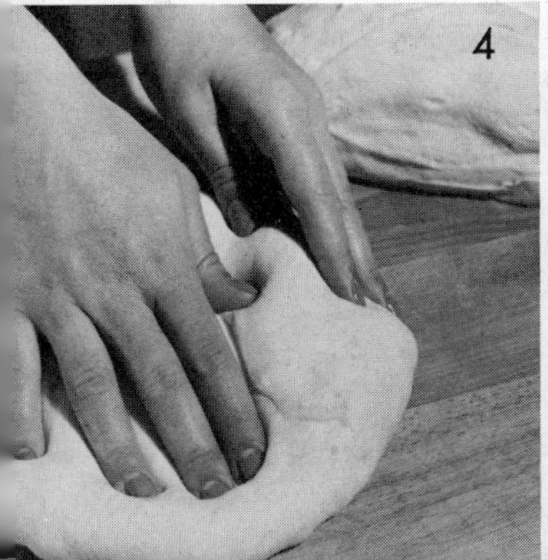
4

5

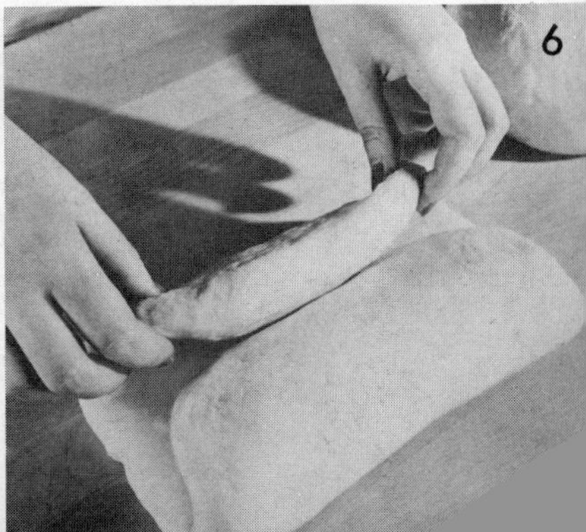
6

▲ Yeast Rolls

Scald (*page 7*)

2 cups milk

Meanwhile, soften

2 pkgs. active dry yeast

in

½ cup warm water, 110°F to 115°F (Or if using compressed yeast, soften 2 cakes in ½ cup lukewarm water, 80°F to 85°F)

Let stand 5 to 10 min.

Meanwhile, put into a large bowl

½ cup sugar
6 tablespoons shortening
2 teaspoons salt

Pour the scalded milk over ingredients in the bowl. When lukewarm, stir mixture, and blend in, beating until smooth

1 cup sifted flour

Stir softened yeast and add, mixing well.

Measure

5 to 6 cups sifted flour

Add about one-half the flour to the yeast mixture and beat until very smooth.

Beat in

2 eggs, well beaten

Then beat in enough remaining flour to make a soft dough. Turn dough onto a lightly floured surface and allow it to rest 5 to 10 min. before starting to knead.

Fantans: Roll dough into rectangle ¼ in. thick. Brush with melted butter or margarine. Cut 1½-in. strips. Stack 7. Cut 1½-in. pieces. Place in muffin-pan wells (bottoms greased).

Parker House: Roll dough into round ¼ in. thick. Cut with floured 2½-in. cutter. Brush with melted butter and margarine. Make off-center crease. Fold smaller side over and seal.

Bowknots: Roll dough into rectangle ¼ in. thick. Cut off strips ½ in. wide, 4 to 5 in. long. With hands, roll and stretch the dough into longer strips. Twist and tie strips into knots.

Crescents: Roll dough into 9-in. rounds, ¼ in. thick. Brush with melted butter or margarine. Cut into 8 wedges. Roll each wedge from the wide end. Seal firmly. Form crescents.

Knead (*page 33*). Form dough into a large ball and place it in a greased, deep bowl just large enough to allow dough to double. Turn dough to bring greased surface to top. Cover with waxed paper and towel and let stand in a warm place (about 80°F) until dough is doubled (about 1 hr.).

Punch down dough with fist; pull edges of dough in to center and turn dough completely over in bowl.* Cover and let rise again until almost doubled (about 45 min.). Again punch down the dough and turn it onto a lightly floured surface. Cover and allow the dough to rest 5 to 10 min.

Follow suggestions for the shaping of rolls (see photos), using amount needed for a single baking. Place rolls about 1 in. apart on greased baking sheets. Brush with

Melted butter or margarine

Cover and let rise again 15 to 25 min. or until dough is light.

Bake at 425°F 15 to 20 min.

4½ to 5 doz. rolls

**Note:* This dough may be kept 3 days in the refrigerator. Grease top of dough and cover. Punch down dough occasionally. Remove enough for a single baking and return remainder to refrigerator immediately. When ready to use, shape rolls and let stand at room temperature for 1 hr. or until light.

Cloverleaf: With hands, shape dough into rolls 1 in. thick. Cut off bits of dough and form balls about 1 in. in diameter. Place three balls in each muffin-pan well (bottoms greased).

Butterflies: Roll dough into rectangle ¼ in. thick, 6 in. wide. Brush with melted butter or margarine. Roll, starting with long side. Cut into 2-in. pieces. Press with knife handle.

Clothespins: Roll dough into rectangle ¼ in. thick. Cut strips ½ in. wide, 6 in. long. Roll and stretch into longer strips. Wrap around greased clothespins, edges touching.

Snails: Roll dough into rectangle ¼ in. thick. Cut off strips ½ in. wide and 4 to 5 in. long. With hands, roll and stretch into longer strips. Coil each strip around index finger.

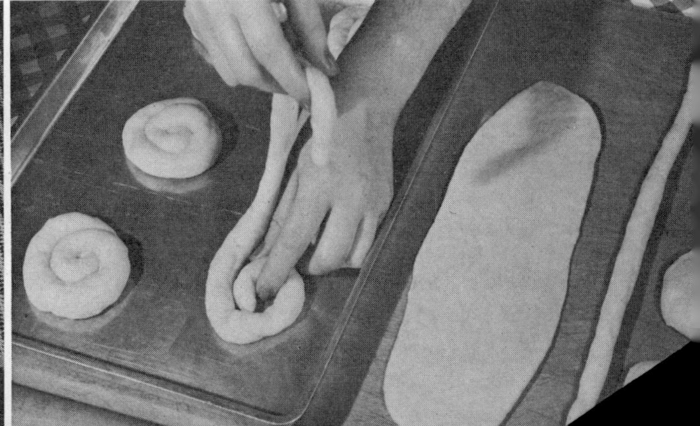

Cinnamon Rolls

△ Cinnamon Rolls

Follow ▲ Recipe (*page 34*) to shaping process. Use one third of dough and roll into a rectangle ¼ in. thick. Brush with melted **butter** or **margarine.** Sprinkle with a mixture of ⅔ cup **sugar,** 2 teaspoons **cinnamon** and ⅓ cup seedless **raisins.** Beginning with longer side, roll dough; press edges to seal. Cut roll into 1-in. slices; place, cut-side down, in a greased pan or muffin-pan wells. Brush with melted butter or margarine. Bake at 350°F 25 to 30 min.

△ Pecan Rolls

Follow ▲ Recipe (*page 34*) to shaping process. Lightly grease bottoms of about 24 muffin-pan wells. Cream together ½ cup **butter** or **margarine,** softened, 1 cup firmly packed **brown sugar** and 1½ teaspoons **cinnamon.** Spread one half of the creamed mixture in bottom of wells. Arrange ½ cup (about 2 oz.) **pecan halves** over mixture and set aside. **Toasted almonds** may be substituted for pecans.

Use one half of the dough; roll into a rectangle ½ in. thick. Spread remaining one half of creamed mixture on dough and sprinkle with ½ cup (about 2 oz.) chopped **pecans.** Beginning with longer side, roll dough and press edges to seal. Cut roll into slices ¾ to 1 in. thick and place, cut side down, in muffin pan-wells. Cover and let rise until doubled.

Bake at 350°F 25 to 30 min. Invert pans on cooling racks. Allow to stand a few seconds before lifting off pans. Cool, pecan side up.

△ Coffee Braid

(*See color photo inside front cover*)

Follow ▲ Recipe (*page 34*). Sift ¼ teaspoon **mace** with the first flour addition. Mix 1 teaspoon grated **lemon peel** (*page 5*) and ½ cup seedless **raisins;** mix into batter before last flour addition. After second rising, divide dough into 3 equal portions. Roll each into a strip about 14 in. long. Braid strips together, tucking open ends under. Cover and let rise about 45 min., or until doubled.

Bake at 350°F 35 to 40 min. While warm, spread with frosting made by blending 1 cup **confectioners' sugar,** 2 tablespoons warm **water** and ½ teaspoon **vanilla extract.** Top with candied **cherries, pecan halves** and bits of candied **citron.**

Sour Cream Kuchen

MRS. JOHN TRAEGER
PORTERVILLE, CALIF.

The contestant modestly described her prize-winning coffee cake as "tasty." We suggest you bake it, taste it, and use your own superlatives.

Set out three 9-in. round layer cake pans.

Scald (*page 7*)
¾ cup milk
Meanwhile, soften
1 pkg. active dry yeast
in
¼ cup warm water 110°F to 115°F (Or if using compressed yeast, soften 1 cake in ¼ cup lukewarm water, 80°F to 85°F)
Let yeast stand 5 to 10 min.

Meanwhile, put into a large bowl
¼ cup sugar
¼ cup butter
1 teaspoon salt
Pour scalded milk over ingredients in bowl. When lukewarm, stir mixture and blend in, beating until smooth
1 cup flour
Stir softened yeast and add, mixing well.

Measure
3 cups sifted flour
Add about one-half the flour to yeast mixture and beat until very smooth.

Beat in
2 eggs, well beaten
Then beat in enough remaining flour to make a soft dough. Form dough into a large ball and place in a greased, deep bowl just large enough to allow dough to double. Turn dough to bring greased surface to top. Cover with waxed paper and a towel and let stand in a warm place (about 80°F) until doubled (about 2 hrs.).

Meanwhile, lightly grease the pans.

When dough has doubled, punch down and turn onto lightly floured surface. Divide into three equal parts and form into smooth balls. Cover and allow to rest 5 to 10 min. Shape into three rounds. Put dough into prepared pans and pat rounds evenly to fit pans. Cover and let rise again until doubled.

Just before dough is doubled, put into a bowl
2 cups firmly packed light brown sugar
Cut in with a pastry blender or two knives until mixture is crumbly
2 tablespoons butter
Set aside.

Blend together thoroughly
1 cup thick sour cream
1 teaspoon vanilla extract
and a mixture of
2 tablespoons confectioners' sugar
1 tablespoon cornstarch
Reserve one half of mixture.

When dough has doubled, spread dough in the pans with remaining sour-cream mixture and then sprinkle with brown-sugar mixture. Sprinkle with about
1 tablespoon cinnamon
Bake at 400°F 20 min., or until golden brown. Remove kuchens from oven and spread with reserved sour-cream mixture. Return to oven and bake 5 min. longer.

Three 9-in. round kuchens

▲ White Bread

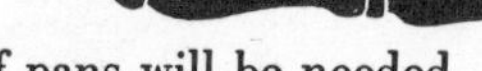

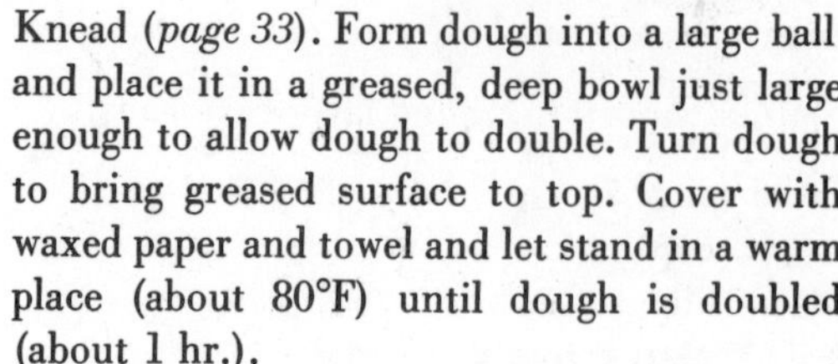

Two 9½x5¼x2¾-in. loaf pans will be needed.

Scald (*page 7*)

2 cups milk

Meanwhile, soften

1 pkg. active dry yeast

in

¼ cup warm water, 110°F to 115°F (Or if using compressed yeast, soften 1 cake in ¼ cup lukewarm water, 80°F to 85°F)

Let yeast stand 5 to 10 min.

Meanwhile, put into a large bowl

2 tablespoons sugar
1½ tablespoons shortening
2½ teaspoons salt

Pour scalded milk over ingredients in bowl. When lukewarm, stir mixture and blend in, beating until smooth

1 cup sifted flour

Stir softened yeast and add, mixing well.

Measure

5 to 6 cups sifted flour

Add about one-half the flour to the yeast mixture and beat until very smooth. Then beat in enough remaining flour to make a soft dough. Turn dough onto a lightly floured surface, and let rest 5 to 10 min.

Knead (*page 33*). Form dough into a large ball and place it in a greased, deep bowl just large enough to allow dough to double. Turn dough to bring greased surface to top. Cover with waxed paper and towel and let stand in a warm place (about 80°F) until dough is doubled (about 1 hr.).

Punch down dough with fist; pull edges of dough in to center and turn dough completely over in bowl. Cover and let rise again until almost doubled (about 45 min.).

Grease bottoms of the loaf pans.

Punch down dough and turn onto a lightly floured surface. Divide into two equal portions and form into smooth balls. Cover and allow to rest 5 to 10 min. Shape into loaves (*page 33*). Place in the greased loaf pans. Cover and let rise until dough is doubled (about 1 hr.).

Bake at 400°F about 50 min., or until loaves are golden brown.

Cool and store as directed (*page 33*).

Two 1-lb. loaves bread

White Bread: Place bread pans on center oven rack so that they do not touch each other.

Tap sides or bottom of each loaf of bread. A hollow sound indicates that the bread is done.

△ Whole Wheat Bread

JOYCE GRAHAM, OMAHA, NEBR.

Follow ▲ Recipe. Increase milk to 2¼ cups. Increase yeast to 2 pkgs. active dry yeast or 2 cakes compressed yeast softened in ½ cup water. Substitute ¼ cup **honey** for the sugar. Increase shortening to ¼ cup and salt to 1 tablespoon. Substitute 1 cup **whole wheat flour** for the cup of sifted flour. Decrease the measured sifted flour to 4 cups, and measure 3 cups whole wheat flour. Add the whole wheat flour and ½ cup of the sifted flour to the yeast mixture. Then beat in enough of the remaining sifted flour to make a soft dough. Proceed through remaining steps of ▲ Recipe.

Bake at 350°F about 45 min., or until loaves are golden brown.

Swedish Rye Bread

MYRTLE C. WORLEY, GOLD BEACH, ORE.

A baking sheet will be needed.

Soften

1 pkg. active dry yeast

in

¼ cup warm water 110°F to 115°F (Or if using compressed yeast, soften 1 cake in ¼ cup lukewarm water, 80°F to 85°F)

Let yeast stand 5 to 10 min.

Meanwhile, put into a large bowl

¼ cup molasses
¼ cup firmly packed brown sugar
1 tablespoon shortening
1 tablespoon salt
1 teaspoon anise seed
½ teaspoon caraway seed

Pour over ingredients in bowl

1½ cups very hot water

When lukewarm, stir mixture and blend in, beating until smooth

1 cup sifted flour

Stir softened yeast and add, mixing well.

Measure

3 to 3½ cups sifted flour
2 cups rye flour

Add the rye flour and beat until very smooth. Then beat in enough of the remaining flour to make a soft dough. Turn dough onto a lightly floured surface and let rest 5 to 10 min.

Knead (*page 33*). Form dough into a large ball and place it in a greased, deep bowl just large enough to allow dough to double. Turn dough to bring greased surface to top. Cover with waxed paper and a towel and let stand in a warm place (about 80°F) until dough is doubled (about 1 hr.).

Punch down dough with fist; pull edges of dough in to center and turn dough completely over in bowl. Cover and let rise again until almost doubled (about 45 min.).

Grease the baking sheet.

Punch down dough and turn onto a lightly floured surface. Divide into two equal portions and form into smooth balls. Cover and allow to rest 5 to 10 min. Place on the greased baking sheet. Cover and let rise until dough is doubled (about 1½ hrs.).

Bake at 400° about 50 min., or until loaves are golden brown.

Cool and store as directed (*page 33*).

2 loaves rye bread

QUICK BREADS

Quick breads get their name from the relatively short time of preparation as compared with yeast breads. The leavening of quick breads is usually achieved by the use of baking powder or baking soda. Popovers are an exception, requiring steam to leaven them. Quick breads include different types of products—muffins, biscuits, loaves (fruit and nut), popovers, corn bread, dumplings, brown bread, waffles, griddlecakes, some doughnuts and fritters.

One method of classifying quick breads is by the proportion of liquid to flour. *Thin batters* (popovers, timbales, griddlecakes)—usually 1½ to 2 cups liquid to 2 cups flour. *Stiff batters* (muffins, fruit and nut loaves)—usually 1 cup liquid to 2 cups flour. *Soft doughs* (doughnuts, baking powder biscuits)—usually ¾ cup liquid to 2 cups flour.

Quick breads do not have the keeping quality that richer products do because they are low in ingredients such as shortening, eggs and sugar.

Most quick breads are at their peak in flavor when served fresh from the oven. Many of the loaves that have higher amounts of sugar and shortening along with fruits and nuts are usually cooled before serving. Some loaves slice more easily and improve in flavor if they are served the following day.

An important reminder—never overmix a quick bread batter or dough.

A Check List for Making Successful Quick Breads

(See For These Recipes—What To Use, How To Do It and Oven Temperatures on *pages 4-7.*)

√ **Read** recipe carefully.

√ **Assemble** all ingredients and utensils.

√ **Have all ingredients** at room temperature unless recipe specifies otherwise.

√ **Select pans** of proper kind and size. Measure inside, from rim to rim.

√ **Use standard measuring cups and spoons.** Use liquid measuring cups (rim above 1-cup line) for liquids. Use nested or dry measuring cups (1-cup line even with top) for dry ingredients. Check liquid measurements at eye level. Level dry measurements with straight-edged knife or spatula.

√ **Preheat oven** 12 to 20 min. at required temperature. Leave oven door open first 2 min.

√ **Place oven rack** so top of product will be almost at center of oven. Stagger pans so no pan is directly over another and they do not touch each other or walls of oven. Place single pan so that center of product is as near center of oven as possible.

√ **Prepare pan**—Grease only bottom of pan or lightly grease baking sheet. If recipe directs, "Set out pan or baking sheet," do not grease pan.

√ **Sift all flour** except whole-grain types before measuring. Spoon lightly into measuring cup; do not jar. Level with straight-edged knife or spatula.

√ **Cream shortening** (alone or with flavorings) by stirring, rubbing or beating with spoon or electric mixer until softened. Add sugar in small amounts; cream after each addition until all graininess disappears and mixture is light and fluffy.

√ **Beat whole eggs** until thick and piled softly when recipe calls for well-beaten eggs.

√ **Beat egg whites** as follows: *Frothy*—entire mass forms bubbles; *Rounded peaks*—peaks turn over slightly when beater is slowly lifted upright; *Stiff peaks*—peaks remain standing when beater is slowly lifted upright.

√ **Beat egg yolks** until thick and lemon-colored when recipe calls for well-beaten yolks.

√ **Fill pans** one-half to two-thirds full.

√ **Apply baking tests** when minimum baking time is up. For *coffee cakes* and for *quick loaf breads,* insert a cake tester or wooden pick in center; if it comes out clean, cake or bread is done.

√ **Remove quick loaf breads and coffee cakes** from pans as they come from the oven, unless otherwise directed. Set on cooling racks to cool.

√ **Wrap cooled quick loaf breads** in waxed paper, aluminum foil or moisture-vapor-proof material; store overnight for easier slicing.

▲ Muffins

Prepare (*page 40*) 12 2½-in. muffin-pan wells.

Melt and set aside
- **¼ cup butter or margarine**

Sift together into a bowl and set aside
- **2 cups sifted flour**
- **⅓ cup sugar**
- **1 tablespoon baking powder**
- **½ teaspoon salt**

Blend thoroughly
- **1 egg, well beaten**
- **1 cup milk**

Blend in the melted shortening. Make a well in center of dry ingredients and add liquid mixture all at one time. With not more than 25 strokes, quickly and lightly stir until dry ingredients are barely moistened. Batter will be lumpy and break from spoon. (Too much mixing will result in muffin tunnels.)

Cut against side of bowl with spoon to get enough batter at one time to fill each muffin-pan well two-thirds full. Place spoon in well and push batter off with another spoon or spatula. Fill any empty wells half-full with water before placing pans in oven.

Bake at 425°F 20 to 25 min., or until muffins are an even golden brown.

Run spatula around each muffin and lift out. If necessary to keep muffins warm before serving, loosen muffins and tip slightly in wells. Keep in a warm place. Serve warm.

1 doz. Muffins

Blueberry Muffins

△ Blueberry Muffins

Follow ▲ Recipe. Rinse and drain 1 cup fresh **blueberries.** Fold into batter with final strokes.

△ Cranberry Muffins

Follow ▲ Recipe. Wash and drain 1 cup **cranberries;** chop coarsely. Mix with 3 tablespoons **sugar.** Mix into sifted dry ingredients.

△ Double-Top Muffins

Follow ▲ Recipe; place a cooked, dried **apricot** half in bottom of each greased muffin-pan well. Spoon batter into wells. Top with mixture of ½ cup firmly packed **brown sugar,** ½ cup **butter** or **margarine,** softened, ⅓ cup sifted **flour** and 1 teaspoon **cinnamon.**

▲ Date-Nut Bread

Prepare (*page 40*) 9½x5¼x2¾-in. loaf pan.

Melt and set aside
⅓ cup shortening
Sift together into a bowl
2 cups sifted flour
¾ cup sugar
4 teaspoons baking powder
¾ teaspoon salt
Mix in
1 cup whole wheat flour
1 cup (about 7 oz.) pitted dates, cut (*page 6*)
1 cup (about 4 oz.) chopped nuts
Set dry ingredients aside.

Mix until blended
1 egg, well beaten
1 cup milk
½ cup molasses
1½ teaspoons vanilla extract
¼ teaspoon orange extract
Blend in the melted shortening.

Make a well in center of dry ingredients and add liquid mixture all at one time. Stir only enough to moisten dry ingredients. Turn batter into pan and spread to corners.

Bake at 350°F about 1 hr., or until bread tests done (*page 40*).

Cool and store as directed (*page 40*).

1 loaf Date-Nut Bread

△ Fruit-Nut Bread

Follow ▲ Recipe. Substitute for dates, ¼ cup each of **currants,** chopped **candied citron, candied cherries** and **candied orange peel.**

Nut Bread

CAROLYN E. ARNOLD, KINGSTON, N. Y.

Prepare (*page 40*) a 9½x5¼x2¾-in. loaf pan.

Melt and set aside
2 tablespoons shortening
Sift together into a bowl
3 cups sifted flour
¾ cup sugar
4 teaspoons baking powder
¾ teaspoon salt
Mix in
¾ cup (about 3 oz.) coarsely chopped nuts
Set dry ingredients aside.

Blend thoroughly
1 egg, well beaten
1½ cups milk
Blend in the melted shortening.

Make a well in center of dry ingredients and add liquid mixture all at one time. Stir only to moisten dry ingredients. Turn batter into pan and spread to corners.

Bake at 350°F about 1 hr., or until bread tests done (*page 40*).

Cool and store as directed (*page 40*).

1 loaf Nut Bread

All-in-One Biscuit Mix

Sift together into a large mixing bowl
8 cups sifted flour
¼ cup baking powder
4 teaspoons salt

Cut in with pastry blender or two knives until mixture resembles coarse corn meal
2 cups lard, hydrogenated vegetable shortening or all-purpose shortening
Store mix in tightly covered container in a cool place. (Biscuit mix made with lard should be stored in refrigerator.)

Note: Before measuring for use in recipe, lightly mix by tossing with fork.

For Rolled Baking Powder Biscuits—Measure 3 cups Biscuit Mix into a bowl. Add ⅔ cup milk all at one time. Stir with a fork; form dough into a ball. On a floured surface knead 10 to 15 times. Roll ½-in. thick. Cut with 2-in. floured cutter. Bake at 450°F 10 to 15 min.

Makes 18 biscuits

Tender-Rich Biscuits

▲ Tender-Rich Buttermilk Biscuits

Set out a baking sheet.

Sift together into a bowl

2 cups sifted flour
2 teaspoons baking powder
1 teaspoon salt

Cut in with a pastry blender or two knives until mixture resembles coarse corn meal

⅓ cup lard

Make a well in the center of the dry ingredients. Pour in all at one time

¾ cup buttermilk

Stir with a fork until dough follows fork. Gently form dough into a ball and put onto a lightly floured surface. Knead lightly with finger tips 10 to 15 times.

Gently roll out dough ½ in. thick. Cut with a floured cutter or knife, using an even pressure to keep sides of biscuits straight. Place biscuits on baking sheet, close together for soft-sided biscuits, or 1 in. apart for crusty sides.

Lightly brush tops with

Milk

Bake at 450°F 10 to 15 min., or until biscuits are golden brown.

About 2 doz. 1½-in. biscuits

△1 Tender-Rich Biscuits

Follow ▲ Recipe; substitute ¾ cup **milk** for buttermilk.

△2 Tender-Rich Drop Biscuits

Follow ▲ Recipe or △1 Recipe. Increase buttermilk or milk to 1 cup. Omit kneading, rolling and cutting. Drop by spoonfuls onto baking sheet.

△3 Tender-Rich Rolled Shortcakes

Follow ▲ Recipe or △1 Recipe. Sift 2 tablespoons **sugar** with dry ingredients. Cut dough with floured knife into squares or into rounds with 3-in. cutter. Or cut dough into halves and roll each portion to fit an 8-in. round layer cake pan. Spread one half of the rounds, or one of the large rounds, with melted **butter** or **margarine.** Top with remaining rounds or round. Place on baking sheet or in layer cake pan and bake as in ▲ Recipe.

△4 Cinnamon Pinwheels

Follow ▲ Recipe or △1 Recipe. Grease the baking sheet. Roll dough into rectangle about ¼ in. thick. Brush dough with 2 tablespoons melted **butter** or **margarine.** Sprinkle with a mixture of ¼ cup firmly packed **brown sugar,** ¼ cup (about 1 oz.) finely chopped **nuts** and 1 teaspoon **cinnamon.** Beginning with long side, roll and press edges together to seal. Cut into 1-in. slices. Do not brush tops with milk. Place flat on baking sheet and bake.

△5 Apple Roll

Follow △ Recipe. Omit the brown sugar mixture. Spread dough with a mixture of 1½ cups (about 2 medium-size) finely chopped **apple,** ½ cup **sugar** and 1 teaspoon **cinnamon.**

Irish Batter Bread

BERTHA L. STICKNEY, HERSEY, MICH.

Prize-winning story of a favorite recipe:

"This recipe was brought to America from Ireland in 1640 and became known to my grandmother in 1829 when she received it, together with a wedding gift, from a Boston cousin. Migrating to Michigan in 1840, by ox-cart, covered wagon and canal boat, she, her husband and six children settled in Owosso. With no grist mill, no wheat, no flour, bread-making became a dreary task. She labored through by pulverizing corn into meal with a mortar and pestle, baking bread in iron bread pans in an open fireplace. For a long time white bread was a delicacy seldom attained.

"Grandmother died in 1910 and among her keepsakes this recipe, yellow from age, the ink faded to a rusty tan, was found in a box, with the Boston cousin's wedding gift—a handsome, purple velvet, beaded pincushion.

"The recipe as it appears here has been somewhat altered to meet modern facilities."

This bread should be stored for 12 to 24 hours before serving.

Grease bottom of a 9½x5¼x2¾-in. loaf pan.

Melt and set aside

2 tablespoons shortening

Sift together into a large bowl and set aside

3 cups sifted flour
½ cup sugar
4 teaspoons baking powder
2 teaspoons cinnamon
1 teaspoon salt

Mix until blended

1 egg, well beaten
1½ cups milk
3 tablespoons grated orange peel (*page 5*)

Blend in the melted shortening. Make a well in center of dry ingredients and add liquid ingredients all at one time with

1 cup (about 5 oz.) currants

Stir to moisten dry ingredients. Beat until smooth. Turn dough into pan and let stand at room temperature for 20 min.

Bake at 325°F 1 hr. to 1 hr. 15 min., or until bread tests done (*page 40*).

Cool and store as directed (*page 40*).

1 loaf bread

Stay-Popped Popovers

Grease thoroughly with cooking oil 6 or 7 heat-resistant glass custard cups; or grease iron popover pans and preheat 15 min. in oven.

Sift together into a bowl and set aside
1 cup sifted flour
½ teaspoon salt
Beat slightly
3 eggs
Beat in
1 cup milk
2 teaspoons melted butter or margarine
Make a well in center of dry ingredients. Pour in liquid mixture. Beat with rotary beater until batter is very smooth. Fill custard cups one-half full of batter.

Bake at 475°F 10 min. Reduce temperature to 350°F and bake 30 min.

Serve immediately. *6 or 7 large popovers*

Note: If a drier interior is desired, make a slit in the side of each baked popover to allow steam to escape. Return to oven with heat turned off and allow popovers to dry 10 min.

▲ Corn-Bread Squares

Prepare (*page 40*) an 8x8x2-in. pan.

Melt and set aside
5 tablespoons shortening
Sift together into a bowl
1 cup sifted flour
¼ cup sugar
1 tablespoon baking powder
¾ teaspoon salt
Mix in
1 cup yellow corn meal
Set dry ingredients aside.

Mix until blended
1 egg, well beaten
1 cup milk
Blend in the melted shortening.

Make a well in center of dry ingredients. Add liquid mixture all at one time. Beat with a rotary beater until just smooth, being careful not to overmix. Turn the batter into pan and spread to corners.

Bake at 425°F about 20 min., or until bread tests done (*page 40*).

Cut into squares and serve. *16 servings*

△ Crisp Corn Sticks

Follow ▲ Recipe. Spoon batter into 12 hot, greased corn-stick pan sections, filling each three-fourths full. Bake at 425°F 10 to 15 min.

Stay-Popped Popovers

Crisp Corn Sticks

▲ Pioneer Griddlecakes

Heat a griddle or heavy skillet over low heat.

Melt and set aside to cool
2 tablespoons shortening
Sift together
2 cups sifted flour
1 tablespoon baking powder
1 tablespoon sugar
¾ teaspoon salt
Blend thoroughly
1 egg, well beaten
1½ cups milk
Blend in the melted shortening.

Make a well in center of the dry ingredients. Add the liquid mixture all at one time, stirring only until blended.

Test griddle; it is hot enough for baking when drops of water sprinkled on surface dance in small beads. Lightly grease griddle or skillet if manufacturer so directs. Pour batter from a pitcher or large spoon into small pools about 4 in. in diameter, leaving at least 1 in. between. Turn griddlecakes as they become puffy and full of bubbles. Turn only once.

Serve immediately with **butter** or **margarine, Panbroiled Link Sausages** (*page 87*) or **Panbroiled Bacon** (*page 87*), **brown sugar, honey, maple sirup, jam** or **jelly.**

To keep cakes warm, place between folds of absorbent paper in a moderate oven.

About 24 griddlecakes

△ Buttermilk Griddlecakes

Follow ▲ Recipe. Substitute 1 teaspoon **baking soda** for baking powder and 2 cups **buttermilk** for milk.

◬ Blueberry Griddlecakes

Follow ▲ Recipe. Add 1 cup rinsed, fresh (or drained, canned) **blueberries.** Serve with topping. Or bake silver-dollar-size griddlecakes; sift **confectioners' sugar** over each. Arrange on plate around **whipped cream** (*page 7*).

Pioneer Griddlecakes and Panbroiled Bacon (page 87)

◬ Corn Meal Griddlecakes

Follow ▲ Recipe or △ Recipe. Reduce flour to 1 cup and mix ¾ cup **corn meal** into the dry ingredients.

▲ Buttermilk Waffles

Heat waffle baker while preparing waffle batter.

Melt and set aside
½ cup butter or margarine
Sift together into a large bowl and set aside
2 cups sifted flour
1 tablespoon sugar
2 teaspoons baking powder
1 teaspoon baking soda
½ teaspoon salt
Beat until thick and lemon-colored
3 egg yolks
Add gradually, blending thoroughly, melted butter or margarine and
2 cups buttermilk
Add liquid mixture all at one time to dry ingredients; mix only until batter is smooth.

Beat until rounded peaks are formed
3 egg whites
Spread the beaten egg whites over the batter and gently fold (*page 6*) together.

Unless temperature is automatically shown on

waffle baker, test heat by dropping a few drops cold water on baker. It is hot enough when drops of water dance in small beads. Pour batter into center of baker. (It is wise to experiment to find the exact amount of batter your baker will hold; use that same measurement in future waffle baking.)

Bake according to manufacturer's directions, or until steaming stops (about 10 min.). Do not raise cover during baking period. Lift cover and loosen waffle with a fork.

Serve immediately with **butter** or **margarine** and warm **maple sirup.** *About 6 waffles*

△ Sweet Milk Waffles

Follow ▲ Recipe. Omit baking soda and increase baking powder to 1 tablespoon. Substitute **milk** for buttermilk.

▲ French Toast

Set out a heavy skillet.

Beat slightly in a shallow dish or pie pan

2 eggs

Mix in and set aside

⅔ cup milk or cream
1 tablespoon sugar
½ teaspoon salt
1 teaspoon vanilla extract

Set out

8 slices bread, white or whole wheat (Slightly dry bread produces firmer French Toast)

Heat in the skillet over low heat

2 to 3 tablespoons butter or margarine

Dip bread slices one at a time into egg mixture. Coat each side well and place in hot skillet at once. Brown over moderate heat, turning once with spatula. If necessary, add more fat to keep slices from sticking.

Serve with **butter** or **margarine, maple sirup, honey, jam** or **confectioners' sugar.**

8 slices French Toast

Note: For oven method, place coated bread slices on a well-greased baking sheet. Brown in oven at 450°F about 10 min. for each side.

△ Oahu Toast

Drain contents of 1 No. 1 flat can **pineapple slices.** Follow ▲ Recipe, omit sugar and substitute **pineapple sirup** for milk. If can does not contain enough sirup, add **water.** Lightly brown pineapple slices in 2 to 3 tablespoons **butter** or **margarine.** Serve one-half pineapple slice with each slice of toast.

▲ Orange Sugar Toast

For Orange Sugar—Blend and set aside

2 tablespoons sugar
1 tablespoon grated orange peel (*page 5*)
2 teaspoons orange juice
⅛ teaspoon nutmeg

For Toast—Remove crusts from

4 slices bread

Set temperature control of range at Broil. Place slices on broiler rack; place in broiler about 3 in. from heat source. When brown, remove and spread untoasted sides with

Butter or margarine

Sprinkle with Orange Sugar and return to broiler rack; broil until sugar is melted.

If desired, cut slices into fancy shapes.

4 slices Orange Sugar Toast

⚠ Cinnamon Caramel Toast

Follow ▲ Recipe. Substitute a mixture of 2 tablespoons **brown** or **maple sugar** and 1 teaspoon **cinnamon** for Orange Sugar.

⚠ English Muffin Crisps

Follow ▲ Recipe or ⚠ Recipe. Substitute 2 split **English muffins** for bread. Butter and toast split sides only. Sprinkle with sugar mixture and continue as in ▲ Recipe.

Brown Sugar Doughnuts and hot coffee

Deep-fry doughnuts and "holes" in heated fat. Fry only as many doughnuts at one time as will float uncrowded one layer deep in the fat. Turn doughnuts with a fork as they rise to surface and several times during cooking (do not pierce). Fry 2 to 4 min., or until lightly browned. Drain doughnuts and "holes" over fat for a few seconds before removing to absorbent paper.

Serve plain or shake 2 or 3 warm doughnuts at a time in a plastic bag containing

½ cup confectioners' sugar

About 2 doz. doughnuts plus "holes"

Brown Sugar Doughnuts

DOROTHY J. MARCUSSEN, RIVERTON, ILL.

The warm sweet smell of fresh doughnuts and the dark fragrance of freshly brewed coffee—a time-tried invitation to comfort and cheer.

Set out a deep saucepan or automatic deep-fryer (*page* 7) and heat fat to 365°F.

Sift together and set aside

5 cups sifted flour
2 teaspoons baking powder
2 teaspoons baking soda
2 teaspoons cinnamon

Beat until thick and piled softly

4 eggs

Add gradually, beating thoroughly after each addition

2 cups firmly packed brown sugar

Blend in dry ingredients alternately with

½ cup thick sour cream

Stir lightly until well blended. Dough will be soft. If dough seems very sticky, measure

½ cup sifted flour

Add enough of the flour to make an easily handled but soft dough. Save remainder for rolling. Chill dough in refrigerator for 1 hr.

Turn dough onto lightly floured surface. Handling very lightly, roll dough ½ in. thick and cut with a lightly floured doughnut cutter.

Halloween Fried Cakes

MRS. MERLA VOUGHT, BOYNE CITY, MICH.

A deep saucepan or automatic deep-fryer will be needed.

Sift together and set aside

4 cups sifted flour
1 tablespoon baking powder
1 teaspoon salt
½ teaspoon baking soda
1 teaspoon pumpkin pie spice

Cream together until lard is softened

2 tablespoons lard
1 teaspoon vanilla extract

Add gradually, creaming well after each addition

1 cup sugar

Add in thirds, beating thoroughly after each addition

2 eggs, well beaten

Blend in

1 cup canned pumpkin

Measure

1 cup buttermilk or sour milk (*page 5*)

Stirring until well blended after each addition, alternately add dry ingredients in fourths, liquid in thirds, to pumpkin mixture. Dough will be soft. Chill in refrigerator about 1 hr.

About 20 min. before ready to deep-fry, heat fat to 365°F (*page* 7).

Turn dough onto a floured surface. Handling

very lightly, roll dough ¼ in. thick and cut with a lightly floured 2-in. doughnut cutter.

Deep-fry doughnuts and "holes" in heated fat. Fry only as many at one time as will float uncrowded one layer deep in the fat. Turn doughnuts with a fork or tongs as they rise to surface and several times during cooking (do not pierce). Fry 3 to 4 min., or until lightly browned. Drain doughnuts and "holes" over fat for a few seconds before removing to absorbent paper.

Serve plain or shake 2 or 3 warm doughnuts at a time in a plastic bag in a mixture of

½ cup granulated sugar
1 to 2½ tablespoons cinnamon

4 doz. doughnuts plus "holes"

▲ Old-Fashioned Apple Fritters

Set out a deep saucepan or automatic deep-fryer (*page* 7) and heat fat to 365°F.

Melt and set aside

1 tablespoon shortening

Sift together into a bowl and set aside

1⅓ cups sifted flour
2 tablespoons sugar
1 teaspoon baking powder
½ teaspoon salt

Wash, pare, core and cut into ¼-in. rings

4 firm apples

Or cut apples into ¼-in. thick lengthwise wedges. Sprinkle over apples

3 to 4 tablespoons lemon juice
2 tablespoons confectioners' sugar

Toss apples lightly. Let stand about 5 min.

Blend thoroughly

2 eggs, well beaten
1 cup milk

Blend in the melted shortening.

Make a well in center of dry ingredients. Add liquid mixture all at one time and mix until batter is smooth.

Drain apple pieces. Using a large fork or slotted spoon, dip apple pieces in batter to coat well, allowing excess batter to drip into bowl before lowering apple pieces into fat. Deep-fry only as many fritters as will float, uncrowded, one layer deep in fat. Turn with a fork as they rise and frequently thereafter (do not pierce). Deep-fry 2 to 3 min., or until golden brown. Drain over fat for a few seconds before removing to absorbent paper.

Serve hot. *5 or 6 servings*

△ Corn-Gold Fritters

Follow ▲ Recipe. Omit apples and sugar. Decrease milk to ⅔ cup and shortening to 1 teaspoon. Add 1 teaspoon **Worcestershire sauce,** ⅛ teaspoon **pepper** and 1⅓ cups (1 12-oz. can) whole kernel **corn,** well drained. Drop by tablespoonfuls into the heated fat. Serve with **Cheese Sauce** (double recipe, *page 181*).

△ Sweet Banana Fritters

Follow ▲ Recipe. Substitute 4 firm **bananas** having green-tipped peel for apples. Peel and cut into halves lengthwise, then into thirds crosswise. Omit confectioners' sugar before dipping into batter.

Dumplings

Sift together

2 cups sifted flour

4 teaspoons baking powder

1 teaspoon salt

Cut in with a pastry blender or two knives until pieces are size of rice kernels

1 tablespoon shortening

Quickly stir in with a fork until just blended

⅔ cup milk

1 tablespoon chopped parsley

Drop by tablespoonfuls on top of stew or fricassee. Dumplings should rest on meat and vegetables; if dumplings settle down on the liquid, they may be soggy. If necessary, pour off excess liquid to prevent this. Cover tightly and cook over medium heat 20 min. without removing cover. *About 6 servings*

Note: ¼ cup chopped **mint** can be substituted for parsley.

Yorkshire Pudding

Pour into an 11x7x1½-in. baking dish and keep hot

¼ cup hot drippings from roast beef

Beat until thick and piled softly

2 eggs

Add to beaten eggs and beat with rotary beater until smooth

1 cup milk

1 cup sifted flour

½ teaspoon salt

Pour into baking dish over hot meat drippings.

Bake at 400°F 30 to 40 min., or until puffed and golden brown.

Cut into squares and serve immediately with **Standing Rib Roast of Beef** (*page 64*).

About 6 servings

Dumplings with stewed chicken

Potato Pancakes

Heat in a heavy skillet over low heat.

Shortening to at least ¼-in. depth

Mix together and set aside

2 tablespoons flour

1½ teaspoons salt

¼ teaspoon baking powder

⅛ teaspoon pepper

Wash, pare and finely grate

6 medium-size (about 2 lbs.) potatoes (about 3 cups, grated)

Set grated potatoes aside.

Blend the dry ingredients into a mixture of

2 eggs, well beaten

1 teaspoon grated onion

Pat the grated potatoes dry with absorbent paper and add potatoes to egg mixture. Mix thoroughly.

When shortening is hot, but not smoking, begin cooking. Using about 2 tablespoons for each pancake, spoon batter onto skillet, leaving at least 1 in. between cakes. Cook over medium heat until golden brown and crisp on one side. Turn pancakes only once and brown second side.

If desired, serve with hot **rosy pink applesauce.**

About 20 medium-size pancakes

Toastee Baskets

Ringlet Shells—To serve four persons, use 12 **bread slices,** about ½ in. thick. Trim off crusts and cut all slices into large squares, rectangles or rounds (making all 12 slices the same shape). Use a biscuit or cookie cutter for cutting the rounds. Set aside four shapes. With a sharp pointed knife or cookie cutter, cut out centers from the 8 remaining shapes to make rings at least ½ in. wide.

Thoroughly brush tops of uncut shapes and both sides of rings with **milk.** Stack 2 rings on each uncut shape. Brush inside and outside with melted **butter** or **margarine.**

Place on a baking sheet and toast at 325°F 12 to 20 min., or until golden brown and crisp.

Croustades—Cut **day-old bread** into slices 1¼ to 2 in. thick. Remove crusts and cut bread into desired shapes—triangles, squares, diamonds; or cut into rounds or fancy shapes with a large biscuit or cookie cutter. If cutter is not deep enough, mark with it and finish cutting with the point of a sharp knife. Following outline of shaped piece, carefully cut out center ¼ to ½ in. from edge, and down to within ¼ to ½ in. of bottom, leaving a neatly cut shell.

Brush outside and inside of shells with melted **butter** or **margarine.**

Place on baking sheet and toast at 325°F 12 to 20 min., or until lightly browned and crisp.

If shells are not used immediately, reheat in oven for a few minutes before filling.

Or deep-fry (*page* 7) unbuttered shells at 375°F until lightly browned. Drain for a few minutes on absorbent paper.

Fill Croustades or Ringlet Shells with creamed eggs, meat, fish, poultry or vegetables.

Shell centers and crusts may be toasted or dried, ground and saved for crumbs. Or centers may be toasted and used as a garnish to top filled Croustades.

Loaf Basket—Neatly trim the crusts from top and sides of a loaf of **unsliced bread.** Using a sharp pointed knife, hollow out center, leaving ¾-in. sides and bottom. Brush inside and out with melted **butter** or **margarine.**
For a cover on the basket, cut a ¾-in. slice from length of loaf before making the basket. Brush both sides with melted **butter** or **margarine.** Place on baking sheet with basket.

Toast at 325°F 15 to 25 min., or until golden brown and crisp.

Fill with any creamed mixture and serve.

Toast Cups—Cut crusts from thin slices of **bread.** Lightly brush both sides with melted **butter** or **margarine** and press each slice into a muffin-pan well, corners pointing up.

Toast at 325°F 12 to 20 min., or until crisp and lightly browned.

Toast Points—Trim crusts from **bread slices.** Toast and spread with **butter** or **margarine.** Cut each slice diagonally in half.

Toast Fingers—Trim crusts from **bread slices.** Toast and spread with **butter** or **margarine.** Cut slices into fingers about 1 in. wide.

Croutons—To prepare about 1½ cups Croutons, melt 2 to 3 tablespoons **butter** or **margarine** in a large, heavy skillet over low heat. Meanwhile, if desired, trim crusts from 2 slices **toasted bread.** Cut bread into ¼- to ½-in. cubes. Put cubes into the skillet and toss until all sides are coated and browned.

What You Should Know About Eggs

The perfection of an egg is one of Nature's miracles. For here is an object lovely in form, filled with nourishment, and possessed of a flavor that is delicious in itself and is an admirable flavor foil for innumerable seasonings and sauces. Few foods match the egg in versatility. Eggs can take us through the day with grace and ease—are equally appealing in the morning, at noon or night.

Grading—Graded eggs in cartons kept in a clean, cold refrigerator by the dealer are safe buys.

Eggs may be graded according to federal, state or private standards. U.S. grades refer to interior quality; sizes refer to weight per dozen.

Grade AA and A eggs are top quality. They have a large amount of thick white and a high, firm yolk. Good for all uses, they are the best choice for poaching, frying or cooking in the shell. Grade B and C eggs have thinner whites and somewhat flatter yolks which may break easily. Offering the same food values as top-grade eggs, these less expensive eggs are a practical buy for scrambling, thickening sauces, making salad dressings and combining with other foods. Quality of eggs should be checked before using by breaking each egg into a small dish.

Most eggs are grouped according to these sizes: extra large, large, medium and small—with a minimum weight per dozen of 27, 24, 21 and 18 ounces respectively. Medium and small eggs are usually more plentiful in summer and early fall and at that time are likely to be a good buy.

Whether the color of the egg shell is brown or white makes no difference in the quality or food value of the egg, though in some localities it does influence price.

Nutrients—Eggs are an important food for children and adults alike because they contain many important nutrients—complete protein, vitamins A and D, the B vitamins, iron and phosphorus.

Storing—As soon as possible after purchasing, put eggs into the refrigerator or store at a cool temperature (large rounded end up). Remove only as many eggs as needed at one time. Washing eggs before storing removes the film or "bloom" which seals the pores of the shell and helps keep out bacteria and odors. If necessary wipe eggs with a damp cloth. Wash eggs just before using.

Food Preparation—The fundamental rule in egg cookery—*Cook eggs with low to moderate, even heat.* This applies to all methods of cooking eggs—and cheese dishes. Too high a heat toughens the protein in eggs and cheese, making eggs leathery and curdled and cheese stringy and separated.

In combining hot mixtures with whole eggs or egg yolks, always *slowly* add the hot mixture (3 or 4 spoonfuls or entire amount) to the beaten egg, stirring or beating constantly.

Separating egg yolks from egg whites is quicker and easier if eggs are about 60°F. Remove eggs from refrigerator about 45 min. before using. Eggs at room temperature, especially egg whites, beat to a larger volume than eggs taken directly from the refrigerator. (For stages of beating eggs see *page 4.*)

Leftover egg whites may be stored in refrigerator; use within 10 days. Uses for egg whites: angel food or white cake, seven-minute frosting, meringue. Store leftover egg yolks in refrigerator; use within 2 or 3 days. Or hard-cook egg yolks; use for salads, sauces, garnish.

▲ Scrambled Eggs

Set out an 8- to 10-in. skillet.

Put into a bowl

6 eggs
6 tablespoons milk or cream
¾ teaspoon salt
⅛ teaspoon pepper

For uniform yellow color beat until blended with rotary beater. For streaks of yellow and white beat slightly.

Heat skillet until just hot enough to sizzle a drop of water. Heat in skillet

3 tablespoons butter or margarine

Pour in egg mixture and cook slowly over low heat. With a fork or spatula lift mixture from bottom and sides of pan as it thickens, allowing uncooked part to flow to bottom. Stir only occasionally. Cook until scrambled eggs are thick and creamy throughout but are still moist.

Serve plain on hot buttered **toast** or **English muffin halves,** or in **Toastee Baskets** (*page 51*). Garnish with **parsley** or **water cress.**

4 servings

△ Kippered Herring Scramble

Remove contents of 1 can (about 3 oz.) **kippered herring** and drain thoroughly on absorbent paper. Discard skin and bones and cut herring into ½-in. pieces. Follow ▲ Recipe; decrease salt to ¼ teaspoon. When eggs just begin to set, quickly mix in fish pieces.

△ Ham or Bacon Scramble

In the top of a double boiler combine the milk of ▲ Recipe with 1 pkg. (3 oz.) **cream cheese** and 2 tablespoons **butter.** Heat over simmering water, stirring occasionally, until cheese is softened and ingredients are blended. Cool slightly. Follow ▲ Recipe; decrease salt to ¼ teaspoon. Add cream cheese mixture gradually to eggs while beating. Add ½ cup diced cooked **ham** or **bacon** to eggs before pouring into skillet. Cream cheese flavor is barely detected but eggs will have an added creaminess.

△ Corn and Cheese Scramble

Follow ▲ Recipe. Blend into the slightly beaten egg mixture 1 cup (about one half of contents of No. 2 can) drained whole kernel **corn,** ¼ cup (1 oz.) grated **cheese** and ½ teaspoon **prepared mustard.** Serve at once with **Panbroiled Link Sausages** (*page 87*).

△ Anchovy Scramble

Follow ▲ Recipe. For each serving, stripe a slice of hot, buttered **toast** with 3 **anchovy fillets.** Heap with scrambled eggs. (It's wise to determine saltiness of anchovies before adding salt to eggs.)

△ Scrambleburgers

Prepare 8 (about 1 lb. bulk pork sausage) **Panbroiled Sausage Patties** (*page 87*). Remove from pan; drain on absorbent paper. Keep hot.

In 2 tablespoons of the **sausage fat,** cook 3 tablespoons each of finely chopped **green pepper** and **onion** until onion is transparent. Proceed with ▲ Recipe, pouring egg mixture over vegetables; scramble. Split, butter and toast cut sides of 8 **buns.** Place sausage patties on bun halves. Top patties with scrambled eggs and cover with remaining bun halves.

Or—Cut the cooked sausage patties into smaller pieces. Combine with cooked onion and green pepper before pouring in eggs.

▲ Eggs Stuffed with Chicken Liver Paste

MRS. ED JENSEN, SIOUX CITY, IOWA

Prepare

5 hard-cooked eggs

Meanwhile, rinse with cold water and drain on absorbent paper

¼ lb. chicken livers

Put livers into a saucepan and add

Hot water to barely cover

Cover saucepan and simmer 10 to 15 min., or until livers are tender when pierced with a fork. Drain and set aside to cool.

Prepare

4 slices Panbroiled Bacon (*page 87*)

Crumble bacon and set aside.

Force chicken livers through a sieve or food mill and set aside.

Cut each egg into halves lengthwise. Remove egg yolks to a bowl and mash with a fork or press through ricer or sieve into the bowl. Mix into egg yolks the liver, crumbled bacon and a mixture of

1 tablespoon chopped parsley or dried parsley flakes
1½ teaspoons minced chives
½ teaspoon onion salt
¼ teaspoon tarragon leaves, crushed
¼ teaspoon salt
¼ teaspoon pepper
Few grains cayenne pepper

Stir in, moistening to a thick, paste-like consistency

1½ to 2 tablespoons mayonnaise

Fill egg whites with liver mixture; sprinkle with

Paprika

Chill thoroughly in refrigerator.

To serve, garnish with **water cress** or **parsley.**

5 servings

△ Deviled Eggs

Follow ▲ Recipe; prepare 9 **hard-cooked eggs.** Omit chicken livers and bacon. To cut eggs, use a narrow, sharp-pointed knife. Mark points in a saw-tooth line at ½-in. intervals lengthwise around each egg. Carefully cut down through marked line to yolk of egg; pull halves apart and carefully remove egg yolk. Omit seasoning mixture. Mix with riced or sieved egg yolks 6 tablespoons **thick sour cream,** 3 tablespoons **salad dressing,** ¾ teaspoon grated **onion,** 3 to 6 drops **tabasco sauce,** and a mixture of ½ teaspoon **garlic salt,** ½ teaspoon **celery salt,** ⅛ teaspoon **Accent** and ⅛ teaspoon **white pepper.** Omit mayonnaise.

Deviled Eggs: Mark sawtooth lines with a knife lengthwise around hard-cooked eggs.

Cut through egg white on marked line, gently pull halves apart; carefully remove egg yolk.

▲ French Omelet

Set out an 8- to 10-in. skillet.

Beat together until well blended but not foamy

6 eggs
6 tablespoons water or milk
¾ teaspoon salt
⅛ teaspoon pepper

Heat the skillet until just hot enough to sizzle a drop of water. Heat in skillet

3 tablespoons butter or margarine

Pour egg mixture into skillet and reduce heat. As the edges of omelet begin to thicken, with a spoon or fork draw cooked portions toward center to allow uncooked mixture to flow to bottom of skillet. Shake and tilt skillet as necessary to aid flow of uncooked eggs. Do not stir.

When eggs no longer flow but surface is still moist, the heat may be increased to quickly brown the bottom of omelet. Loosen edges carefully and fold in half. Slide onto a warm serving platter. Garnish. *4 to 6 servings*

Note: Omelets to which other ingredients are added are often cooked in smaller portions, pancake-fashion, or the larger ones are cut into wedges and served.

△ Country-Style Omelet

Panbroil 6 to 8 slices **bacon** until crisp (see Panbroiled Bacon, *page 87*). In 2 tablespoons of the **bacon fat,** brown 1 cup cooked, cubed **potatoes.** Coarsely crumble bacon and combine with browned potatoes. Proceed with ▲ Recipe, pouring egg mixture over bacon and potatoes in skillet. If necessary, add more fat. Stir slightly to allow egg mixture to settle under potatoes and bacon.

△ Cheese Omelet *

Follow ▲ Recipe, adding to egg mixture 1 teaspoon **Worcestershire sauce,** 3 tablespoons minced **parsley** and ¼ cup (1 oz.) grated **cheese.** Sprinkle an additional ¼ cup grated cheese over omelet while it is cooking.

△ Chicken Liver Omelet

Clean ¼ lb. **chicken livers.** To coat evenly, shake livers in plastic bag containing a mixture of ⅓ cup **flour,** ½ teaspoon **salt** and ¼ teaspoon **paprika.** Brown livers with 2 tablespoons minced **onion** in 3 tablespoons **butter** or **margarine,** turning frequently. Follow ▲ Recipe, enclosing chicken livers in omelet just before serving. (Cut livers into smaller pieces if necessary.)

△ Jam or Jelly Omelet *

Follow ▲ Recipe. Just before folding omelet, spread with ⅓ to ½ cup **jam** or **jelly.**

△ Sausage Omelet Fold *

Prepare **Panbroiled Link Sausages** (*page 87*), allowing at least two links per serving. Drain on absorbent paper; keep hot. Proceed with ▲ Recipe, enclosing sausages in folded omelet before serving. Serve at once with **Tomato Sauce** (*page 188*).

△ Sauce-Topped Omelet *

Prepare **Mushroom Sauce** (*page 181*), **Cheese Sauce** (*page 181*) or **Tomato Sauce** (*page 188*). Follow ▲ Recipe. Pour sauce over omelet after it has been placed on serving plate. One cup hot cooked **peas** may be added.

△ Cantonese Omelet *

Panfry in 2 to 3 tablespoons **butter** or **margarine,** 2 tablespoons finely chopped **onion** and ½ cup sliced **mushrooms** (*page 6*) or drained **bean sprouts.** Mix in 1 cup of a combination of cut-up cooked **shrimp** (see Cooked Shrimp, *page 126*) and chopped, cooked **pork** and ½ teaspoon **soy sauce.**

Continue heating for 2 to 3 min. Add **salt** and **pepper** to taste. Keep hot while proceeding with ▲ Recipe. Enclose vegetable-meat combination in folded omelet before serving.

Eggs on Noodle Casserole

Eggs on Noodle Casserole

Grease a shallow 2-qt. casserole or 8 large ramekins.

Prepare

5 hard-cooked eggs

Meanwhile, cook (*page 141*)

3 cups (8 oz.) noodles

When noodles are tender, drain and put into the casserole.

Prepare (*page 4*) and set aside

½ cup (1 to 2 slices) buttered fine, dry bread crumbs

Cut the eggs crosswise into halves. Remove egg yolks to a bowl and mash with a fork or press through ricer or sieve into a bowl. Mix in

2 tablespoons anchovy paste
1 tablespoon minced parsley
1 teaspoon minced onion

Stir in, moistening the egg-yolk mixture to a thick, paste-like consistency, about

2 tablespoons undiluted evaporated milk
2 to 3 teaspoons lemon juice

Pile mixture lightly into the egg-white cavities; leave tops roughly rounded. Arrange eggs on the noodles and set aside.

Mix in a saucepan and heat

1⅔ cups undiluted evaporated milk
1¼ cups (10½- to 11-oz. can) condensed tomato soup

Place over low heat, stirring occasionally, until heated. Pour sauce over eggs and noodles and top with buttered bread crumbs.

Bake at 350°F 20 to 25 min., or until crumbs are lightly browned. *8 servings*

Egg Croquettes

Prepare and set aside

4 hard-cooked eggs

Prepare in double-boiler top over direct heat

2 cups Medium White Sauce (double recipe, *page 181*; increase flour to ½ cup and salt to 1 teaspoon)

Vigorously stir about ¼ cup of the hot sauce, 1 tablespoon at a time, into

3 eggs, slightly beaten

Quickly blend into sauce. Cook over simmering water 3 to 5 min., stirring slowly to keep mixture cooking evenly. Remove sauce from simmering water and cool slightly by setting double-boiler top in bowl of cold water.

Peel and dice the hard-cooked eggs and gently mix them with the sauce. Cool completely; chill mixture in refrigerator 1 hr. or longer. Set out a deep saucepan or an automatic deep-fryer (*page 7*) and heat fat to 375°F.

Shape cold egg mixture into croquettes (balls or cones), using about ¼ cup of mixture for each. Roll them in

1½ cups (4 to 5 slices) fine, dry bread crumbs

Then dip them into a mixture of

1 egg, well beaten
1 tablespoon milk

Again roll them in bread crumbs. Shake off loose crumbs.

Deep-fry croquettes 3 to 5 min., or until golden brown. Fry only one layer of croquettes at a time; do not crowd. Turn them occasionally to brown evenly. Remove croquettes with slotted spoon; drain over fat for a few seconds before removing to absorbent paper.

12 croquettes

▲ Cheese Soufflé

Set out a 1½-qt. casserole; do not grease. (If necessary, a 1-qt. casserole with straight sides may be used. Fold a 2-ft. piece of waxed paper in half lengthwise; place waxed paper around casserole, cut-side down, overlapping ends of waxed paper. Secure waxed paper around casserole by tying with a string.)

Grate and set aside

6 oz. sharp Cheddar cheese (1½ cups, grated)

Prepare

1 cup Thick White Sauce (*page 181*; increase flour and butter to ¼ cup each; add ½ teaspoon dry mustard and ⅛ teaspoon paprika with seasonings)

Cool slightly and add grated cheese all at one time. Stir sauce rapidly until cheese is melted.

Beat until thick and lemon-colored

4 egg yolks

Cheese Soufflé: Use folded piece of waxed paper and string to increase capacity of a 1-qt. casserole.

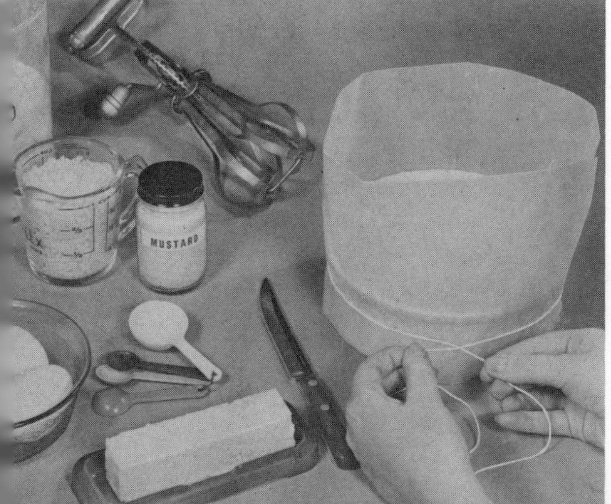

Slowly spoon sauce into egg yolks, while stirring vigorously.

Beat until rounded peaks are formed

4 egg whites

Gently spread egg-yolk mixture over beaten egg whites. Carefully fold (*page 6*) together until just blended. Turn mixture into casserole. Insert the tip of a spoon 1 in. deep in casserole, 1 to 1½ in. from edge; run a line around mixture. (Inner part of the mixture will form a "hat" when baked.)

Bake at 325°F about 50 min., or until a silver knife comes out clean when inserted halfway between center and edge of soufflé.

Serve at once (while top hat is at its height).

6 servings

△ Fresh Mushroom Soufflé

Follow ▲ Recipe. Decrease cheese to 1 cup. Clean (*page 6*) and finely chop ½ lb. **mushrooms.** Cook slowly with ¼ cup minced **onion** in 2 tablespoons **butter** or **margarine** until onion is transparent and mushrooms are lightly browned and tender; gently move and turn with fork or spoon. Using slotted spoon, remove vegetables from skillet and blend into sauce just before folding into egg whites.

⚠ Little Soufflés

Follow ▲ Recipe or △; divide soufflé mixture among six 4- to 4½-in. ungreased individual casseroles. Bake 25 to 30 min., or until soufflés test done.

Rice-Cheese Puffs

Prepare

1¾ cups Perfection Boiled Rice (one-half recipe, *page 147*)

While the rice is cooking, finely grate and set aside

3 oz. sharp Cheddar cheese (¾ cup, grated)

Melt in a medium-size saucepan over low heat

4 teaspoons butter or margarine

Blend in

4 teaspoons flour
½ teaspoon Accent
¼ teaspoon salt
Few grains pepper

Heat until mixture bubbles. Remove from heat. Add gradually while stirring constantly

⅓ cup milk

Return to heat and bring rapidly to boiling, stirring constantly; cook 1 to 2 min. longer.

Cool sauce slightly and add the grated cheese all at one time. Stir sauce rapidly until cheese is melted. Blend in

½ teaspoon grated onion
¼ teaspoon Worcestershire sauce
¼ teaspoon dry mustard
5 drops tabasco sauce
Few grains cayenne pepper

Mix with the cooked rice and place in refrigerator to chill (about 1 hr.).

Set out a deep saucepan or an automatic deep-fryer (*page 7*) and heat fat to 375°F.

Remove rice mixture from refrigerator. Shape into 2-in. balls, using about 1 tablespoon of the mixture for each ball. Dip balls into a mixture of

1 egg, slightly beaten
1 tablespoon milk

Coat balls by rolling in

½ cup (1 to 2 slices) fine, dry bread crumbs

Deep-fry only as many balls at one time as will float uncrowded one layer deep in the heated fat. Fry 1 to 2 min., or until balls are golden brown. Turn them with a fork as they rise to surface and several times during cooking (do not pierce). Remove balls with a slotted spoon; drain over fat for a few seconds before removing to absorbent paper.

Serve hot with

Tomato Sauce (*page 188*), or
Quick Tomato Sauce (*page 183*)

About 1 doz. puffs

Macaroni and Cheese

Thoroughly grease a 2-qt. casserole.

Grate and set aside

½ lb. Cheddar cheese (about 2 cups, grated)

Prepare (*page 4*) and set aside

½ cup (1 to 2 slices) buttered fine, dry bread crumbs

Cook (*page 141*)

2 cups (8-oz. pkg.) macaroni

While macaroni is cooking, prepare

2 cups Thin White Sauce (double recipe, *page 181*; increase salt to 1 teaspoon and Accent to ¾ teaspoon)

Cool sauce slightly. Stir grated cheese all at one time into the slightly cooled white sauce. Blend the sauce with the cooked and drained macaroni and turn into the casserole. Sprinkle the buttered crumbs around edge of casserole. If desired garnish with chopped **parsley.**

Bake at 350°F about 20 min., or until crumbs are lightly browned. *6 or 7 servings*

Macaroni and Cheese

Egg Foo Yung

MRS. J. E. BUSENHART, ARNOLD, MO.

Set out a large, heavy skillet.

For Foo Yung Sauce—Prepare and set aside

1 cup quick chicken broth (*page 7*)

Melt in a saucepan over low heat

2 tablespoons butter or margarine

Blend in

2 tablespoons flour
1 teaspoon sugar
¼ teaspoon salt

Heat until mixture bubbles. Remove from heat. Add gradually, stirring constantly, the broth.

Mix in

1 teaspoon soy sauce

Cook rapidly, stirring constantly, until sauce thickens. Cook 1 to 2 min. longer. Cover and keep warm over hot water.

For Foo Yung Patties—Drain contents of

1 No. 2 can bean sprouts (about 2½ cups, drained)

Clean (*page 6*) and finely chop

1 medium-size onion (about ½ cup, chopped)

Mix together and set aside the bean sprouts, chopped onion and

½ cup diced, cooked ham

Combine and beat until thick and piled softly

6 eggs
¾ teaspoon salt
¼ teaspoon Accent

Heat skillet until just hot enough to sizzle a drop of water. Heat in skillet

6 tablespoons shortening or cooking oil

Meanwhile, blend the ham-bean-sprout mixture into the beaten eggs.

Slowly pour about ½ cup of the mixture at a time into the skillet, forming a patty. Cook until bottom of patty is browned. Turn and brown other side. Drain on absorbent paper.

Serve Egg Foo Yung patties hot, with the Foo Yung Sauce. If desired accompany with **Perfection Boiled Rice** (*page 147*). *6 servings*

Egg Loaf

MRS. VIRGIL E. HILLS, WARREN, ME.

Grease an 8½x4½x2½-in. loaf pan.

Prepare and mix together in a small bowl.

½ cup sliced, cooked carrots
½ cup chopped, cooked celery
½ cup cooked peas
2 chopped hard-cooked eggs
1 tablespoon chopped parsley
1 teaspoon minced onion

Prepare

½ cup Medium White Sauce (one-half recipe, *page 181*)

Stirring vigorously, slowly pour white sauce into a mixture of

4 eggs, beaten
½ teaspoon salt
⅛ teaspoon pepper
¼ teaspoon Accent

Blend in the vegetable-egg mixture. Turn into the greased loaf pan.

Bake at 350°F 40 min., or until a silver knife comes out clean when inserted halfway between center and edge of baking dish.

Serve immediately. If desired, accompany with **Cheese Sauce** (*page 181*). *About 6 servings*

What You Should Know About Meat

Meat is king of the American dinner table—the food that holds the center spot in the menu and the hub around which most meals are planned. Preferences vary from region to region: New England and California love lamb, ham is the favorite in the South, in the Midwest pork and beef vie for favor and in the West and Southwest beef is tops.

America is almost unique in the world in the abundance of its meat supplies and the manner in which this abundance is taken for granted. Historically there are good reasons why this came to be. The first colonists found an amazing, almost untouched supply of wild game in the woods and the fields; and as the pioneers pushed westward, they encountered an inexhaustible abundance on the great western plains. Where fruit, grain and vegetables might be scarce, because the land was not yet cultivated and the supplies the pioneers carried with them were exhausted, there was no end to the meat that was theirs for the shooting. And the high meat diet on which the pioneers fed undoubtedly had much to do with the hardiness, toughness and spirit which settled our country.

Meat is an excellent source, perhaps the best, of the complete proteins from which strong bodies are built, with which they are repaired, and which supply those bodies with heat and energy and help them to resist infections. Protein to perform these functions can be obtained from a diet which contains no meat at all, but not so readily and, for most persons, not so palatably. In addition to the high protein content, meat is also rich in the minerals and vitamins which regulate all body functions.

Add to the presence of all these nutrients in meat, which make it such a fine body-building food, the fact that it is extremely palatable and that it has a high satiety value—that is, it satisfies not only when it is eaten but for a longer time thereafter than any other food. All these characteristics add up to good reason why the American diet is built around meat and why the selection and preparation of meat is a vital part of a homemaker's job.

SELECTION—Pioneer homemakers had little choice in the matter of their meat; they cooked what the hunter brought home. The modern homemaker, on the other hand, sees a vast array of meats spread out before her whenever she visits her favorite meat market. Her skill as a cook starts with her ability to select not only the right cut of meat for the method of preparation she means to use, but to select meat of good quality; for the quality of the meat itself determines to a large extent the quality of the cooked food. An experienced family meat buyer learns to recognize the characteristics of meat at a glance; she is aided by a knowledge of meat inspection and grading stamps.

Inspection Stamp—All meats processed by packers who ship their products across state lines must pass Federal inspection. The round purple Federal inspection stamp ("U. S. INSP'D & P'S'D") guarantees that the meat is from healthy animals slaughtered under sanitary conditions and that it is wholesome. Meats handled by packers who market locally must pass city and state inspections. These inspections guarantee wholesomeness, not quality.

Grade Stamp—Quality grading is a separate operation and may be done according to government grade standards or according to packers' own standards, which are usually closely in line with government grades. Grade and brand names are stamped on the meat with a roller stamp which leaves its mark along the full length of the carcass. The purple ink used for both inspection and grade stamps is a harmless vegetable dye which need not be cut away before cooking.

Official U. S. Quality Grades are "Prime," the absolutely top quality found in meat from prize animals, which is seldom seen in the retail market; "Choice," the highest quality usually available for home use; "Good," "Commercial" and "Utility." These grades are applied to beef, veal and (with the exception of the "Commercial" grade) to lamb. Pork is not officially graded, except by the packer. Where grade stamps are in evidence, the homemaker can rely on them as indexes to the quality of the meat. But in many cases, as in selecting precut and pre-packaged meats, her own knowledge of the appearance of quality is a valuable guide.

What To Look For In Beef—Beef of good to prime quality, whatever the cut, is thick-fleshed and compact, implying a plump, stocky animal; in lower grades the flesh is thinner, indicating that the animal was rangy and angular. There is a good covering of fat, which becomes thinner and patchier in lower grades, and a generous marbling or flecking of fat through the lean (almost absent in the lowest grades). Color in all grades varies from light to dark red. Bones of young beef are red and porous; as the animal matures they become harder and white.

What To Look For In Veal—Veal, which always comes from a young animal (calves three months to a year old), is very different in appearance from beef. The lean is a light grayish-pink in color, has no marbling and very little covering fat. The bones are red and porous; in the youngest veal the ends may still be pliable. Veal is fine-grained and less firm than beef of comparable grade; because the animal is young, veal is likely to be tender.

What To Look For In Lamb—Ninety-three per cent of all sheep in this country are marketed as lambs and yearlings; only seven per cent as mutton (lamb more than one year old). The bones, fat and color of lean are all indications of the age of lamb. Young lamb has red bones, which become white as the animal matures. The lean is light to dark pink in lambs, darkening to light red in yearlings and light to dark red in mutton. Lamb fat is rather soft and creamy or pinkish in color; with maturity it becomes white and much harder, even brittle.

What To Look For In Pork—Pork usually comes from animals under a year old and is almost always tender; the quality of American pork is quite uniform, with fewer grades than other meats. The color of young pork is grayish pink, which becomes pinker in older animals. The flesh is firm, fine in grain, well marbled (flecked) with fat and covered with a layer of firm white fat.

Pre-Packaged Meats—In recent years it has become possible to buy meats on a self-service basis in many supermarkets. The meats are cut, weighed, packaged and priced by the meat dealer, and are placed in refrigerated open cases for selection by the homemaker. Because they are wrapped in a transparent material, she can see the exact number of pieces she is buying, judge the quality and quickly compare prices and values.

STORAGE—As soon as possible after purchase, meat should be placed in the home refrigerator. Remove fresh meat from the meat-market wrappings and rewrap it loosely in waxed or parchment paper. For best keeping, put it into the meat-keeping compartment of the refrigerator.

In general, the smaller the proportion of cut surfaces exposed, the longer the meat will keep without deterioration. Ground meat, chops and mechanically tenderized steaks should not be stored more than one to three days. Due to the spicing, fresh pork sausage keeps better than other ground meats, usually up to a week. Beef roasts, legs of lamb and similar large cuts will keep in good condition as long as a week. Variety meats such as hearts, kidneys and liver are highly perishable and should be used within two days. Pre-packaged table-ready sliced meats and frankfurters are exceptions to the loose-wrapping rule; they will keep two or three weeks if left in their original moisture-proof wrappings, or if snugly re-wrapped at home in moisture-proof material.

Longer storage periods are possible in the freezer compartment of the refrigerator, which has a temperature of 25°F or lower. For freezing in this compartment, meats should be closely wrapped in a freezer wrapping material. Even the most perishable meats and ground beef will keep for two or three weeks under these conditions.

Fresh meats can be stored in home freezers at a temperature of 0°F or below for much longer periods. They should first be wrapped in freezer wrapping material which is moisture-vapor-proof. Maximum frozen storage periods recommended are: for ground meat and sausage, 1 to 3 months; fresh pork, 3 to 6 months; veal and lamb, 6 to 9 months; beef 6 to 12 months.

METHODS OF COOKING—Since the first cave-family discovered that meat tasted better when cooked, only two ways of cooking meat have ever been devised: by dry heat and by moist heat. There are several methods of cooking by dry heat: roasting, broiling, panbroiling and frying. There are two methods of cooking by moist heat: braising and cooking in liquid. Most of these methods have been in use for thousands of years, from cave days to the present, but in the comparatively few years since the experimental method was first applied to cooking, more has been learned about the techniques that give cooked meat the best appearance, texture and flavor than in all the millennia that went before.

In general, dry-heat methods are used for the more tender cuts of meat with little connective tissue. Exceptions to this rule are the smaller cuts (steaks, chops and cutlets) of pork and veal, though both are classed as tender meats. Both pork and veal need longer cooking, pork to develop its rich flavor and veal to soften its connective tissue. Long cooking by dry heat tends to dry them out; therefore a moist-heat method, braising, is the method of choice for pork and veal cuts other than roasts.

Roasting—To roast, in modern usage, is to cook in an oven, uncovered and without the addition of any liquid.

Thousands of laboratory tests on all kinds of roasts have revealed many facts about the roasting method which today can be stated as rules. These rules have as their objective the desired degree of doneness combined with maximum palatability and juiciness, the most appetizing appearance and minimum shrinkage.

Rules worth noting:

1. A constant low oven temperature should be maintained.
2. Even though time-weight relationship tables are followed carefully, the only accurate test for doneness is the internal temperature as registered by a roast meat thermometer.
3. Searing (initial high temperature) does not keep in juices but increases their loss.
4. Cooked fat side up, the roast will be self-basting.
5. Covering the roast or adding water produces moist-heat cooking and is not done in roasting.
6. Seasoning may be added before or after cooking; penetration is to a depth of only about ½ inch.
7. A time allowance of 20 to 30 minutes should be added to total roasting time in order that the roast may "set" in advance of carving; this makes carving easier and slices neater.

A low oven temperature throughout roasting cooks the meat more uniformly, with less shrinkage and loss of juices and fat; the covering fat is not charred and the meat is more palatable. A low temperature means less work for the homemaker, too, because there is less spattering of fat, less burning of fat on pans, racks and oven walls, less need for watching and an easier clean-up job.

Even with a constant temperature, it is not possible to predict accurately by means of time-weight tables when any particular piece of meat will be cooked done. The shape of the roast, the proportion of lean to fat, the amount of bone, the aging of the meat—all affect the time that will be required to produce the desired degree of doneness. Time tables are useful in estimating about how much total time will be required, but the only accurate test of actual doneness is the roast meat thermometer which registers the temperature at the center of the roast. When using a roast meat thermometer, the bulb of the thermometer should be inserted as nearly as possible to the center of the largest muscle, but should not come into contact with fat or bone.

Even after the establishment of a low temperature as desirable for roasting, some persons continued to sear meats to "seal in" juices. It has been disproved in test after test that searing results in any saving of juices; rather, it actually increases their loss. It does produce more drippings and a richer brown color in the drippings, which may make a richer brown and a more flavorful gravy.

Broiling—To broil is to cook by direct heat, over hot coals or under a flame or heating element.

As in roasting, a moderately low temperature for broiling produces more uniform cooking, less shrinkage, better appearance, more tender meat, less smoking and spattering of fat and no charring. Broiling temperature is controlled by regulating the distance between the source of heat and the surface of the meat. In broiling too, time tables are only a guide to total broiling time. However, it is quite easy to check on doneness of these comparatively thin pieces of meat without use of a thermometer, by cutting into the meat next to the bone with a sharp knife, and observing the color.

Meat for broiling should not be seasoned until after cooking, because salt tends to draw juices out from the exposed cut surface. Season the first side with a mixture of salt, pepper and Accent just before turning to broil the second side, and season the second side when cooking is complete.

Broiling as a cooking method is reserved for tender steaks and chops of beef and lamb. Veal and pork, although tender meats, are not usually broiled for reasons already explained (*page 62*). Ham steaks, however, are frequently broiled.

Panbroiling—To panbroil is to cook by heat transmitted through the hot metal of a skillet, but without added fat or water.

Panbroiling is used for the same cuts as is broiling. Fat should be poured off as it collects, to insure even cooking; the pan should not be covered. To test for doneness, cut a small gash close to the bone and note the color of the meat at the center.

Frying—To fry is to cook in fat, whether in a large amount (deep-frying) or a small amount (panfrying). Meats most frequently fried are thin steaks and chops and liver. They are usually floured or breaded to produce a brown, flavorful crust. In panfrying the meat is browned in a small amount of fat and then cooked at moderate temperature until done, turning frequently. If the skillet is covered or water is added, the procedure becomes braising rather than true frying.

Braising—To braise meat is to brown it in a small amount of fat; then to simmer it gently either in its own juices (by covering the skillet) or in a small amount of added liquid, which may be water, milk, cream, meat stock, vegetable juice or other liquid. The cooking done after browning may be done either on top of the range or in the oven.

The method is used in cooking pot roasts, veal and pork chops and steaks. These are all either less tender cuts of beef, such as round or flank steak, or small cuts of veal and pork which as previously stated require thorough cooking.

Cooking in Liquid—Stews require that the meat be cooked in liquid. Hams and corned beef are also cooked this way in some cases; veal cuts may be simmered as a preliminary to obtaining diced cooked veal for other recipes. Organs such as heart and tongue, which are much-exercised muscles, are often cooked in liquid.

Meats cooked in liquid should always be simmered rather than boiled; that is to say, cooked at a low temperature, as for meats cooked by dry heat methods.

How To Do It

COAT MEAT PIECES (as for stew) evenly by shaking a few pieces at a time in a plastic bag containing a mixture of flour and seasonings.

GRIND COOKED MEAT—Trim meat from bone; remove any excess fat. Put meat through medium blade of food grinder.

LARD MEAT by laying bacon strips or other fat on top of roast (usually veal); or by inserting fat strips into the lean with a larding needle to increase juiciness and improve flavor.

UNMOLD MEAT LOAVES—With spatula, gently loosen meat from sides of pan. Pour off excess juices; invert onto platter and remove pan. For meat loaves with topping, pour off excess juices and lift loaf onto platter with two wide spatulas.

POUND MEAT—To increase tenderness in less tender cuts of meat, place meat on flat working surface and repeatedly pound it with a meat hammer; turn meat and repeat on other side.

TURN MEAT during broiling, panbroiling or panfrying by inserting fork into the fat rather than the lean portion, thus avoiding loss of juices from lean.

THICKEN COOKING LIQUID—Pour ½ cup cold water into a screw-top jar; sprinkle ¼ cup flour onto the water (or use amounts specified in recipe). Cover jar tightly and shake until well blended. Slowly pour one-half of mixture into cooking liquid, stirring constantly. Bring to boiling. Gradually add only what is needed of remaining mixture for consistency desired. Bring to boiling after each addition. After final addition, cook 3 to 5 min. longer.

▲ Standing Rib Roast of Beef

This roast is flavor-perfect and succulent—the prime favorite of all lovers of beef.

Set out a shallow roasting pan.

Wipe with a clean, damp cloth

3-rib (6 to 8 lbs.) standing rib roast of beef

(Have meat dealer loosen chine bone to make carving easier.) Place roast, fat side up, in roasting pan. Season with a mixture of

1½ teaspoons salt
1 teaspoon Accent
⅛ teaspoon pepper

Insert roast meat thermometer in center of thickest part of lean; be sure bulb does not rest on bone or in fat.

Roast at 300°F, allowing 18 to 20 min. per pound for rare; 22 to 25 min. per pound for medium; and 27 to 30 min. per pound for well-done meat. Roast is also done when roast meat thermometer registers 140°F for rare; 160°F for medium; and 170°F for well-done meat.

Meat drippings may be used for **Brown Gravy** (*page 187*), or **Norwegian Wine Gravy** (*page 188*). For a special treat, serve **Yorkshire Pudding** (double recipe, *page 50*) as an accompaniment. *About 12 servings*

Note: To prepare roast of beef on an outdoor grill see OUTDOOR COOKING (*page 10*).

Standing Rib Roast of Beef

△ Rolled Rib Roast of Beef

Follow ▲ Recipe. Substitute **rolled beef rib roast** for the standing rib roast. Roast at 300°F, allowing 28 to 32 min. per pound for rare; 34 to 38 min. per pound for medium; and 40 to 45 min. per pound for well-done meat.

Grandma's Beef Pot Roast

MRS. A. L. CHRISTENSEN, METUCHEN, N. J.

Set out a heavy sauce pot having a tight-fitting cover; or use a Dutch oven.

Wipe with a clean damp cloth

3 to 4 lb. rump roast of beef

Set aside.

Heat in the sauce pot over medium heat

2 tablespoons olive oil

Add and cook until onion is transparent, stirring occasionally

1 cup (about 2 medium-size) coarsely chopped onion (*page 6*)
4 cloves garlic (*page 6*), minced; or crushed in a garlic press

With a slotted spoon, remove onion to a small dish. Put the meat into the sauce pot, brown on all sides over medium heat.

Meanwhile, dissolve

2 beef bouillon cubes or 1 teaspoon concentrated meat extract

in

1 cup hot tomato juice

When meat is browned, return the onion to the sauce pot. Add the tomato bouillon and

1 cup claret
½ cup chopped celery leaves
2 teaspoons chopped parsley
6 whole cloves
2 bay leaves

and a mixture of

1½ teaspoons salt
1 teaspoon Accent
½ teaspoon paprika
¼ teaspoon pepper

Bring liquid just to boiling, stirring and scraping bottom of pot to loosen all drippings. Reduce heat; cover and simmer (do not boil) 2½ to 3 hrs., or until meat is tender when pierced with a fork. Add hot water or wine if necessary during cooking period.

Remove meat to warm serving platter. If desired, thicken cooking liquid (*page 63*; use 1 to 2 tablespoons flour-water mixture.)

6 to 8 servings

Rolled Pot Roast with Sour Cream Gravy

Heat in a Dutch oven over medium heat

3 tablespoons fat

Wipe with a clean, damp cloth

4 lb. rolled pot roast of beef

Add the meat to fat and brown on all sides over medium heat.

Meanwhile, clean (*page 6*), cut into quarters and set aside

1 medium-size onion

Season the browned meat with a mixture of

1 teaspoon salt
1 teaspoon Accent
⅛ teaspoon pepper

Add the onion and

¼ cup water
1 bay leaf

Cover tightly; simmer (do not boil) about 3 hrs. If necessary to add more water during cooking period, add hot water.

About 15 min. before meat is tender, cook and drain (*page 141*)

3 cups (about 4 oz.) noodles

Rolled Pot Roast with Sour Cream Gravy

Using a fork, blend with the noodles

3 tablespoons butter

Serve buttered noodles in warm serving bowl or on platter with the pot roast.

For Gravy—When meat is tender, remove from liquid and keep warm. Strain liquid and return it to Dutch oven. Set over medium heat.

Put into a 1-pt. screw-top jar

½ cup water

Sprinkle onto the liquid

1 tablespoon flour

Cover jar tightly and shake until mixture is well blended. Slowly pour mixture into cooking liquid, stirring constantly. Bring rapidly to boiling, continuing to stir; cook 3 to 5 min.

Remove Dutch oven from heat. Stirring vigorously with a French whip, whisk beater or fork, add to mixture in Dutch oven, in very small amounts, a mixture of

1½ cups thick sour cream
1½ tablespoons lemon juice
1½ teaspoons grated lemon peel (*page 5*)
¾ teaspoon sugar

Place over low heat and stir constantly until thoroughly heated (3 to 5 min.); do not boil.

Serve gravy with pot roast and noodles.

About 12 servings

Broiled Beef Steaks

Broiled Beef Steaks

Wipe with a clean, damp cloth

Beef steaks, such as porterhouse, T-bone, sirloin or club, cut about 1 in. thick.

(Allow ⅓ to ½ lb. meat per serving.)

Set temperature control of range at Broil.

Arrange beef steaks on broiler rack. Place in broiler with tops of steaks 2 in. from heat source; broil 8 to 10 min. (The short cooking time for rare steaks; the longer cooking time for medium-done steaks.)

Meanwhile, for each pound of meat, mix together

1 teaspoon salt
½ teaspoon Accent
¼ teaspoon pepper

When steaks are browned on one side, sprinkle with one half of seasoning mixture. Turn and broil second side 8 to 10 min. Test for doneness by cutting a slit along the bone and noting color of meat. Season second side. For 2-in. steaks, broil with top of steaks 3 in. from heat source, allowing 15 to 20 min. on each side. Cut through fat on outside edge of each steak at 1-in. intervals; be careful not to cut through lean.

Serve steaks with

Butter-Fried Mushrooms (*page 153*)
Butter-Fried Onion Slices (*page 153*)

Note: To prepare beef steaks on an outdoor grill see Outdoor Cooking (*page 10*).

Panbroiled Beef Steaks

Heat a large, heavy skillet.

Wipe with a clean, damp cloth

Beef steaks, such as porterhouse, T-bone, sirloin or club, cut ¾ to 1 in. thick.

(Allow ⅓ to ½ lb. meat per serving.)

Place steaks in skillet and brown meat slowly over medium heat. Maintain a temperature which allows juices to evaporate rather than collect in pan. With too low heat, the meat will simmer in its own juices and become dry and less tender when cooked. If necessary turn meat occasionally for even browning. Pour off fat as it accumulates.

For each pound of meat, mix together

1 teaspoon salt
½ teaspoon Accent
¼ teaspoon pepper

When steaks are browned on one side, turn and sprinkle one half of seasoning over top. Brown other side and sprinkle with seasoning just before serving. Allow 10 to 20 min. total cooking time, depending on degree of doneness desired. Test for doneness by cutting a slit along the bone and noting color of meat.

Beef Brochettes

Set out six 8-in. skewers.

Wipe with a clean, damp cloth
1½ lbs. beef sirloin
Cut into 12 cubes. Set aside.

Clean (*page 6*), cut into halves lengthwise
6 small (about 1 lb.) onions
Set aside.

Clean (*page 6*, do not slice), remove stems from and set aside
12 large mushrooms
(Mushroom stems may be used in other food preparation.)

Cut into halves
6 slices bacon
Thread onto each skewer in the following order: onion half, bacon, beef, mushroom; repeat. Do not crown pieces on skewer.

Brush meat and vegetables generously with
Melted butter or margarine
Set temperature control of range at Broil.

Arrange skewers on broiler rack. Place in broiler with tops of brochettes about 3 in. from heat source.

Broil about 10 min., frequently turning and brushing brochettes with melted butter or margarine. Test for doneness by cutting a slit in beef cube and noting color of meat.

Sprinkle broiled brochettes with a mixture of
1 teaspoon salt
½ teaspoon Accent
⅛ teaspoon pepper
Serve at once. *6 servings*

Teriyaki Steak

MRS. JAMES LOTZGESELL
SAN FRANCISCO, CALIF.

Set out a large, shallow dish.

Blend together thoroughly
⅓ cup soy sauce
1 tablespoon wine vinegar
2 tablespoons sugar
1 tablespoon dark brown sugar
1½ teaspoons ginger
1 clove garlic (*page 6*), minced; or or crushed in a garlic press
Wipe with a clean, damp cloth
3 lbs. steak cut at least 1 in. thick (top round steak may be used)
Put steak in the dish; pour marinade (liquid mixture) over meat. Marinate (*page 6*) 30 min., turning meat once or twice.

Set temperature control of range at Broil.

Remove steak from marinade and place it on the broiler rack. Put into broiler with top of steak 3 in. from heat source.

Broil 9 to 12 min. (The shorter cooking time is for rare steak; the longer cooking time is for medium-done steak.) Turn and broil second side 9 to 12 min. If desired, brush steak occasionally with the marinade. Test for doneness by cutting a slit near the bone and noting color of meat. Serve immediately. *6 servings*

Beef Brochettes

▲ Beef Stroganoff

WILLA J. SESSIONS, TAMPA, FLA.

Set out a heavy 10-in. skillet having a tight-fitting cover.

Wipe with a clean, damp cloth

2 lbs. round steak, cut ½ in. thick

Cut into 2x½x½-in. strips. Coat meat evenly (*page 63*) with a mixture of

⅓ cup flour
1 teaspoon salt
¾ teaspoon Accent
⅛ teaspoon pepper

Heat in the skillet over low heat

⅓ cup butter or margarine

Add the meat strips and

½ cup (1 medium-size) finely chopped onion (*page 6*)
1 small clove garlic (*page 6*), minced; or crushed in a garlic press

Cook over medium heat, frequently moving and turning meat to brown evenly on all sides.

Meanwhile, prepare

1 cup quick meat broth (*page 7*)

When meat is browned, slowly add the broth. Add

1 tablespoon sherry

Bring liquid rapidly to boiling; reduce heat, cover and simmer (do not boil) 20 to 25 min., or until meat is tender.

While meat is cooking, prepare

Butter-Fried Mushrooms (½ recipe, *page 153*; use 3 tablespoons butter)

Blend together

1 cup thick sour cream
1 teaspoon Worcestershire sauce

When meat is tender, remove skillet from heat. Stirring vigorously, add to mixture in skillet, in very small amounts, the sour-cream mixture. Add the mushrooms. Return to heat. Continue cooking over low heat, keeping mixture moving with a spoon, 3 to 5 min., or until thoroughly heated; do not boil.

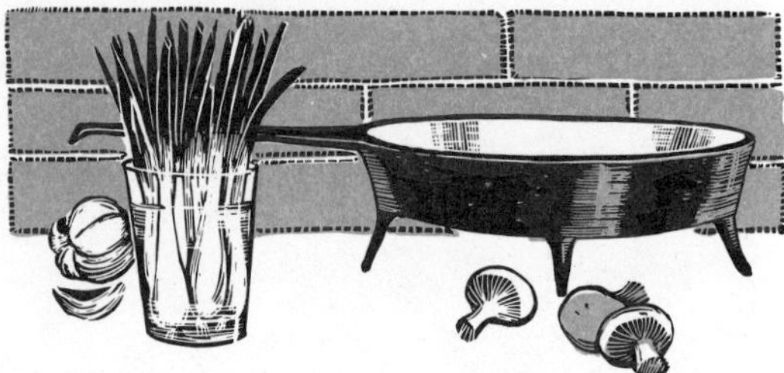

Turn the meat mixture into a warm serving dish. Serve immediately. Accompany with

Whipped Potatoes (*page 158*),
Noodles (*page 141*) or
Perfection Boiled Rice (*page 147*)

6 servings

△ Beef Stroganoff Par Excellence

Follow ▲ Recipe; substitute **boneless beef,** such as tenderloin, sirloin, or rib for the round steak. Increase quick meat broth to 2 cups. Blend 3 tablespoons **tomato paste** with the sour cream and Worcestershire sauce.

Braised Short Ribs De Luxe

ALICE M. WALCKER, PORTLAND, ORE.

Set out a large heavy kettle, or sauce pot having a tight-fitting cover; or use a Dutch oven.

Wipe with a clean, damp cloth

3 lbs. beef short ribs

Cut into serving-size pieces. Coat meat evenly (*page 63*) with a mixture of

⅓ cup flour
2 teaspoons salt
1 teaspoon Accent
¼ teaspoon pepper

Heat in the kettle over medium heat

⅓ cup fat

Add the meat and brown on all sides over medium heat.

Meanwhile, clean (*page 6*) and thinly slice

2 medium-size onions, (about 1 cup, sliced)

Prepare

½ cup chopped green pepper (*page 6*)

Add onion and green pepper to meat with

1 clove garlic (*page 6*), minced; or crushed in a garlic press

Add to kettle a mixture of

1 cup water
¼ cup ketchup

Bring liquid rapidly to boiling; reduce heat, cover and simmer (do not boil) over low heat until meat is tender when pierced with a fork (about 2 hrs.). Turn meat occasionally. Add small amounts of hot water as needed.

Remove meat to warm serving platter.

Add to the cooking liquid

1½ cups water

Bring rapidly to boiling; reduce heat and simmer gently several minutes. If desired, thicken cooking liquid (*page 63*; add flour-water mixture one tablespoon at a time). Serve hot.

6 servings

▲ Beef Short Ribs with Vegetables

Set out a large, heavy kettle or sauce pot having a tight-fitting cover; or use a Dutch oven.

Wipe with a clean, damp cloth

3 lbs. beef short ribs

Cut into serving-size pieces. Coat meat evenly (*page 63*) with a mixture of

⅓ cup flour
2 teaspoons salt
1 teaspoon Accent
⅛ teaspoon pepper

Heat in the kettle over medium heat

⅓ cup fat

Add the meat pieces and brown on all sides over medium heat.

While meat is browning, clean (*page 6*), thinly slice and set aside

1 medium-size onion

When meat is brown, remove kettle from heat and slowly pour in

2 cups hot water

Add the sliced onion. Cover tightly and bring water to boiling over high heat. Reduce heat and simmer (do not boil) about 1½ hrs., or until meat is almost tender (at which time vegetables should be added). Add hot water as necessary.

Before time to add vegetables to ribs, wash and cut off stem ends from

½ lb. green beans

Set beans aside.

Wash, pare, and cut into halves

6 medium-size (about 2 lbs.) potatoes

Add prepared vegetables to kettle with

1 teaspoon salt
¼ teaspoon Accent
⅛ teaspoon pepper

Cover kettle and continue to simmer.

Meanwhile, clean (*page 6*)

12 stalks celery

Cut crosswise into 3-in. pieces and put into kettle. Cover and simmer about 35 min., or until meat and vegetables are tender when pierced with a fork. With a slotted spoon, remove meat and vegetables from kettle to hot serving platter; keep warm. Thicken cooking liquid for gravy (*page 63*; use ¼ cup water and 2 tablespoons flour).

Serve hot. *6 servings*

△ Spicy Short Ribs and Fruit

Follow ▲ Recipe; omit vegetables. When ribs have simmered 1 hr., add 1 cup (about 5 oz.) **dried apricots** and 1 cup (about 5 oz.) pitted **prunes.** Remove about 1 cup cooking liquid. Blend into liquid a mixture of ½ cup **sugar,** ½ teaspoon **cinnamon,** ½ teaspoon **allspice** and ¼ teaspoon ground **cloves.** Blend in 3 tablespoons **vinegar.** Pour mixture over ribs. Continue to simmer 30 min. or until meat and fruit are tender. Serve with cooking liquid.

Hamburger Steak Dinner

Mix together lightly in a large bowl

2 lbs. ground beef
½ cup milk
1 egg, beaten
4 teaspoons Worcestershire sauce

and a mixture of

2 teaspoons salt
1 teaspoon Accent
¼ teaspoon pepper

Set temperature control of range at Broil.

Shape meat mixture into an oval about 1½ in. thick. Put meat on broiler rack. Place in broiler with top of meat 3 in. from heat source.

Broil about 10 to 12 min. or until browned on one side. Turn and broil second side. Remove to warm serving plate. Serve with

Parsley New Potatoes (*page 158*)
Butter-Fried Onion Slices (*page 153*)

8 servings

Sauerbraten

ADELE S. WEILER, DEL NORTE, COLO.

A heavy 4-qt. kettle having a tight-fitting cover or a Dutch oven will be needed. Set out a deep 3- or 4-qt. bowl.

Wipe with a clean, damp cloth

4 to 5 lb. pot roast of beef (rump, chuck, blade or round)

Put the meat into the bowl. Set aside.

Combine in a saucepan and heat just to boiling

2 cups vinegar
2 cups water
1 large onion (*page 6*), sliced
2 tablespoons sugar
2 teaspoons salt
10 peppercorns
6 whole cloves
2 bay leaves

Remove from heat; cool slightly. Pour mixture over meat in bowl. Add

1 lemon, rinsed and cut into ¼-in. slices

Cool, cover bowl tightly and put into refrigerator. Marinate (*page 6*) for 3 days, turning meat once a day.

Set out the kettle and cover.

Remove meat from marinade and drain thoroughly. Strain and reserve marinade.

Heat in the kettle over low heat

2 to 3 tablespoons butter or margarine

Add the pot roast and brown on all sides over medium heat. Slowly add 2 cups of the reserved marinade (reserve remaining marinade for gravy). Bring liquid rapidly to boiling. Reduce heat; cover kettle tightly and simmer (do not boil) 2½ to 3 hrs., or until meat is tender when pierced with a fork. Add more of the marinade, if necessary.

Remove meat to a warm platter and keep warm. Pour cooking liquid from kettle and set aside for gravy.

For Gravy—Melt in the kettle

¼ cup butter or margarine

Thoroughly blend in

¼ cup flour

Heat until mixture bubbles and is golden brown, stirring constantly. Remove from heat. Add gradually, stirring constantly

3 cups liquid (reserved cooking liquid and enough reserved marinade or hot water to equal 3 cups liquid)

Return to heat. Add, stirring in

8 gingersnaps (about 2 oz.), crumbled

Bring to boiling; cook rapidly, stirring constantly, until gravy thickens. Cook 1 to 2 min. longer.

Serve meat and gravy with **Dumplings** (*page 50*), **Potato Pancakes** (*page 50*) or **Noodles** (*page 141*). *10 to 12 servings*

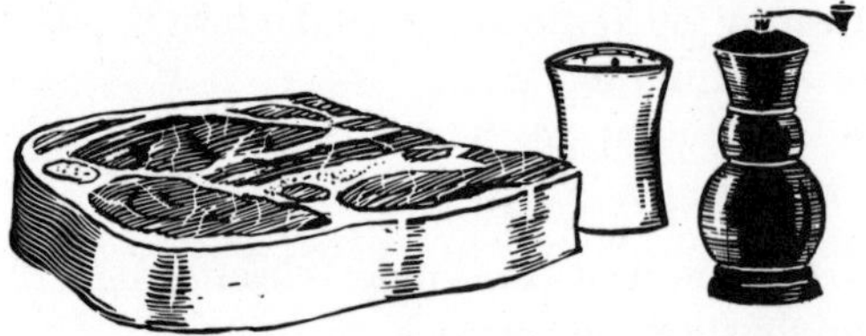

▲ Spicy Brown Beef Stew

Set out a large heavy kettle having a tight-fitting cover; or use a Dutch oven.

Wipe with a clean, damp cloth

2 lbs. beef for stewing (chuck, round or brisket)

Cut meat into 1½-in. pieces. Coat meat evenly (*page 63*) with a mixture of

⅓ cup flour
2 teaspoons salt
½ teaspoon Accent
⅛ teaspoon pepper

Heat in the kettle over medium heat

3 tablespoons fat

Add meat and brown on all sides over medium heat, occasionally moving and turning pieces. When meat is browned, pour off the excess fat.

While meat is browning, clean (*page 6*), chop and set aside

1 medium-size onion (½ cup, chopped)

Slowly pour into the kettle or Dutch oven

1 qt. hot water

Add to kettle the chopped onion and

1 tablespoon salt
1 teaspoon Worcestershire sauce
1 teaspoon lemon juice
2 bay leaves
½ teaspoon pepper
½ teaspoon Accent
Few grains cloves

Cover and bring liquid rapidly to boiling. Reduce heat and simmer (do not boil) about 1½ hrs., or until meat is almost tender.

About 15 min. before adding vegetables to stew, clean (*page 6*)

12 small onions

Set aside.

Wash, scrape and cut into pieces

8 medium-size carrots

Add prepared vegetables to kettle or Dutch oven. Cover and simmer 30 to 45 min. longer, or until meat and vegetables are tender.

While vegetables are cooking, prepare and set aside to keep warm

Whipped Potatoes (*page 158*)

Just before removing meat and vegetables from kettle, if desired, dissolve in a small amount of hot water

2 teaspoons concentrated meat extract

With slotted spoon, remove meat and vegetables from stew to hot dish. Stir into the cooking liquid the dissolved concentrated meat extract. Thicken cooking liquid (*page 63*).

Return meat and vegetables to kettle and heat thoroughly. Spoon Whipped Potatoes in a ring onto serving dish. Fill center of and surround potato ring with the stew. *8 to 10 servings*

△ Individual Pastry-Topped Pies

Follow ▲ Recipe; omit Whipped Potatoes. Grease 5 or 6 small casseroles. Prepare **Pastry for 1-Crust Pie** (*page 242*). Roll pastry into a rectangle about ⅛ in. thick. Cut 5 or 6 strips of pastry 1 in. wide. Cut remaining pastry into strips ½ in. wide. Turn heated stew into casseroles. Moisten rims of casseroles with water. Place one of the 1-in. pastry strips around inside edge of each casserole, pressing strip onto edge. Carefully arrange narrower strips to form lattice pattern (*page 242*), leaving about ¼ in. between the strips. Trim strips so ends extend about ¼ in. beyond edge of casserole. Fold the ends of the strips over the pastry on edge of casseroles; press to seal.

Bake at 425°F 25 to 30 min., or until pastry is lightly browned.

New England Dinner

▲ New England Dinner

A typical New England "boiled" dinner.

Set out a large sauce pot or kettle having a tight-fitting cover; or use a Dutch oven.

Wipe with a clean, damp cloth
4 to 6-lb. piece of corned beef
Put the meat into the sauce pot and add
Water to cover
Cover sauce pot tightly and bring water just to boiling over high heat. Reduce heat and simmer (do not boil) 3 to 5 hrs. (allow 40 to 50 min. per pound), or until meat is tender when pierced with a fork.

About an hour before meat is tender, clean (see Sweet-Sour Beets, *page 150*) and cook (*page 149*) 30 to 45 min., or until just tender
6 medium-size (about 1 lb.) beets
While beets are cooking, wash and scrape
6 medium-size (about 1½ lbs.) carrots
Wash and pare (do not cut)
6 medium-size (about 2 lbs.) potatoes
Skim off any excess fat from cooking water in sauce pot. Add the potatoes and carrots. Cover and continue to simmer.

When carrots and potatoes have cooked about 20 min., remove outer wilted leaves and any blemishes from
1 small head cabbage
Wash thoroughly and cut from top to bottom into wedges. Remove heavy ribs of outer leaves. Put cabbage into the sauce pot about 8 to 12 min. before end of cooking time. Cook, loosely covered, just until tender.

When the beets are tender, peel off and discard skins. Add to beets
2 tablespoons butter or margarine
Keep beets warm while arranging meat platter. When carrots, potatoes, cabbage, and meat are tender, remove meat from cooking liquid and place it on a large, warm platter. Surround with the vegetables. Serve immediately.

6 to 8 servings

△ Corned Beef and Cabbage

Follow ▲ Recipe; omit beets and carrots. Use 1 large head **cabbage,** quartered or cut into wedges. Thicken the cooking liquid (*page 63*) and serve with the meat and vegetables.

Hamburgers

Set out a large, heavy skillet.

Mix lightly
1½ lbs. ground beef
with a mixture of
1½ teaspoons salt
¾ teaspoon Accent
¼ teaspoon pepper
Shape into 6 patties about ¾ in. thick or 8 patties about ½ in. thick.

Heat in the skillet over medium heat
1 tablespoon fat
Place patties in skillet and cook until brown on one side. Turn and brown other side. (Allow 10 to 15 min. for cooking thick patties and 6 to 10 min. for cooking thin patties.) Remove from skillet to warm serving platter. Serve hot garnished with **parsley.**

6 to 8 servings

Note: Hamburgers or any of the following variations may be served on toasted, buttered **buns,** if desired.

Italian-Style Meat Balls

EMMA G. PUTNAM, SANTA CRUZ, CALIF.

This recipe is typical of the interesting ways in which Italian cooks incorporate spinach into other foods for an accent of flavor.

Heat in a large, heavy skillet having a cover
1 teaspoon olive oil
Add and cook until onion is transparent, occasionally moving pieces with a spoon
½ cup (1 medium-size) chopped onion (*page 6*)
⅓ cup finely chopped green pepper (*page 6*)
Add contents of skillet to a bowl containing
1 lb. ground beef
1 cup chopped cooked spinach, well drained
1 egg, beaten
3 tablespoons grated Parmesan cheese
and a mixture of
½ teaspoon Accent
¼ teaspoon salt
¼ teaspoon pepper
Mix lightly. Form mixture into 1½-in. balls.

Heat in the skillet over medium heat
2 tablespoons fat
Add meat balls to skillet and brown over medium heat. Turn balls frequently to obtain an even browning and to keep balls round.

Pour over the browned meat balls a mixture of
2 cups (2 8-oz. cans) tomato sauce
1 tablespoon grated Parmesan cheese
Cover and simmer 30 to 40 min.

Serve with
Spaghetti (*page 141*)

About 4 servings

Norwegian Meat Balls and Gravy

MRS. WILLIAM L. ABLE, PATEROS, WASH.

A delicious reminder of the ground-meat miracles in traditional Scandinavian cookery.

Heat in a large, heavy skillet over low heat
2 tablespoons butter
Add and cook over medium heat until onion is transparent, stirring occasionally
⅓ cup finely chopped onion (*page 6*)
Mix together lightly the onion and
1 lb. ground beef
¼ lb. ground lean pork
½ cup (½ slice) soft bread crumbs
½ cup milk
1 egg, beaten
and a mixture of
2 teaspoons sugar
1¼ teaspoons salt
¾ teaspoon Accent
½ teaspoon nutmeg
¼ teaspoon allspice
Shape meat mixture into 1-in. balls.

Heat in the skillet over low heat
2 tablespoons butter
Add the meat balls and brown over medium heat. Shake pan frequently to obtain an even browning and to keep balls round. Reduce heat, cover skillet and continue to cook about 10 min., shaking pan occasionally. Remove meat balls to warm serving dish; set aside and keep warm.

Blend into the fat in the skillet
3 tablespoons flour
1 teaspoon sugar
½ teaspoon salt
¼ teaspoon pepper
Heat until mixture bubbles and flour is lightly browned. Remove from heat. Add gradually, stirring in, a mixture of
1 cup water
¾ cup cream
Bring rapidly to boiling, stirring constantly; cook 1 to 2 min. longer. Pour gravy over meat balls in dish. Serve at once. *6 servings*

Best-Ever Stuffed Meat Loaf

Grease a 9½x5¼x2¾-in. loaf pan and set out a large, heavy skillet.

For Wheat-Germ Bread Stuffing—Toast, cut into cubes and set aside

6 slices bread (about 4 cups cubes)

Prepare and set aside

1 cup quick meat broth (*page 7*)

Clean (*page 6*), finely chop and set aside enough celery to yield

1 cup chopped celery (about 2 large stalks)

Heat in the skillet over low heat

¼ cup butter or margarine

Add the toasted-bread cubes. Turn occasionally until they are coated evenly on all sides with butter and are golden brown in color.

Remove skillet from heat source. Add to skillet, mixing lightly with the bread cubes, one half the meat broth (reserve remainder for meat-wheat-germ mixture), the celery and

¼ cup wheat germ
¼ cup finely chopped green pepper (*page 6*)
¼ cup minced onion
1 egg, beaten

and a mixture of

¼ teaspoon salt
¼ teaspoon Accent
⅛ teaspoon pepper

Set stuffing aside.

For Tomato Topping—Put into a bowl

¾ cup (6-oz. can) tomato paste

Blend in

⅓ cup firmly packed brown sugar
1 teaspoon prepared mustard
½ teaspoon Worcestershire sauce

Set topping aside.

Best-Ever Stuffed Meat Loaf

For Meat Loaf—Put into a large bowl

2 lbs. ground beef
½ cup wheat germ
2 tablespoons minced onion

and a mixture of the reserved meat broth and

2 teaspoons salt
½ teaspoon Accent
⅛ teaspoon thyme
⅛ teaspoon pepper

Mix together lightly.

Divide meat mixture into two equal portions. Lightly pack one portion into the loaf pan. Spread Wheat-Germ Bread Stuffing evenly over top of meat layer. Lightly pack remaining meat mixture evenly over stuffing. Spread Tomato Topping evenly over top of loaf.

Bake at 350°F about 1 hour.

Drain off excess liquid. Carefully remove loaf to a warm platter. Garnish as desired.

8 servings

Tamale Perfection

A South-of-the-Border inspiration.

Grease a 2-qt. casserole.

Put into a large, heavy, cold skillet
¼ lb. bulk pork sausage
Break into small pieces with fork or spoon. Add
1½ tablespoons cold water
Cover and cook slowly 8 min. Remove cover and pour off fat. Mix in with fork or spoon, breaking meat into pieces
1 lb. ground beef
Brown meat over medium heat, stirring occasionally. Pour off fat as it collects.

When meat begins to brown, add
1 cup (about 2 medium-size) finely chopped onion (*page 6*)
½ cup finely chopped celery (*page 6*)
⅓ cup finely chopped green pepper (*page 6*)
Cook until meat is well browned and onion is transparent, stirring occasionally.

Add slowly and mix in
2¼ cups (No. 2 can) tomatoes, sieved
1¼ cups (12-oz. can, drained) whole kernel corn
Blend in a mixture of
2 teaspoons chili powder
1 teaspoon salt
½ teaspoon Accent
¼ teaspoon pepper
Cover and simmer about 15 min.

Pit and slice enough ripe olives to yield
1 cup sliced ripe olives
Set aside.

Mix together and add gradually to skillet, stirring continually
1 cup cold water
½ cup yellow corn meal
Cook over low heat until thickened, stirring slowly. Stir in the sliced olives. Turn into casserole.

Tamale Perfection

Bake at 350°F 1 hr.

Remove from oven and sprinkle with
¾ cup (3 oz.) grated sharp Cheddar cheese
Return to oven and bake 5 min. longer, or until cheese is melted.

Garnish with
Whole ripe olives
Sprigs of parsley

8 servings

Beef and Pork Loaf

Set out a 9½x5¼x2¾-in. loaf pan.

Mix together lightly
1¼ lbs. ground beef
½ lb. ground lean pork
2 cups (2 slices) soft bread crumbs
¼ cup minced onion
1 cup milk
1 egg, beaten
and a mixture of
2 teaspoons salt
1 teaspoon Accent
¼ teaspoon pepper
Pack lightly into loaf pan, rounding top.

Bake at 350°F about 1½ hrs. Unmold (*page 63*) onto warm serving platter. Serve warm.

About 8 servings

Shish Kabobs and tossed salad

▲ Lamb Kabobs

For Marinade—Mix together thoroughly

3/4 cup tarragon vinegar
1/3 cup salad oil
2 teaspoons salt
3/4 teaspoon Accent
1/2 teaspoon pepper

Add

1 bay leaf
1/2 clove garlic (*page 6*)

For Kabobs—Wipe with a clean, damp cloth

1 1/2 lbs. boneless lamb (shoulder or leg)

Cut into 1½-in. cubes. Cover lamb with marinade and set in refrigerator for at least 24 hrs., turning meat several times.

Set out six 8-in. skewers.

Clean (*page 6*), cut into halves from top to base and set aside

6 small (about 1 lb.) onions

Clean (*page 6*, do not slice), remove stems from and set aside

12 large mushrooms

(Mushroom stems may be used in other recipes as desired.)

Rinse and pat dry with absorbent paper

6 chicken livers

Cut into halves and wrap around livers

3 slices bacon

Thread onto each skewer in the following order: lamb, onion half, mushroom, liver, lamb, onion half and mushroom. Do not crowd pieces on skewer.

Brush meat and vegetables generously with

Melted butter or margarine

Arrange skewers on broiler rack.

Set temperature control of range at Broil.

Place in broiler with tops of kabobs about 3 in. from source of heat. Broil 15 to 20 min., turning kabobs several times and brushing with melted butter or margarine. Test for doneness by cutting a slit in lamb cubes and noting color of meat. Season kabobs with a mixture of

1 teaspoon salt
1/4 teaspoon Accent
1/8 teaspoon pepper

Serve at once. *6 servings*

△ Shish Kabobs

Follow ▲ Recipe; increase lamb to 2 lbs.; omit mushrooms, chicken livers, and bacon. Clean and cut into quarters 3 small **green peppers.** Beginning with an onion half, thread onto each skewer in the following order: onion half, lamb, green pepper, lamb; repeat.

Roast Leg of Lamb with spiced peaches and buttered peas

Crown Roast of Lamb

Set out a shallow roasting pan with rack.

Wipe with a clean, damp cloth
4- to 6-lb. (12 to 16 rib) crown roast of lamb
(Have meat dealer remove backbone to make carving easier.) Rub lamb with a mixture of
2 teaspoons salt
1 teaspoon Accent
¼ teaspoon pepper
Cover each rib bone with a piece of
Salt pork or bacon
If desired, insert into meaty portion in center of crown
2 cloves garlic (*page 6*), slivered
Place lamb, rib bones up, on rack in pan. Insert roast meat thermometer between ribs into center of thickest part of meat, being sure bulb does not rest in fat.

Roast lamb uncovered at 300°F 3 to 4½ hrs., or until thermometer registers 180°F. (Allow about 45 min. per lb.)

Remove from oven to warm serving plate. Replace bacon with paper frills.

Fill center of crown with cooked small whole **potatoes,** fresh **peas,** tiny **carrots** or **cauliflowerets.** *6 to 8 servings*

Note: Center of roast may be filled before roasting with seasoned, ground **lamb trimmings,** or a **bread** or **sausage stuffing.** Proceed as above, allowing about 1 hr. longer for roasting time.

▲ Roast Leg of Lamb

Set out a shallow roasting pan with rack.

Wipe with a clean, damp cloth
5- to 6-lb. leg of lamb
Do not remove the fell (thin papery covering).

Rub lamb with a mixture of
2 teaspoons salt
1 teaspoon Accent
¼ teaspoon pepper
Place lamb skin side down on rack in pan. Insert roast meat thermometer in center of thickest part of meat, being sure that bulb does not rest on bone or in fat.

Roast lamb uncovered at 300°F about 3 hrs., allowing 30 to 35 min. per pound. Meat is medium done when thermometer registers 175°F and well done at 180°F.

Place a paper frill around end of leg bone.

Serve on warm platter. Garnish with **parsley** or **mint leaves.** *About 10 servings*

△ Roast Leg of Lamb, French Style

Follow ▲ Recipe. Before roasting, cut several small slits in surface of meat. Insert into each slit 1 sliver of **garlic.** Melt 3 tablespoons **butter.** Use butter to brush meat frequently during roasting. Remove meat from pan and pour off fat from drippings in pan.

Make gravy by stirring into drippings in pan 1 cup cold **quick meat broth** (*page 7*) or **water.** Bring to boiling over direct heat, stirring constantly. Season with a mixture of ½ teaspoon **salt,** ¼ teaspoon **Accent** and ¼ teaspoon **pepper.**

▲ Irish Stew

Set out a large kettle having a tight-fitting cover; or use a Dutch oven.

Wipe with a clean, damp cloth

2 lbs. boneless lamb for stew

Cut meat into 2-in. pieces. Coat meat evenly (*page 63*) with a mixture of

⅓ cup flour
2 teaspoons salt
½ teaspoon Accent
⅛ teaspoon pepper

Heat in the kettle over medium heat

3 tablespoons fat

Add lamb and brown on all sides over medium heat, moving and turning pieces occasionally. Pour off excess fat. Remove from heat and slowly pour into the kettle

1 qt. hot water

Cover and bring liquid to boiling over high heat. Reduce heat; simmer (do not boil) about 1½ hrs., or until meat is almost tender. Add small amounts of hot water as necessary.

Add vegetables to kettle about 45 min. before end of cooking period. About 15 min. before adding vegetables to stew, clean (*page 6*) and set aside

6 small onions

Clean (*page 6*; do not remove leaves) and cut crosswise into slices ½ in. thick

4 stalks celery, with leaves

Set pieces aside.

Wash, scrape or pare, cut into ½-in. pieces and set aside

4 small carrots

Wash, pare and quarter

6 medium-size (about 2 lbs.) potatoes
1 medium-size turnip

Add the prepared vegetables to the stew with

1½ teaspoons salt
½ teaspoon Accent
⅛ teaspoon pepper

Cover and simmer about 45 min., or until meat and vegetables are tender when pierced with a fork. With slotted spoon, remove meat and vegetables from stew to hot dish. Thicken cooking liquid (*page 63*).

Return meat and vegetables to kettle and heat thoroughly. Serve hot. *8 to 10 servings*

△ Savory Lamb Stew

Follow ▲ Recipe; omit turnip. Add to stew with seasonings ¼ teaspoon **savory,** ¼ teaspoon **basil** and ¼ teaspoon **marjoram.**

△ Irish Stew with Dumplings

Follow ▲ Recipe. After adding vegetables to stew, prepare **Dumplings** (*page 50*). Bring stew to boiling. Drop dumpling mixture by tablespoonfuls on top of stew. (Dumplings should rest on meat and vegetables; if dumplings settle down into the liquid, they may be soggy.) If necessary, remove some of the liquid temporarily to prevent this. Cover tightly and cook over medium heat 20 min. without removing cover. Remove stew and dumplings to hot serving dish.

△ Lamb Pies

Follow ▲ Recipe; omit celery and turnip. Substitute 2 medium-size **onions,** sliced, for the small whole onions. Cube potatoes and slice the carrots ¼ in. thick. Stir into the finished stew 1 cup (8-oz. can, drained) **peas.**

Set out 8 individual casseroles.

Lamb Pies

After adding vegetables to stew, prepare **Tender-Rich Biscuits** (*page 43*; roll dough ¼ in. thick and cut to fit tops of casseroles; bake as for biscuits). Spoon stew into the casseroles and top each with a baked biscuit.

Spicy Lamb Shanks

EVELYN N. REED, WHITE RIVER JUNC., N. H.

Set out a large, heavy skillet and a large, shallow baking dish with aluminum foil to cover.

Wipe with a clean, damp cloth
4 lamb shanks, about 1 lb. each
(Have meat dealer crack shin bone.)

Coat shanks evenly with a mixture of
¼ cup flour
1 teaspoon salt
¾ teaspoon Accent
¼ teaspoon pepper
Heat in the skillet over medium heat
¼ cup fat
Put shanks in the skillet. Brown well on all sides. Remove shanks to baking dish. Add
½ cup water
Cover; bake at 300°F about 1½ hrs., or until meat is almost tender when pierced with fork.

Meanwhile, prepare
1⅔ cups dried apricots (cook until almost tender)
1 cup dried prunes (cook until almost tender)
Drain. Remove and discard pits from prunes. Put fruit into a saucepan. Add
1 cup water
½ cup sugar
3 tablespoons vinegar
½ teaspoon cinnamon
½ teaspoon allspice
¼ teaspoon cloves
¼ teaspoon salt
Bring rapidly to boiling and simmer 5 min.

Drain fat from cooked shanks. Add the cooked fruit mixture. Cover and bake 30 min. longer. Serve hot. *4 servings*

Barbecued Lamb Shanks

MRS. JOHN SWETKA, RED BLUFF, CALIF.

Set out a large, shallow baking dish having a tight-fitting cover and a large, heavy skillet.

Wipe with a clean, damp cloth
4 lamb shanks, about 1 lb. each
(Have meat dealer crack shin bone.)

Coat shanks evenly with a mixture of
¼ cup flour
1 teaspoon salt
½ teaspoon Accent
¼ teaspoon pepper
Heat in the skillet over medium heat
¼ cup fat
Place shanks in the skillet. Brown well on all sides. Remove shanks to baking dish. Meanwhile, mix together in a saucepan
1 cup ketchup or chili sauce
½ cup water
¼ cup wine vinegar
4 teaspoons Worcestershire sauce
2 teaspoons sugar
2 teaspoons paprika
1 teaspoon dry mustard
1 teaspoon salt
½ teaspoon Accent
½ teaspoon pepper
5 drops tabasco sauce
1 cup (about 2 medium-size) chopped onion (*page 6*)
2 cloves garlic (*page 6*), minced; or crushed in garlic press
Heat sauce to boiling. Remove from heat and pour over meat.

Bake, covered, at 300°F 1½ to 2 hrs., or until meat is tender when pierced with a fork. Turn and baste shanks frequently.

Serve with
Perfection Boiled Rice (*page 147*)
4 servings

Spring Roast Ham

▲ Spring Roast Ham

Set out a shallow roasting pan with rack.

For Ham—Follow directions on wrapper or wipe with a clean, damp cloth

10-lb. smoked whole ham

Place ham fat side up on rack. Insert roast meat thermometer in center of thickest part of lean, being sure bulb does not rest on bone or in fat.

Roast uncovered at 300°F.

When ham has roasted about 2 hrs., prepare Pineapple Glaze.

For Pineapple Glaze—Blend together

½ cup firmly packed brown sugar
1½ teaspoons cornstarch
½ teaspoon dry mustard

Add and stir in

1 cup (9-oz. can) crushed pineapple

Bring to boiling and cook until mixture is transparent and slightly thickened, stirring constantly. Keep warm.

To Glaze Ham—Remove ham from oven after it has cooked about 2½ hrs. Remove rind (if any) being careful not to remove fat. Making diagonal cuts, score fat surface of ham to make diamond pattern; or use scalloped cookie cutter to make flower pattern.

Place in center of each pattern

Whole clove

Spread ham with Pineapple Glaze. Return to oven and continue roasting about 45 min., or until internal temperature reaches 160°F. (Total roasting time is about 3 hrs., allowing 18 to 20 min. per pound.)

Remove ham to warm serving platter; remove roast meat thermometer. *About 20 servings*

△ Spring Roast Half Ham

Follow ▲ Recipe. Substitute 5 lb. **shank** or **butt half smoked ham** for whole ham. Allow 22 to 25 min. per pound of ham. Substitute the following for Pineapple Glaze. Mix together ½ cup firmly packed **brown sugar,** 2 teaspoons **flour** and ½ teaspoon **dry mustard.** Stir in 1 tablespoon **vinegar.** After ham has roasted about 1½ hrs., remove from oven, trim, score and spread with the glaze. Press into glaze **maraschino cherry halves, pineapple chunks** and whole **cloves** to form an attractive design. Roast until internal temperature reaches 160°F. *About 10 servings*

Broiled Ham Slice

Wipe with a clean, damp cloth

1 smoked ham slice, cut ¾ to 1 in. thick

Allow ⅓ to ½ lb. meat per serving.

Set temperature control of range at Broil.

Place ham slice (or slices) on broiler rack. Place in broiler with top of slice 2 in. from heat source; broil about 8 to 10 min. Turn and broil second side about 8 to 10 min., or until ham is tender when pierced with a fork. If desired, serve with **Zippy Mustard Sauce** (*page 183*).

Stuffed Ham Slices

Stuffed Ham Slices

Set out a 13½x8¾x1¾-in. baking dish.

Wipe with a clean, damp cloth

2 smoked ham slices, cut 1 in. thick

Place one ham slice in the baking dish.

Mix together

4 cups (4 slices) soft bread cubes
½ cup (2½ oz.) seedless raisins
¼ cup firmly packed brown sugar
½ teaspoon dry mustard

Lightly toss with bread mixture

⅓ cup butter or margarine, melted

Spoon stuffing evenly over ham slice in dish. Top stuffing with second ham slice. Insert around edge of top slice of ham

Whole cloves

Drain, reserving sirup

1 No. 2 can sliced pineapple (about 10 slices pineapple)

Place two slices of pineapple in each corner of baking dish. Cut the two remaining pineapple slices into wedges. Brush top ham slice with reserved pineapple sirup. Arrange wedges to resemble flower petals on top of ham.

Bake stuffed ham slices uncovered at 300°F about 1½ hrs. Baste with reserved pineapple sirup several times during baking.

Garnish with **parsley.** *6 to 8 servings*

▲ Baked Ham Slice

Wipe with a clean, damp cloth and place in an 11¾x7½x1¾-in. baking dish

1 smoked ham slice, cut ½ in. thick

(Allow ⅓ to ½ lb. meat per serving.)

Insert into ham slice at 1-in. intervals

Whole cloves

Sprinkle over ham a mixture of

2 tablespoons brown sugar
2 tablespoons fine, dry bread crumbs
1 teaspoon grated orange peel (*page 5*)
½ teaspoon dry mustard

Rinse and cut into ¼-in. slices

1 orange

Arrange slices on ham. Garnish with

Maraschino cherries, cut into rings

Carefully pour over top of ham slice

¾ cup orange juice

Bake at 300°F about 20 min. Remove cloves from ham slice before serving.

△ Pineapple Baked Ham Slice

Follow ▲ Recipe. Substitute **lemon peel** for orange peel, canned **pineapple juice** for orange juice and 3 canned **pineapple slices** for the orange slices.

△ Ginger Baked Ham Slice

Follow ▲ Recipe. Substitute **lemon peel** for orange peel and **ginger ale** for orange juice. Omit orange and cherry garnish.

△ Plum Baked Ham Slice

Follow ▲ Recipe. Substitute **sirup** drained from 1 No. 2 can of **Italian plums** for orange juice. Arrange plums around ham slice. Omit orange and cherry garnish.

Glazed Smoked Shoulder Butt

Glazed Smoked Shoulder Butt

It's the splash of beer in the glaze that gives such an indefinably wonderful taste to smoked butt prepared in this way. For a special treat serve with a big bowl of hot potato salad.

Set out a large, heavy sauce pot or kettle having a tight-fitting cover.

Wipe with a clean, damp cloth
2 smoked boneless pork shoulder butts, about 1½ lbs. each
Put shoulder butts into the sauce pot. Add
Hot water (enough to cover meat)
6 whole cloves
4 peppercorns
Bring liquid rapidly to boiling; reduce heat, cover and simmer (do not boil) 45 min. Cool meat in cooking liquid; drain.

Set out a shallow roasting pan with rack.

Place shoulder butts on rack. Stud tops with
Whole cloves
Blend together thoroughly
1 cup thick applesauce
⅔ cup firmly packed brown sugar
½ cup beer
1 teaspoon cinnamon
¼ teaspoon nutmeg
Spread mixture thickly over top and sides of each butt.

Bake at 350°F 1 hr., or until meat is tender when pierced with a fork.

Serve hot or cold with **caraway-seasoned sauerkraut** (1 teaspoon caraway seeds per No. 2½ can sauerkraut). *About 6 servings*

Barbecued Spareribs

MRS. BOYD BENFIELD, NEWTON, N. C.

Set out a shallow roasting pan; omit rack.

Wipe with a clean, damp cloth
4 lbs. spareribs, cracked through center
Cut into serving-size pieces. Rub pieces with a mixture of
1 tablespoon salt
1 teaspoon pepper
1 teaspoon Accent
Put pieces into the roasting pan, meaty side up. Roast at 350°F 30 min., turning once.

Meanwhile, heat in a saucepan over low heat
¼ cup butter or margarine
Add
1 cup finely chopped onion (*page 6*)
1 cup finely chopped celery (*page 6*)
Cook over medium heat until onion is transparent, stirring occasionally. Add a mixture of
2 cups ketchup
2 cups water
⅓ cup Worcestershire sauce
¼ cup vinegar
¼ cup firmly packed brown sugar
¼ teaspoon cayenne pepper
Heat to boiling. Remove from heat. Stir in
½ cup lemon juice
Pour sauce over ribs; cover pan. Continue baking, basting frequently with the sauce, until meat is tender (1 to 1½ hrs.). If sauce becomes too thick, add more water. Uncover the last 15 to 20 min. *6 to 8 servings*

Orange Pork Chops

MRS. NEWMON A. SMITH, STEENS, MISS.

A grand-prize winner, this original recipe creates boldly and imaginatively with everyday ingredients and brings a burst of startlingly fresh flavor to an old favorite.

Set out a large, heavy skillet and a large, shallow baking dish or 2-qt. casserole having a tight-fitting cover.

Wipe with a clean, damp cloth

6 pork chops, cut about 1 in. thick

Heat in the skillet over medium heat

1 teaspoon fat

Put chops into skillet; brown on both sides.

Clean (*page 6*) and cut into ¼-in. slices and set aside

2 medium-size (about ½ lb.) onions

Blend together

¾ cup (6-oz. can) frozen orange juice concentrate, thawed
⅔ cup water
1 tablespoon lemon juice

and a mixture of

2 tablespoons brown sugar
1½ teaspoons ginger
1 teaspoon poultry seasoning
1 teaspoon marjoram
½ teaspoon Accent
½ teaspoon salt

Arrange the browned chops in the baking dish. Place onion slices on top of chops. Pour the orange juice mixture over the chops. Cover.

Bake at 350°F 1 hr., or until meat is tender and *thoroughly* cooked. (To test for doneness, cut slit near bone; no pink should be visible.)

6 servings

Orange Pork Chops

Pork Chops and Lima Beans

MILDRED HABASEK, BERWYN, ILL.

This dish proves that juicy pork chops and protein-rich limas were made for each other.

Set out a shallow 2-qt. casserole or baking dish and a large, heavy skillet.

Wipe with a clean, damp cloth

4 pork chops, cut ¾ to 1 in. thick

Heat in the skillet over medium heat

1 teaspoon fat

Put chops into skillet and brown lightly on both sides over medium heat.

While chops are browning, set aside to drain contents of

1 No. 2 can (2¼ cups, drained) lima beans

Drain, reserving liquid for use in other food preparation, contents of

1 No. 2 can tomatoes (about 1 cup, drained)

Sieve the tomatoes; mix in the casserole with the lima beans and

½ cup chopped onion (*page 6*)
1 tablespoon dark molasses
1 teaspoon salt
¼ teaspoon Accent

Season chops with a mixture of

2 teaspoons salt
1 teaspoon Accent
½ teaspoon pepper

Arrange the chops over the lima-bean mixture.

Bake at 350°F 1 hr., or until meat is tender and *thoroughly* cooked. (To test for doneness, cut a slit near the bone; no pink color should be visible.)

4 servings

Roast Loin of Pork

Roast Loin of Pork

What flavor surpasses crisp tawny roast pork?

Set out a roast meat thermometer and a shallow roasting pan.

Wipe with a clean, damp cloth

3- to 5-lb. pork loin roast

(Have meat dealer loosen chine bone.) Rub pork with a mixture of

4 teaspoons dry mustard
1 teaspoon salt
1 teaspoon Accent
¼ teaspoon pepper

Place pork, fat side up, in pan. (Bones form a natural rack.) Insert roast meat thermometer in center of thickest part of meat, being sure the bulb does not rest in fat or on bone.

Roast pork uncovered at 350°F 2 to 3 hours. (Allow 35 to 40 min. per pound.) Meat is done when internal temperature of meat reaches 185°F. Remove roast from oven; remove thermometer. Place roast on warm serving platter. Garnish as desired. *6 to 10 servings*

Bar-B-Q'd Pork Steaks

AAGOT HANSON, EAGLE GROVE, IOWA

Set out a large, shallow baking dish or roasting pan.

Wipe with a clean, damp cloth

6 pork steaks, arm or blade, cut ¾ to 1 in. thick

Heat in a heavy skillet over medium heat

1 teaspoon fat

Put steaks into skillet; brown on both sides over medium heat.

While steaks are browning, combine in a saucepan and heat to boiling

1½ cups ketchup
1½ cups water
¼ cup vinegar
¼ cup Worcestershire sauce
2 teaspoons salt
2 teaspoons chili powder
2 teaspoons paprika
1 teaspoon pepper
½ teaspoon Accent

Clean (*page 6*) and thinly slice

2 large (about ⅔ lb.) onions

Season the steaks with a mixture of

1 teaspoon salt
1 teaspoon Accent
¼ teaspoon pepper

Arrange steaks in the baking dish; cover with the onion slices. Pour sauce over all.

Bake at 350°F 50 to 60 min., or until pork is tender and *thoroughly* cooked. (To test for doneness, cut a slit near the bone; no pink color should be visible.) Baste frequently with sauce.

Serve with onion slices and sauce spooned over steaks. *6 servings*

Note: **Pork chops** may be substituted for the pork steaks.

▲ Frilly Frankfurters

Set out an 11¾x7½x1¾-in. baking dish.

Prepare
1 cup Whipped Potatoes (one-fourth recipe, *page 158*)
Add and mix thoroughly
¼ cup finely chopped onion
¼ cup chopped sweet pickle
3 tablespoons chopped pimiento
Set aside.

Make a lengthwise slit almost through
6 frankfurters
Open the slit frankfurters and spread the cut surfaces with
¼ cup prepared mustard
Arrange frankfurters in the baking dish with cut surfaces up; pile potato mixture lightly over top.

Bake at 350°F 20 min., or until lightly browned.

For Broiling—Arrange frankfurters on broiler rack. Pile whipped potato mixture lightly on frankfurters.

Set temperature control of range at Broil.

Place broiler rack in broiler with top of potatoes 4 to 5 in. from source of heat; broil 7 to 8 min., or until lightly browned. *6 servings*

△ Franks with Cheese Frills

Follow ▲ Recipe. Omit chopped ingredients. Blend the Whipped Potatoes with ¾ cup (3 oz.) grated **Cheddar cheese.** Bake or broil as in ▲ Recipe.

Note: To prepare frankfurters on an outdoor grill see Outdoor Cooking (*page 10*).

Bacon-Wrapped Frankfurters

Set out a large, shallow baking dish.

Set out
12 slices bacon
Cut almost through lengthwise
12 frankfurters
Mix together
1 cup sweet pickle relish
2 tablespoons prepared mustard
Fill the frankfurters with the relish mixture. Starting at one end, wrap one slice of bacon around each frankfurter; secure ends with wooden picks. Put frankfurters in baking dish.

Bake at 375°F 25 min., or until bacon is crisp.
6 servings

Pigskin Special

(Ground "Frank" Meat Loaf)

MRS. W. L. ISBELL, BROOKSTON, IND.

Lightly grease a 9½x5¼x2¾-in. baking pan.

Grind (*page 63*) and put into a bowl
1 lb. frankfurters
Add and mix thoroughly
1 cup (3 slices) fine, dry bread crumbs
2 tablespoons finely chopped onion
2 tablespoons chopped green pepper
½ teaspoon sage
1 cup milk
2 eggs, beaten
Pack mixture lightly into the baking dish.

Bake at 350°F 45 min. Pour off excess liquid and unmold (*page 63*).

Spread over top of loaf
2 tablespoons ketchup or chili sauce
Serve loaf hot or cold. *About 6 servings*

Glazed Canadian-Style Bacon

Place on a rack in a shallow baking pan
1½ lbs. Canadian-style bacon (one piece)
Insert in upper surface
10 to 12 whole cloves
Spread over surface a mixture of
¼ cup firmly packed brown sugar
1½ tablespoons dry mustard
Roast uncovered at 300°F 30 min.

Pour over meat
½ cup apple cider or juice
Basting occasionally, continue cooking 15 to 25 min. longer, or until meat is tender.

6 servings

▲ Cranberry-Glazed Canadian-Style Bacon

Arrange in an 11¾x7½x1¾-in. baking dish
10 slices (about 1 lb.) Canadian-style bacon, cut about ¼ in. thick
Sprinkle slices with a mixture of
1 tablespoon grated orange peel (*page 5*)
½ teaspoon sugar
⅛ teaspoon cloves
Few grains nutmeg
Spread over slices
1 cup whole cranberry sauce
Bake uncovered at 350°F about 25 min.

5 servings

Broiled Canadian-Style Bacon with peaches

△ Broiled Canadian-Style Bacon

Follow ▲ Recipe for amount of Canadian-style bacon. Set temperature control of range at Broil. Arrange slices on broiler rack. Place in broiler with top of meat 3 in. from source of heat. Broil about 5 min. on each side, or until browned. Spoon about ½ cup whole **cranberry sauce** into cavities of 5 **canned peach halves** and place on broiler rack after bacon is turned.

Note: Any **jelly** may be used to glaze Canadian-style bacon or to fill cavities of peaches.

Gourmet Canadian-Style Bacon

Lightly grease 4 ramekins.

Clean, separate into flowerets, soak and cook (*page 149*)
1 medium-size head cauliflower
Brush a cold skillet with
Melted fat
Arrange in the skillet
8 slices (about ⅔ lb.) Canadian-style bacon, cut about ¼ in. thick
Cook slowly, browning on each side. Pour off any fat that collects during cooking. Place 2 slices in each ramekin.

Shred and set aside
8 oz. process American cheese (2 cups, shredded)
Prepare
2 cups Medium White Sauce (double recipe, *page 181*)
Cool sauce slightly. Add three-fourths of the cheese all at one time; stir until blended. Add
1 tablespoon onion juice
½ teaspoon paprika
Divide cauliflower evenly among ramekins. Pour sauce over cauliflower in each ramekin.

Bake at 350°F 10 min.

Sprinkle with the remaining cheese and
½ cup buttered crumbs (*page 4*)
Return to oven and bake 10 min. longer, or until cheese is melted and crumbs are lightly browned. *4 servings*

Panbroiled Bacon

(*See photo on page 46*)

Cooking at one time only as many slices as will lie flat in skillet, place in a cold skillet
½ lb. bacon slices
Cook slowly over low heat, turning bacon frequently. Pour off fat as it collects. When bacon is evenly crisped and browned, remove from skillet and drain on absorbent paper. Serve hot. *10 to 12 slices bacon*

▲ Little Sausages with Apple Rings

Prepare
24 Panbroiled Link Sausages (*on this page*)
Remove links to absorbent paper. Keep warm. Drain any remaining fat from skillet and wipe skillet with absorbent paper.

For Apple Rings—Wash and core
4 medium-size (about 1⅓ lbs.) apples
Cut each apple crosswise into about 5 slices (½ to ¾ in. thick). Place apple slices flat in the skillet. Add
⅓ cup pineapple juice
Set over medium heat. Cover and cook about 5 min. on one side. Turn slices and cook about 5 min. longer, or until slices are tender. Remove from skillet and serve with sausage links. *6 to 8 servings*

△ Little Sausages with Glazed Apple Rings

Follow ▲ Recipe for preparing sausage links.

Little Sausages with Apple Rings

For Glazed Apple Rings—Melt in a small skillet over low heat ¼ cup **butter** and ¼ cup firmly packed **brown sugar.** Add **apple rings** and cook about 5 min. on one side. Carefully coat slices with sirup and cook until tender.

Panbroiled Sausage Patties

Shape into 5 or 6 flat patties and put into a cold skillet
1 lb. bulk pork sausage
(Or put sausage into skillet and break into pieces with fork.) Add
3 tablespoons water
Cover and cook slowly 5 min. Remove cover. Pour off fat. Brown, turning occasionally. Pour off fat as it collects. Cook 20 to 30 min., or until browned. Remove to absorbent paper. *5 or 6 sausage patties*

Panbroiled Link Sausages

Put into a large cold skillet
12 (about ¾ lb.) link sausages
Add
2 tablespoons water
Cover and cook slowly 8 to 10 min. Remove cover and pour off fat. Brown links over medium heat, turning as necessary (do not prick links with a fork). Remove links to absorbent paper to drain.

Calf's Liver with Bacon

Calf's Liver with Bacon

Set out a large, heavy skillet.

Prepare, reserving bacon drippings

12 slices Panbroiled Bacon (*page 87*)

Wipe with a clean, damp cloth and, if necessary, remove tubes and outer membrane from

6 slices (about 1½-lbs.) veal or calf's liver, cut about ½ in. thick

Coat slices evenly with a mixture of

½ cup flour
1 teaspoon Accent
¾ teaspoon salt
¼ teaspoon pepper

Meanwhile, return to skillet and heat 3 tablespoons of the reserved bacon drippings. Put liver slices in skillet and brown on both sides over medium heat; do not overcook. Arrange on warm serving plate with bacon slices. Serve at once. *6 servings*

Liver Loaf

Grease a 9½x5¼x2¾-in. loaf pan. Set out a large skillet having a tight-fitting cover.

Wipe with a clean, damp cloth, and, if necessary, remove tubes and outer membrane from

¾ lb. pork liver

Put liver in skillet with

1 cup hot water

Cover and simmer 5 min. Drain; set liver aside to cool.

Meanwhile, combine and mix lightly

¾ lb. bulk pork sausage
1½ cups cracker crumbs
¼ cup ketchup
2 tablespoons lemon juice
1 tablespoon Worcestershire sauce
2 eggs, beaten
½ cup milk

and a mixture of

1½ teaspoons salt
½ teaspoon chili powder
½ teaspoon Accent
¼ teaspoon pepper

Grind (*page 63*) the liver. Mix lightly with the sausage mixture. Pack lightly into loaf pan.

Bake at 350°F about 1½ hours. Unmold (*page 63*). *6 to 8 servings*

Liver Balls in Onion Gravy

Set out a large skillet and a small skillet, each having a tight-fitting cover.

Wipe with a clean, damp cloth and, if necessary, remove tubes and outer membrane from

½ lb. liver (beef, lamb, pork or veal)

Put liver into the small skillet with

¾ cup hot water

Cover and simmer 5 min. Drain; set liver aside.

Meanwhile, prepare in the large skillet, reserving drippings

4 slices Panbroiled Bacon (*page 87*)

While bacon is cooking, mix in a large bowl

1 egg, beaten
¼ cup milk
¼ cup chopped onion
3 tablespoons well-drained, chopped sweet pickle
⅓ cup (1 slice) fine, dry bread crumbs

and a mixture of

½ teaspoon salt
¼ teaspoon Accent
⅛ teaspoon pepper

Crumble bacon and add to bread-crumb mixture. Grind (*page 63*) the liver. Add to bacon mixture and mix lightly. Shape into 1½-in. balls. Return reserved drippings to skillet and heat. Brown liver balls in skillet over medium heat, turning occasionally to brown evenly.

Meanwhile, prepare and set aside

2 cups quick meat broth (double recipe, *page 7*)

With slotted spoon, remove browned liver balls from skillet; set aside to keep warm.

Heat in the skillet over low heat

½ cup butter or margarine

Add and cook until onion is transparent, occasionally moving and turning with a spoon

¼ cup chopped onion
3 tablespoons (about 1 small) chopped carrot
1 bay leaf

Blend into mixture in skillet

4½ tablespoons flour

Heat until mixture bubbles, stirring constantly. Remove from heat.

Gradually add broth, stirring constantly. Bring rapidly to boiling, stirring constantly; cook 1 to 2 min. longer. Add liver balls and simmer about 30 min. Remove bay leaf.

Meanwhile, heat in the small skillet

2 tablespoons butter or margarine

Add and cook until transparent, occasionally moving and turning with a fork

1 large onion (*page 6*), sliced thinly

Garnish liver balls and gravy with onion slices.

About 4 servings

Smoked Tongue Platter

Smoked Tongue Platter

Put into a large, heavy sauce pot having a tight-fitting cover

1 smoked beef tongue

Add enough boiling water to cover the tongue. Cover and simmer 3 to 4 hrs. or until tender. (Or cook according to directions on package.) When tongue is cool enough to handle, slit skin on underside of tongue and peel it off. Cut away roots and gristle. If not used immediately, cool tongue in cooking liquid. Drain; store in refrigerator.

Slice tongue and arrange slices in a ring on serving platter. Fill center of ring with

Garden Potato Salad (*page 168*)

Garnish with

Parsley
Sliced hard cooked eggs

6 to 8 servings

Veal Shoulder Roll Surprise

Stuffed Roast Breast of Veal

MRS. L. A. KING, JACKSONVILLE, FLA.

Set out a shallow roasting pan with rack.

Wipe with a clean, damp cloth

3 to 4-lb. breast of veal with pocket

(Have meat dealer cut meat away from ribs to form a pocket for stuffing.) Rub roast with a mixture of

1¼ teaspoons salt
¾ teaspoon Accent

Set meat aside.

Clean, cook (*page 149*) and drain

1 lb. spinach

Mix the cooked spinach with

3 cups (3 slices) soft bread cubes
½ cup (2 oz.) grated Cheddar cheese
¼ cup milk
2 tablespoons butter or margarine
½ teaspoon minced parsley

and a mixture of

½ teaspoon salt
¼ teaspoon Accent
⅛ teaspoon pepper

Lightly spoon spinach mixture into pocket. Skewer or sew to keep stuffing in place. Put meat, rib side down, on rack in pan. Place over top of roast

4 slices bacon

Roast uncovered at 300°F about 2½ hrs., or until meat is tender. *4 to 6 servings*

Veal Shoulder Roll Surprise

Set out a roast meat thermometer and a shallow roasting pan with rack.

Set out

1 pt. Blueberry-Lemon Jam (*page 308*)

Wipe with a clean, damp cloth

4-lb. veal shoulder roll

Cut one end of the cord tied around the roll; remove and set cord aside.

Carefully unroll veal and spread jelly over it in a layer about ¼ in. thick. Reroll the veal and again tie with cord.

Rub the roll with a mixture of

2 teaspoons salt
1 teaspoon Accent
¼ teaspoon pepper

Put veal roll on rack in roasting pan. Insert roast meat thermometer at top center of roll, being sure that bulb rests in center of the roll.

Lay over the veal

4 slices bacon or salt pork

Roast veal uncovered at 300°F. Remove veal from oven after 2 hrs. Remove slices of bacon or salt pork. Spread top of roll with Blueberry-Lemon Jam.

Return veal to oven and continue roasting about ½ hr., or until internal temperature of veal reaches 170°F. (The total roasting time should be about 2½ hrs., allow about 40 min. per pound.)

Remove from oven; remove thermometer and keep veal hot. Remove cord from roll just before carving.

Serve with additional Blueberry-Lemon Jam.

About 8 servings

Breaded Veal Chops

Set out a large, heavy skillet having a tight-fitting cover.

Wipe with a clean, damp cloth
4 veal chops or small cutlets
Coat chops with a mixture of
¼ cup flour
1 teaspoon salt
½ teaspoon Accent
¼ teaspoon pepper
Heat in the skillet over medium heat
2 tablespoons fat
Meanwhile, dip the chops into a mixture of
1 egg, slightly beaten
2 tablespoons milk or water
Coat the chops with
1 cup fine, dry bread or cracker crumbs
Put chops into skillet and brown on both sides over medium heat. Remove from heat and pour off remaining fat. Slowly add to skillet
½ cup tomato juice or water
Cover skillet and cook over low heat about 1 hr. or until meat is tender when pierced with a fork. Add small amounts of liquid as needed.

Serve with
Quick Tomato Sauce (*page 183*)

4 servings

Breaded Veal Chops

Veal Chops Hungarian

A zestful sour cream gravy gives flavor contrast.

Set out a large, heavy skillet having a tight-fitting cover.

Wipe with a clean, damp cloth
6 veal chops, rib or loin, cut about ¾ in. thick
Coat chops evenly with a mixture of
¼ cup flour
1 teaspoon salt
½ teaspoon Accent
¼ teaspoon pepper
Heat in the skillet over medium heat
2 to 3 tablespoons fat
Add the chops and brown evenly on both sides. Spoon over chops
½ cup (1 medium-size) chopped onion (*page 6*)
Sprinkle with
½ teaspoon paprika
Add to the skillet
½ cup hot water
Cover skillet tightly. Simmer over low heat 45 min., or until chops are tender when pierced with a fork.

Meanwhile, cook and drain (*page 141*)
3 cups (about 4 oz.) broad noodles
Remove chops to hot platter. Remove skillet from heat.

For Gravy—Mix together
1 cup thick sour cream
2 tablespoons water
and a mixture of
1 tablespoon paprika
½ teaspoon salt
½ teaspoon Accent
⅛ teaspoon pepper
Pour into the skillet; set over low heat. Heat thoroughly, stirring constantly. Do not boil.

Toss the drained noodles with
Butter or margarine
Arrange noodles around chops. Spoon the gravy over the chops. Serve at once.

6 servings

Poultry includes all domesticated birds used for food: chicken (including capon), turkey, goose, duckling, guinea and squab. Recently the Rock-Cornish game hen, a delicious hybrid, has been added. Wild duck and pheasant are game birds which are handled like domestic poultry. Rabbit, either domestic or wild, has meat so similar to poultry that it is included here.

CLASSES—Chickens and turkeys are classified according to size, age and sex. Age influences tenderness of the meat and therefore determines the cooking method. Size determines the cooking time.

Chicken—*Broiler*, either sex, 1½ to 2½ lbs. ready-to-cook weight, 10 to 12 weeks old; *fryer*, either sex, 2 to 3 lbs. ready-to-cook weight, 12 to 16 weeks old; *roaster*, either sex, usually over 3½ lbs., usually under 8 months; *capon*, unsexed male, usually under 10 months, 4 lbs. or over, exceptionally good flavor, especially tender, with large proportion of white meat; *stewing chicken*, female, usually more than 10 months, 3 to 5 lbs. ready-to-cook weight.

Turkey—*Fryer-roaster*, either sex, usually under 16 weeks, 4 to 8 lbs. ready-to-cook weight; *young hen or tom*, female or male, usually under 8 months, 8 to 24 lbs. ready-to-cook weight; *mature hen or tom*, over 10 months, less tender and seldom found on the consumer market.

Duck—*Duckling*, either sex, 8 to 9 weeks old, 3½ to 5 lbs. ready-to-cook weight (the only class in which ducks are marketed commercially).

Goose—Classifications less well established, but weights range from 4 to 8 lbs. ready-to-cook weight for young birds, up to 14 lbs. for mature birds.

STYLES—*Dressed poultry* refers to birds which have been bled and feather-dressed but have head, feet and viscera intact. *Ready-to-cook poultry* is fully cleaned inside and out and is ready for cooking; it may or may not be tagged or stamped with official inspection or grade labels. (Since 1953, only ready-to-cook poultry is permitted to carry United States Department of Agriculture grades on individual birds; but the use of official inspection and grading services is entirely voluntary on the part of the packers.) Ready-to-cook poultry is marketed either fresh, ice-chilled or quick-frozen. In many markets, chicken and turkey halves, quarters, pieces and giblets are sold separately, fresh or quick-frozen. These pieces—especially breast, thighs and drumsticks—greatly simplify cooking and serving poultry and facilitate meal-planning. Quick-frozen *stuffed* turkeys must be cooked without thawing. DO NOT FREEZE YOUR OWN STUFFED TURKEYS as the time required to freeze them with stuffing encourages the growth of bacteria.

BUYING GUIDES—Where tags or stamps provide information as to quality established by inspection and grading or both, this is the consumer's most reliable guide in the selection of poultry. The grading and inspection program of the United States Department of Agriculture employs three easily recognizable marks: 1) *inspection mark*, indicating that the bird has been processed under sanitary conditions and is wholesome food; 2) *grade mark*, indicating the quality, class and kind—there are three grades, A, B and C; 3) *grade and inspection mark*. Poultry bearing the combined grade and inspection marks is guaranteed to be of top quality.

When grading and inspection labels are not present, the consumer may be guided by some of the standards used in official grading. Young birds have smooth, soft, thin skin, little fat and flexible-tipped breastbones; as the bird ages, the skin coarsens, more fat is deposited along the backbone and the breastbone becomes more rigid.

Grade A quality requires that a bird be well-formed and full-fleshed, with no defects, tears or bruises in the skin, clean and free from pinfeathers.

STORAGE—Poultry is a perishable food and must be safeguarded against spoilage or deterioration of flavor by proper care. *Quick-frozen* poultry must be kept frozen until ready to use and once thawed must not be refrozen. In thawing frozen poultry before cooking, directions on the label should be followed. *Fresh or ice-chilled* poultry should be purchased only at markets where the birds are kept refrigerated. To store poultry of this style at home, remove it from the meat dealer's wrappings and rewrap it loosely; then store in the coldest part of the refrigerator (about 40°F). Cut-up poultry should be held no more than 24 hours before using; whole birds with the giblets wrapped separately may be stored up to two days.

PREPARATION FOR COOKING—*Ready-to-cook* poultry, whole or in pieces, should be rinsed in cold water, drained immediately and patted dry. It should never be allowed to soak in water, as soaking dissipates flavor. *Dressed* poultry should be drawn immediately, preferably at the market. Remove pinfeathers with a sharp-pointed knife or a strawberry huller. Singe the bird over a flame, turning quickly until all down and hair are burnt off. Then wash as for ready-to-cook poultry.

Before roasting, neck and body cavities of whole birds are rubbed with a mixture of salt and Accent, then usually stuffed (never stuff until ready to roast), trussed and roast-meat thermometer inserted. Poultry pieces generally are coated with a mixture of flour, salt, pepper, Accent and other seasonings if desired, before frying or browning; before broiling, they are seasoned with salt, pepper and Accent.

COAT POULTRY PIECES EVENLY—Put a mixture of flour and seasonings into a bowl or onto a piece of waxed paper. Coat one or a few pieces of poultry at a time. Or shake a few pieces at a time in a plastic or clean paper bag containing the flour mixture.

COOKING POULTRY—Two general principles apply to the cooking of all kinds of poultry: 1) Cook at low to moderate constant heat for a suitable length of time. High temperatures shrink the muscle tissue and make the meat tough, dry and hard. Poultry should always be cooked until well done; the meat should separate easily from the bone and should be tender to the fork. An exception is wild duck, which is traditionally served rare. 2) Suit the method of cooking to the age or class of the bird. Young birds of all kinds may be broiled, fried or roasted in an open pan. Older, less tender birds require cooking by moist heat, either in a covered casserole or Dutch oven, or in water or steam.

STUFFING POULTRY FOR ROASTING—Ingredients for a stuffing should be mixed *just before needed* and the bird should be stuffed *just before roasting*. Never stuff bird a day in advance and store in refrigerator or freezer. These are safety precautions to prevent food poisoning, since stuffing is the perfect medium for disease-producing bacteria. *Immediately* after the meal is served, remove the stuffing from the bird and store, covered, in the refrigerator. Use leftover stuffing within 2 or 3 days and heat thoroughly before serving.

Any extra stuffing which cannot be put into the bird may be put in a greased, covered baking dish or wrapped in aluminum foil and baked in the oven during the last hour of roasting.

TESTS FOR DONENESS OF ROAST POULTRY—A roast-meat thermometer, if used, should register 190°F when bird is done (insert in center of inside thigh muscle). The thickest part of drumstick feels soft when pressed with fingers protected with clean cloth or paper napkin. Or drumstick moves up and down or twists out of joint easily.

STORING COOKED POULTRY—Cooked poultry, gravy and stuffing should not be left at room temperature for longer than it takes to finish the meal. Never store bird with stuffing; remove stuffing and store it covered in refrigerator; cover gravy and refrigerate. If only one side of a roast bird has been carved, wrap remainder of bird in waxed paper, aluminum foil or moisture-vapor-proof material; store in refrigerator. If more than one half of the meat has been used, remove the remaining meat from the bones and wrap tightly before storing. Cooked pieces should be tightly wrapped and refrigerated. Do not keep cooked poultry, however carefully stored, for more than a few days.

CUT-UP COOKED CHICKEN—For recipes in this book that call for *cut-up cooked chicken*, use stewed chicken or canned chicken.

Roast Chicken with Giblet Gravy (page 187) and buttered carrots

Roast Chicken

(See photo on page 187)

Set out a shallow roasting pan with rack.

Clean

1 roasting chicken, 3 to 4 lbs., ready-to-cook weight

Cut off neck at body, leaving on neck skin. (If chicken is frozen, thaw according to directions on package.) Rinse and pat dry with absorbent paper; set aside. Reserve giblets for gravy; or use in other food preparation.

Prepare and cool

Herb Stuffing (*page 108*; see note) or Apple Stuffing for Poultry (*page 108*)

Rub cavities of chicken with a mixture of

1 teaspoon Accent
½ to 1 teaspoon salt

Lightly fill body and neck cavities with stuffing. To close body cavity, sew or skewer and lace with cord. Fasten neck skin to back and wings to body with skewers. Tie drumsticks to tail. Brush skin thoroughly with

Melted fat

Place chicken breast side up or down, as desired, on rack in roasting pan. If roast-meat thermometer is used, place it in center of inside thigh muscle. (When chicken is done, roast-meat thermometer will register 190°F.) Place fat-moistened cheesecloth over top and sides of chicken. Keep cloth moist during roasting by brushing occasionally with fat from bottom of pan.

Roast uncovered at 325°F about 3 hrs., or until chicken tests done (*page 93*). If bird was started breast down, turn breast up when about three-quarters done.

When chicken is tender, remove from oven. Remove thermometer and keep bird hot. Allow to stand in pan 15 to 30 min. before serving. This allows chicken to absorb its juices and become easier to carve. This also allows time to prepare gravy and garnishes.

To serve, remove cord and skewers. Place chicken on heated platter. Serve with

Dumplings (*page 50*)
Brown Gravy (*page 187*) or Giblet Gravy (*page 187*; use drippings for part or all of liquid)

About 6 servings

▲ Broiled Chicken

DORIS WADE, DANVILLE, IND.

Clean, rinse and pat dry with absorbent paper

2 broiling chickens, 1½ to 2 lbs. each, ready-to-cook weight

(Have meat dealer split birds into halves lengthwise and remove backbone, neck and keel bone.) Reserve giblets for use in other food preparation.

Brush pieces with

Juice of 1 lemon (about 3 tablespoons)

Set the remaining lemon juice aside. Season chicken pieces with a mixture of

1 tablespoon salt
1 teaspoon Accent
1 teaspoon paprika
¼ teaspoon pepper

Melt

⅓ cup butter or margarine

Brush pieces with some of the melted butter; reserve remainder for basting sauce. Set out

3 tablespoons sugar

Sprinkle one half of the sugar over the chicken pieces; add remainder to reserved butter with the remaining lemon juice.

Set temperature control of range at Broil. Arrange the chicken pieces skin side down in broiler pan (not on rack). Bring wing tips onto backs under the shoulder joint. Press down.

Place pan in broiler so that surface of chicken is 7 to 9 in. from heat source. Broil 10 min. without turning pieces. Continue to broil chicken 30 to 40 min., brushing pieces frequently (about every 10 min.) with the butter mixture; turn chicken occasionally to brown evenly. Chicken is done when browned and when drumstick moves easily. *4 servings*

△ Wine-Broiled Chicken

BARBARA MALMUTH, LOS ANGELES, CALIF.

Follow ▲ Recipe. Decrease sugar to 1 teaspoon; do not sprinkle over chicken. Add the sugar, ½ teaspoon **garlic salt** and ⅓ cup **sherry** to basting sauce.

Note: To prepare chicken on an outdoor grill see OUTDOOR COOKING (*page 10*).

Golden Crusty Chicken

Set out a deep saucepan or automatic deep-fryer (*page 7*); heat fat to 350°F.

Clean

1 frying chicken, 2 to 3 lbs. ready-to-cook weight

Broiled Chicken, Corn-on-the-Cob and Baked Potatoes cooked on an outdoor grill (page 10)

Disjoint chicken and cut into serving-size pieces. (If chicken is frozen, thaw according to directions on package.) Rinse and pat dry with absorbent paper. Set aside.

Sift together

1 cup sifted flour
2½ teaspoons salt
1 teaspoon Accent
1 teaspoon sugar
½ teaspoon pepper
¼ teaspoon paprika

Blend together and add to flour mixture

1 egg, slightly beaten
1 cup milk

Mix until batter is thoroughly blended. Dip pieces of chicken into batter; coat well. Allow any excess coating to drip off before lowering chicken into the heated fat.

Fry only as many pieces at one time as will lie uncrowded one layer deep in the fat. Fry chicken about 10 to 13 min., or until tender and golden brown. (Liver requires only about 1 min. frying time.) Turn pieces with tongs several times during cooking. Drain over fat a few seconds; remove to absorbent paper.

Serve hot. *2 to 4 servings*

Fried Chicken: Coat chicken pieces evenly. Place skin side down in skillet. Turn with tongs.

Cook covered 25 to 40 min. Uncover last 10 min. to crisp skin. Garnish with parsley.

▲ Fried Chicken

Set out a Dutch oven or a large, heavy skillet having a tight-fitting cover.

Clean

1 frying chicken, 2 to 3 lbs. ready-to-cook weight

Disjoint chicken and cut into serving-size pieces. (If chicken is frozen, thaw according to directions on package.) Rinse and pat dry with absorbent paper.

Coat chicken (*page 93*) with a mixture of

½ cup flour
1 teaspoon paprika
1 teaspoon salt
½ teaspoon Accent
¼ teaspoon pepper

Heat in the skillet over medium heat

Fat (or use cooking oil) to at least ½-in. depth

Starting with meaty pieces of chicken, place them skin side down in skillet. Put in less meaty pieces as others brown. To brown all sides, turn pieces as necessary with tongs or two spoons. When chicken is evenly browned, reduce heat and add

1 to 2 tablespoons water

Immediately cover skillet. Cook slowly 25 to 40 min., or until thickest pieces of chicken are tender when pierced with a fork. Uncover the last 10 min. to crisp skin.

Serve with **Brown Gravy** (Method 1, *page 187*; use pan drippings and milk for liquid).

2 to 4 servings

△ Maryland-Fried Chicken

Coat chicken pieces with seasoned flour (omit paprika) as in ▲ Recipe. Dip them into a mixture of 2 **eggs** beaten with 3 tablespoons **water.**

Roll pieces in 1½ cups fine dry **bread crumbs, corn meal,** fine **cracker crumbs** or finely crushed **corn flakes.** Let stand 5 to 10 min. to "seal" coating. Cook as in ▲ Recipe.

▲ Oven "Barbecued" Chicken

ARLETTA WHALEY, OTWELL, IND.

Set out a shallow baking pan, a large, heavy skillet and a small saucepan.

Clean

1 frying chicken, 2 to 3 lbs. ready-to-cook weight

Disjoint chicken and cut into serving-size pieces. (If chicken is frozen, thaw according to directions on package.) Rinse and pat dry with absorbent paper.

Coat chicken (*page 93*) with a mixture of

½ cup flour
1 teaspoon paprika
1 teaspoon salt
½ teaspoon Accent
¼ teaspoon pepper

Heat in the skillet over medium heat

½ cup fat

Starting with meaty pieces of chicken, place them skin side down in skillet. Put in less meaty pieces as others brown. To brown all sides, turn pieces as necessary with tongs or two spoons. Arrange pieces one layer deep in the baking pan.

While chicken browns, combine in saucepan

1⅓ cups (14-oz. bottle) ketchup
1 cup water
½ cup finely chopped onion (*page 6*)
2 tablespoons vinegar
1 tablespoon Worcestershire sauce
1 clove garlic (*page 6*), minced; or crushed in garlic press
1 tablespoon sugar
1 tablespoon paprika
1 teaspoon salt
¼ teaspoon pepper

Bring sauce to boiling, stirring occasionally. Remove from heat; add

¼ cup lemon juice

Pour sauce over chicken pieces in baking pan.

Turning and basting chicken frequently with the sauce, bake at 325°F about 45 min., or until thickest pieces are tender when pierced with a fork. *About 4 servings*

△ Broiler Barbecued Chicken

Prepare sauce as in ▲ Recipe; set aside. Substitute 2 **broiling chickens,** about 1½ lbs. each, ready-to-cook weight, for the frying chicken. (Have meat dealer split birds into halves lengthwise and remove backbone, neck and keel bone.) Brush chicken halves with ¼ cup melted **butter** or **margarine.** Arrange pieces skin side down in broiler pan (not on rack); brush with the sauce. Set temperature control of range at Broil. Place pan 7 to 9 in. from heat source. Broil 40 to 50 min., turning and basting frequently with the sauce.

Serve immediately.

Oriental Barbecued Chicken

MRS. YOTSUO FUKE, HILO, HAWAII

Do you have a yen for a perked-up chicken dish? Then try this zesty recipe from Hawaii.

Clean

1 frying chicken, 2½ to 3 lbs. ready-to-cook weight

Disjoint and cut into serving-size pieces. (If chicken is frozen, thaw according to directions on package.) Rinse chicken pieces and drain on absorbent paper.

Mix together in a large, shallow dish

½ cup soy sauce
¼ cup sugar
3 drops tabasco sauce
1½ teaspoons ginger
½ teaspoon Accent
Few grains paprika
1 clove garlic (*page 6*), minced; or crushed in garlic press

Turn chicken pieces in the soy-sauce marinade. Cover and set aside in a cool place several hours or overnight, turning pieces occasionally. Remove chicken from marinade. (Reserve marinade for basting.)

Set out

8 slices bacon

Wrap each chicken piece with a bacon slice. Secure slices with wooden picks. Place chicken pieces in a large shallow baking dish.

Frequently turning pieces and basting with reserved marinade, bake at 350°F 1½ hrs., or until thickest pieces of chicken are tender when pierced with a fork.

Serve immediately with

Perfection Boiled Rice (*page 147*)

4 servings

Creamed Chicken in Pastry Shells

Creamed Chicken in Pastry Shells

Set out a heavy 2-qt. saucepan.

Prepare, bake and set aside

8 4½-in. pastry shells (one- and one-half times recipe for Pastry for Little Pies and Tarts, (*page 243*; flute shells, see photo)

Dice and set aside enough chicken to yield

2½ cups diced cooked chicken

Heat in the saucepan over low heat

2 tablespoons butter or margarine

Add

½ cup (4-oz. can, drained) sliced mushrooms
¼ cup finely chopped green pepper (*page 6*)
2 tablespoons finely chopped onion

Cook until onion is transparent and mushrooms are lightly browned, occasionally moving and turning with a spoon. Add, stirring constantly

2½ cups (2 10½- to 11-oz. cans) condensed cream of chicken soup
½ cup milk
2 tablespoons finely sliced pimiento
¼ teaspoon Accent

Blend in the chicken. Heat, but do not boil.

Spoon the hot mixture into the prepared pastry shells. Serve immediately. *8 servings*

Chicken à la King

Set out a 2-qt. saucepan.

Cut into chunks and set aside enough cooked chicken to yield

3 cups cooked chicken

Prepare and set aside

1½ cups quick chicken broth (*page 7*; use 2 chicken bouillon cubes)

Cook and set aside (drain if necessary)

1 10-oz. pkg. frozen peas

Meanwhile, clean and slice (*page 6*)

½ lb. mushrooms

Heat in the saucepan over low heat

⅓ cup butter, margarine, or chicken fat

Add the mushrooms. Cook slowly about 5 min., frequently moving and turning with a spoon. With slotted spoon remove mushrooms, allowing fat to drain back into saucepan; set mushrooms aside.

Blend into butter in saucepan a mixture of

¼ cup flour
1 teaspoon salt
½ teaspoon Accent
Few grains pepper

Heat until mixture bubbles; cook 3 to 5 min. Remove from heat. Add gradually, stirring constantly, the chicken broth and

1½ cups cream

Return mixture to heat; cook until thickened. Add the chicken, peas, mushrooms and

¼ cup (2-oz. can, drained) pimiento strips

Cook mixture slowly until chicken is thoroughly heated. If desired, transfer mixture to a chafing dish.

Serve over **waffles, rusks,** or **Toast Points** (*page 51*), or in **Toast Cups** (*page 51*).

6 servings

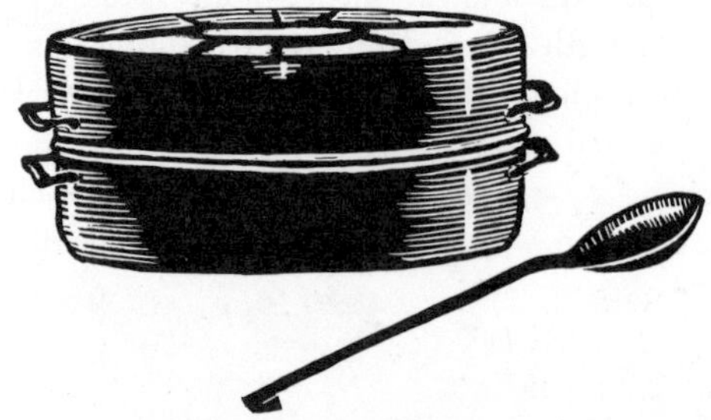

Chicken Livers Orientale

Set out a large, heavy skillet.

Drain, reserving sirup, and set aside

1 No. 2 can pineapple chunks (about 2 cups, drained)

Clean thoroughly, rinse with cold water, and set aside to drain on absorbent paper

2 lbs. chicken livers

Blanch (*page 5*) and set aside

1 cup (5½ oz.) almonds

Mix together in a medium-size saucepan

¼ cup firmly packed brown sugar
¼ cup sugar
¼ cup cornstarch

Add gradually, while stirring constantly, a mixture of the reserved pineapple sirup and

1½ cups (12-oz. can) pineapple juice
4 to 6 tablespoons vinegar
1 tablespoon soy sauce

Bring rapidly to boiling, stirring constantly. Cook 3 min. longer, stirring occasionally. Set aside and keep hot.

Heat in the skillet over low heat

½ cup butter or margarine

Put livers in skillet. Turning occasionally, cook about 10 min., or until lightly browned. Add pineapple chunks, almonds, and sauce. Moving mixture gently with a spoon, cook a few min. longer, or until pineapple is heated.

Spoon mixture into chafing dish to keep warm while serving. Serve over

Perfection Boiled Rice (*page 147*)

6 to 8 servings

Curried Chicken with Almonds

Cut into strips and set aside enough cooked chicken to yield

4 cups cooked chicken

Coarsely chop and set aside

½ cup (about 2¾ oz.) unblanched, toasted almonds (*page 6*)

Clean and slice (*page 6*)

¼ lb. mushrooms

Heat in a chafing pan (or large skillet) over direct heat

⅓ cup butter or margarine

Add mushrooms to chafing pan with

¼ cup finely chopped onion
¼ cup finely chopped celery

Cook over medium heat until onion is transparent and mushrooms are delicately browned, occasionally moving and turning pieces.

Gently push vegetables to one side of the pan and blend into butter a mixture of

½ cup flour
2 teaspoons curry powder
1½ teaspoons Accent
1 teaspoon salt

Heat until mixture bubbles, stirring constantly. Remove from heat. Add gradually to chafing pan, stirring constantly

2 cups cream
2 cups chicken broth; or quick chicken broth (*page 7*)

Return to heat and bring rapidly to boiling, stirring constantly, and carefully mixing in the vegetables; cook 1 to 2 min. longer. Blend in the chicken. Cook until chicken is thoroughly heated, occasionally stirring gently. Sprinkle chopped almonds over top.

Serve with **Perfection Boiled Rice** (*page 147*) and curry condiments, such as freshly grated **coconut,** golden **raisins,** Indian **chutney** and **Broiled Bananas** (*page 161*). *6 to 8 servings*

Curried Chicken with Almonds and Broiled Bananas (page 161)

Chicken Fricassee, Biscuits and Cream Gravy

Chicken Fricassee with Biscuits and Cream Gravy

Set out a Dutch oven or a sauce pot having a tight-fitting cover.

For Chicken—Clean

1 stewing chicken, 4 to 5 lbs., ready-to-cook weight

(If frozen, thaw according to directions on package.) Disjoint and cut into serving-size pieces. Rinse; pat chicken pieces and giblets dry with absorbent paper.

Heat in the sauce pot over low heat

¼ cup butter or margarine

Add the chicken pieces. Brown over medium heat, occasionally moving and turning pieces.

Pour over the browned chicken

3 cups hot water

Add

1 small onion (*page 6*)
3 sprigs parsley
2 3-in. pieces celery with leaves
1 small bay leaf
2 or 3 peppercorns
2 teaspoons Accent
1 teaspoon salt

Cover and simmer 2 to 3 hrs., or until thickest pieces of chicken are tender when pierced with a fork.

While chicken is cooking, prepare

Tender-Rich Buttermilk Biscuits (*page 43*)

Remove chicken to hot serving platter; cover to keep warm while preparing gravy. Strain and reserve the broth for gravy.

For Gravy—Heat in a small saucepan over low heat

¼ cup butter or margarine

Blend in a mixture of

¼ cup flour
¼ teaspoon pepper

Heat until mixture bubbles and flour is lightly browned. Remove from heat. Add gradually, stirring constantly, the reserved chicken broth (about 2 cups) and

½ cup cream

Cook slowly, stirring constantly, until gravy thickens. Cook 1 to 2 min. longer.

To Serve—Split 6 of the biscuits into halves and arrange them around the chicken pieces on the serving platter. (Set remaining biscuits aside to keep warm.) Pour part of the gravy over the chicken and biscuits on the platter. Serve remaining gravy in a small bowl or gravy boat with the remaining biscuits.

6 to 8 servings

▲ Roast Rock Cornish Game Hen

Set out a shallow roasting pan with a rack.

Prepare and set aside for stuffing

Wild Rice with Mushrooms (one-half recipe, *page 161*; add all mushrooms to rice)

Clean

4 Rock Cornish game hens, about 1 lb. each

Rinse and pat dry with absorbent paper.

Rub cavities of the four hens with

2 teaspoons salt
¼ teaspoon Accent

Lightly fill body cavities with the stuffing. To close body cavities, sew or skewer and lace with cord. Fasten neck skin to backs and wings to bodies with skewers. Put game hens breast-side up on rack in roasting pan.

Set out

¼ cup unsalted butter, melted

Brush each hen with the butter.

Roast uncovered at 350°F.

Frequently baste hens during roasting period with drippings from roasting pan.

Roast 1 to 1½ hrs., or until hens test done. To test doneness, move leg gently by grasping end bone; drumstick-thigh joint moves easily when hens are done. (Protect fingers from heat with paper napkin.)

Place game hens on a heated platter; keep warm while preparing gravy. Before serving, remove skewers and garnish hens with

Sprigs of water cress

For Gravy—Prepare

½ cup quick meat broth (*page 7*)

Set aside to cool.

Leaving brown residue in roasting pan, pour the drippings into a bowl. Allow fat to rise to surface; skim off fat and reserve. Remaining drippings are meat juices which should be used as part of the liquid in the gravy. Measure into roasting pan 1½ tablespoons of the reserved fat. Blend in

1½ tablespoons flour
¼ teaspoon Accent
⅛ teaspoon salt
⅛ teaspoon pepper

Stirring constantly, heat until the mixture bubbles. Remove from heat and add gradually, stirring constantly and vigorously, the broth and ½ cup of the drippings. Return to heat and bring mixture rapidly to boiling, stirring constantly. Cook 1 to 2 min. longer. While stirring, scrape bottom and sides of pan to blend in brown residue. Remove from heat and stir in

2 tablespoons Madeira wine

Pour into a gravy boat and serve hot.

4 servings

△ Roast Squab

Follow ▲ Recipe. Substitute 4 **squabs,** ¾ to 1 lb. each, ready-to-cook weight, for the Rock Cornish game hens.

Roast Rock Cornish Game Hen

Roast Ducklings with Orange Rice Stuffing

Roast Ducklings with Orange Rice Stuffing

Set out a shallow roasting pan with rack.

Clean

2 ducklings, 4 lbs. each, ready-to-cook weight

Cut off necks at bodies, leaving on neck skin. (If frozen, thaw according to directions on package.) Rinse and pat ducklings dry with absorbent paper; set aside. Reserve giblets for use in other food preparation.

Prepare and cool

Orange-Rice Stuffing (*page 111*)

Set out

1 cup orange juice

Rub cavities of ducklings with a mixture of

1 to 2 teaspoons salt
1 to 2 teaspoons Accent

Lightly fill body and neck cavities with the stuffing. To close body cavity, sew or skewer and lace with cord. With skewers, fasten neck skin to back and wings to body. Place ducklings breast side up on rack in roasting pan. Brush with the orange juice.

Roast at 325°F. After 30 min., brush ducklings with juice; brush frequently thereafter. Roast 3 hrs., or until ducklings test done (*page 93*).

Remove skewers and cord. Serve ducklings on heated platter. Garnish with **orange slices.** If desired, accompany with Orange Gravy.

For Orange Gravy—Leaving brown residue in roasting pan, pour into a bowl

Drippings

Allow fat to rise to surface; skim off fat and reserve. Remaining drippings are meat juices and orange juice which should be used as part of the liquid in the gravy.

Measure into the roasting pan 3 tablespoons of the reserved fat. Blend in a mixture of

3 tablespoons flour
¼ teaspoon salt
¼ teaspoon Accent
⅛ teaspoon pepper

Stirring constantly, heat until mixture bubbles. Remove from heat and add slowly, stirring constantly and vigorously

2 cups liquid (cooled drippings plus orange juice)

Return to heat and cook rapidly, stirring constantly, until gravy thickens. Cook 1 to 2 min. longer. While stirring, scrape bottom and sides of pan to blend in brown residue.

About 8 servings

▲ Roast Ducklings with Giblet Gravy

Set out a shallow roasting pan with rack.

Clean

2 ducklings, 4 lbs. each, ready-to-cook weight

Cut off necks at bodies, leaving on neck skin. (If frozen, thaw according to directions on package.) Rinse and pat ducklings dry with absorbent paper; set aside. Refrigerate giblets.

Prepare

Chestnut Stuffing for Roast Duckling (*page 110*), or Apple Stuffing for Poultry (*page 108*)

Set aside.

Rub cavities of ducklings with a mixture of

1 to 2 teaspoons salt
1 to 2 teaspoons Accent

Lightly fill body and neck cavities of ducklings with the stuffing. To close body cavities, sew or skewer and lace with cord. With skewers fasten neck skin to back and wings to body. Place breast side up on rack in roasting pan.

Roast uncovered at 325°F about 3 hrs., or until ducklings test done (*page 93*).

To serve, remove skewers and cord. Place ducklings on a heated platter; cover and keep hot. Prepare **Giblet Gravy** (*page 187*; cook giblets during last half of roasting period).

About 8 servings

△ Roast Ducklings
(Unstuffed)

Follow ▲ Recipe; omit stuffing. If desired, place quartered, cored, unpared **apples,** halved **onions,** or ribs of **celery** inside duckling. Roast 2 to 2½ hrs., or until duckling tests done.

▲ Roast Goose with Prune Stuffing

Set out a shallow roasting pan with rack.

For Prune Stuffing—Stew, remove pits and set aside

1 cup (about 7 oz.) large dried prunes

Meanwhile, cook in salted water just to cover, about 30 to 40 min., or until tender

1 lb. lean pork (all visible fat removed), cut in pieces

Drain and put through food chopper. Set aside.

Prepare

½ cup chopped onion (*page 6*)
¼ cup chopped green olives

Heat in a skillet over medium heat

1 tablespoon fat

Add the onion; cook until transparent, occasionally moving with a spoon. Mix in the pork; season with a mixture of

1 teaspoon salt
1 teaspoon Accent
¼ teaspoon pepper

Remove skillet from heat; stir in

2 egg yolks, slightly beaten

Remove ¼ cup of pork stuffing and combine with the olives. Fill pitted prunes with this mixture and gently mix prunes with remaining stuffing.

To Prepare Goose—Clean, removing any layers of fat from body cavity and opening

1 goose, 10 to 12 lbs. ready-to-cook weight

Cut off neck at body, leaving on neck skin. (If goose is frozen, thaw according to directions on package.) Rinse and pat dry with absorbent paper. (Reserve giblets for use in other food preparation.) Rub cavities of goose with **salt.**

Lightly spoon stuffing into body and neck cavities. To close body cavity, sew or skewer and lace with cord. Fasten neck skin to back with skewer. Loop cord around legs and tighten slightly. Place breast side down on rack in roasting pan.

Roast uncovered at 325°F for 3 hrs. Remove fat from pan several times during this period. Turn goose breast side up. Roast 1 to 2 hrs. longer, or until it tests done (*page 93*). (Total roasting time: about 25 min. per pound.)

To serve, remove skewers and cord. Place goose on heated platter. Garnish as desired.

8 servings

△ Roast Goose with Apple Stuffing

Follow ▲ Recipe; substitute **Apple Stuffing for Poultry** (*page 108*) for the prune stuffing.

Roast Goose with Prune Stuffing

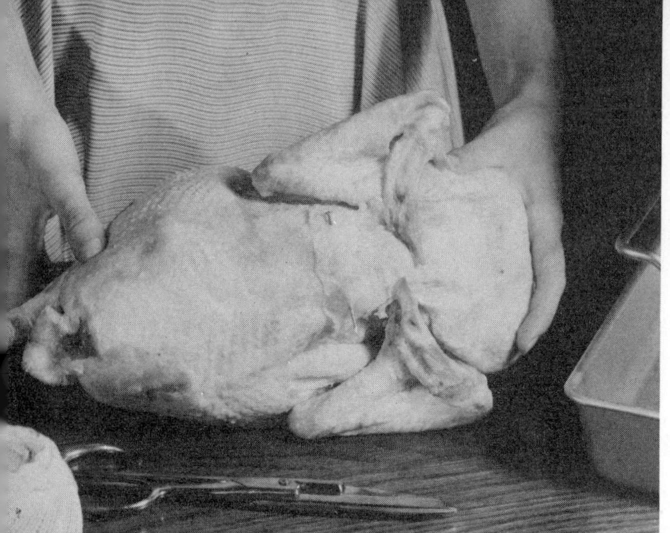

Roast Turkey: Fasten neck skin to back of bird with a skewer. Bring wing tips onto the back.

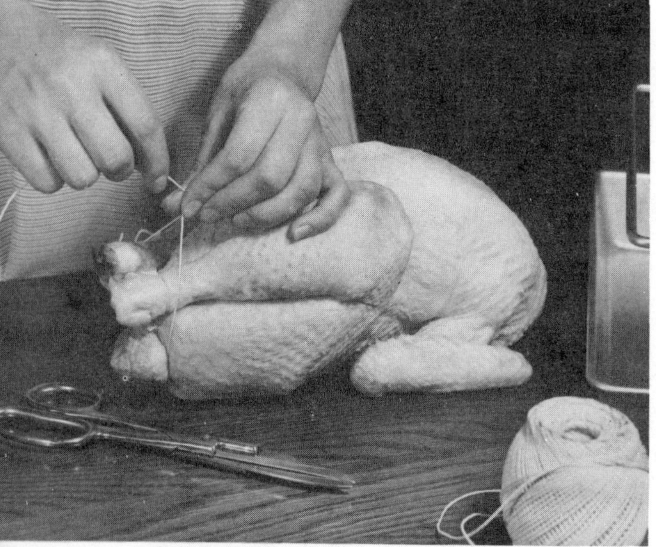

Tie drumsticks of the turkey to the tail with cord. Brush the skin thoroughly with melted fat. Roast.

Test for doneness by pressing thickest part of drumstick with fingers. Meat feels soft to touch.

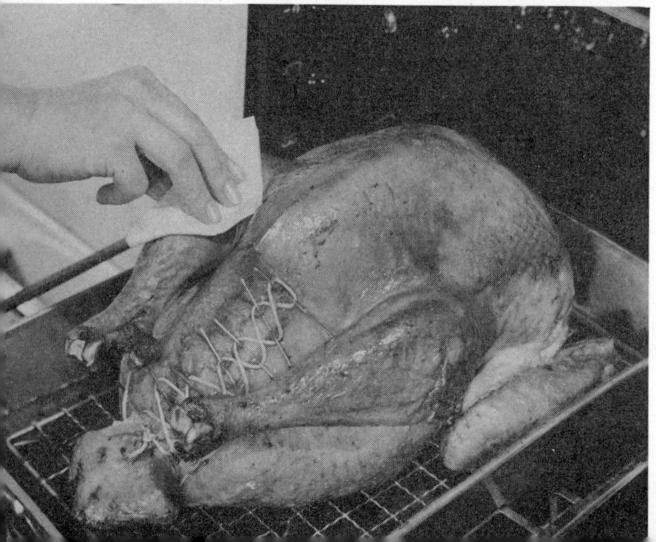

▲ Roast Turkey

Set out a shallow roasting pan with rack.

Clean

1 turkey, 10 to 12 lbs. ready-to-cook weight

Cut off neck at body, leaving on neck skin. (If turkey is frozen, thaw according to directions on package.) Rinse, drain and pat dry with absorbent paper; set aside. Reserve giblets.

Prepare

Herb Stuffing or Oyster Stuffing (*page 108*) or Giblet Stuffing for Roast Turkey (*page 110*)

Rub cavities of turkey with a mixture of

2 teaspoons Accent
1 to 2 teaspoons salt

Lightly fill body and neck cavities with stuffing. To close body cavity, sew or skewer and lace with cord. Fasten neck skin to back with skewer. Tie drumsticks to tail. Bring wing tips onto back. Brush skin thoroughly with

Melted fat

Place breast side up on rack in roasting pan. If roast-meat thermometer is used, place it in center of inside thigh muscle. (When turkey is done, roast-meat thermometer will register 190°F.) Place fat-moistened cheesecloth over top and sides of turkey. Keep cloth moist during roasting by brushing occasionally with fat from bottom of pan.

Roast uncovered at 325°F 4 to 4½ hrs., or until turkey tests done (*page 93*). Remove turkey from oven. Remove roast-meat thermometer and keep turkey hot. Allow to stand 30 to 40 min. before serving. This allows turkey to absorb its juices and become easier to carve. This also allows time to prepare gravy and garnishes. Remove cord and skewers. Serve turkey on hot platter. Garnish with **parsley.** Serve with

Cranberry sauce
Brown Gravy or Giblet Gravy (*page 187*)

If desired, put paper frills on drumsticks.

About 16 servings

△ Roast Half Turkey

Follow ▲ Recipe; use **half** or **quarter turkey,** 3½ to 5 lbs., ready-to-cook weight. Rub cut side with one-half salt mixture. Skewer skin along cut side to prevent shrinking. Tie leg to tail and wing flat against breast. Place skin-side up on rack. Roast at 325°F 2 hrs.

Meanwhile, prepare **Stuffing for Half Turkey** (*page 108*). Spoon stuffing onto a piece of aluminum foil. Cover stuffing with the half turkey and return turkey and stuffing to rack. Roast 1 to 1½ hrs. longer, or until turkey tests done (*page 93*). *About 8 servings*

△ Roast Turkey in Aluminum Foil

Follow ▲ Recipe for preparing turkey; omit stuffing turkey. (If desired, bake stuffing separately.) Wrap turkey securely in medium weight aluminum foil; close with a drugstore or lock fold to prevent leakage of drippings. Place turkey, breast side up in roasting pan (omit rack).

Roast at 450°F about 3 hrs., or until turkey tests done (*page 93*). About 15 to 20 min. before end of cooking time, remove from oven. Quickly fold foil back away from bird to edges of pan. If using roast-meat thermometer, insert it at this time. Return bird to oven and complete cooking. (Turkey will brown sufficiently in this time.)

Turkey-Rice Dinner

Grease a 2-qt. casserole.

Prepare
Perfection Boiled Rice (*page 147*)
Meanwhile, blanch (*page 5*) and sliver
½ cup (about 3 oz.) almonds
With fork, toss almonds with
½ cup soft bread crumbs
¼ cup butter or margarine, melted
Set aside.

Dice and set aside enough turkey to yield
2 cups diced cooked turkey
Prepare and set aside
1½ cups Thin White Sauce (1½ times recipe, *page 181*; if available, use turkey broth for one half of liquid. Add 2 or 3 drops tabasco sauce)
With a fork, gently mix drained rice and
12 pimiento-stuffed olives, sliced
Mix the diced turkey with
½ cup (4-oz. can, drained) sliced mushrooms
½ teaspoon Accent
Spoon one third of the rice into casserole. Add one half of the turkey mixture; repeat and top with remaining rice. Pour sauce over all. Sprinkle with crumb-almond mixture.

Bake at 350°F 25 to 30 min., or until top is crusty and golden brown. *6 to 8 servings*

Note: **Noodles** or **Macaroni** (*page 141*) may be substituted for the rice.

Creamed Turkey and Oysters

Cut into chunks enough cooked turkey to yield
2 to 3 cups cooked turkey
Set in refrigerator until ready to use.

Drain, reserving liquid
1 pt. oysters
Pick over oysters to remove any shell particles. Set oysters and liquid aside.

Prepare in a chafing dish (or saucepan)
3 cups Medium White Sauce (three times recipe, *page 181*; use milk or cream for liquid)
Blend into sauce
⅓ cup (2¼-oz. can) deviled ham
½ teaspoon Accent
Add the turkey and reserved oysters and liquid, gently blending in. Heat thoroughly.

Meanwhile, prepare **Toast Cups** (*page 51*).

Fill toast cups with the creamed mixture. Serve at once. *8 servings*

▲ Roast Wild Duck with Wild Rice Stuffing

Set out a shallow roasting pan with rack.

Singe and clean

2 wild ducks, 2 to 3 lbs. each

Cut out oil sac at base of tail; cut off neck at body, leaving on neck skin. Wash ducks in cold, running water; dry with absorbent paper.

Prepare and set aside

Wild Rice Stuffing (½ recipe, *page 111*)

Set out

4 slices bacon or salt pork

Rub cavities of ducks with a mixture of

1 to 2 teaspoons salt
1 to 2 teaspoons Accent

Lightly fill body and neck cavities of ducks with the stuffing. To close body cavities, sew or skewer and lace with cord. With skewers fasten neck skin to back and wings to body. Put ducks breast side up on rack in roasting pan. Place bacon or salt pork over breasts.

Roast uncovered at 400°F to 450°F 20 to 25 min. for very rare, 30 to 40 min. for medium-rare. (Wild duck is traditionally served rare.) If desired, baste occasionally with

1 cup orange juice, cider or red wine

To serve ducks, remove skewers and cord. Place on heated platter; cover ducks and keep hot while preparing gravy and garnishes.

For Gravy—Scrape pan drippings into a small saucepan. Put into 1-pt. screw-top jar

½ cup water

Sprinkle onto it

1 tablespoon flour

Cover tightly and shake until mixture is well blended. Gradually stir into liquid in pan. Bring rapidly to boiling, stirring constantly until thickened. Cook 3 to 5 min.

About 4 servings

△ Roast Wild Goose

Follow ▲ Recipe; substitute a **wild goose** for ducks. Use full recipe of stuffing. Increase bacon if necessary. Roast at 325°F about 3 hrs. Baste frequently.

Roast Wild Duck

MRS. H. L. BLEVINS, APPALACHIA, VA.

Set out a shallow roasting pan with rack.

Singe and clean

2 wild ducks, 2 to 3 lbs. each

Cut out oil sac at base of tail; cut off neck at body, leaving on neck skin. Wash ducks in cold, running water; dry with absorbent paper.

Set out

3 apples
2 onions (*page 6*)
1 orange
4 slices bacon

Rub cavities of ducks with a mixture of

1 teaspoon salt
1 teaspoon Accent
¼ teaspoon pepper
⅛ teaspoon ginger

Rub surface of ducks with cut side of

½ lemon

Quarter the apples, onions, and orange. Put pieces inside cavities of ducks. Refrigerate ducks 2 hrs. Discard filling and place ducks breast side up on rack in roasting pan. Lay bacon strips over breasts. Pour over birds

2 cups quick meat broth (*page 7*)
3 tablespoons melted butter

Roast uncovered at 375°F to 400°F about 30 min. (Wild duck is traditionally served rare.)

Baste occasionally with pan gravy.

About 4 servings

△ Fruit-Filled Wild Duck

Follow ▲ Recipe; do not refrigerate ducks. Close openings of filled ducks with small skewers. Substitute 2 cups **orange juice** or **red wine** for meat broth. Omit butter.

Roast Pheasant

Set out a shallow roasting pan with rack.

Prepare

Wild Rice and Mushrooms (*page 161*; add all mushrooms to rice)

Set aside for stuffing.

Clean

2 young pheasant, about 2 lbs. each

Cut off necks at bodies, leaving on neck skin. (If frozen, thaw according to directions on package.) Rinse and pat dry with absorbent paper. (Reserve giblets for use in other food preparation.) Rub cavities with a mixture of

1 to 2 teaspoons salt
1 to 2 teaspoons Accent

Lightly fill body and neck cavities with the stuffing. To close body cavities, sew or skewer and lace with cord. With skewers, fasten neck skin to back and wings to body.

Place pheasant breast side up on rack in roasting pan. Brush with

¼ cup unsalted butter, melted

Roast uncovered at 325°F, brushing pheasant frequently during roasting period with drippings from pan. Roast 1½ to 2 hrs., or until pheasant tests done (*page 93*).

Keep pheasant warm while preparing

Brown Gravy (*page 187*; add 2 tablespoons red wine)

Before serving, remove skewers and cord.

4 servings

Rabbit Stew

Set out a large kettle or sauce pot having a tight-fitting cover.

Heat to boiling in a large saucepan

2½ cups water

Meanwhile, sort and wash thoroughly

1 cup (about ½ lb.) dried large lima beans

Add beans gradually to water so boiling will not stop. Simmer 2 min.; remove saucepan from heat. Set beans aside to soak 1 hr.

Meanwhile, clean (*page 6*), cut into thin slices and set aside

2 medium-size (about ½ lb.) onions

Finely dice, and set aside, enough bacon to yield

½ cup diced bacon

Wipe with a clean, damp cloth and cut into serving-size pieces

1 rabbit, 2½ to 3-lbs., ready-to-cook weight

(If frozen, thaw according to directions on package.) Set aside.

Put diced bacon in kettle and heat over low heat. Add the onion slices and cook over medium heat until onion is transparent and bacon is lightly browned (not crisp). With slotted spoon, remove bacon and onion to a small dish.

Put rabbit pieces into the kettle and cook until lightly browned, turning pieces with tongs or two spoons to brown evenly. Add more fat if necessary.

Add to the browned rabbit

Hot water (enough to half-cover)

Return bacon and onion to kettle. Add

1 tablespoon salt
1 teaspoon Accent
¼ teaspoon pepper
⅛ teaspoon thyme
1 clove garlic (*page 6*), minced; or crushed in a garlic press
1 bay leaf

Bring liquid rapidly to boiling; reduce heat, cover and simmer (do not boil) 45 min.

Meanwhile, wash, scrape or pare, and slice

1 lb. carrots (about 2½ cups, sliced)

Drain lima beans and add to kettle with sliced carrots. Continue cooking about 45 min., or until rabbit and vegetables are tender. Add more boiling water as needed. During last 15 min. of cooking time, add

2 green peppers (*page 6*), sliced in rings

If desired, thicken cooking liquid (*page 63*). Remove bay leaf.

6 to 8 servings

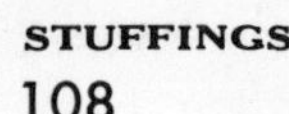

Apple Stuffing for Spareribs

Wash, quarter, core, pare, dice and set aside
- **1 medium-size apple (1 cup, diced)**

Heat in a skillet over medium heat
- **¼ cup butter or margarine**

Add and cook until transparent, occasionally moving and turning with a spoon
- **½ cup (1 medium-size) chopped onion (*page 6*)**

Meanwhile, toss together the diced apple and
- **2 cups (about 2 slices) soft bread crumbs or cubes**

and a mixture of
- **1 teaspoon salt**
- **¼ teaspoon Accent**
- **1 teaspoon celery seed**
- **¼ teaspoon marjoram**
- **⅛ teaspoon pepper**

Blend with onion and fat. Toss mixture with
- **¼ cup apple cider (use only enough barely to moisten bread)**

About 3½ cups stuffing

▲ Herb Stuffing

Mix together
- **¾ cup melted butter or margarine**
- **2 teaspoons salt**
- **½ to 1 teaspoon Accent**
- **1 teaspoon sage (or ½ teaspoon each of thyme, rosemary and marjoram)**
- **¼ teaspoon pepper**

Lightly toss seasoned butter with a mixture of
- **2 qts. (about 8 slices) soft bread cubes**
- **¾ cup milk**
- **⅓ cup chopped celery with leaves**
- **⅓ cup chopped onion**

Spoon stuffing into neck and body cavities of turkey—do not pack. (See STUFFING POULTRY FOR ROASTING, *page 93*.)

Stuffing for 10-lb. turkey

△ Oyster Stuffing

Drain 1 pt. **oysters,** reserving liquid. Pick over to remove any shell particles. Simmer oysters in reserved liquid 3 min., or until edges begin to curl. Chop if oysters are large.

Follow ▲ Recipe. Substitute **poultry seasoning** for sage. Add oysters to bread cubes. **Oyster liquid** may be substituted for part of the milk.

△ Stuffing for Half Turkey

Follow ▲ Recipe or △ Recipe, allowing ⅔ cup stuffing per serving. Spoon stuffing onto aluminum foil and place under turkey the last 1 to 1½ hrs. of roasting time.

△ Apple Stuffing for Poultry

Follow ▲ Recipe; increase onion to ½ cup and substitute ½ teaspoon **marjoram** for sage. Wash, quarter, core, pare, dice and toss with the bread mixture 2 medium-size **apples** (about 2 cups, diced).

For one 10- to 12-lb. goose, prepare one-half recipe Apple Stuffing; for one chicken or two ducklings, prepare one-third recipe.

△ Toasted-Bread Stuffing

Follow ▲ Recipe; omit soft bread cubes and milk. Increase onion to 1 cup, celery to ¾ cup. Toast until golden brown and thoroughly dried 11 slices **white bread.** Put bread into a bowl. Pour **milk** or **water** over bread and let stand until slices swell. Squeeze out moisture; pull bread apart. Remove bread to a large bowl. Pour the seasoned butter over the bread. Add the chopped vegetables and 2 **eggs,** well beaten. Mix together lightly with 2 forks.

Note: These stuffings may also be used for chicken, goose or duckling. Allow about 1 cup bread cubes per pound of ready-to-cook weight of bird; if weight is 10 lbs. or less, subtract 1 cup from total; if weight is more than 10 lbs., subtract 2 cups from the total number. Proportionately increase or decrease remaining ingredients in recipe.

Celery-Almond Stuffing

Finely chop and set aside

½ cup (about 3 oz.) blanched, toasted almonds (*page 5*)

Finely dice enough celery to yield

3 cups finely diced celery (*page 6*)

Prepare and set aside

¾ cup quick chicken broth (*page 7*)

Mix together

¾ cup butter, melted
2 teaspoons poultry seasoning
1 teaspoon salt
½ teaspoon Accent
¼ teaspoon pepper

Lightly toss butter mixture with the almonds, celery, chicken broth and

2 qts. (about 8 slices) soft bread crumbs
⅓ cup finely chopped onion

Spoon stuffing into neck and body cavities of turkey—do not pack. (See STUFFING POULTRY FOR ROASTING, *page 93*.)

Stuffing for 10-lb. turkey

Molly's Bread Stuffing

(For Poultry and Game)

MRS. BILL SETZER, JOHNSON CITY, TENN.

Molly was a Southern mountain woman who earned her living as a cook for a short time. Innocent of book-learnin' though she was, Molly knew her native mountain cooking lore. Her bread stuffing is especially good with game.

Put in a large cold skillet

½ lb. (about 8) sausage links
2 tablespoons water

Cover and cook slowly 8 to 10 min. Remove cover and pour off fat. With a fork, break links into small pieces. Add

1 small onion, finely chopped

Cook over medium heat, until onion is transparent and sausage is lightly browned, frequently moving and turning with a spoon.

Add

½ cup butter

When butter has melted, stir in a mixture of

3 cups (9 slices) fine, dry bread crumbs
1 cup corn-bread crumbs
½ teaspoon sage
½ teaspoon salt
¼ teaspoon Accent
⅛ teaspoon pepper

Heat, stirring gently and constantly, until crumbs absorb butter. Remove from heat.

Spoon stuffing lightly into small game animals or birds. (See STUFFING POULTRY FOR ROASTING, *page 93*.)

About 3 cups stuffing

▲ Chestnut Stuffing for Roast Duckling

Set out a shallow baking dish.

Wash and make a long slit through shell on both sides of

2 lbs. chestnuts

Put chestnuts into the dish and brush them with

1½ tablespoons cooking oil

Set in 450°F oven for 20 min.

Remove chestnuts from oven, allow to stand until just cool enough to handle, and with a sharp pointed knife remove shells and skins. Put into boiling salted water to cover and boil 20 min., or until tender.

Meanwhile, heat in a skillet over low heat

¼ cup butter

Add to butter and cook over medium heat until onion is transparent, occasionally moving and turning pieces with a spoon

1 small onion (*page 6*), chopped
½ cup chopped celery (*page 6*)

Remove skillet from heat; add and mix well

1 cup (about 1 slice) soft bread crumbs
1 tablespoon chopped parsley

and a mixture of

1 teaspoon salt
¼ teaspoon Accent
⅛ teaspoon pepper

When chestnuts are tender, put one half through ricer or food mill. Coarsely chop remaining chestnuts. Combine chestnuts with bread-crumb mixture. Toss lightly with

½ cup cream

Just before roasting, spoon stuffing into neck and body cavities of bird—do not pack. (See STUFFING POULTRY FOR ROASTING, *page 93*.)

About 3½ cups stuffing
(Enough for two 4-lb. ducklings)

Note: For a 10- to 12-lb. turkey, double recipe; increase bread crumbs to 5 cups.

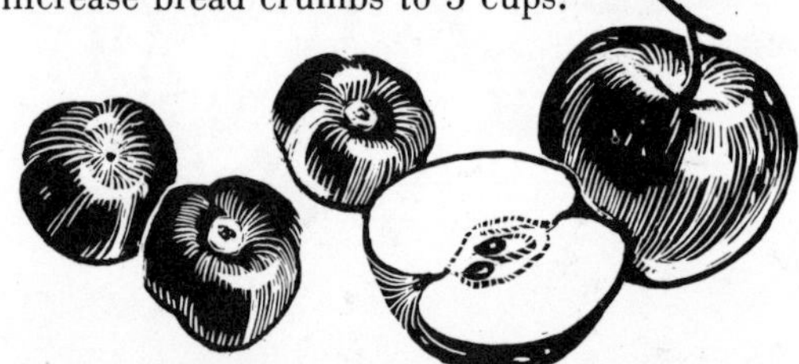

△ Apple-Chestnut Stuffing

Follow ▲ Recipe; wash, quarter, core and dice 1 medium-size cooking **apple** (about 1 cup, diced). Mix the apple into the stuffing before addition of cream.

Giblet Stuffing for Roast Turkey

Set out a small skillet.

Prepare and cook, simmering until tender, 2 to 2½ hrs.

Turkey giblets (gizzard, heart, liver) and neck

Remove giblets and neck from broth; allow meat to cool slightly. Remove neck meat from bones and chop with giblets; put into a large mixing bowl. Set aside. Strain and reserve the giblet broth.

Heat in the skillet over medium heat

¾ cup butter or margarine

Add to fat and cook until onion is transparent, occasionally moving and turning with a spoon

½ cup (about 1 medium-size) chopped onion (*page 6*)

Remove from heat and stir in a mixture of

2 teaspoons salt
½ teaspoon Accent
¼ teaspoon pepper
¼ teaspoon paprika

Set out

2 qts. (about 11 slices) dry bread cubes
2 tablespoons chopped parsley

Add gradually to bread cubes, tossing lightly

¾ cup reserved giblet broth
2 eggs, well beaten

Add the chopped giblets, the onion mixture and the chopped parsley.

Just before roasting turkey, spoon stuffing into neck and body cavities—do not pack. (See STUFFING POULTRY FOR ROASTING, *page 93*.)

Enough stuffing for a 10- to 12-lb. turkey

Orange-Rice Stuffing

Heat in a heavy 2-qt. saucepan over low heat

3 tablespoons butter or margarine

Add and cook over medium heat until onion is transparent, occasionally moving and turning pieces with a spoon

1 cup diced celery with leaves (*page 6*)

2 tablespoons chopped onion

Add to saucepan and bring to rapid boiling

1½ cups water

1 cup orange juice

2 tablespoons grated orange peel (*page 5*)

1½ teaspoons salt

½ teaspoon Accent

⅛ teaspoon marjoram

⅛ teaspoon thyme

Add gradually so boiling will not stop

1 cup uncooked rice

Stir to blend thoroughly. Cover saucepan tightly; reduce heat to very low and cook about 25 min. without removing cover. Cool slightly. Spoon stuffing into neck and body cavities of bird—do not pack. (See STUFFING POULTRY FOR ROASTING, *page 93*.)

4 cups stuffing
(Enough for two 4-lb. ducklings or one 4- to 5-lb. roasting chicken)

To Stuff Poultry: Stuff just before putting in the oven. Lightly fill body and neck cavities with stuffing.

Wild Rice Stuffing

MRS. A. E. BOYCE, RIVERDALE, N. DAK.

Set out a 3-qt. saucepan having a tight-fitting cover.

Heat in the saucepan over low heat

⅓ cup butter or margarine

Add, stirring constantly

2 cups wild rice

Cook, stirring frequently, until rice is very hot and tips are lightly browned. Add

1 cup chopped onion (*page 6*)

1 cup chopped celery (*page 6*)

Continue cooking until onion is transparent, frequently moving mixture with a spoon. Add, stirring in

4 cups chicken broth or quick chicken broth (*page 7*)

¼ teaspoon Accent

Bring to boiling. Cover tightly and simmer until rice is tender and liquid is absorbed (about 30 min.).

Meanwhile, chop and set aside

1 cup (about 4 oz.) walnuts

Heat in a small skillet over low heat

1 tablespoon butter or margarine

Add

½ cup chopped mushrooms (*page 6*)

Cook over medium heat until lightly browned, frequently moving and turning pieces with a spoon. Set aside.

Remove rice mixture from heat. Turn into a large mixing bowl. Add the walnuts, mushrooms, and a mixture of

½ teaspoon celery salt

½ teaspoon poultry seasoning

½ teaspoon salt

Dash nutmeg

Blend together lightly but thoroughly. Spoon lightly into cavities of poultry or game. (See STUFFING POULTRY FOR ROASTING, *page 93*.)

About 7 cups stuffing

Fish

AVAILABILITY—Fresh fish are best prepared as soon as possible after being caught. When fresh, they have red gills, bright eyes, and bright-colored scales adhering tightly. The flesh is firm and elastic, and practically free from odor. Fresh fish should be packed in ice until purchased; at home, wrap in aluminum foil or moisture-vapor-proof material and store in the refrigerator.
Frozen fish is available the year around in market forms such as steaks, fillets and sticks. It should be solidly frozen and *never refrozen after thawing;* packages should be in perfect condition.
Smoked fish is a delicacy; salmon, whitefish and haddock (finnan haddie) are popular varieties.
Canned fish is easy to store (in a cool, dry place) and convenient to serve. Sardines, tuna, cod, salmon, mackerel and kippered herring are some of the varieties. Fish cakes and balls are also canned.

MARKET FORMS—Whole or round fish are just as they come from the water; before cooking they must be scaled and the entrails removed; the head, tail and fins may be removed if desired.
Drawn fish have only the entrails removed; before cooking they must be scaled; the head, tail and fins may be removed if desired.
Dressed fish have been scaled and the entrails, head, tail and fins removed; ready-to-cook.
Fish steaks are cross sections of larger dressed fish; ready-to-cook as purchased.
Fish fillets are the sides of a dressed fish, cut lengthwise away from the backbone; practically boneless.
Fish sticks are uniform pieces of fish dipped in batter, breaded and frozen; they resemble French fried potatoes in appearance and can be purchased uncooked or precooked. Precooked sticks are deep-fried before freezing and need only to be heated.

PURCHASING GUIDE—For *whole or round fish* allow 1 lb. per serving. *Dressed fish* or *fish steaks* allow ½ lb. per serving. Allow ⅓ lb. per serving of *fish fillets* or *frozen fish sticks.*

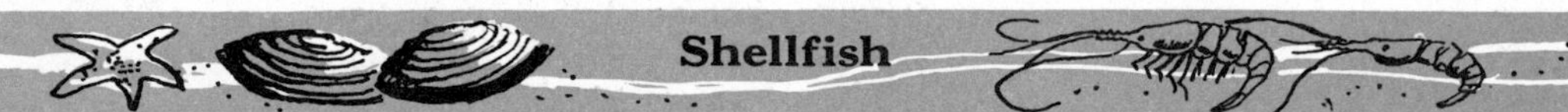

Shellfish

MARKET FORMS—Live shellfish are those which should be alive when purchased, such as crabs, lobsters, clams and oysters (except when purchasing cooked lobsters and crabs in the shell).
Shucked shellfish have been removed from their shells; oysters, clams and scallops come this way.
Headless shellfish are shrimp and rock-lobster tail (spiny lobster) which are marketed in this form.
Cooked meat is the edible portion of the shellfish, cooked and ready to eat; shrimp, crab and lobster meat are marketed this way.
Frozen shellfish now available are shrimp, crab, lobster, rock-lobster tails, scallops and oysters.

OYSTERS—*Oysters in the shell* must have tightly closed shells; this indicates that they are alive and usable. Oysters in the shell, kept in the refrigerator at 40°F, will remain good for several days. They are generally sold by the dozen. *Fresh or frozen shucked oysters* are sold by the pint or quart. They should be plump, with a natural creamy color, free from shell particles and with clear liquid. Fresh shucked oysters packed in cans and labeled "Perishable, Keep Refrigerated" must be refrigerated in the home. Frozen oysters should not be thawed until ready to use and never refrozen.

CLAMS—The market species of the Atlantic coast are the *hard-shelled, soft-shelled* and *surf clams. Quahog* is the common name for the hard-shelled clam in New England, where "clam" generally refers to the soft-shelled variety. In Middle Atlantic states and southward, "clam" usually means the hard-shelled clam. Dealers' names for smaller sizes of hard-shelled clams are *little necks* and *cherrystones;* these are served raw on the half shell. The larger sizes, used for soups and chowders, are *chowders. Steamers* are the smaller sizes of soft-shelled clams and *in-shells,* the larger sizes. Common species of the Pacific coast are *pismo, razor, little neck* (different from Atlantic coast hard-shelled clam) and *butter.*

Clams in the shell should be alive when purchased. Hard-shelled clams having gaping shells that do not close when handled are not alive and not usable. There will be some contraction of the siphon or neck of other varieties when the live clam is touched. Shell clams kept in the refrigerator at 40°F will remain alive several days. *Fresh shucked clams,* sold by the pint or quart, should be plump, with clear liquid, and free from shell particles. They are packed in metal or waxed containers and should be refrigerated or packed in ice; they will stay fresh for a week or 10 days if properly handled. *Frozen shucked clams* should not be thawed until ready to use and never refrozen. Clams are canned whole or minced, or as chowder. Clam juice, broth and nectar are also canned.

SCALLOPS—The edible portion is the muscle that opens and closes the scallop shells. There are two kinds, the tiny *bay scallop* and the larger *sea scallop.* Fresh scallops and thawed frozen scallops, should have a sweetish odor.

SHRIMP—*Fresh shrimp* with heads removed are sold by the pound either fresh or frozen. Shrimp are graded according to the number per pound—jumbo (under 25); large (25 to 30); medium (30 to 42); or small (42 and over). *Cooked shrimp* with shells removed are sold by the pound; the meat is pink. *Canned shrimp* are available in several sizes of cans and may be used in place of cooked shrimp.

LOBSTER—Lobster may be purchased *live in the shell, cooked in the shell,* as *lobster meat* or *canned.* Live lobsters are dark bluish-green to brownish-olive in color; they must be alive up to the moment of cooking. The weight may vary from ¾ to 3 lbs. Lobsters cooked in the shell are red in color; they are not generally available in large quantities. Lobster meat is picked from cooked lobsters and chilled. It is sold by the pound, fresh or frozen.

How to Kill and Clean a Lobster—Live lobsters may be killed by plunging into boiling water (*page 122*). Or lobsters may be killed by the following method. Place lobster on a cutting board with back or smooth shell up. Hold a towel firmly over head and claws. Quickly insert the point of a sharp heavy knife into center of the small cross on the back of the head. This kills the lobster by severing the spinal cord. Before removing knife, bear down heavily, cutting through entire length of body and tail. Pull halves apart; remove and discard the stomach (a small sac which lies in the head) and the spongy lungs (which lie in upper body cavity between meat and shell). Remove and discard the dark intestinal vein running through center of body. Crack claws with nutcracker.

Lobster may be cooked as directed in **Lobster Thermidor** (*page 124*). Or broil lobster shell side down about 10 min. on preheated broiler pan with top of lobster 3 to 4 in. from source of heat. Brush frequently with melted butter.

ROCK-LOBSTER TAIL—The trade name for crayfish or spiny lobster tail; the meaty tail is the only portion marketed. Usually sold frozen, the meat should be a clear whitish color. Shell color depends on the kind. *Canned rock-lobster meat* is available.

CRABS—Crabs may be purchased *live, cooked in the shell,* as *crab meat* or *canned.* Live crabs are either hard-shelled or soft-shelled. Soft-shelled crabs are blue crabs that have been caught immediately after having shed their old, hard shells. Hard-shelled crabs are sold cooked in the shell. Crab meat comes from cooked crabs and is sold by the pound. It is very perishable and should be refrigerated or packed in ice. Cooked crab meat may be one of the following: *Blue Crab*—Lump meat comes from the large muscles which operate the swimming legs; it is white in color and is sometimes called "special" or "back fin" lump crab meat. Flake meat is the remaining portion of the body meat; it is also white. Claw meat is brownish meat removed from the claws. *Rock Crab*—Meat is brownish in color; there is only one grade. *Dungeness Crab*—Claw and body meat is reddish in color. *King Crab*—Meat from the King Crab of Alaska is removed mostly from the legs, frozen and packed. Entire leg sections, cooked and frozen, are also marketed.

▲ Creamed Finnan Haddie and Cracker Tips en Casserole

Grease 6 individual casseroles or one 2-qt. casserole or baking dish.

In the top of a double boiler or in a covered saucepan, soak for 1 hour

2 lbs. finnan haddie (smoked haddock)

in

Milk to cover

Heat slowly 20 min. Drain, reserving milk for sauce. Set aside.

Prepare, coarsely chop and set aside

2 hard-cooked eggs

Melt in top of double boiler over low heat

3 tablespoons butter or margarine

Blend in

3 tablespoons flour

Heat until mixture bubbles. Remove from heat and add gradually, stirring constantly, the milk "stock" from the fish. (If "stock" measures less than 1½ cups liquid, add enough cream to make this amount.) Return to heat. Cook rapidly, stirring constantly, until sauce thickens. Remove from heat and vigorously stir about 3 tablespoons of the sauce into

2 egg yolks, slightly beaten

Immediately return mixture to double boiler.

Cook over simmering water 3 to 5 min. Stir slowly and constantly to keep mixture cooking evenly. Remove from simmering water; cool slightly.

Remove skin and bones from fish. Flake (*page 6*) fish and combine with the sauce. Gently stir in the chopped eggs and

3 tablespoons capers

Pour mixture into the casserole. Insert into mixture on a diagonal

10 to 12 crisp thin crackers, lightly buttered (leave about one half of each cracker exposed)

Bake at 375°F 10 to 12 min. to heat mixture thoroughly and to lightly brown the crackers.

Garnish with **parsley.** Serve at once.

6 servings

Creamed Codfish and Cracker Tips

△ Creamed Codfish and Cracker Tips

Follow ▲ Recipe; substitute **codfish** for finnan haddie. If cod is salted, cover with **water** and heat slowly to boiling. (If dry and/or very salty, drain and again cover with water and bring to boiling.) Drain, cover with **milk** and proceed as in ▲ Recipe.

Fried Kippers in Cream

Set out a large, heavy skillet.

Cover with cold water and bring to boiling

4 kippered herring

Drain, dry with absorbent paper and set aside.

Heat in the skillet

3 to 4 tablespoons butter or margarine

Add and cook until transparent, turning occasionally

3 medium-size onions (*page 6*), cut into ¼-in. slices and separated into rings

Remove onions and keep warm.

Place herring in skillet. Brown over low heat about 5 min. on each side.

Meanwhile, scald (*page 7*)

1¼ cups cream

Slowly pour one half of the cream into skillet with herring and simmer 2 min. Add remaining cream and simmer 3 min. longer.

Serve at once. Garnish with the onion rings.
4 servings

▲ Broiled Fish Steaks

Set temperature control of range at Broil and grease a broiler rack.

Wipe with a clean, damp cloth
2 lbs. fish steaks, such as cod, halibut or salmon
(If using frozen steaks, thaw according to directions on package.) If desired, bring ends of each steak together and fasten with a small skewer to give oval shape. Arrange steaks on the greased broiler rack. Brush tops of steaks with one half of a mixture of
¼ cup butter or margarine, melted
1 tablespoon chopped parsley or chives
Place broiler rack in broiler with top of steaks 2 in. from source of heat; broil 5 to 8 min. (depending upon thickness of steaks). Season steaks with one half of a mixture of
1 teaspoon salt
¾ teaspoon Accent
⅛ teaspoon pepper
Turn steaks carefully and brush second side with remaining butter mixture. Broil 5 to 8 min. longer, or until fish flakes easily (*page 6*).

Sprinkle second side with remaining seasoning mixture. Remove carefully to warm serving platter. Serve with **lemon wedges** or
Hollandaise Sauce (*page 182*)
4 servings

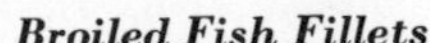

Broiled Fish Fillets

△ Broiled Fish Fillets

Follow ▲ Recipe. Substitute **fish fillets** for the steaks. Place them skin side down on the greased rack. Broil 10 to 12 min. without turning. Brush fillets with melted **butter** or **margarine** during broiling.

Note: To prepare fish on an outdoor grill see OUTDOOR COOKING (*page 10*).

Broiled Trout

Set temperature control of range at Broil and grease a broiler rack.

Wipe with a clean, damp cloth
4 small cleaned and scaled trout, about 10 oz. each
(If using frozen trout, thaw according to directions on package.) Do not cut off tails or heads; game fish are usually served with the head and tail on. Arrange trout on the greased broiler rack. Brush with one half of a mixture of
¼ cup butter or margarine, melted
1 tablespoon lemon juice
Place broiler rack in broiler with top of trout 2 in. from source of heat; broil 5 to 8 min. (depending upon thickness of trout).

Season trout with one half of a mixture of
2 teaspoons salt
1 teaspoon Accent
½ teaspoon paprika
¼ teaspoon pepper
Turn trout carefully and brush second side with remaining butter mixture. Sprinkle second side with remaining seasoning mixture. Broil 5 to 8 min. longer, or until fish flakes easily (*page 6*).

Remove carefully to a warm serving platter. Garnish with **parsley.** Serve trout with **lemon wedges.**
4 servings

▲ Baked Stuffed Fish

Line a large shallow baking pan with aluminum foil or parchment paper.

For Stuffing—Crush (*page 6*)

½ lb. crackers (or enough to yield 3 cups crumbs)

Turn crumbs into a bowl; set aside.

Heat in a skillet over low heat

⅔ cup butter or margarine

Add, and cook slowly until onion is transparent, occasionally moving with a spoon

¾ cup chopped celery (*page 6*)
¼ cup finely chopped onion

Add to crumbs with a mixture of

2 tablespoons lemon juice
2 teaspoons minced parsley
¼ teaspoon rosemary
½ teaspoon salt
½ teaspoon Accent
¼ teaspoon pepper

Toss lightly with a fork to mix thoroughly. Add

¼ cup hot water

Mix thoroughly and set aside.

For Fish—Rinse body cavity thoroughly with cold water, drain, and pat dry with absorbent paper

4- to 5-lb. dressed fish (such as whitefish, lake trout, shad or bass, with backbone removed)

Rub cavity of fish with

1 tablespoon salt
¾ teaspoon Accent

Lightly pile (do not pack) stuffing into fish. Fasten open edges with skewers or close with wooden picks. Put stuffed fish in baking pan and brush outside surface with

Cooking or salad oil

Bake at 350°F 45 to 50 min., or until fish flakes easily (*page 6*). *8 servings*

△ Planked Fish Supreme

Follow ▲ Recipe for preparing and baking fish. (To season, brush a hardwood plank with unsalted fat. Heat in a 250° oven 1 hr. Cool.)

To Stuff a Fish: Lightly pile stuffing into body cavity. Close cavity with skewers or wooden picks.

While fish is baking, prepare **Duchess Potatoes** (*page 159*); do not spoon potatoes onto baking sheet.

Lightly grease the seasoned plank with unsalted fat. Put into oven to heat. When fish is cooked, transfer to the heated plank. Force potatoes through a pastry bag and No. 7 decorating tube into a spiral-shaped border on the plank. Cover exposed plank as completely as possible. Brush potatoes lightly with melted **butter** or **margarine.** Put planked fish and potatoes into a 400°F oven 10 min., or until potatoes are lightly browned.

Arrange on the plank buttered **Brussels sprouts** and **lemon wedges.** Accompany with **Quick Tomato Sauce** (*page 183*).

Planked Fish: Place baked fish on a heated, greased plank. Arrange vegetables. Set in oven.

▲ Panfried Fish Fillets

Set out a large, heavy skillet.

Wipe with a clean, damp cloth
2 lbs. fish fillets, such as perch, sole or haddock
(If fish is frozen, thaw according to directions on package.) Cut into serving-size pieces and set aside.

Mix in a shallow pan and set aside
2 cups (about 6 slices) fine, dry bread crumbs
1 teaspoon salt
½ teaspoon Accent
¼ teaspoon pepper
Beat slightly in a shallow bowl
2 eggs
1 tablespoon milk
Heat in the skillet over low heat
¼ cup butter, margarine or bacon drippings
Dip fillets into egg mixture; then coat with crumb mixture. Put into the skillet and brown lightly on both sides, turning only once. Cook only until fish flakes easily (*page 6*). Transfer fish to warm serving platter, scraping loose and removing any bits of fish which may have stuck to the skillet. Cover fish to keep warm.

Heat in the skillet until lightly browned
½ cup butter or margarine
Stir in
¼ cup lemon juice
2 tablespoons finely chopped parsley
Heat thoroughly and pour over fish.

5 to 6 servings

△ Panfried Whole Fish

Substitute dressed small **whole fish,** such as lake perch, blue gills, sunfish or crappies, for the fish fillets. Proceed as in ▲ Recipe.

Codfish Cakes

A deep saucepan or automatic deep-fryer will be needed.

Set out
1 lb. salt codfish
Cover with cold water to freshen. Let stand in the cold water at least 4 hrs. Change water 3 or 4 times during that period. (Or follow directions on package.) Drain fish and remove any pieces of bone. Flake (*page 6*) and set fish aside.

About 20 min. before ready to deep-fry, heat fat to 365°F (*page 7*).

Meanwhile, wash, pare and cut into pieces
4 to 6 medium-size (about 2 lbs.) potatoes
Combine fish and potatoes in a saucepan. Cook covered in boiling water to cover about 20 min., or until potatoes are tender when pierced with a fork.

Thoroughly drain and mash potatoes and fish. Whip in until mixture is fluffy
2 tablespoons butter or margarine
and a mixture of
2 eggs, beaten
½ teaspoon paprika
¼ teaspoon Accent
⅛ teaspoon pepper
Deep-fry by dropping spoonfuls of the mixture into the hot fat. Drop only as many at one time as will float uncrowded one layer deep. Turn cakes as they brown, cooking each 2 to 5 min., or until golden brown. Drain on absorbent paper.

Serve with
Tomato Sauce (*page 188*) or Medium White Sauce (*page 181*)

6 servings

Poached Fish Veronique: Cut paper to fit. Roll fish fillets and fasten with wooden picks.

Fit greased paper cover over pan. Simmer fish. Hole in paper allows steam to escape.

▲ Poached Fish with Horse-radish Sauce

Set out a large, heavy skillet having a tight-fitting cover.

Wipe with a clean, damp cloth

1½ lbs. fish fillets, such as perch or bass

(If fish is frozen, thaw according to directions on package.) Tie fish loosely in cheesecloth to prevent breaking; place in the skillet. Add, in order

Boiling water (enough to just cover fish)
½ cup dry white wine
1 small onion (*page 6*), chopped
2 tablespoons chopped parsley
1 teaspoon salt
½ teaspoon Accent
⅛ teaspoon pepper

Cover skillet and simmer about 10 min., or until fish flakes easily (*page 6*).

Meanwhile, prepare

Horse-radish Sour Cream Sauce (*page 184*)

Pour sauce into serving dish; set aside.

Drain fish, reserving stock; remove cheesecloth. (Strain stock and use in other food preparation.) Place fish on warm platter. Serve with the sauce. *4 servings*

△ Poached Fish with Butter Sauce

Follow ▲ Recipe; omit Horse-radish Sour Cream Sauce. Pour strained stock into saucepan. Simmer until liquid is reduced to 1 cup. Thicken with 1 tablespoon **Brown Roux** (*page 187*) or 1 **egg yolk.** Add 1 tablespoon **butter,** stirring until well blended. Heat thoroughly. Pour over fish, or serve in a separate dish.

Poached Fish Veronique

Set out a large, heavy skillet having a tight-fitting cover. Cut a circle of white paper to fit skillet; cut a small hole in center to allow steam to escape. Butter one side of the paper.

Wipe with a clean, damp cloth

1½ lbs. fish fillets (such as perch, bass, haddock or sole)

(If frozen, thaw according to directions on package.) Roll fillets; fasten with wooden picks.

Season with a mixture of

1 teaspoon salt
1 teaspoon Accent
¼ teaspoon pepper

Set fillets aside.

Heat in the skillet over low heat

2 tablespoons butter or margarine

Add and cook over medium heat until onion is transparent, stirring constantly

1 tablespoon minced onion

Place the fish in the skillet. Add

½ cup dry white wine

Place paper circle, buttered-side down, on top of the fillets. Bring liquid to boiling; cover and simmer about 10 min., or until fish flakes easily (*page 6*). Carefully remove fish to serving platter. Pour off and reserve the cooking liquid.

Melt in the skillet over low heat

1 tablespoon butter

Blend in

2 teaspoons flour

Heat until mixture bubbles. Remove from heat. Add gradually, stirring constantly, the reserved cooking liquid and

¼ cup cream

Return to heat and cook, stirring constantly, until mixture thickens; cook 1 to 2 min. longer.

Spoon sauce over fish. Garnish with **lemon wedges** and seedless **white grapes.** (If desired, the grapes may be added to the sauce.)

Serve at once. *4 servings*

Sweet-Sour Salmon Steaks

MRS. C. S. LOBEL, INDIO, CALIF.

Put into a Dutch oven or a deep kettle or sauce pot having a tight-fitting cover

1½ cups water
1 medium-size onion (*page 6*), sliced
1 carrot, sliced
1 lemon, thinly sliced
1 teaspoon Accent
½ teaspoon salt
3 or 4 peppercorns
½ bay leaf

Bring liquid to boiling.

Meanwhile, wipe with a clean, damp cloth

4 salmon steaks, about ½ lb. each

(If using frozen salmon, thaw according to directions on package.) Arrange the steaks on a large square of cheesecloth. Pull up corners of cheesecloth and tie together. Lower salmon into the kettle. Cover and simmer 10 min.

Melt in a small saucepan over low heat

2 tablespoons butter or margarine

Add, blending in

1 cup firmly packed brown sugar

Continue cooking, stirring frequently until sugar is melted.

Meanwhile, combine

14 gingersnaps, crushed (about 1 cup crumbs)
1 cup vinegar

Remove from heat. Gradually add vinegar mixture, stirring until smooth. Set aside.

Remove kettle from heat. Remove salmon from liquid; carefully remove cloth. Strain the cooking liquid and return it to kettle. Add

¼ cup dark, seedless raisins

Blend in the vinegar mixture. Return to heat and bring liquid to boiling, stirring constantly. Carefully lower salmon steaks into the liquid. (Arrange steaks only one layer deep, if possible.) Cover tightly and simmer gently 5 min., or until salmon flakes easily (*page 6*). Remove kettle from heat; cool salmon in the liquid. Serve warm, or chill in refrigerator. (For a more pronounced sweet-sour flavor, chill overnight.) When ready to serve, carefully remove steaks to serving dish. If desired, accompany with some of the cooking liquid.

4 servings

Sweet-Sour Salmon Steaks

Hot Salmon Loaf

Heat water for boiling water bath (*page 6*). Grease bottom of a 9½x5¼x2¾-in. loaf pan.

Using the fine blade of food chopper, grind enough toasted almonds to yield
1¼ cups (about 7 oz.) ground toasted almonds (*page 6*)
Finely flake (*page 6*)
2 cups (1-lb. can) salmon
Set almonds and fish aside.

Prepare
1½ cups Medium White Sauce (one and one-half times recipe, *page 181*)
Vigorously stir about 3 tablespoons of hot sauce into
3 egg yolks, slightly beaten
Immediately return egg-yolk mixture to sauce, stirring vigorously.

Stir into the sauce the salmon, almonds and
1½ cups (1½ slices) soft bread crumbs
¼ cup finely chopped onion
4 drops tabasco sauce
and a mixture of
2 teaspoons salt
½ teaspoon Accent
½ teaspoon pepper
½ teaspoon paprika
Beat until rounded peaks are formed
3 egg whites
Spread beaten egg whites over salmon and fold (*page 6*) together. Turn mixture into pan.

Bake in boiling water bath at 350°F about 1 hr. and 10 min.

Unmold (*page 63*). Garnish with **parsley** and **lemon slices** and serve at once.

About 6 servings

▲ Sea Food Potpourri

Grease a 2-qt. casserole.

Prepare
3 hard-cooked eggs
Meanwhile, combine gently with a fork
1 cup (7-oz. can, drained) tuna, coarsely flaked (*page 6*)
1 cup (6- to 7-oz. can, drained) crab meat, stiff bony tissue removed
⅔ cup (5-oz. can, drained) shrimp, black veins removed and discarded (*page 126*) and shrimp cut into halves
Drain, reserving liquid, and set aside
1 cup (8-oz. can) sliced mushrooms
Grate and set aside
4 oz. Cheddar cheese (1 cup, grated)
Prepare
2 cups Thin White Sauce (double recipe, *page 181*; substitute reserved mushroom liquid for part of milk)
Cool slightly. Add cheese all at one time. Stir sauce rapidly until cheese is melted. Blend in
3 tablespoons finely chopped chives
10 ripe olives, pitted and sliced
Arrange one half of the sea food in casserole. Slice the eggs and arrange one half of the slices on sea food. Add mushrooms and one half of the sauce. Repeat layers. Cover with remaining sauce and
½ cup coarsely crushed potato chips
Bake at 350°F 20 to 30 min., or until well browned. *8 servings*

△ Sea Food and Biscuits

Follow ▲ Recipe. Omit potato chips. Prepare dough for **Tender-Rich Biscuits** (one-half recipe, *page 43*; if desired, add 1 tablespoon finely chopped **parsley** to flour-shortening mixture.) Cut 1-in. square biscuits. Arrange casserole layers. Bake at 425°F 10 min. Remove from oven and arrange biscuits in diagonal lines across top of casserole; leave spaces between biscuits. Increase oven temperature to 450°F and bake 10 to 15 min. longer, or until biscuits are lightly browned.

▲ Crab Meat Ramekins

Set out a double boiler. Grease 6 ramekins or individual casseroles.

Drain, remove and discard bony tissue and separate contents of

2 7-oz. cans (1¾ cups) crab meat

Set aside.

Prepare in top of double boiler

1 cup Thin White Sauce (*page 181*)

Remove from heat and vigorously stir about 3 tablespoons of the sauce into

2 egg yolks, slightly beaten
¼ to ½ teaspoon Accent

Immediately stir mixture into hot sauce in double-boiler top and cook over simmering water 3 to 5 min.; stir slowly to keep mixture cooking evenly.

Remove from heat; add gradually, stirring in

¼ cup minced green pepper (*page 6*)
1 tablespoon lemon juice
1½ teaspoons onion juice

Add crab meat, gently blending with a spoon.

Turn mixture into ramekins. Top with

¾ cup buttered dry bread crumbs (*page 5*)

Bake at 350°F 20 to 25 min., or until crumbs are lightly browned. *6 servings*

△ Crab Meat and Tomato Ramekins

Follow ▲ Recipe. Substitute **Medium White Sauce** (*page 181*; use tomato juice for milk) for Thin White Sauce. Use ½ cup crumbs; combine with ¼ cup grated **Parmesan cheese.**

Crab Meat Ramekins with mixed vegetable salad, potato chips and iced coffee

Crab 'n' Oysters

JANE H. BARBER, WATCH HILL, R.I.

Set out a double boiler.

Drain, reserving liquid

2 doz. (about 1 qt.) large oysters

Pick over oysters to remove any shell particles.

Drain, remove and discard bony tissue from

½ cup (about 2 oz.) fresh lump crab meat

Set oysters and crab meat aside.

Melt in top of double boiler

¼ cup butter or margarine

Blend in

1 tablespoon flour

Heat until mixture bubbles. Remove from heat. Add gradually, stirring in, the reserved oyster liquid and

¼ cup ketchup
¼ cup cream
1 teaspoon Worcestershire sauce
½ teaspoon salt
½ teaspoon Accent

Return to heat and bring rapidly to boiling, stirring constantly. Cook 1 to 2 min. longer. Remove from heat. Add all at one time, stirring constantly

2 tablespoons grated Cheddar cheese

Continue stirring until cheese is melted. Stir in the crab meat.

Return to heat and heat to simmering. Add the oysters. Cook until edges of oysters begin to curl; do not overcook or oysters will be tough.

Serve hot over toast. *6 servings*

"Boiled" Lobster

Fill a large deep kettle or sauce pot having a tight-fitting cover about ⅔ full (or enough to cover the lobster) with

Hot salted water (1 tablespoon salt per qt. water)

Bring water rapidly to boiling. Grasp by the back, below the large claws, and plunge head first into the water—one at a time

2 live lobsters, about 1½ lbs. each

Cover, bring water again to a rolling boil. Reduce heat and simmer 15 to 20 min. Drain and cover with cold water to chill. Drain again. Place bottom side up on a cutting board.

Twist off the two large claws, the smaller ones and the tail. With a pair of scissors cut (or with a sharp knife slit) the bony membrane on the underside of tail. Spread tail shell apart and remove meat. Remove and discard the intestinal vein. With a sharp knife slit in one piece underside of body of lobster, cutting completely through entire length of body. Remove and discard the intestinal vein running lengthwise through center of body. Remove and discard stomach (a small sac which lies in the head) and spongy lungs (which lie in upper body cavity between meat and shell).

If present, remove and reserve the tomalley (green liver) and the coral (bright red roe) to be used along with the lobster meat or as a garnish. Remove the small amount of meat present in the body shell. Disjoint the large claws and crack with a nutcracker. A nut pick or cocktail fork may be helpful in removing meat from small joints and claws. Put meat into a bowl or jar, cover and refrigerate until ready to use. *About 2 cups lobster meat*

Note: If lobster is to be served hot, do not plunge into cold water after cooking. Use tongs to remove to cutting board. Leave small claws and tail intact. Slit entire length of body and tail, cutting through meat to shell. Remove and discard the vein, lungs and stomach. Crack large claws with a nutcracker. Serve with melted **butter** and **lemon wedges.**

Broiled Rock-Lobster Tails

Thaw according to directions on package
1 12-oz. frozen rock-lobster tail for each person
Prepare and set aside Crumb Topping.

For Crumb Topping—Melt in a saucepan over medium heat
2 tablespoons butter or margarine
Stir in
½ cup (about 1½ slices) fine, dry bread crumbs
Remove saucepan from heat and stir in
½ teaspoon lemon juice
½ teaspoon onion juice
and a mixture of
⅛ teaspoon salt
⅛ teaspoon Accent
Few grains pepper
Set temperature control of range at Broil and grease a broiler rack.

Melt in a small saucepan over medium heat and set aside to keep warm
½ cup butter
Snip through and remove thin shell on underside of each lobster tail; remove vein. Holding tail in both hands, bend it towards shell side to crack; or insert a skewer lengthwise through meat—this keeps tail flat. (If you buy fresh rock-lobster tails, your dealer may do this.)

Place tails flesh side down on broiler rack. Set rack under broiler with top of lobster tails 4 in. or more from heat source. Broil 6 to 8 min. Turn tails flesh side up with tongs and brush with melted butter. Broil about 4 min.; brush again with melted butter. Sprinkle some of the Crumb Topping over top of each lobster tail. Broil about 2 min. longer, or until meat is completely white and opaque.

Sprinkle with
Paprika
Serve immediately with additional melted butter and **lemon wedges.**

Note: To prepare rock-lobster tails on an outdoor grill see OUTDOOR COOKING (*page 10*).

▲ Lobster Newburg in Pastry Shells

Prepare, bake and set aside to cool
Pastry for Little Pies or Tarts (*page* 243; use six 3-in. tart pans. Or use commercial patty shells.)

For Lobster Newburg—Drain, cut into ½-in. pieces and set aside
1½ cups (two 6-oz. cans) lobster meat
Heat in a skillet over low heat
¼ cup butter or margarine
Blend in
2 cups cream
¾ teaspoon salt
½ teaspoon Accent
⅛ teaspoon pepper
⅛ teaspoon nutmeg
Bring just to boiling. Stir in the lobster meat and cook over low heat until meat is thoroughly heated. Vigorously stir about 3 tablespoons of this hot mixture into
4 egg yolks, slightly beaten
Immediately blend into hot mixture. Stirring constantly, continue to cook just until mixture thickens. (Do not overcook or allow mixture to boil as sauce will curdle.) Remove immediately from heat. Blend in about
1 tablespoon sherry
Spoon into the pastry shells. Sprinkle with **paprika.** *6 servings*

△ Crab Meat Newburg

Follow ▲ Recipe; substitute 1½ cups (two 6½-oz. cans) **crab meat** for the lobster. Remove and discard bony tissue from meat.

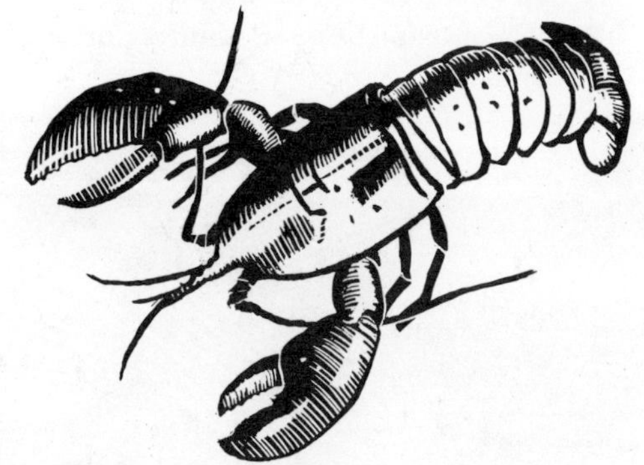

Rock-Lobster Thermidor

▲ Lobster Thermidor

Kill and clean (*page 113*)

3 live lobsters, about 1½ lbs. each

(Live lobsters may be killed at the market.)

Heat in a large heavy skillet having a tight-fitting cover

6 tablespoons butter

Put lobster halves, meat-side down, into the skillet. Place claws on top. Cover; cook slowly 12 to 15 min., or until tender.

Meanwhile, prepare and set aside

1½ cups Medium White Sauce (one and one-half times recipe, *page 181*; stir into sauce 3 tablespoons heavy cream after removing from heat)

Heat in a saucepan

3 tablespoons butter

Add and cook over medium heat until onion is transparent and mushrooms browned

⅔ cup chopped mushrooms
2 tablespoons chopped shallots or onion

Occasionally move and turn mixture. Remove from heat and set aside.

Blend into one half of the white sauce

3 tablespoons heavy cream
2 tablespoons white wine
1 teaspoon finely chopped chervil or parsley
½ teaspoon Worcestershire sauce

and a mixture of

¾ teaspoon Accent
½ teaspoon dry mustard
¼ teaspoon salt
⅛ teaspoon cayenne pepper

Add to mushroom mixture. Cook over low heat until thoroughly heated, moving and turning mixture gently with a spoon.

Gently pry the cooked lobster meat from shells, starting at tail. Reserve shells. Remove meat from large claws. Cut the lobster meat into 1-in. pieces and blend into the sauce.

Preheat shells, cavity-side up, at 325°F about 7 min. Fill with lobster mixture.

Pour remaining white sauce into the top of a double boiler. Stir over low heat until heated. Vigorously stir about 3 tablespoons sauce into

1 egg yolk, slightly beaten

Immediately return mixture to top of double boiler. Stirring constantly, cook over simmering water 3 to 5 min. Remove from heat and spoon over lobster mixture in the shells. Sprinkle over the filled shells

2 tablespoons grated Parmesan cheese (1 teaspoon cheese per shell)

Set temperature control of range at Broil.

Place baking sheet on broiler pan with top of food 2 to 3 in. from heat source. Broil 2 to 3 min., or until lightly browned. *6 servings*

△ Rock-Lobster Thermidor

Follow ▲ Recipe. Substitute six 8-oz. **rock-lobster tails** for the whole lobsters. Cook the tails (see Imperial Lobster, *on this page*). Cut through and remove thin shell on underside of each tail. Carefully remove meat. Omit Parmesan cheese and browning in broiler. Reheat filled shells thoroughly in 325° F oven.

Imperial Lobster

(Rock-Lobster Tails)

MRS. WALTER W. HISSEY
CATONSVILLE, MD.

This superb, prize-winning dish, fit for the most imperial taste, was created on the eastern seaboard of the United States where shellfish cookery has been a high art for many years.

Lightly butter 4 ramekins or individual casseroles. If desired, use 6 crab-shaped ramekins.

Set out a baking sheet.

Fill a kettle having a tight-fitting cover about two-thirds full with hot water. Bring salted water (1 teaspoon salt per qt. of water) to a rapid boil. Put into the boiling water

3 medium-size frozen rock-lobster tails
1 teaspoon Accent

Cover and bring rapidly just to boiling; reduce heat. Simmer about 11 min. for lobster tails weighing about 10 oz. (or 1 min. longer than individual weight in ounces; add 2 min. if tails are frozen).

Drain lobster tails; rinse under a stream of running cold water until cool enough to handle; drain again. Place on a cutting board, shell side down. Cut through and remove thin shell on underside of each tail. Split lengthwise through the meat. Remove the meat; cut into small pieces and set aside.

While lobster tails are cooking, heat in a small skillet over low heat

1 tablespoon butter

Add and cook over medium heat until tender, occasionally moving and turning with a spoon

¾ cup (about 1 large) chopped green pepper (*page 6*)

Set aside to cool slightly.

Mix thoroughly in a bowl

2 egg yolks, slightly beaten
⅓ cup mayonnaise
1 teaspoon Worcestershire sauce
1 teaspoon prepared mustard
½ teaspoon dry mustard
2 or 3 drops tabasco sauce

Add and mix in the lobster and green pepper.

Set ramekins on the baking sheet and spoon mixture into them. Dot top of each with

Butter (about 1 teaspoon each)

Bake at 500°F about 15 min., or until mixture is heated thoroughly and lightly browned.

4 to 6 servings

Shrimp Sauté

MRS. A. E. BOYCE, RIVERDALE, N. DAK.

Set out a heavy skillet or saucepan.

Remove tiny legs and peel shells from

1½ lbs. fresh shrimp with shells

Cut a slit to just below surface along back (outer curved surface) of shrimp to expose the black vein. With knife point, remove vein in one piece. Rinse shrimp quickly in cold water. Drain on absorbent paper.

Heat in the skillet

¼ cup butter or margarine

Add the peeled shrimp and

3 to 4 teaspoons finely chopped parsley
1 clove garlic (*page 6*), minced; or crushed in a garlic press

Cook, stirring frequently, until shrimp turn pink (about 10 min.). Add, stirring constantly

⅓ cup sherry

and a mixture of

¾ teaspoon salt
¼ teaspoon Accent
⅛ teaspoon pepper

Cook 2 min. longer. Serve hot. Serve some of the cooking liquid as sauce. *About 4 servings*

Cooked Shrimp: Drop shrimp into a boiling mixture of water, lemon juice, salt and Accent.

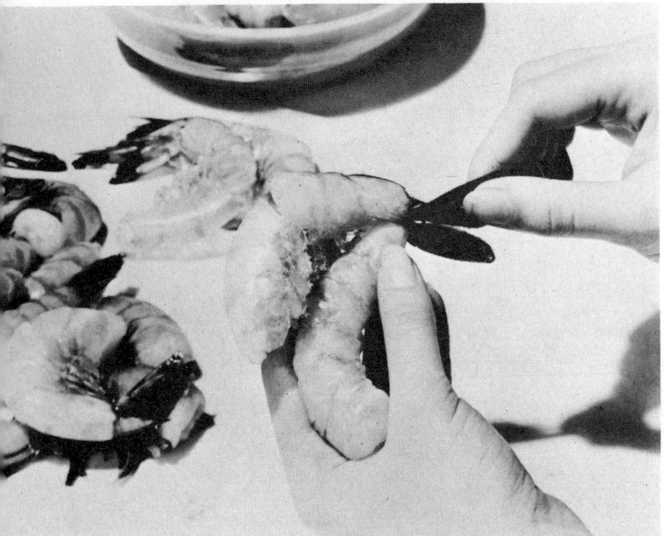

Chill the shrimp in cold water. Drain. Strip away the tiny legs and remove shells from cooked shrimp.

Cut a slit along outer curved surface of shrimp to expose black vein. Remove vein in one piece.

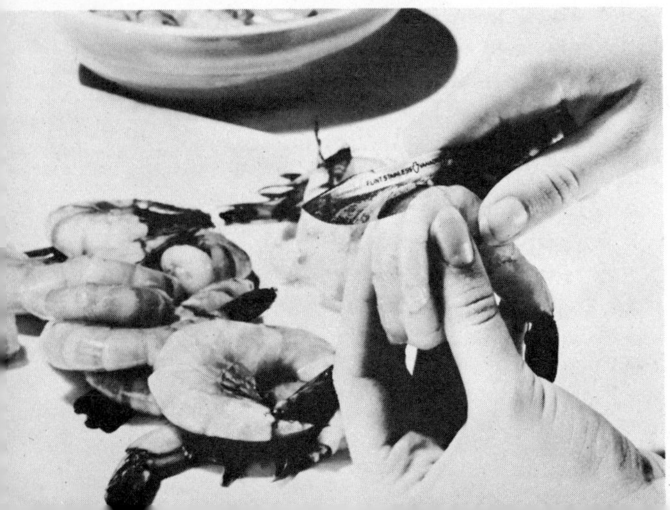

Cooked Shrimp

Wash in cold water

1 lb. fresh shrimp with shells

Drop shrimp into a boiling mixture of

2 cups water
3 tablespoons lemon juice
1 tablespoon salt
½ teaspoon Accent

Cover tightly. Simmer 5 min., or only until shrimp are pink and tender. Drain and cover with cold water to chill. Drain shrimp again. Remove tiny legs. Peel shells from shrimp.

Cut a slit to just below surface along back (outer curved surface) of shrimp to expose the black vein. With knife point remove vein in one piece.* Rinse shrimp quickly in cold water. Drain on absorbent paper. Refrigerate. Serve with

Creamy Sea Food Cocktail Sauce (*page 185*), or Zippy Cocktail Sauce (*page 185*), or Shrimp Remoulade Sauce (*page 184*)

**Note:* Veins present in canned shrimp are removed in the same way.

Creole-Style Shrimp with Rice

Set out a 2-qt. casserole.

Wash in cold water

1½ lbs. fresh or frozen large shrimp with shells

Drop shrimp into a boiling mixture of

3 cups water
3 tablespoons lemon juice
1 tablespoon salt
1 teaspoon Accent
3 or 4 sprigs parsley
1 clove garlic, peeled (*page 6*) and split
1 bay leaf
Small piece celery with leaves
3 peppercorns

Cover tightly. Simmer 5 min., or only until

shrimp are pink and tender. Drain and cover with cold water to chill. Drain, peel and remove vein (see Cooked Shrimp, *page 126*). Put shrimp into casserole and set aside.

Heat in a skillet over low heat
- **¼ cup butter or margarine**

Add and cook slowly until onion is transparent, occasionally moving and turning mixture with a spoon
- **1 cup (about 4 stalks) diced celery (*page 6*)**
- **⅔ cup (about 1½ large) chopped onion (*page 6*)**
- **½ cup (about 1 medium-size) finely chopped green pepper (*page 6*)**

Thoroughly blend in
- **1 cup water**
- **¾ cup (6-oz. can) tomato paste**
- **1 tablespoon minced parsley**
- **½ teaspoon salt**
- **¼ teaspoon Accent**
- **4 or 5 drops tabasco sauce**

Pour mixture into casserole. Mix gently to distribute shrimp evenly.

Heat in oven at 350°F about 30 min.

Meanwhile, prepare
- **Perfection Boiled Rice (*page 147*)**

Serve shrimp mixture over hot rice.

6 servings

Fresh Shrimp Curry

Cook and clean
- **2 lbs. fresh shrimp with shells (see Cooked Shrimp, *page 126*)**

Set aside.

Heat in a heavy 3-qt. saucepan
- **⅓ cup butter or margarine**

Add and cook over medium heat until onion is golden yellow, stirring occasionally
- **3 tablespoons chopped onion**
- **3 tablespoons chopped celery**
- **3 tablespoons chopped green apple**
- **12 peppercorns**
- **1 bay leaf**

Fresh Shrimp Curry

Blend in a mixture of
- **⅓ cup flour**
- **2½ teaspoons curry powder**
- **½ teaspoon Accent**
- **¼ teaspoon sugar**
- **⅛ teaspoon nutmeg**

Heat until mixture bubbles. Remove from heat and add gradually, stirring constantly
- **2½ cups milk**

Return to heat and bring rapidly to boiling. Stirring constantly, cook until mixture thickens. Cook 1 to 2 min. longer.

Remove from heat; stir in
- **2 teaspoons lemon juice**
- **½ teaspoon Worcestershire sauce**

Strain mixture through a fine sieve, pressing vegetables against sieve to extract all sauce. Set aside to keep warm.

Heat in a skillet over low heat
- **½ cup butter or margarine**

Add the cooked shrimp and cook over medium heat, moving and turning gently with a spoon, until shrimp are lightly browned. Pour the contents of the skillet into the sauce and blend thoroughly.

Serve at once with **Perfection Boiled Rice** (*page 147*) and **curry condiments,** such as freshly grated coconut, golden raisins, preserved kumquats, chutney, and chopped roasted peanuts.

4 servings

Shrimp Imperial

Cook and clean

1½ lbs. fresh shrimp with shells (see Cooked Shrimp, *page 126*; use 3 cups water)

Reserve three whole shrimp for garnish; cut remainder into halves. Chill in refrigerator.

Set out a double boiler.

Grate and set aside

3 oz. Cheddar cheese (about ¾ cup, grated)

Prepare (*page 6*) and set aside

¾ cup (about 1 large) chopped green pepper
½ cup (about 1 medium-size) minced onion

Heat in top of double boiler over low heat

¼ cup butter

Add the onion and green pepper and cook until onion is transparent and pepper is tender, occasionally moving mixture with a spoon. Blend in a mixture of

3 tablespoons flour
1 teaspoon salt
½ teaspoon Accent
⅛ teaspoon pepper

Heat until mixture bubbles. Remove from heat. Add gradually, stirring constantly

1 cup undiluted evaporated milk
1 cup water

Return to heat and bring rapidly to boiling, stirring constantly; cook 1 to 2 min. longer.

Vigorously stir about 3 tablespoons of hot mixture into

2 egg yolks, slightly beaten

Immediately blend into mixture in double boiler. Cook over simmering water 3 to 5 min. Stir slowly to keep mixture cooking evenly. Stir in the cooked shrimp and

½ cup (4-oz. can, drained) sliced mushrooms
3 tablespoons chopped pimiento
1 tablespoon finely chopped parsley
1 tablespoon prepared horse-radish
1 teaspoon Worcestershire sauce

Cook, stirring occasionally, until shrimp and mushrooms are thoroughly heated.

Pour into a large serving dish and sprinkle with the grated cheese. Garnish with the reserved shrimp and

Parsley sprigs
Strips of pimiento

Serve in **Toast Cups** (*page 51*), or on buttered **toast.**

6 servings

Scallops Baked in Shells

Scallops in a sauce with a redolent bouquet.

Butter 6 baking shells or ramekins.

Set out

2 lbs. scallops

(If using frozen scallops, thaw according to directions on package.) Rinse scallops in cold water. Set aside to drain on absorbent paper.

Heat in a saucepan

2 cups dry white wine
Herb bouquet (*page 5*)

Add the scallops to the wine with

½ teaspoon salt
½ teaspoon Accent

Cover and simmer about 10 min., or until scallops are tender. Remove herb bouquet. Drain scallops, reserving the liquid. Cut the scallops into pieces and set aside.

Clean (*page 6*) and chop

½ lb. mushrooms

Put the mushrooms into a saucepan with

6 chopped shallots (or ¼ cup minced onion)
1 tablespoon minced parsley
3 tablespoons butter
2 tablespoons water
1 teaspoon lemon juice
¼ teaspoon Accent

Cover and simmer 5 to 10 min. Add the vegetable mixture to the scallops; set aside.

Melt in the saucepan

¼ cup butter

Scallops Baked in Shells

Blend in

¼ cup flour

Heat until mixture bubbles. Remove from heat. Add gradually, stirring in, the reserved liquid. Return mixture to heat and bring rapidly to boiling, stirring constantly; cook 1 to 2 min. longer. Remove from heat.

Stirring vigorously, gradually add the sauce to a mixture of

2 egg yolks, slightly beaten
¼ cup heavy cream

Stir in the scallop mixture. Fill shells or ramekins, piling high in center. Sprinkle with

⅓ cup (1 slice) buttered dry bread crumbs (page 4)

Set shells on a baking sheet and place in oven at 450°F 8 to 10 min. (or place in broiler 4 in. from source of heat); bake until crumbs are browned.

Serve hot. *6 servings*

▲ Deep-Fried Scallops

Set out a deep saucepan or automatic deep-fryer (*page 7*) and heat fat to 365°F.

Set out

2 lbs. scallops

(If using frozen scallops, thaw according to directions on package.) Rinse scallops in cold water. Set aside to drain on absorbent paper.

Put into a shallow pan or dish and set aside

1 cup (about 3 slices) fine, dry bread crumbs

Mix together in a bowl

2 eggs, slightly beaten
2 tablespoons milk
2 tablespoons paprika
1 teaspoon salt
1 teaspoon Accent
¼ teaspoon pepper
⅛ teaspoon cayenne pepper

Dip scallops, one at a time, into egg mixture and then coat by rolling in bread crumbs.

Deep-fry in the heated fat only as many scallops at one time as will lie uncrowded one layer deep in the fat. Fry 2 or 3 min., or until brown. Turn scallops as they rise to surface and several times during cooking. Remove scallops with a slotted spoon; drain over fat for a few seconds before removing them to absorbent paper.

Serve hot with **lemon wedges** and melted **butter** or **Tartar Sauce** (*page 184*).

6 to 8 servings

△ Deep-Fried Oysters

Follow ▲ Recipe. Substitute 1 qt. large **oysters** for the scallops. Drain and pick over to remove any shell particles. (Reserve liquid for use in other food preparation.) Coat oysters by rolling in bread crumbs; dip in egg mixture; coat again in bread crumbs. Heat fat to 375°F and deep-fry as in ▲ Recipe.

△ Deep-Fried Shrimp

Follow ▲ Recipe. Substitute 2 lbs. fresh **shrimp** with shells for the scallops. Peel and remove vein (see Shrimp Sauté, *page 125*). Heat fat to 350°F. Deep-fry as in ▲ Recipe.

Steamed Clams

Best clams for steaming are the soft-shelled.

Set out a kettle having a tight-fitting cover.

Wash, scrub and very thoroughly rinse
24 to 30 clams (allow about 6 to 8 clams per person)
Put clams into the kettle. Add
1 cup water
Cover tightly and steam over low heat until shells open. Remove from liquid. (Liquid may be strained and used for clam juice cocktails or in other food preparation.)

Serve clams from the shell. Accompany with
Melted butter

About 4 servings

Clam Fritters

MRS. MARCUS F. JENSEN
DOUGLAS, ALASKA

If you've never tasted clam fritters, try these.

Set out a deep saucepan or automatic deep-fryer (*page 7*) and heat fat to 365°F. Set out a large bowl.

Drain, reserving juice
1 cup shucked clams
Rinse clams and put through food chopper.

Mix together in the bowl the clams and
¼ cup juice from clams
¼ cup milk
1 egg, slightly beaten
3 tablespoons butter, melted
Set mixture aside.

Sift together into a bowl
1 cup sifted flour
2½ teaspoons baking powder
¼ teaspoon salt
⅛ teaspoon pepper
¼ teaspoon paprika
Add clam mixture to the dry ingredients all at one time. Mix only until well blended. Drop by teaspoonfuls into hot fat. Fry 2 to 3 min. Drain on absorbent paper. *6 servings*

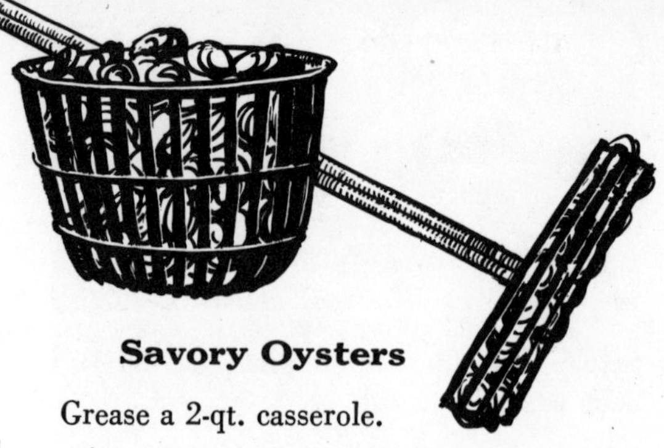

Savory Oysters

Grease a 2-qt. casserole.

Prepare coarse crumbs from
6 slices crisp toast (2 cups crumbs)
Set aside.

Heat slowly about 5 min. in a large skillet, stirring occasionally
½ cup butter or margarine
⅔ cup (6¾-oz. can, drained) mushrooms, finely sliced
⅓ cup chopped green pepper (*page 6*)
½ clove garlic (*page 6*; insert wooden pick for easy removal)
Remove skillet from heat; discard garlic. Stir in toast crumbs, blending well. Set aside.

Drain thoroughly, reserving liquid
1 qt. oysters
Pick over oysters to remove any shell particles. Combine ¼ cup of reserved oyster liquid with
¼ cup cream or rich milk
1 teaspoon Worcestershire sauce
Set aside oysters and liquid.

Mix together
1 teaspoon salt
1 teaspoon paprika
½ teaspoon Accent
⅛ teaspoon mace
Dash of cayenne pepper
Line bottom of casserole with one third of crumb mixture. Top with layers of one half of the oysters, one half of the seasonings and one third of the crumb mixture. Repeat oyster and seasoning layers. Spoon remaining reserved liquid over oysters before topping with remaining crumb mixture.

Bake at 375°F 20 to 30 min., or until crumbs are golden brown. *6 to 8 servings*

▲ Oysters Rockefeller I

There is a saying in New Orleans that whoever eats Oysters Rockefeller feels as rich as the famous tycoon. This is one of the most distinguished dishes of a region noted for its imaginative cooking. There are many variations.

Set out a shallow baking dish and fill ¼ in. deep with coarse salt.

Prepare
2 cups Medium White Sauce (double recipe, *page 181*)
Remove thickened sauce from heat and vigorously stir about 3 tablespoons hot sauce into
1 egg, slightly beaten
Immediately return to mixture in saucepan and cook over low heat 1 to 2 min., stirring constantly. Set sauce aside and keep it warm.

Cook (*page 149*) in heavy saucepan contents of
2 12-oz. pkgs. frozen chopped spinach
Drain thoroughly and set aside.

Meanwhile, place flat side of shell up and carefully open, by inserting the tip of a knife between edges of shell opposite hinges
2 doz. shell oysters
Loosen the oysters from the top shell and place them in the deep half of the shell. Discard the top shells. Arrange oysters-in-the-shells in the prepared baking dish. (If shell oysters are not available, use 1 pt. shucked oysters and purchased clam shells.)

Set out
2 tablespoons sherry
Sprinkle ¼ teaspoon wine over each oyster. Set baking dish aside.

Heat in a heavy skillet over low heat
2 tablespoons butter or margarine
Add and cook over medium heat until onion is transparent, stirring occasionally
1 tablespoon finely chopped onion

Oysters Rockefeller II

Add to the skillet the drained spinach, 2 tablespoons of the white sauce and
1 tablespoon minced parsley
½ teaspoon Worcestershire sauce
6 drops tabasco sauce
and a mixture of
¼ teaspoon salt
¼ teaspoon Accent
Few grains nutmeg
Few grains pepper
Mix thoroughly and heat 2 to 3 min. Spoon the spinach mixture over the oysters; then spoon the remaining white sauce over the spinach. Sprinkle over sauce
Grated Parmesan cheese
Bake at 375°F 15 to 20 min., or until lightly browned.

Serve immediately. *4 to 6 servings*

△ Oysters Rockefeller II

Follow ▲ Recipe; omit Medium White Sauce and egg. Blend 2 tablespoons **cream** with the cooked spinach. Top spinach mixture with ¾ cup buttered, fine, dry **bread crumbs** (*page 4*); then sprinkle with the cheese.

Perhaps the majority of the recipes in this section belong to the class of wonderful family fare. Of course there are a number of exceptions; for example, the **Red 'n' White Salad Mold** (*page 171*) combines cooked chicken with cranberry sauce and pineapple in a manner worthy of your most special luncheon guests. But many others of these recipes are for the hearty, homey type of dish which satisfies the family and saves work for you.

There are old favorites here—**Chili Con Carne** (*page 135*), **Baked Beans** (*page 139*) and **Flavor-Filled Macaroni and Cheese** (*page 142*). There are delightful new dishes, too—creamed foods, main-dish salads and many oven main dishes, including casseroles, pies and scallops.

TYPES—A true *casserole* mixture contains meat, fish, poultry, eggs or cheese, sometimes more than one of them, combined in a well-flavored sauce, sometimes with rice or some pasta product: all turned into an ovenware dish and baked. A *pie* is a quite similar mixture topped with a crust of pastry, biscuits or mashed potatoes, and baked. A *scallop* has the foods arranged in alternate layers, usually with a well-seasoned white sauce, and it usually has a topping of buttered crumbs, or sometimes crumbs and cheese or simply grated cheese. Many of these oven dishes may be fully prepared ahead of time and stored in the refrigerator or freezer to be cooked when needed.

BAKING—The baking dish in which these mixtures are cooked is generally of heat-resistant glass, pottery or enameled iron ware. It is important to choose a dish of the right size. The mixture, whatever its type, should come to about one-half to two-thirds inch below the rim of the casserole; if the dish is fuller, the mixture may overflow when it bubbles up; if less full, the sides of the dish will interfere with proper heat circulation and may prevent browning of the surface.

Most oven main dishes are cooked uncovered, since a brown surface is usually desired. However, when some ingredient in the mixture requires long cooking, the casserole may be covered during the first part of the cooking time to produce steaming and prevent excessive browning; uncovering for a short time just before taking from the oven browns the surface sufficiently.

INGREDIENTS—Ground meat is called for in many recipes in this section. For best flavor in any ground meat dish, always purchase meat that is freshly ground. Many homemakers like to order the cut of beef they favor—round, chuck, brisket or whatever it may be—and have it ground while they wait. A coarse single grind insures juiciness. The same suggestion applies to pork and lamb.

After ground meat is brought home, it should be removed from the meat dealer's wrappings and stored *lightly* covered (not wrapped) in the coldest part of the refrigerator, preferably for not longer than two days. Light handling of ground meat, both in shaping and during cooking, keeps the texture light and juicy. In general, allow about 1 teaspoon salt and ½ teaspoon Accent per pound of meat.

Cheese is another ingredient which appears frequently in casserole cookery. It may be a principal ingredient of the casserole mixture or an important garnish—important because of the rich, tangy flavor imparted by even a light topping of grated cheese, or crumbs and cheese, to almost any food combination. The cheese which is used probably more often than any other in American cookery is Cheddar, mild or sharp as family preference dictates; but dozens of other varieties of cheese, many of them originating in far corners of the world, are now being produced domestically and are therefore available quite generally.

Cheese is of three types: natural, process, and a blend called "cheese food." *Natural cheese*, which is the basis of both other types as well, is made directly from milk—usually cows' milk, though some special cheeses are made from the milk of goats or ewes. The cheese-making process concentrates into the cheese almost all the proteins and most of the fat, minerals and vitamins of the milk; hence all cheese is highly nutritious food. The special character of different varieties of cheese is determined by the manner in which they are aged and "ripened" by bacterial action and molds. Some aging and ripening takes place in all cheeses except cream cheese, cottage cheese and Neufchâtel.

Natural cheese may be soft, semisoft, hard or very hard. *Soft cheeses* include both unripened cream and cottage cheese and some ripened varieties such as Camembert and Brie (both table rather than cooking cheeses). Familiar examples of *semisoft cheeses* are Roquefort and Blue, usually used in spreads and salad dressings, though occasionally in cooked dishes too. The most common cooking cheeses are *hard cheeses*, including Cheddar and Swiss (both Emmentaler and Gruyère). The best-known of the *very hard cheeses* are Parmesan and Romano, which are most frequently used grated as a topping for cooked foods; these are often purchased already grated, though if purchased in the piece and grated as needed, the unused portion will keep almost indefinitely. Many other varieties in these classifications are becoming increasingly recognized and used, including Italian Ricotta and Mozzarella, Norwegian Mysost and Gjetost, Dutch Edam and Gouda, and Swiss Sapsago. Some have cooking uses, others are primarily table cheeses. Most are now produced in this country.

Process cheeses are a development of recent years. They are produced from natural cheeses by methods developed to insure uniformity of flavor, texture, moisture content and cooking quality. They are often blends of more than one variety of cheese; but even when only one variety is used, cheeses selected at different stages of ripeness are blended, thus insuring uniformity.

In processing, the natural cheeses are ground up, mixed together by heating and stirring with an emulsifying agent until melted, and measured into molds lined with a completely moisture-vapor-proof packaging material; the packages are immediately closed and sealed and the cheese is cooled in its air-tight package. This process "fixes" the flavor of the cheese because it destroys the enzymes, bacteria and molds which in natural cheese continue the ripening process until the cheese is used. Process cheeses have good keeping qualities.

Cheese foods are made like process cheeses, but certain dairy products (such as cream, milk or dry mild solids) are added; at least 51 per cent of the weight must be natural cheese. *Process cheese spreads* are made like cheese foods, except that they must be spreadable at room temperature.

Other foods used in luncheon and supper dishes so frequently that they deserve special mention are members of the *pasta* family: macaroni, spaghetti and egg noodles. Pasta comes in many forms other than the three most familiar ones, so much variety in appearance is possible. Shells, bows, little star shapes, elbows, very fine noodles and very wide ones (*lasagne*), slender *vermicelli* and *matassa*, fat *mostaccioli* and *tufoli* are only a few of the available forms. All combine well with meat and cheese, because they absorb and spread flavors rapidly.

Pasta products require careful cooking for maximum palatability. Specific directions on individual packages should be followed; but in general, all pasta should be cooked in a large amount of furiously boiling salted water, for just long enough to make the pasta tender but still firm to the teeth (what the Italians term "al dente"). Use of too little water in cooking produces a sticky texture and a pasty taste; too long cooking makes pasta soft and watery. Cooked pasta should be drained immediately in a colander or sieve, rinsed with hot water to remove loose starch (or with cold water if the product is to be used in a salad), and preferably used at once. Actual cooking time varies from 5 to 20 minutes, depending on the variety.

The Know-How of Freezing Casseroles

Add to your leisure hours and your family's enjoyment by making full use of your freezer. On the days when you feel like cooking, cook double or triple your usual amounts—part to be served immediately and the remainder to be frozen and served for future meals.

Freezing changes the texture of some foods. Since some strong flavors become undesirable you may prefer to add some seasonings at serving time. Salt tends to lose its strength. Some fats are likely to become rancid if stored too long. Hard-cooked egg white becomes tough. Usually it is best to omit rice, noodles, spaghetti and macaroni from casserole mixtures—just cook and add at serving time. Vegetables may be omitted; cook and add them to casserole mixtures just before serving. Crisp casserole toppings, such as bread crumbs, should be added 10 to 15 minutes before the end of oven-thawing period.

Preparation for the Freezer—Foods for the freezer must be of top quality and handled carefully but rapidly from shopping bag to freezer. Be sure that fruits and vegetables are carefully sorted and scrupulously cleaned—but never water-soaked. Use clean equipment. Cook meats and vegetables until barely tender to avoid mushy textures. Cool food rapidly by setting the pan containing the food in a larger pan of ice and water (stir occasionally to hasten cooling). When food is completely cooled, package and freeze.

Packaging for the Freezer—Packaging is all-important for proper freezing. Package food in quantities that will be used at a single meal; never refreeze a thawed food. Different shapes and types of foods require different containers and wrappings. Choose moisture-vapor-proof wrapping material and containers of correct size and shape. A tight seal is of utmost importance.

Pack solidly to force out air, leaving space at top of container for expansion of foods—about ½ inch in pint containers and about 1 inch in quarts.

Some mixtures may be layered in containers to hasten removal and thawing; divide layers of about 1 inch with double thicknesses of strong, pliable material.

Food may be frozen in a casserole if freezer space permits and if the kind of casserole used can be subjected to sudden, extreme temperature changes. Put cover over casserole of completely cooled food and tape-seal or wrap; freeze. When frozen, remove casserole from freezer and place over very low heat 1 or 2 minutes, or until contents loosen from casserole; slide onto a large piece or into a bag of moisture-vapor-proof material. Seal, label and freeze. When the vegetable is to be added to the casserole just before serving, package the frozen vegetable and casserole mixture first separately and then together so that the complete casserole dish is in one package.

Labeling for the Freezer—The freezer-storage life of combination or casserole dishes is short; use them within a few days or at the most, in a few weeks. Don't hoard—a rapid turnover of casserole freezer foods is freezer-wisdom and freezer-economy and indicates good freezer management.

Equip yourself with an efficient freezer pen, pencil or crayon. Write plainly on each package its contents, date of freezing and intended use. It is well, too, to keep a handy record near the freezer with the same information. Check off foods as they are used. Store systematically and conveniently.

Serving from the Freezer—Time needed for thawing frozen cooked foods varies with the food, thickness of frozen block and thawing method. Use the method which will least change appearance and texture. Foods to be thawed before heating or serving may be thawed at room temperature or in the food compartment of the refrigerator in their freezer containers. Foods that scorch easily are best when tightly covered and reheated from a frozen state in top of double boiler over simmering water or in the oven, stirring no more than necessary. Set freezer containers in warm water until contents loosen enough to be removed. Unwrap frozen mixtures which were first casserole frozen, and later removed from the casserole for storage. Grease the same top-of-range casserole; return mixture to it. Thaw over direct, low heat or in oven.

Correct freezer-to-table preparation is the last important step to quality freezer casseroles.

Beef Pinwheels

Lightly grease a baking sheet.

Heat in a heavy skillet over medium heat

1 tablespoon fat

Add and cook until browned, breaking into small pieces with fork or spoon

½ lb. ground beef

When meat is almost browned, add and cook until onion is transparent

2 tablespoons finely chopped onion
1 tablespoon minced parsley
¼ teaspoon salt
¼ teaspoon Accent
Few grains pepper

Remove from heat and moisten with

2 to 3 tablespoons chili sauce

Set meat mixture aside.

Prepare dough for

Tender-Rich Biscuits (*page 43*)

Roll dough into rectangle ½ in. thick. Spread ground meat mixture over biscuit dough. Beginning with longer side of rectangle, roll tightly, without stretching, into a long roll; pinch ends to seal. Slice into ½-in. pinwheels.

Place on the baking sheet.

Bake at 450°F 10 to 15 min., or until browned.

Serve hot. (If desired, accompany with **Brown Gravy,** *page 187.*) *About 6 servings*

△ Ham Pinwheels

Follow ▲ Recipe. Substitute for the ground beef 1½ cups **ground cooked ham;** omit cooking in the fat. Substitute for the chopped onion, salt and chili sauce, ⅓ cup **sweetened condensed milk,** ¼ cup **pickle relish,** 2 tablespoons minced **parsley** and 2 teaspoons **prepared mustard.** Complete pinwheels as in the ▲ Recipe.

△ Luncheon Meat Pinwheels

Follow △ Recipe. Substitute 1½ cups **ground luncheon meat** for ham.

Chili con Carne

Heat in a large skillet having a tight-fitting cover

2 tablespoons fat

Add and cook until onion is transparent, occasionally moving and turning with a spoon

½ cup (about 1 medium-size) chopped onion (*page 6*)

Add and cook over medium heat until lightly browned, breaking into small pieces with fork or spoon

1 lb. ground beef

Add slowly, stirring constantly

2 cups (1-lb. can) kidney beans
2 cups (1-lb. can) cooked tomatoes, cut in pieces

and a mixture of

1 tablespoon chili powder
1½ teaspoons salt
¾ teaspoon Accent
⅛ teaspoon pepper
⅛ teaspoon cayenne pepper

Cover and simmer over low heat about 1 hour, stirring occasionally.

Serve hot with rolls or bread sticks and

Southwestern Salad Bowl (*page 172*)

4 to 6 servings

Chili con Carne

Fresh Vegetable Chow Mein

ETHELYN BEORGEON, OCONTO, WIS.

Set out a small skillet and a large, heavy skillet having a tight-fitting cover.

Wipe with a clean, damp cloth and cut into ¾-in. cubes
1¼ lbs. pork steak
1 lb. lean beef
Heat in the large skillet over low heat
2 tablespoons butter
Add the beef and pork and cook over medium heat until well browned, occasionally moving and turning pieces with fork or spoon.

Meanwhile, clean (*page 6*), separate into stalks and cut into thin strips 1-in. long
½ large bunch celery
Clean (*page 6*) and finely chop
3 medium-size onions
Drain contents of
1 8-oz. can bamboo shoots
Add the vegetables to the skillet with enough water to just cover meat and vegetables. Cover and cook over low heat until meat and vegetables are tender (about 40 min.).

Prepare, slice and set aside
2 hard-cooked eggs
Meanwhile, blend together until smooth
4 tablespoons soy sauce
2 tablespoons cornstarch
1 teaspoon Accent
Add slowly to cooking liquid while stirring constantly. Bring liquid to boiling; cook over low heat about 15 min. longer.

Spread in a shallow pan, contents of
1 can (about 3¾ oz.) Chinese noodles
Heat in 300°F oven about 10 min.

Drain and set aside contents of
1 8-oz. can water chestnuts
Clean (*page 6*) and cut into small pieces
1 medium-size green pepper
Rinse, remove and discard stem ends, peel and cut into thin slices
2 medium-size tomatoes
Add the chestnuts, green pepper and tomatoes to the hot mixture; cook 2 to 3 min. longer.

Melt in the small skillet over low heat
2 tablespoons butter
Add and cook until lightly browned, occasionally moving and turning pieces with fork or spoon
½ cup (4-oz. can, drained) mushrooms
Rinse and cut into thin slices
1 orange
Cut each slice in half and set aside.

Spread noodles over bottom of large serving platter. Cover with the pork-beef mixture; spoon the mushrooms over meat. Garnish top with the sliced hard-cooked eggs. Place the orange slices around edge of platter.

About 8 servings

China Boy

(Ham-Egg-Rice Scramble)

MRS. J. A. McCONNELL, PORTLAND, ORE.

Set out a 10-in. skillet and a heavy 2-qt. saucepan having a tight-fitting cover.

Bring to boiling in the saucepan
1¼ cups water
¼ teaspoon salt
Add gradually so boiling will not stop
½ cup rice
(The Rice Industry no longer considers it necessary to wash rice before cooking.) Reduce heat to very low. Blend in
1 tablespoon butter
Cover saucepan tightly and cook, without removing cover, about 25 min., or until all the water is absorbed and a rice kernel is entirely soft when pressed between fingers.

Meanwhile, grind enough cooked ham to yield
1½ cups ground cooked ham
Set ham aside.

Heat in the skillet over low heat
2 tablespoons butter
Add
¾ cup (about 1 large) chopped onion
Cook until onion is transparent, occasionally moving and turning with a spoon. Add ham and cook until ham is thoroughly heated, occasionally moving and turning mixture with fork or spoon. Remove from heat. Add all at one time and blend well
3 eggs, slightly beaten
Return skillet to heat. As soon as eggs are cooked (1 to 2 min.), remove mixture from heat. Add the cooked rice, blending in thoroughly.

Serve immediately. *4 to 6 servings*

Hawaiian Supper

MRS. BILLIE L. OWENS, TOPEKA, KANS.

Set out a large, heavy skillet.

Prepare and set aside
2½ cups slivered cooked ham
⅓ cup chopped green pepper (*page 6*)
Heat in the skillet over medium heat
2 tablespoons fat
Add the ham and the green pepper. Cook until ham is lightly browned, occasionally moving and turning mixture with a spoon.

Meanwhile, drain, reserving sirup, and set aside the contents of
1 9-oz. can pineapple tidbits
Cook according to directions on package
1⅓ cups packaged precooked rice
Add to the water with the rice
⅛ teaspoon cloves
Set aside to keep warm.

Mix together thoroughly
2 tablespoons brown sugar
1½ tablespoons cornstarch
Blend in to form a smooth paste
1½ tablespoons vinegar
Add gradually, stirring to blend, the reserved pineapple sirup and
¾ cup water
1½ teaspoons prepared mustard
⅛ teaspoon pepper
Pour the cornstarch mixture into the skillet. Cook, stirring constantly, until the mixture thickens and is transparent. Stir in the tidbits and cook until heated thoroughly.

Using a fork, blend into the rice
2 tablespoons butter or margarine
Serve the ham mixture over the rice.
4 or 5 servings

Stuffed Peppers

Stuffed Peppers

Set out a shallow 2-qt. baking dish and a medium-size saucepan.

Rinse and cut into halves lengthwise

4 large green peppers

Remove and discard stems, all white fiber and seeds; rinse cavities. Drop pepper halves into boiling salted water to cover and simmer 5 min. Remove peppers from water and invert. Set aside to drain.

Meanwhile, cook

½ cup packaged precooked rice (see directions on package)

While rice is cooking, cut into small pieces and set aside enough cooked ham to yield

2 cups cooked ham pieces

Cut into 8 slices and set aside

¼ lb. Cheddar cheese

Heat in the saucepan

½ cup butter or margarine

Add ham and toss lightly with a fork to blend. Blend in the rice and

2 tablespoons minced onion
2 tablespoons finely chopped celery

Mix together and blend in

¼ teaspoon dry mustard
¼ teaspoon garlic salt
¼ teaspoon Accent
⅛ teaspoon pepper

Lightly fill pepper halves with ham-rice mixture, heaping slightly. Place one slice of cheese on top of each pepper. Place peppers in baking dish. Pour around peppers

1½ cups tomato juice

Bake at 350°F about 20 min. Increase heat to 400°F and bake 10 min. longer, or until cheese is lightly browned.

Spoon the hot tomato juice over peppers.

4 servings

Crusty Croquettes

A deep saucepan or automatic deep fryer will be needed.

Prepare and set aside

2 cups finely chopped or ground cooked chicken

Prepare

1 cup Thick White Sauce (*page 181*)

Blend in

1 tablespoon finely chopped parsley
1 tablespoon lemon juice
½ teaspoon onion juice

and a mixture of

½ teaspoon salt
½ teaspoon Accent
¼ teaspoon celery salt

Add the chicken and gently blend in. Chill mixture in refrigerator until firm.

Fill saucepan with fat; heat to 375°F (*page 7*).

Shape the chilled chicken mixture into balls, cones or cylinders. Roll in

1 cup (3 slices) fine, dry bread crumbs

Dip into a mixture of

1 egg, slightly beaten
1 tablespoon milk

Again coat in bread crumbs, shaking off loose crumbs. Deep-fry croquettes, turning often to brown evenly. Drain on absorbent paper.

Serve immediately. *6 servings*

Note: Finely chopped or ground cooked **meat,** or flaked cooked **fish** may be substituted for the chicken.

Flavor-Rich Baked Beans

Grease 8 individual casseroles (or 1 bean pot or casserole) having tight-fitting covers.

Heat to boiling in a large, heavy saucepan
1½ qts. water
Meanwhile, sort and wash thoroughly
2⅓ cups (about 1 lb.) pea (navy) beans
Gradually add beans to water so that boiling will not stop. Reduce heat and simmer 2 min.; remove from heat. Set aside to soak 1 hr.

Cut into 1-in. chunks and set aside
½ lb. salt pork (with rind removed)
Add pork chunks to soaked beans with
½ cup chopped celery (*page 6*)
½ cup (about 1 medium-size) chopped onion (*page 6*)
1 teaspoon salt
¾ teaspoon Accent
Cover tightly and bring mixture to boiling over high heat. Reduce heat and simmer 45 min., stirring once or twice. Drain beans, reserving liquid. Put an equal amount of beans and salt pork chunks into each casserole. Set aside.

Mix together in a saucepan 1 cup of the reserved bean liquid and
¼ cup ketchup
¼ cup molasses
2 tablespoons brown sugar
1 teaspoon dry mustard
½ teaspoon pepper
¼ teaspoon ginger
Bring to boiling. Pour an equal amount of the liquid mixture into each casserole.

Cover casseroles and bake at 300°F about 2½ hrs. If necessary, add more reserved bean liquid to beans during baking. Remove covers and bake ½ hr. longer.

Serve with **Boston Brown Bread.** *8 servings*

Double-Quick Baked Beans

Double-Quick Baked Beans

Grease 4 individual casseroles or a shallow 1-qt. baking dish.

Mix together
¼ cup ketchup
3 tablespoons minced onion
2 tablespoons molasses
2 tablespoons brown sugar
½ teaspoon salt
¼ teaspoon Accent
2 drops tabasco sauce
Blend thoroughly with
2 cups (1 1-lb. can) baked beans
Turn into the casseroles or baking dish. Cut crosswise into pieces
4 slices bacon (or use salt pork)
Put a few pieces on top of bean mixture in each casserole. (Or leave slices whole and arrange on top of beans in baking dish.)

Bake at 375°F 20 to 30 min., or until heated thoroughly.

Serve with **Boston Brown Bread.** *4 servings*

Pot o' Dried Beef and Macaroni

Grease a shallow 1½-qt. casserole.

Set out

1½ cups (about 4 oz.) drief beef, shredded

Melt in a large skillet over low heat

2 tablespoons butter

Add 1 cup dried beef (reserve remaining ½ cup for topping) and

1⅓ cups (two 6¾-oz. cans, drained) sliced mushrooms

Cook over medium heat until edges of beef are curled and mushrooms are lightly browned, frequently moving and turning mixture with fork or spoon. Set skillet aside in a warm place while preparing sauce.

Grate

6 oz. Cheddar cheese (about 1½ cups, grated)

Prepare

3 cups Medium White Sauce (3 times recipe, *page 181*; use 1 cup cream for one-third of the liquid; omit salt)

Cool sauce slightly. Add cheese to sauce all at one time, stirring until cheese is melted.

Cook and drain (*page 141*)

1½ cups shell macaroni

Reserve 1 cup sauce and 1 cup macaroni.

Mix remaining sauce and macaroni together. Turn into casserole. Top with the browned mushrooms and dried beef. Arrange reserved macaroni over dried beef and pour reserved sauce over all. Tuck reserved dried beef into sauce to form an attractive pattern on top of casserole. Sprinkle with **paprika.**

Bake at 350°F 20 to 30 min., or until heated thoroughly. *6 to 8 servings*

Pot o' Dried Beef and Macaroni

Dried Beef Wiggle

MRS. RUSSELL P. YEATON, VERONA, N. J.

Heat in a 2-qt. saucepan over low heat

¼ cup butter or margarine

Add

½ cup finely chopped green pepper (*page 6*)
2 tablespoons minced onion

Cook until onion is transparent, stirring occasionally. Add

1½ cups (about 4 oz.) dried beef, shredded

Cook over medium heat until edges of beef curl and beef is lightly browned, frequently moving and turning with fork or spoon.

Remove beef and vegetables with a slotted spoon. Set aside.

Using drippings in pan as part of the fat, prepare

3 cups Medium White Sauce (three times recipe, *page 181*; omit salt)

Return beef and vegetables to the thickened sauce. Add, stirring in

1 cup drained whole kernel corn
⅛ teaspoon pepper

Heat until corn is thoroughly heated. Serve over **toast,** in **patty shells** or in **Toast Cups** (*page 51*). *About 6 servings*

Tomatoes Stuffed with Rice and Cheese

Butter an 8x8x2-in. baking dish.

For Filling—Prepare
2 cups Perfection Boiled Rice (two-thirds recipe, *page 147*)
Meanwhile, grate
2 oz. Cheddar cheese (about ½ cup, grated)
Mix 2 tablespoons grated cheese with
⅓ cup (about ½ slice) soft bread crumbs
2 tablespoons melted butter or margarine
Set prepared crumbs aside.

Heat in skillet
2 tablespoons butter or margarine
Add and cook until lightly browned
½ cup (4-oz. can, drained) sliced mushrooms
Stir remaining grated cheese and mushrooms into rice. Add
1 teaspoon Worcestershire sauce

For Tomatoes—Rinse
6 large, firm tomatoes
Cut a ¼-in. slice from top of each tomato. With a sharp knife, cut down around inside of tomatoes, about ¼ in. from edges, being careful not to cut through bottoms. With a spoon, scoop out center pulp. Sieve pulp and combine with rice mixture. Season each tomato with part of a mixture of
¾ teaspoon salt
½ teaspoon Accent
Lightly fill tomatoes with rice mixture, heaping slightly. Place in baking dish. Top with buttered crumb mixture.

Bake at 375°F 15 to 20 min. *6 servings*

▲ Macaroni

Heat to boiling in a large saucepan
3 qts. water
1 tablespoon salt
Add gradually
2 cups (8-oz. pkg.) uncooked macaroni (elbows, other shapes or tubes broken into 1- to 2-in. pieces)
Boil rapidly, uncovered, 10 to 15 min.

Test tenderness by pressing a piece against side of pan with fork or spoon. Drain macaroni by turning it into a colander or large sieve; rinse with hot water to remove loose starch. *About 4 cups cooked Macaroni*

△ Spaghetti

Follow ▲ Recipe. Substitute for the macaroni an equal amount of broken or unbroken **spaghetti.**

△ Noodles

Follow ▲ Recipe for the cooking of commercial or **Homemade Noodles** (*page 143*). Substitute 3 cups (about 4 oz.) **noodles** for macaroni. Boil 6 to 10 min., or until tender.

Deviled Ham and Macaroni Ring

Flavor-Filled Macaroni and Cheese

Deviled Ham and Macaroni Ring

Grease a 1½-qt. ring mold. Heat water for boiling water bath (*page 6*).

Cook, drain (*page 141*) and set aside
2 cups (8 oz.) macaroni (elbows, other small shapes, or tubes broken into 1- to 2-in. pieces)
Meanwhile, grate and set aside
4 oz. sharp Cheddar cheese (about 1 cup, grated)
Prepare and set aside
1 cup chopped green pepper (*page 6*)
⅔ cup chopped onion (*page 6*)
3 to 4 tablespoons minced parsley
Beat in a large bowl until well blended
1 egg, well beaten
1 cup milk
½ teaspoon prepared mustard
½ teaspoon salt
¼ teaspoon Accent
⅛ teaspoon pepper
Add the drained macaroni, grated cheese, green pepper, onion and parsley. Mix lightly until thoroughly blended.

Around bottom and sides of mold, spoon, at intervals, contents of
2 2¼-oz. cans deviled ham
Turn macaroni mixture into ring mold.

Bake in boiling water bath at 350°F 50 to 60 min., or until mixture is set.

Shortly before macaroni ring is done, prepare
Quick Tomato Sauce (*page 183*)
Remove ring from oven. Run a spatula around edge of mold and around center ring to loosen. Unmold onto a warm serving platter. Garnish as desired. *About 6 servings*

▲ Flavor-Filled Macaroni and Cheese

Thoroughly grease a shallow, 2-qt. casserole.

Cook, drain (*page 141*) and set aside
2 cups (8-oz. pkg.) macaroni (use small shapes or break tubes into 2-in. pieces)
Meanwhile, grate and set aside
6 oz. Cheddar cheese (1½ cups, grated)
Prepare
2 cups Thin White Sauce (double recipe, *page 181*; mix ¼ teaspoon dry mustard and a dash of paprika with flour before blending into fat)
Cool sauce slightly.

Add grated cheese to sauce all at one time;

stir rapidly until cheese is melted. Blend in

1/3 cup minced onion
1/2 teaspoon Worcestershire sauce
1/4 teaspoon Accent

Place one half of the macaroni in the casserole and cover with one half of the sauce; repeat.

Set out

8 slices (1/2 lb.) Cheddar cheese

Rinse, remove stem ends and cut into slices

3 medium-size (about 1 lb.) tomatoes

Alternate and overlap cheese and tomato slices in a border around top of macaroni. Lightly brush tomatoes with

Melted butter or margarine

Bake at 350°F 25 to 30 min., or until cheese slices are softened. *6 to 8 servings*

△ Bacon Bits Macaroni

Follow ▲ Recipe. Prepare **Panbroiled Bacon** (*page 87*); crumble and mix it with sauce.

Mostaccioli and Cheese

Set out an 8x8x2-in. baking dish.

Prepare

Tomato Sauce (*page 188*)

Heat to boiling in large saucepan

3 qts. water
1 tablespoon salt

Gradually add

2 cups (8-oz. pkg.) mostaccioli

Boil rapidly, uncovered, 12 to 15 min., or until mostaccioli is tender. Test tenderness by pressing a piece against side of pan with fork or spoon. Drain by turning into a colander or large sieve. Return drained mostaccioli to saucepan and mix with 2 tablespoons Tomato Sauce. Place one half of mostaccioli into baking dish. Add in layers

1 cup diced Mozzarella cheese
2 tablespoons grated Parmesan cheese
1/4 teaspoon pepper

Cover with remaining mostaccioli. Cover with Tomato Sauce.

Bake at 350°F about 15 to 20 min., or until tomato sauce is bubbling.

Serve with remaining hot Tomato Sauce. Sprinkle with

Grated Parmesan or Romano cheese

4 to 6 servings

Homemade Noodles

Sift together into a bowl

1 cup sifted flour
1/2 teaspoon salt

Make a well in center of flour and add

1 egg, slightly beaten

While blending ingredients, add gradually

1 to 2 tablespoons water or milk

Dough should be stiff. Turn dough out onto a lightly floured surface. Shape into a ball and knead (*page 33*). Cover and let rest 5 min.

Roll dough on lightly floured surface 1/8 in. thick. If dough sticks, loosen from surface with knife or spatula; sprinkle flour underneath. Turn dough over and roll until paper thin. Allow dough to partially dry (about 1 hr.)

Cut dough into lengthwise strips, 2½ in. wide, and stack on top of each other. Slice into short strips 1/16 to 1/8 in. wide. Separate noodles and allow to dry thoroughly. (Noodles can be stored in a tightly covered container.)

To cook, see **Noodles** (*page 141*).

About 1/8 lb. noodles

Homemade Noodles: Cut partially dried dough into strips; stack the strips, slice and spread to dry.

Supperette à la Pizza

MRS. NONA BLANK, LAKE WORTH, FLA.

Set out two baking sheets.

Heat in a skillet

1 to 2 tablespoons fat

Add and cook over medium heat until browned, breaking into pieces with fork or spoon

½ lb. ground beef

Remove from heat and blend in

¾ cup (6-oz. can) tomato paste

and a mixture of

1¼ teaspoons oregano
¼ teaspoon garlic salt
¼ teaspoon salt
¼ teaspoon pepper
¼ teaspoon Accent

Set aside.

Set out

10 thin slices Mozzarella cheese
Ready-to-bake biscuits (1 8-oz. container)

Pat biscuits into 4-in. rounds and place on baking sheets. Top each with one slice mozzarella cheese. Top each cheese slice with 3 tablespoons of tomato-paste-meat mixture.

Sprinkle each biscuit generously with

Grated Parmesan cheese

Bake at 450°F 8 to 10 min., or until crust is browned. *5 servings*

Stuffed Cabbage Rolls

Stuffed Cabbage Rolls

Grease a shallow, 2-qt. top-of-range casserole having a tight-fitting cover.

Remove and discard wilted outer leaves, rinse and cut about one-half the core from

1 medium-size head (about 2 lbs.) cabbage

Remove 8 large leaves. Shred enough of the remaining cabbage to yield 2 cups. Spread shredded cabbage in casserole. Add

1 bay leaf
1 clove garlic (*page 6*), uncut; (insert wooden pick for easy removal)

Set casserole aside.

Pour boiling water into a large saucepan to 1-in. level. Add large cabbage leaves with

½ teaspoon salt

Cover and simmer 2 to 3 min., or until leaves begin to soften; drain.

Meanwhile, heat in a large heavy skillet

2 to 3 tablespoons butter or margarine

Add and cook over medium heat, occasionally moving pieces with a spoon, until onion is transparent

1 cup finely chopped onion (*page 6*)

Remove from heat and mix in thoroughly

⅔ lb. ground beef (break into small pieces with fork or spoon)
⅔ cup packaged precooked rice
¼ cup thick sour cream
½ teaspoon Worcestershire sauce

and a mixture of

¾ teaspoon salt
½ teaspoon Accent
⅛ teaspoon pepper

Place ¼ cup of the mixture in center of each cabbage leaf. Roll each leaf, tucking ends in toward center. Fasten securely with wooden picks; place on shredded cabbage in casserole. Pour over the rolls a mixture of

3½ cups (1 No. 2½ can) tomatoes, sieved
½ teaspoon salt
¼ teaspoon Accent
Few grains pepper

Cover and simmer over low heat 45 to 60 min., or until tender when pierced with a fork.

About 10 min. before rolls are tender, pile lightly on the rolls

½ cup thick sour cream

Cover casserole and complete cooking.

Place rolls in warm serving dish. Remove bay leaf, garlic and wooden picks. Spoon sauce over rolls and serve with the shredded cabbage.

4 servings

Beef and Potato Scallop

MRS. F. B. JACKSON, ELDRED, PA.

Lightly grease a 2½-qt. casserole.

Grate and set aside

4 oz. Cheddar cheese (about 1 cup, grated)

Wash, pare, cut into cubes and set aside

4 medium-size potatoes (about 4 cups, cubed)

Prepare

2 cups Thin White Sauce (double recipe, *page 181*)

Cool slightly. Add ¾ cup of the grated cheese to the sauce all at one time, stirring until cheese is melted. Set aside to keep warm.

Mix together the potatoes and

1½ cups (about 4 oz.) dried beef, shredded
1½ tablespoons minced green pepper
1½ teaspoons minced onion
½ teaspoon celery salt
¼ teaspoon Accent
⅛ teaspoon pepper

Add the cheese sauce; blend thoroughly. Turn mixture into casserole and top with remaining grated cheese.

Bake at 350°F 1 hr., or until potatoes are tender when pierced with a fork. *6 servings*

Meat-Crusted Corn Pie

Set out a 9-in. pie pan.

Heat in a large skillet over low heat

2 tablespoons butter or margarine

Add and cook until transparent, occasionally moving with a spoon

½ cup (about 1 medium-size) chopped onion (*page 6*)

Drain contents of

1 1-lb. can whole kernel corn (about 1¾ cups, drained)

Add to the skillet, blending with fork or spoon, the corn and

1¼ cups (10½- to 11-oz. can) condensed tomato soup

and a mixture of

1 teaspoon salt
½ teaspoon marjoram
¼ teaspoon chili powder

Simmer uncovered about 10 min., stirring occasionally.

Meanwhile, mix together lightly

¾ lb. ground beef
¼ lb. ground pork
½ cup uncooked brown granular wheat cereal
3 tablespoons minced onion
1 egg, beaten
½ cup milk
1 tablespoon Worcestershire sauce

and a mixture of

1 teaspoon salt
½ teaspoon Accent
⅛ teaspoon pepper

Turn into pie pan. Gently pat mixture to evenly cover bottom, sides and rim of pan. Pour corn mixture into shell.

Bake at 350°F 35 to 45 min.

Garnish with **green pepper rings.**

About 6 servings

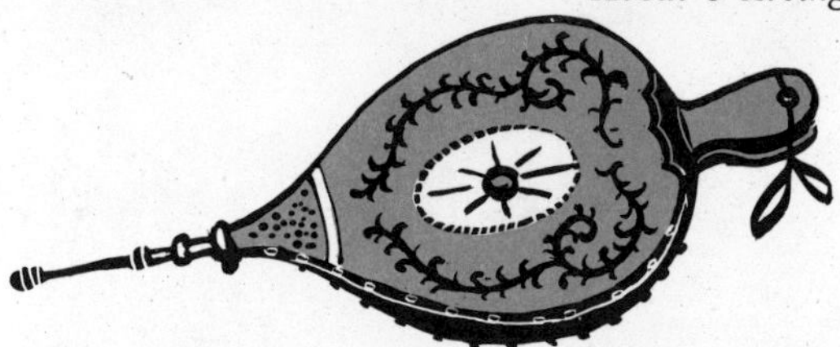

Pizza: Place the dough in the center of the pizza pan. Use fingers to spread dough on the bottom.

Spoon the sieved tomatoes over dough and arrange thin slices of Mozzarella cheese over the tomatoes.

Bake the pizza about 30 minutes or until the crust is golden brown and cheese is melted and bubbly.

▲ Italian Tomato-Cheese Pizza

Lightly grease two 15-in. round pizza pans, two large round griddles or two 15½x12-in. baking sheets.

Soften

½ pkg. (1 teaspoon) active dry yeast in
2 tablespoons warm water, 110°F to 115°F (If using compressed yeast, soften ½ cake in 2 tablespoons lukewarm water, 80°F to 85°F.)

Let stand 5 to 10 min.

Meanwhile, pour into a large bowl

1 cup warm water

Blend in

2 cups sifted flour
1 teaspoon salt

Stir softened yeast and add, mixing well.

Measure

2 cups sifted flour

Add about one-half the flour to yeast mixture and beat until very smooth. Mix in enough flour to make a soft dough. Turn onto a lightly floured surface. Allow to rest 5 to 10 min.

Knead (*page 33*). Form dough into a large ball and place it in a greased, deep bowl just large enough to allow dough to double. Turn dough to bring greased surface to top. Cover with waxed paper and towel; let stand in a warm place (about 80°F) until doubled, about 2 hrs.

Punch down with fist. Fold edges toward center and turn completely over in bowl. Divide into two equal portions and form into balls.

Place one ball in center of each pan. Push dough down in center with hand and spread to ⅛-in. thickness. Shape edge by pressing dough between thumb and forefinger to make ridge.

Force through a sieve

3 cups drained canned tomatoes

Use one half (about 1½ cups) of sieved tomatoes to cover the dough on each pan.

Top each pizza with one-half (4 oz.) of

8 oz. Mozzarella cheese, sliced thin

Sprinkle over each pizza, in order listed, one-half of

- **½ cup olive oil**
- **¼ cup grated Parmesan cheese**
- **1 teaspoon salt**
- **½ teaspoon pepper**
- **2 teaspoons oregano**

Bake at 400°F 25 to 30 min., or until browned.

Cut into wedges. Serve hot. *6 to 8 servings*

△ Mushroom Pizza

Follow ▲ Recipe. Place on *each* pizza 1 cup (8-oz. can, drained) **button mushrooms.**

△ Sausage Pizza

Follow ▲ Recipe. Place on *each* pizza 1 lb. hot **Italian sausage,** cut into ¼-in. pieces.

△ Anchovy Pizza

Follow ▲ Recipe. Omit Mozzarella cheese and Parmesan cheese. Sprinkle ¼ teaspoon **oregano** over each pizza. Arrange on *each* 8 **anchovy fillets,** cut into ¼-in. pieces.

△ Miniature Pizzas

Follow ▲ Recipe. Roll dough and cut into 3½-in. rounds with cookie cutter. Shape edges of rounds as in ▲ recipe. Top *each* pizza with 2 tablespoons canned **tomatoes,** sieved, and a slice of **Mozzarella cheese.** Sprinkle over cheese 1 teaspoon **olive oil,** ½ teaspoon grated **Parmesan cheese, salt, pepper** and **oregano.**

Bake at 400°F 15 to 20 min., or until crust is browned. *About 24 miniature pizzas*

△ English Muffin Pizza

Split 12 **English muffins** and spread cut sides with **butter** or **margarine.** Toast under the broiler until lightly browned. Top each half as for △ Recipe and bake at 400°F 5 to 8 min., or until tomato mixture is bubbling hot.

Perfection Boiled Rice

Bring to boiling in a deep saucepan

- **2 qts. water**
- **1 tablespoon salt**
- **1 teaspoon Accent**

So boiling will not stop, add gradually

- **1 cup rice**

(The Rice Industry no longer considers it necessary to wash rice before cooking.) Boil rapidly, uncovered, 15 to 20 min., or until a kernel of rice is entirely soft when pressed between fingers.

Drain rice in colander or sieve and rinse with hot water to remove loose starch. Cover colander and rice with a clean towel and set over hot water until rice kernels are dry and fluffy. *About 3½ cups cooked rice*

Quick Cooking Rice

Cooked rice prepared from packaged precooked rice may be substituted for Perfection Boiled Rice if directions on the package are followed carefully for amounts and timing.

Boiled Wild Rice

Bring to boiling in a deep saucepan

- **3 cups water**
- **1 teaspoon salt**

Meanwhile, wash in a colander or sieve

- **1 cup wild rice**

Add rice gradually to water so boiling will not stop. Cook covered 30 to 40 min., or until a kernel of rice is tender when pressed between fingers; do not remove cover during this time.

If necessary, drain rice in a colander or sieve. If not used immediately, keep rice hot by placing colander over hot water and covering with a folded towel. *About 3 cups rice*

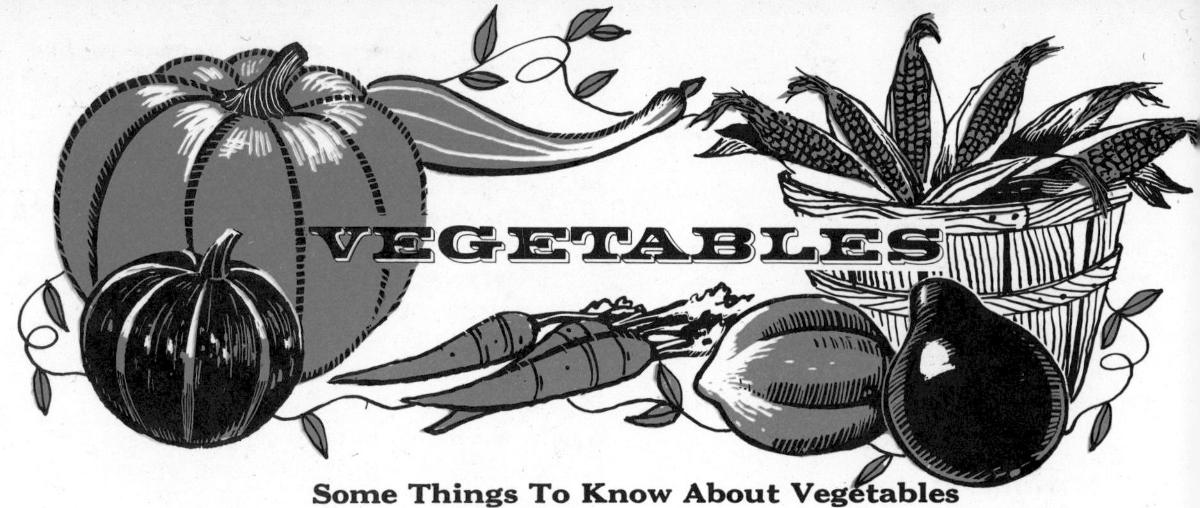

Some Things To Know About Vegetables

Nothing bespeaks the bounty of our land and the variety of its climate more dramatically than the handsome vegetables available in all seasons. What a blessing they are to the beauty of our tables and the nutritive value of our menus! Regarded originally as "boiled" drudges, valued chiefly for the seasoning that could be extracted from them, vegetables are enjoyed and prized today for their own special qualities of excellence.

SELECTION—Choose vegetables, whether fresh, frozen or canned, according to the intended use. For example, appearance is of prime importance when selecting vegetables for a vegetable plate while of lesser importance for soup vegetables.

Fresh Vegetables should be firm and blemish-free. Buy from a reliable dealer who practices good methods of handling vegetables and has a quick turnover of the more perishable items.

Vegetables at the peak of their season are usually more flavorful and lower priced than when they are available out of season.

When selecting vegetables at the market refrain from pinching, squeezing or unnecessary touching. Handle gently to prevent bruising.

Garden-Fresh Vegetables should be picked just before using if possible.

Frozen Vegetables should be solidly frozen and never refrozen after thawing. The package should be in perfect condition.

Canned Vegetables, as are all canned foods shipped between states, are subject to the regulations of the Federal Food, Drug and Cosmetic Act.

Can labels must state the net weight or net fluid contents of the can and, in general, carry descriptions of the style of pack, size, maturity, seasoning, amount of food and number of servings.

Dietetic-packed canned foods, including vegetables, are available for those on special diets such as low-sodium, diabetic or weight reduction.

STORAGE—Proper storage facilities are necessary to keep vegetables in good condition.

Fresh Vegetables—Store less perishable vegetables, such as cabbage, potatoes, dry onions, winter squash and rutabagas, in a cool, dry, well-ventilated place without beforehand washing. Keep onions separate from other vegetables. Store potatoes in a dark place and not directly on the floor.

Wash other vegetables such as greens, carrots and radishes before storing; drain thoroughly and gently pat dry with a soft, clean towel or absorbent paper. Place in refrigerator in vegetable drawers or plastic bags, or wrap tightly in waxed paper, moisture-vapor-proof material or aluminum foil to prevent vegetables from wilting unless refrigerator maintains a high humidity. *Never soak vegetables* when washing them. If they are wilted, put them in cold water for a few minutes. Shake off all moisture left from washing or crisping—drain thoroughly and gently pat dry.

Store peas and lima beans in the pod to keep fresh. Pods may be washed before storing; quickly rinse peas and lima beans after shelling.

Frozen Vegetables—Store in home freezer or in freezing compartment of refrigerator until ready to use. If package starts to thaw, use as soon as possible.

Canned Vegetables—Store in a cool, dry place away from heat-producing objects. If either end of can is bulged or swollen, discard the can because this is a sign of spoilage. Rust on a can and dents in a can do not indicate spoilage unless there is evidence of leakage.

PREPARATION—Vegetables are excellent sources of vitamins and minerals. Protect your investment of money and time spent in wise selection and storage by proper and careful preparation. Follow the methods given in How to Cook Vegetables and in recipes.

Leave edible peel on vegetables or use vegetable parer or sharp knife to keep parings thin. Many vitamins and minerals hide just under the peel—do not heedlessly throw them away. Cook whole beets without paring to retain red color.

Since the useable minerals and many vitamins in vegetables readily dissolve in water, DO NOT DISCARD COOKING LIQUID if any remains.

Clean Spinach—Cut off and discard tough stems, roots and bruised or wilted leaves. Wash leaves thoroughly by lifting up and down several times in a large amount of cold water, changing water as necessary. Lift leaves out of water each time before pouring off water. When free from sand and gritty material, transfer to a large, heavy saucepan.

Soak cauliflower, broccoli, artichokes and Brussels sprouts in salted water 20 to 30 min. before they are cooked to remove small insects and dust.

How to Cook Vegetables

To prepare taste-tempting vegetables and to retain their abundant minerals and vitamins, cook them carefully and quickly. DO NOT OVERCOOK, whether fresh, frozen or canned.

Accent—Add at beginning of cooking period, when vegetables are buttered or sauced and seasoned for service, or sprinkle over raw vegetables and greens.

BAKING—Bake such vegetables as potatoes, tomatoes and squash without removing skins. Pare vegetables for oven dishes; follow directions given with specific recipes.

BOILING—Have water boiling rapidly before adding vegetables. Add salt and Accent at beginning of cooking period (¼ teaspoon of each per cup of water). After adding vegetables, again bring water to boiling as quickly as possible. If more water is needed, add boiling water. Boil at a moderate rate and cook vegetables until just tender.

In general, cook vegetables in a covered pan in the smallest amount of water and in the shortest length of time possible. Exceptions for amounts of water or for covering are:

Potatoes—cooked in water to cover.

Green Vegetables (peas, green or lima beans)—loosely covered.

Spinach—partially covered pan with only the water which clings to leaves after final washing.

Asparagus—arranged in tied bundles with stalks standing in a small, deep pan containing at least 2 in. of boiling water—pan loosely covered.

Broccoli—tied, stalks (over ½ in. thick, split lengthwise) standing in a deep pan containing boiling water up to flowerets—pan loosely covered.

Strong-flavored Vegetables (cauliflower, mature cabbage and Brussels sprouts)—cooked loosely covered in a large amount of water. To restore color of red cabbage, add a small amount of vinegar at the end of the cooking period, just before draining.

A desirable boiled vegetable is free from excess water, retains its original color and is well seasoned. Pieces are uniform in size and attractive.

Canned Vegetables—Heat to boiling point in liquid from can.

Home-Canned Vegetables—Boil 10 min. (not required for tomatoes and sauerkraut).

Dried (dehydrated) Vegetables—Soak and cook as directed for specific recipes.

Frozen Vegetables—Do not thaw before cooking (thaw corn on cob and partially thaw spinach). Break frozen block apart with fork during cooking. Use as little boiling salted water as possible for cooking. Follow directions on package.

BROILING—Follow directions with specific recipes.

FRYING and DEEP-FRYING—Follow directions with specific recipes.

PANNING—Finely shred or slice vegetables. Cook slowly until just tender in a small amount of fat, in a covered, heavy pan. Occasionally move pieces with spoon to prevent sticking and burning.

STEAMING—Cooking in a pressure saucepan is a form of steaming. Follow directions given with saucepan as overcooking may occur in seconds.

Note: Some saucepans having tight-fitting covers may lend themselves to steaming vegetables in as little as 1 teaspoon water, no water, or in a small amount of butter, margarine or shortening.

Buttered Lima Beans

Set out a deep saucepan.

Shell, discarding pods, and rinse

2 lbs. green lima beans (about 1⅓ cups or ⅔ lb. shelled)

Cook (*page 149*) 20 to 30 min., or until just tender when pierced with a fork.

When beans are tender, drain, and blend in until melted

3 tablespoons butter or margarine

and a mixture of

½ teaspoon salt
½ teaspoon Accent
⅛ teaspoon pepper

Serve immediately. *4 or 5 servings*

Buttered Lima Beans, Corn-on-the-Cob and Raw Vegetable Relishes (page 166)

▲ Sweet-Sour Beets

(Harvard Beets)

Set out a 2-qt. saucepan having a tight-fitting cover.

Leaving on 1- to 2-in. stem and the root end (this helps beets retain red color), cut off leaves from

1 lb. (about 5) medium-size beets

Wash and cook (*page 149*) 30 to 45 min., or until just tender.

When beets are tender, drain if necessary and reserve liquid in a measuring cup. Set aside.

Plunge beets into running cold water. Peel off and discard skin, stems and root ends from beets. Dice or slice beets and set aside.

Mix together in the saucepan

2 tablespoons sugar
1 tablespoon cornstarch
½ teaspoon salt
¼ teaspoon Accent

Pour into reserve beet liquid

Cold water (enough to make ¾ cup liquid)

Stirring constantly, gradually add liquid to mixture in saucepan with

3 tablespoons vinegar

Stirring constantly, bring rapidly to boiling and cook 3 min. Add the beets and

2 tablespoons butter or margarine

Keeping mixture moving with a spoon, bring again to boiling; cover and simmer 8 to 10 min.

Serve immediately. *4 servings*

△ Beets in Orange Sauce

Follow ▲ Recipe. Decrease beet-water mixture to ½ cup. Substitute ⅓ cup **orange juice** for vinegar. Add ¼ teaspoon grated **orange peel** (*page 5*). Garnish with **hard-cooked eggs,** chopped.

French Fried Onions

French Fried Onions

Set out a deep saucepan or automatic deep-fryer (*page 7*) and heat fat to 365°F.

Meanwhile, clean (*page 6*) and cut into slices ¼ in. thick

3 medium-size (about ½ lb.) onions

Separate slices into rings and set aside.

Melt and set aside to cool

1 tablespoon butter or margarine

Sift together into a bowl and set aside

1¼ cups sifted flour
½ teaspoon salt
½ teaspoon Accent
⅛ teaspoon pepper

Beat until thick and piled softly

2 eggs

Blend in

¾ cup milk
1 teaspoon Worcestershire sauce

Blend in the butter or margarine. Make a well in center of dry ingredients; add liquid mixture all at once. Blend just until smooth.

Dip onion rings in batter with fork or slotted spoon to coat evenly. Deep-fry only as many at one time as will float uncrowded one layer deep in fat. Fry 2 to 3 min., or until golden brown. Turn onion rings with a fork as they rise to surface and several times during cooking. Drain over fat a few seconds before removing to absorbent paper. *About 6 servings*

▲ Braised Onions

Set out a shallow 2-qt. casserole having a cover.

Clean (*page 6*) and cut into crosswise halves

8 medium-size (about 1½ lbs.) onions

Prepare

1 cup quick meat broth (*page 7*)

Pour into the casserole. Place onions in liquid, cut-side down. Sprinkle with a mixture of

1 tablespoon sugar
½ teaspoon salt
¼ teaspoon Accent
Few grains pepper

Dot onions generously with

Butter or margarine

Cover and bake at 350°F 45 to 50 min., or until onions are tender. During baking, baste two or three times with liquid in casserole. Remove casserole from oven and sprinkle onions with a mixture of

½ cup (2 oz.) grated Cheddar cheese
⅓ cup fine, dry bread crumbs
½ teaspoon paprika

Return to oven and bake uncovered 8 to 10 min., or until crumbs are lightly browned.

6 servings

△ Braised Turnips

Follow ▲ Recipe. Substitute 2 to 2½ lbs. medium-size **turnips** for onions. Wash, pare and cut into ¼-in. slices. Double the amounts of seasonings. Arrange one half of turnip slices in the bouillon. Sprinkle with one half of seasoning mixture. Dot with **butter** or **margarine.** Repeat layering.

Cover and bake 40 to 45 min., or until turnips are tender. Complete as in ▲ Recipe.

Corn-on-the-Cob

(See color photo, inside back cover, and photo on page 150)

Set out a large saucepan.

Remove husks, corn silk and blemishes from
4 ears corn
If ears are large, cut into halves. Cook covered in boiling water to cover. (For mature corn, add ½ teaspoon **sugar** per qt. water.)

Boil corn at a moderate rate about 6 to 12 min., or until just tender.

Remove corn with fork or tongs onto platter. Serve hot with **salt, pepper, Accent** and lots of **butter** or **margarine.** *4 servings*

Note: To prepare corn-on-the-cob on an outdoor grill see OUTDOOR COOKING *(page 10)*.

Plantation Corn Pudding

Grease a 1½ qt. casserole. Heat water for boiling water bath *(page 6)*.

Scald *(page 7)*
1¾ cups milk
Add
1 tablespoon butter or margarine
While milk scalds, beat slightly
4 eggs
Blend eggs with
2 cups (1-lb. can) cream-style corn
2 tablespoons slivered pimiento
2 tablespoons finely chopped green pepper (page 6)
2 tablespoons grated onion
and a mixture of
1 teaspoon sugar
1 teaspoon salt
½ teaspoon Accent
¼ teaspoon pepper
Stirring vigorously, gradually add the milk to the corn mixture; pour into the casserole.

Bake in boiling water bath at 300°F 45 to 60 min., or until a silver knife comes out clean when inserted halfway between center and edge of casserole. *6 servings*

▲ Scalloped Corn

Butter a 1-qt. casserole.

Combine
2½ cups (No. 2 can) cream-style corn
½ cup milk
3 tablespoons melted butter or margarine
Thoroughly blend in
1 cup fine, dry bread or cracker crumbs
3 tablespoons finely chopped onion (page 6)
3 tablespoons finely chopped green pepper (page 6)
2 tablespoons brown sugar
and a mixture of
1 teaspoon salt
¼ teaspoon Accent
¼ teaspoon pepper
Turn into the casserole. Dot with
2 teaspoons butter or margarine
Bake corn at 350°F 30 min., or until lightly browned. *6 servings*

△ Corn-Tomato Scallop

Follow ▲ Recipe. Substitute **whole kernel corn** (No. 2 can, drained) for cream-style corn. Substitute 1¾ cups (one-half of No. 2½ can) **tomatoes,** cut in pieces, for milk.

Scalloped Eggplant

MRS. JESSIE JACK, MITCHELLVILLE, IOWA

Grease a 1-qt. casserole.

Prepare and set aside
3 hard-cooked eggs
Prepare and set aside
¾ cup garlic-buttered cracker crumbs (clean 1 clove garlic and cut into halves; add to 2 to 3 tablespoons melted butter or margarine and allow to stand until garlic flavor is absorbed; proceed as for buttered crumbs, *page 4*)
Meanwhile, wash, pare and cut into 1-in. cubes
1 medium-size (about 1 lb.) eggplant
Cook (*page 149*) about 7 min., or until just tender. If necessary, drain.

Prepare
1 cup (about 2 medium-size) coarsely chopped green pepper (*page 6*)
½ cup (about 1 medium-size) coarsely chopped onion (*page 6*)
Scald (*page 7*)
¾ cup milk
Add to scalded milk
2 tablespoons butter
Dice the hard-cooked eggs and gently toss them with the chopped green pepper, onion, eggplant, cracker crumbs and a mixture of
1½ teaspoons salt
¼ teaspoon pepper
¼ teaspoon Accent
Spoon mixture into the casserole.

Pour scalded milk over mixture. Sprinkle with
¼ cup (1 oz.) grated Cheddar cheese
Bake uncovered at 300°F about 55 min.
4 to 6 servings

Butter-Fried Mushrooms

Set out a large, heavy skillet.

Clean and slice (*page 6*)
1 lb. mushrooms
Set mushrooms aside.

Heat in the skillet over low heat
⅓ to ½ cup butter
Add the sliced mushrooms.

Cook slowly, carefully turning occasionally, until lightly browned and tender.

Season with
Salt
Pepper
Accent
Serve immediately. *6 servings*

Butter-Fried Onion Slices

Set out a large, heavy skillet.

Clean (*page 6*) and slice ¼ in. thick
6 medium-size onions
Heat in the skillet over low heat
¼ cup butter
Fry onion slices, one layer at a time, in the butter until lightly browned on both sides, turning only once with spatula or pancake turner to keep the slices from separating into rings. Season with
Salt
Pepper
Accent
Serve immediately. *4 to 6 servings*

Stuffed Artichokes Sicilian

Set out a 10-in. skillet having a tight-fitting cover.

With a sharp knife, cutting straight across, cut off 1 in. of the tops from

4 medium-size artichokes

Cut off stems about 1 in. from base and remove outside lower leaves. With scissors, clip off tips of leaves and discard. Soak (*page 149*) artichokes.

Meanwhile, mix together and set aside

⅔ cup (2 slices) fine, dry bread crumbs
1 clove garlic (*page 6*), thinly sliced
1 teaspoon grated Parmesan cheese
1 teaspoon chopped parsley
1 teaspoon salt
¾ teaspoon pepper
¼ teaspoon Accent

Rinse artichokes thoroughly in clear water and drain.

Spread leaves apart; place in each artichoke

3 slices garlic

Sprinkle crumb mixture between leaves and over top of artichokes. Sprinkle with

1 tablespoon chopped parsley

Place the artichokes upright in the skillet containing

2 cups water

Sprinkle artichokes with

2 tablespoons olive oil

Cover and cook about 30 min., or until a leaf can be easily pulled from artichoke.

To Eat Artichokes—Pull out leaves, one by one. Eat only the tender part of leaf by drawing it between teeth. Discard less tender tip. Continue with each leaf until choke or fuzzy part in center is reached. Remove choke with knife and fork and discard. Cut heart or base into pieces and eat with a fork. *4 servings*

▲ Asparagus Parmesan

Butter a 1½-qt. casserole or shallow baking dish.

Break off and discard lower parts of stalks as far down as they will snap from

1½ lbs. asparagus

Wash remaining portions of stalks thoroughly. If necessary, remove scales to dislodge any sand. Cook (*page 149*) 10 to 20 min., or until asparagus is just tender. (Or cook contents of two 10-oz. pkgs. frozen asparagus, *page 149*).

Melt in small saucepan and add to casserole

½ cup butter or margarine

Place cooked asparagus in the casserole and sprinkle with a mixture of

½ cup (about 2 oz.) grated Parmesan or Romano cheese
1 teaspoon salt
½ teaspoon pepper
½ teaspoon Accent

Bake at 450°F 5 to 10 min., or until cheese is melted. *6 servings*

△ Asparagus Hollandaise

Follow ▲ Recipe for cooking asparagus. Omit the cheese mixture and baking period. Serve cooked asparagus on a warm platter with **Hollandaise Sauce** (*page 182*).

▲ French-Style Green Beans in Mustard Sauce

Wash, break off ends and French (cut lengthwise into fine strips)

1½ lbs. (about 5 cups) green beans

Cook (*page 149*) 15 to 20 min., or until tender. (Or cook contents of two 10-oz. pkgs. frozen French-style green beans, *page 149*).

While beans are cooking, prepare

Creamy Mustard Sauce (*page 183*)

When beans are tender, drain. Put beans into hot serving dish. Pour sauce over beans and serve immediately. *About 6 servings*

⚠ French-Style Green Beans and Onions

Follow ▲ Recipe, omitting Mustard Sauce. Clean (*page 6*) 8 to 12 small whole **onions.** Cook (*page 149*) 15 to 25 min., or until just tender. Drain and combine with cooked green beans. Pour over vegetables a mixture of ¼ cup melted **butter** or **margarine,** ½ teaspoon **salt,** ¼ teaspoon **pepper** and ¼ teaspoon **Accent.** Toss gently. Heat slowly 5 min., or until thoroughly heated.

⚠ French-Style Green Beans with Almonds

Follow ▲ Recipe, omitting Mustard Sauce. Coarsely chop ¼ cup (about 1½ oz.) toasted, blanched **almonds** (*page 5*). Add almonds to cooked green beans with a mixture of 3 tablespoons melted **butter** or **margarine,** ½ teaspoon **salt,** ¼ teaspoon **Accent,** ¼ teaspoon **lemon juice** and ¼ teaspoon **rosemary** or **savory.** Toss gently.

Green Beans Supreme

Set out a medium-size saucepan and a shallow 1-qt. baking dish.

Shred and set aside

4 oz. process cheese food (about 1 cup, shredded)

Wash, break off ends and French (cut lengthwise into fine strips)

1 lb. (about 3 cups) green beans

Cook (*page 149*) 15 to 20 min., or until just tender. (Or cook contents of two 10-oz. pkgs. frozen French-style green beans, *page 149*.)

Heat in the saucepan over low heat

2 tablespoons butter or margarine

Green Beans Supreme

Add and cook over medium heat, occasionally moving and turning with a spoon

2 tablespoons minced onion

Cook until onion is transparent. Remove from heat and blend in a mixture of

1 tablespoon flour
½ teaspoon salt
½ teaspoon paprika
¼ teaspoon dry mustard
¼ teaspoon Accent

and

½ teaspoon Worcestershire sauce

Heat until mixture bubbles. Remove from heat. Add gradually, stirring constantly

1 cup undiluted evaporated milk

Return to heat and bring rapidly to boiling, stirring constantly; cook 1 to 2 min. longer.

When beans are tender, drain if necessary, and add to sauce. Toss mixture gently with a spoon until blended. Spoon into the baking dish. Sprinkle with the shredded cheese food and

2 tablespoons fine, dry bread crumbs

Set temperature control of range at Broil. Place baking dish on broiler rack. Place in broiler with the top of the mixture 2 to 3 in. from source of heat.

Broil 5 min., or until bread crumbs are lightly browned and cheese is melted.

4 to 6 servings

▲ French Fried Potatoes

(*See color photo, inside back cover, right-hand side*)

To keep last-minute dinner flurries down to a manageable size, prepare French Fries by Method 1. It speeds up the job by getting it partially done before serving time.

Method 1—Set out a deep saucepan or automatic deep-fryer (*page 7*) and heat fat to 300°F.

Meanwhile, wash and pare

6 medium-size (about 2 lbs.) potatoes

Cut potatoes with knife or fancy cutter. Trim off sides and ends to form large blocks. Cut lengthwise into about ⅜-in. slices; stack evenly. Cut lengthwise into sticks about ⅜-in. wide. Pat dry with absorbent paper.

Fry about 1 cup at a time in hot fat until potatoes are transparent but not browned. Remove from fat and drain on absorbent paper.

Just before serving, heat fat to 360°F. Return potatoes to fat, frying 1 cup at a time. Fry until crisp and golden brown.

Drain on absorbent paper.

Sprinkle with

Salt
Accent

(For variety substitute seasoned salt or garlic salt for salt.) Serve immediately or keep warm in 300°F oven. *6 servings*

Method 2—Heat fat to 360°F. Prepare potatoes as in Method 1 and deep-fry until tender and golden brown.

△ Lattice Potatoes

Follow ▲ Recipe, Method 2, for frying. Heat fat to 370°F. Wash and pare potatoes. For lattice effect, cut potatoes with a fancy fluted cutter into thin crosswise slices, turning potato each time to make lattice. Pat slices dry with absorbent paper. Deep-fry until potatoes are crisp and golden brown.

Guatemala Potatoes

AMELIE M. KINZER, VAN NUYS, CALIF.

Grease a shallow 1½-qt. casserole having a tight-fitting cover.

Set aside to drain, reserving liquid in a 2 cup measure, contents of

1 No. 2 can tomatoes (1 cup, drained)

Break tomatoes into pieces with a spoon.

Wash, pare and thinly slice

6 medium-size (about 2 lbs.) potatoes (about 4 cups, sliced)

Coat potato slices evenly by shaking them in a plastic bag in a mixture of

3 tablespoons flour
1½ teaspoons salt
½ teaspoon pepper
½ teaspoon Accent

Clean (*page 6*) and cut into thin slices

2 large onions

Carefully place one half of potato slices in even layers in baking dish. Add one half of the onion slices and one half of the tomatoes.

Repeat layers.

Top with

6 slices bacon

Pour 1½ cups of the reserved tomato liquid over the mixture.

Bake covered at 375°F 30 min. Remove cover and bake 35 min. longer, or until potatoes are tender when pierced with a fork and bacon is cooked. *6 servings*

▲ Hashed Brown Potatoes

Set out a large, heavy skillet.

Leftover cooked potatoes may be used. Or—Wash and cook (*page 149*)

6 or 7 medium-size (about 2 lbs.) potatoes

Cook about 25 to 35 min., or until potatoes are tender when pierced with a fork.

Drain potatoes. To dry them, shake pan over

low heat. Peel and dice or chop potatoes and put into a bowl. Add

⅓ cup milk

and a mixture of

1 teaspoon salt
¼ teaspoon Accent
¼ teaspoon paprika

Mix gently.

Heat in the skillet

3 to 4 tablespoons fat

Turn potatoes into the skillet, pressing down to form an even layer. Cook slowly without stirring until crusty and browned on under side. Turn with a pancake turner or spatula, and brown other side. (Add more fat to skillet if necessary.) Quickly turn potatoes onto a warm platter. *6 servings*

△ O'Brien Potatoes

Follow ▲ Recipe for cooking potatoes. Dice or chop. Heat fat in skillet and add ¼ cup chopped **onion,** 2 tablespoons minced **pimiento** and 2 tablespoons minced **green pepper.** Add potatoes, milk and seasonings. Cook, occasionally moving and turning with a spoon, until potatoes are lightly browned.

△ Skillet Browned Potatoes

Follow ▲ Recipe; omit milk. Cook 12 small, whole potatoes. Leave whole. Heat fat in skillet. Pan-fry potatoes, turning them in hot fat until lightly browned and crisp. After frying, sprinkle potatoes with seasonings given in ▲ Recipe.

△ Fried Sweet Potatoes

Follow ▲ Recipe; use **sweet potatoes.** Peel cooked potatoes and slice evenly into all crosswise or all lengthwise slices. Omit milk and seasonings. Heat fat, add potatoes and season with 1 teaspoon **salt** and 1 tablespoon **brown sugar.** Pan-fry over medium heat, turning pieces frequently and carefully until browned.

Jungle-"Fried" Potatoes

MRS. JOE KNOWLES, BELLEVILLE, ILL.

Set out a 10-in. skillet having a tight-fitting cover.

Wash and pare

3 medium-size (about 1 lb.) potatoes

With a sharp knife or vegetable slicer, cut into thin uniform crosswise slices.

Clean (*page 6*) and chop

1 large onion (about ¾ cup, chopped)

Put potato slices and onion in the skillet.

Add

Water (enough to cover potato slices)

Cover skillet and cook over medium heat about 7 min., or until potatoes are just tender when pierced with a fork. Remove cover and add

¼ teaspoon salt
¼ teaspoon pepper
⅛ teaspoon Accent

Cook uncovered over low heat, turning occasionally, about 5 min., or until the water is evaporated.

Serve immediately. *3 or 4 servings*

Parsley New Potatoes

Wash
24 (about 3 lbs.) small new potatoes
Cook (*page 149*) about 20 min., or until potatoes are tender when pierced with a fork.

Meanwhile, melt in a small saucepan
½ cup butter or margarine
Stir in
¼ cup finely chopped parsley
1 teaspoon salt
½ teaspoon Accent
¼ teaspoon pepper
Keep mixture warm.

Drain potatoes. To dry potatoes, shake pan over low heat. Peel potatoes immediately.

Place potatoes in warm serving dish. Pour parsley butter over potatoes and turn them to coat well.

Serve immediately. *6 to 8 servings*

Spud'n-Cheese Puffs

FAY KESSINGER, ROACHDALE, IND.

Lightly butter a baking sheet.

Wash, pare and cook (*page 149*)
4 medium-size (about 1⅓ lbs.) potatoes
Cook about 25 to 35 min., or until potatoes are tender when pierced with a fork. Drain.

While potatoes are cooking, grate and set aside
4 oz. (about 1 cup) grated sharp Cheddar cheese

To dry potatoes, shake pan over low heat. To heat potato masher, food mill or ricer, and a mixing bowl, scald them with boiling water.

Mash or rice potatoes thoroughly. Whip in until potatoes are fluffy
¼ cup butter or margarine
½ cup milk or cream (added gradually)
and a mixture of
2 teaspoons baking powder
½ teaspoon salt
¼ teaspoon pepper
¼ teaspoon Accent
Whip into potatoes the grated cheese and
1 teaspoon finely chopped onion
Shape mixture into balls or patties, using ¼ cup mixture for each. Carefully roll potato balls or patties in
1½ cups finely crushed corn flakes
Place on the baking sheet.

Bake at 400°F 20 min., or until heated thoroughly and browned. *6 servings*

▲ Whipped Potatoes

Wash, pare and cook (*page 149*)
6 medium-size (about 2 lbs.) potatoes
Cook about 25 to 35 min., or until tender when pierced with a fork. Drain.

To dry potatoes, shake pan over low heat. To heat potato masher, food mill or ricer and a mixing bowl, scald them with boiling water.

Mash or rice potatoes thoroughly. Whip in until potatoes are fluffy
3 tablespoons butter or margarine
⅓ to ½ cup hot milk or cream (added gradually)
and a mixture of
1 teaspoon salt
¼ teaspoon Accent
⅛ teaspoon white pepper
Whip potatoes until light and fluffy. If necessary, keep potatoes over hot water and cover with folded towel until ready to serve.

About 4 cups Whipped Potatoes

Dinner on a Plank—Duchess Potatoes, broiled ground meat, onions and tomatoes

△ Duchess Potatoes

Follow ▲ Recipe. Beat in 2 **egg yolks** (or 1 whole egg for softer mixture) after addition of hot milk. Spoon potatoes into small mounds on greased baking sheet or force through a pastry bag and a No. 7 star tube into spiral-shaped servings. Brush with melted **butter.** Bake at 450°F about 10 min., or until browned. With spatula, carefully remove potatoes from baking sheet.

Note: Duchess Potatoes are used for planked meals. Force potatoes through pastry bag and No. 7 star tube onto seasoned plank around meat or fish and vegetables forming a spiral-shaped border. Cover exposed plank as completely as possible. Brush with melted butter; bake or broil as directed in recipes until potatoes are lightly browned.

Scalloped Sweet Potatoes

WANDA HUFFMAN, EVANS, COLO.

Grease a 1½-qt. casserole having a tight-fitting cover.

Wash

4 medium-size (about 1⅓ lbs.) sweet potatoes

Cook covered in boiling salted water to cover for 10 min. Drain. To dry potatoes, shake pan over low heat. Peel. With a sharp knife, cut into crosswise slices ⅛ in. thick. Set aside.

Mix together

¼ cup sugar
2 tablespoons grated orange peel (*page 5*)
½ teaspoon salt

Wash, cut away peel and cut into crosswise slices ¼ in. thick

2 large oranges

Set out

¼ cup butter

Arrange one half of the potato slices in an even layer in the casserole. Cover with one half of the orange slices and sprinkle with one half of the sugar mixture. Dot with 2 tablespoons of the butter. Repeat layering.

Pour over casserole

⅔ cup orange juice

Bake covered at 375°F about 40 min., or until potatoes are tender when pierced with a fork.

4 or 5 servings

Candied Sweet Potatoes

Set out a large, heavy skillet and a large saucepan having a cover.

Wash

6 medium-size (about 2 lbs.) sweet potatoes or yams

Cook (*page 149*) 25 to 35 min., or until potatoes are just tender when pierced with a fork. Drain. To dry potatoes, shake pan over low heat. Peel potatoes and set aside.

Heat in the skillet over low heat

⅓ cup butter or margarine

Blend in

⅓ cup firmly packed brown sugar
¼ teaspoon salt

Heat until mixture bubbles. Add potatoes. Cook over medium heat, turning potatoes several times, about 20 min., or until potatoes are well-glazed and thoroughly heated.

4 to 6 servings

Tomato Broil

Mix and set aside

2 tablespoons fine cracker crumbs
1 teaspoon sugar
¼ teaspoon salt
¼ teaspoon Accent
⅛ teaspoon pepper

Rinse, cut away stem ends from and cut into halves crosswise

2 large tomatoes

Brush with

Melted butter or margarine

Sprinkle with the crumb mixture. Arrange tomato halves on broiler rack.

Set temperature control of range at Broil. Place broiler rack under broiler with top of tomatoes about 3 in. from source of heat. Broil 10 min., or until crumbs are lightly browned. *4 servings*

Scalloped Tomatoes

Grease a 1½-qt. casserole.

Toast until very crisp and cut into cubes

3 slices bread

Meanwhile, clean (*page 6*) and chop

2 medium-size (about ½ lb.) onions (about 1 cup, chopped)

Drain and break into pieces with a spoon, the contents of

1 No. 2½ can tomatoes (about 2 cups, drained)

Mix in the casserole one half of the chopped onion, the tomatoes and

½ cup cheese-cracker crumbs

and a mixture of

1½ teaspoons sugar
½ teaspoon Accent
½ teaspoon salt

Cover with the remaining chopped onion.

Spoon over mixture

¾ cup thick sour cream

Toss bread cubes over cream.

Lightly brush bread cubes with

Melted butter or margarine

Bake at 325°F 20 min., or until mixture is thoroughly heated.

Serve in sauce dishes. *6 servings*

Vegetable Medley

ESTEL E. COX, JACKSONVILLE, ORE.

Set out a 10-in. skillet having a tight-fitting cover.

Remove and discard wilted outer leaves, rinse, cut into quarters (discarding core) and coarsely shred

1 small head (about ¾ lb.) cabbage (about 3 cups, shredded)

Set aside.

Clean (*page 6*) and cut crosswise into ¼-in. slices enough celery to yield

1 cup (about 4 stalks) sliced celery

Clean (*page 6*) and coarsely chop enough green pepper to yield

1 cup (about 2 medium-size) chopped green pepper

Clean (*page 6*) and cut into thin slices

1 medium-size onion

Heat in the skillet over medium heat

1 tablespoon shortening

Add the cabbage, celery, green pepper and onion to the melted shortening.

Season with a mixture of

1 teaspoon salt
½ teaspoon Accent
¼ teaspoon pepper

Cover and cook over medium heat. Occasionally moving and turning mixture with a spoon, cook about 7 min. or until vegetables are nearly tender but still slightly crisp.

4 servings

Wild Rice with Mushrooms

Set out a medium-size skillet.

Bring to boiling in a deep saucepan

3 cups water
1 teaspoon salt
½ teaspoon Accent

Meanwhile, wash in a colander or sieve

1 cup wild rice

Add rice gradually to water so that boiling will not stop. Boil rapidly, covered, 30 to 40 min., or until a kernel of rice is entirely tender when pressed between fingers. Drain rice in a colander or sieve.

If necessary to keep rice warm, place colander over hot water and cover with a folded towel.

While rice is cooking, clean and slice

½ lb. mushrooms (*page 6*)

Heat in the skillet

¼ cup butter

Add mushrooms with

2 tablespoons finely chopped onion

Cook slowly, occasionally turning and moving gently with a spoon, until mushrooms are lightly browned. Remove from heat and reserve about ¼ cup mushrooms for garnish. Combine remaining mushrooms, onion, wild rice and

⅓ cup butter, melted

Toss gently until mushrooms and butter are evenly distributed throughout rice. Turn hot mixture into a warm serving dish and garnish with reserved mushrooms. *6 to 8 servings*

Wild Rice with Mushrooms

Broiled Bananas

(*See photo on page 99*)

Bananas are versatile, and today's taste-wise homemakers use them as vegetables.

Peel

6 firm bananas having all-yellow or slightly green-tipped peel

Arrange bananas on broiler rack. Brush generously with

Melted butter or margarine

Sprinkle with

Few grains salt

Set temperature control of range at Broil. Place in broiler with top of bananas 3 in. from source of heat for 5 min., or until bananas are lightly browned and tender when pierced with a fork.

Carefully transfer to a warm serving plate; garnish with sprigs of parsley. *6 servings*

Squash Supreme

MRS. STANLEY CARLSON
MARSHALL, MINN.

An original and very interesting presentation of one of the hardiest and most delightful members of the squash family.

Set out a 13x9½x2-in. baking dish.

Wash and cut into halves lengthwise
2 medium-size acorn squash
Remove seeds and fibers. Place cut-side down in baking dish. Pour in boiling water to ¼-in. depth in baking dish. Bake at 400°F 30 min.

Meanwhile, prepare and set aside
2 cups (about 8 stalks) finely chopped celery (*page 6*)
⅔ cup (about 3 small) finely chopped onion (*page 6*)
⅔ cup (about 2½ oz.) grated cheese
Heat in a skillet over low heat
¼ cup butter
Add the chopped onion and celery and cook over medium heat, occasionally moving and turning mixture with a spoon. Cook about 10 min., or until onion is transparent and celery is tender.

Meanwhile, dissolve
2 beef bouillon cubes
in
¼ cup hot water
Add to celery-onion mixture and blend well. Remove from heat and cool slightly. Add the grated cheese all at one time. Blend in, with a mixture of
1 teaspoon dry mustard
1 teaspoon paprika
1 teaspoon salt
½ teaspoon Accent
When squash has baked 30 min., remove baking dish from oven. Reduce temperature to 350°F. Turn squash and fill cavities with cheese mixture.

Return to oven and bake 25 to 30 min. longer, or until squash is tender when pierced with a fork. *4 servings*

Summer Squash with Dill

Set out a 3-qt. heavy saucepan having a tight-fitting cover.

Wash, trim off ends and cut into thin crosswise slices
2 lbs. summer squash
(Choose young, tender squash; it is not usually necessary to pare them. Pare only if the outside seems tough.)

Put squash into the saucepan with
½ cup boiling water
2 teaspoons finely chopped fresh dill or ¼ teaspoon dill seeds
½ teaspoon salt
¼ teaspoon Accent
Cover saucepan and cook squash 15 to 20 min., or until just tender. Drain if necessary.

Mix together in top of double boiler
1 cup thick sour cream
1 tablespoon lemon juice
2 teaspoons sugar
½ teaspoon paprika
Cook over simmering water, stirring constantly, 3 to 5 min., or until sauce is thoroughly heated. Carefully mix sauce with the squash and serve immediately. *6 servings*

Zucchini Provençale

Set out a 3-qt. saucepan having a tight-fitting cover and a 2-qt. casserole.

Wash, trim off ends, cut crosswise into ⅛-in. slices and set aside
8 to 10 (2½ lbs.) small zucchini squash
Clean and slice (*page 6*)
¼ lb. mushrooms

Coarsely chop enough onion to yield

⅔ cup (about 3 small) coarsely chopped onion (*page 6*)

Heat in the saucepan

3 tablespoons olive oil

Add zucchini, mushrooms and onion. Cover saucepan and cook zucchini mixture over low heat 10 to 15 min., or until tender, occasionally turning mixture and moving it gently with a spoon.

Meanwhile, set out

⅔ cup (about 3 oz.) grated Parmesan cheese

Remove zucchini mixture from heat; lightly mix in about one half of the grated cheese with a fork. Spoon in a mixture of

1½ cups (2 6-oz. cans) tomato paste
1 clove garlic (*page 6*), minced; or crushed in a garlic press
1 teaspoon salt
½ teaspoon Accent
⅛ teaspoon pepper

Blend lightly but thoroughly. Turn into the casserole. Sprinkle with the remaining cheese.

Bake at 350°F 20 to 30 min. *8 servings*

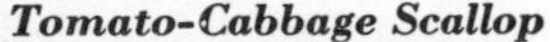

Tomato-Cabbage Scallop

Tomato-Cabbage Scallop

Grease 6 ramekins.

Crush finely

3 cups corn flakes

Mix in evenly and set aside

1 cup (4 oz.) grated Cheddar cheese

Remove and discard wilted outer leaves, rinse, cut into quarters (discarding core) and coarsely shred

1 1-lb. head cabbage (about 4 cups, shredded)

Cook (*page 149*) over medium heat about 7 min., or until cabbage is tender; drain well.

Heat in a large saucepan over low heat

3 tablespoons butter or margarine

Add and cook over medium heat, occasionally moving and turning with a spoon

½ cup (about 1 medium-size) chopped onion (*page 6*)

Cook until onion is transparent. Blend in a mixture of

3 tablespoons flour
1 teaspoon salt
½ teaspoon Accent
⅛ teaspoon pepper

Heat until mixture bubbles. Remove saucepan from heat.

Add gradually, stirring in

2½ cups (No. 2 can) tomatoes, cut in pieces
⅓ cup chopped green pepper (*page 6*)

Cook rapidly, stirring constantly, until mixture thickens. Pour one third of tomato mixture into ramekins and add one half of cabbage; repeat. Cover with final one third of tomato mixture. Top with corn-flake mixture.

Bake at 375°F about 25 min. *6 servings*

The Good Salad

Salads bring to the table an ineffable touch of freshness. Composed of fresh or cooked foods, touched to piquancy by the right dressing and usually accompanied by a flash of green, they appeal to eye and taste and satisfy both. Today's salad recipes, conspicuously missing from cookbooks 50 years ago, show a riot of inventiveness in creating new combinations of ingredients for interesting and tantalizing results.

Salads are exciting! Look at the variety—salads made with fruits, vegetables and hearty protein foods; salads tossed, molded or frozen; salads for appetizer, main course, accompaniment or dessert.

Salads are worthwhile eating! Look at the appetite appeal of these health-giving foods—fresh vegetables and fruits chock-full of needed vitamins and minerals; protein-rich meat and fish, poultry, cheese and eggs; salad greens and raw vegetables for bulk, necessary for good digestion.

A salad is only as good as its makings so select the ingredients with care. Greens should be fresh, crisp and dry, vegetables garden-fresh, and fruits firm, fully ripe and free from blemish. When using canned products choose those of good quality and appearance. Meat, poultry, fish, cheese and eggs should be fresh. Use only the appetizing leftovers.

A salad should have a carefree look, not too carefully arranged to look overhandled nor too carelessly prepared to look untidy. A salad should fit the serving dish, not skimpily nor too full.

A salad is complemented by the dressing so suit it to the salad. Dressings should coat the greens, not drown them; they should accompany the salad, not hide it.

GELATIN TECHNIQUES—Recipes will remind you:

Lightly oil molds with a flavorless salad or cooking oil (not olive oil). Invert mold to drain excess oil.

Rinse molds with cold water when shiny coating of oil is not desirable; invert to drain.

Soften gelatin in liquid as specified in recipes.

Dissolve softened gelatin *completely* as recipe directs, over very hot water or in very hot liquid.

Chill gelatin mixtures in the refrigerator, stirring occasionally, or over ice and water, stirring frequently, until of desired consistency. Chill gelatin mixtures until slightly thicker than consistency of thick, unbeaten egg white before adding remainder of ingredients, such as chopped or whole foods which would sink to bottom of mold if the gelatin were not sufficiently thickened. When gelatin mixture is already thick because of ingredients or is not a clear mixture, chill until it begins to gel (gets slightly thicker) before adding chopped or whole foods.

Prevent separation of layered molds by chilling gelatin mixtures until slightly set (each mixture is of same consistency); layers should be of almost same consistency when turning one mixture onto another so that they will be fused when unmolded.

Unmold gelatin by running tip of knife around edge of mold to loosen and to permit air to get into mold. Invert mold onto chilled serving plate. If mold does not loosen because of air lock, wet a clean towel in hot water and wring almost dry. Wrap hot towel around mold for a few seconds only. If mold still does not loosen, repeat.

Beat whipping cream to a medium consistency (piles softly), not soft peaks, when it is to be blended with a gelatin mixture.

SALAD GREENS AND PREPARATION—The many kinds of greens star in the tossed salad and form the background of other salads. Select greens that are fresh, blemish-free and firm. In general, wash before storing, drain thoroughly and gently pat dry with a soft, clean towel or absorbent paper. Place in the refrigerator in vegetable drawers or plastic bags, or wrap tightly in waxed paper, moisture-vapor-proof material or aluminum foil to prevent greens from wilting, unless refrigerator maintains a comparatively high humidity.

Never soak greens when washing them. If necessary, crisp them by placing them for a short time in ice and water. Before using, remove every bit of moisture left from washing or crisping.

Lettuce—Discard bruised and wilted leaves; rinse; drain; dry. *Cups*—Remove core from head lettuce with sharp, pointed knife; let cold water run into core cavity to loosen leaves; drain; gently pull leaves from head; cut off heavy, coarse ends; pat dry. *Head* or *Iceberg*—firm, compact head of medium-green outside leaf, pale green heart. *Butterhead* or *Boston*—soft, lighter head of light green outside leaf, light yellow heart; not as crisp as iceberg. *Romaine* or *Cos*—green elongated head with coarser leaf and stronger flavor than iceberg. *Bibb* or *Limestone*—head similar to Boston in size and shape; deep green leaves with delicate flavor. *Leaf*—many varieties grown commercially and in the home garden; leafy bunches of curly-edged leaves.

Cabbage—Store in cool place without washing. Discard bruised and wilted outside leaves, rinse, cut into quarters and remove core; chop or shred as directed in recipes. *Early* or *new*—pointed heads. *Danish-type*—staple winter cabbage; compact head. *Savoy*—round head of yellowish, crimped leaves. *Celery* or *Chinese*—long, oval-shaped head of pale green to white leaves; characteristics of romaine and cabbage. *Red*—very tight head of purple leaves.

Endive—Discard bruised and wilted leaves; rinse; drain; dry. *Curly endive* (often called chicory)—bunchy head with narrow, ragged-edged curly leaves; dark green outside, pale yellow heart; pleasant bitter taste. *Broad-leaf endive* (often called escarole)—bunchy head of broad leaves that do not curl at tips; dark green outer leaves, pale yellow heart; not as bitter as curly endive. *French endive* (Witloof chicory)—thin, elongated stalk usually bleached white while growing.

Kale—Curly-leafed green of cabbage family; dark green; may have slightly browned edges caused by cold weather in growing season. Trim off tough stems and bruised or wilted leaves; wash; drain; dry.

Parsley—Discard coarse stems and bruised leaves; wash gently but thoroughly in cold water; drain and shake off excess water; pat dry. Store in tightly covered jar or plastic bag in refrigerator.

Spinach—Discard tough stems, roots and bruised or wilted leaves. Wash leaves thoroughly by lifting up and down several times in a large amount of cold water. Lift leaves out of water each time before pouring off water; repeat in clean water until all sand and grit are removed. Drain; pat dry.

Water Cress—See PARSLEY. Water cress also may be stored before it is washed. Stand a tied bunch in a jar or bowl holding enough cold water to reach about halfway up stems. Cover and store in refrigerator. When using, snip off amount needed, rinse, drain and shake off excess water. Or store cleaned water cress in a plastic bag in refrigerator.

Other Greens—*Field salad*—spoon-shaped leaves; *finocchio*—anise-flavored stalk (like celery); *Swiss chard*—use tops only (like beet greens);—*beet, dandelion, mustard, turnip greens*—use tops only.

SALAD DRESSINGS—A twist of the wrist and a turn or two of the imagination—endless variations are possible from the basic French, mayonnaise and cooked dressings. Others are the sweet or sour cream, cream or cottage cheese and yogurt dressings and the bacon-vinegar type for wilted greens.

Mayonnaise has caused many a tear when it has broken or separated because the oil was added too rapidly at the beginning. The problem is to re-form (re-emulsify) the mayonnaise; the solution is to gradually add the mayonnaise, beating constantly, to 1 egg yolk, 1 tablespoon cold water, small quantity of vinegar or small portion of good mayonnaise. Mayonnaise will separate if frozen or kept in the coldest part of the refrigerator.

French dressings need to be shaken before using to mix thoroughly and re-form the emulsion.

Salad dressings should be stored covered in a cool place or in the refrigerator.

Raw Vegetable Relishes

(*See photo on page 150*)

Use raw vegetables for colorful, easy-to-prepare relishes. Select only those that are in prime condition—crisp, fresh, preferably young and tender. Clean them thoroughly; with a sharp knife trim ends, where necessary, and cut the vegetables into varied shapes as suggested. Chill thoroughly in ice and water or in refrigerator before serving. Sprinkle lightly with Accent.

Carrot Curls—Cut tender cleaned carrots into halves lengthwise. Using a vegetable parer, shave into paper-thin strips. Curl around finger. Fasten with wooden pick and chill in ice and water until curled. Drain and remove pick before serving.

Carrot Sticks—Cut tender cleaned carrots into narrow strips about 3 in. long. Chill in the refrigerator.

Cauliflowerets—Remove outside leaves and stalk from cauliflower head. Separate cauliflower into small flowerets. Let stand in cold salted water 20 to 30 min. to remove any dust or small insects which settle in the cauliflower. Drain and chill in the refrigerator.

Double Celery Curls—Cut tender cleaned celery into 2½- to 3-in. lengths. Slit each into narrow parallel strips from either end almost to center. Chill in ice and water until curled. Drain before serving.

Fluted Cucumber Slices—Draw tines of a fork lengthwise over entire surface of rinsed cucumbers. Cut into thin slices.

Green Pepper Strips—Rinse whole green peppers and cut into halves lengthwise. Carefully remove all white fiber and seeds; slice lengthwise into strips. For rings, slice cleaned whole green peppers crosswise.

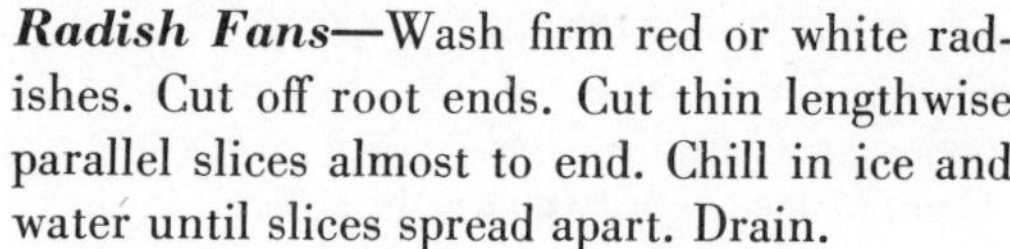

Radish Fans—Wash firm red or white radishes. Cut off root ends. Cut thin lengthwise parallel slices almost to end. Chill in ice and water until slices spread apart. Drain.

Radish Roses—Wash firm red radishes. Cut off root ends. On each, leave a bit of stem and a fresh leaf or two for garnish. With a sharp knife, mark petals. Pare each petal thinly from tip almost to stem. Chill in ice and water until petals spread apart. Drain before serving.

Scallions (green onions)—Cut off roots and trim green tops to 2 to 3 in., discarding any wilted or bruised parts. Peel and rinse.

Tomato Wedges—Rinse firm tomatoes and put into boiling water about ½ min., or until skin loosens. Peel, cut out stem ends and chill. Place chilled tomato on flat surface and cut lengthwise into six or eight wedges.

Wilted Lettuce

Rinse, pat dry and separate into leaves
1 large head lettuce
Place in a large bowl and cover. Set aside in refrigerator.

Dice and panbroil (*page 87*), reserving fat
6 slices bacon
Set bacon aside.

Put into the skillet ¼ cup of the reserved bacon fat and
½ cup vinegar
¼ cup water
3 tablespoons sugar
½ teaspoon salt
¼ teaspoon Accent
Heat mixture to boiling, stirring well. Stir in the bacon. Immediately pour vinegar mixture over the lettuce and toss lightly to thoroughly coat lettuce leaves.

Serve at once. *About 6 servings*

Caesar Salad

Set out a large salad bowl.

Combine

¼ cup salad or olive oil
¼ cup lemon juice
¼ teaspoon Worcestershire sauce
1 clove garlic (*page 6*), cut in halves

Chill in refrigerator 1 hr.

Wash, discarding bruised leaves, and thoroughly dry (use as much of each green as desired)

Curly endive
Lettuce
Romaine
Water cress

Tear enough greens into bite-size pieces to yield about 2 qts. Put into large plastic bag or vegetable freshener. Place in refrigerator to chill at least 1 hr.

When the dressing is chilled, remove from refrigerator and remove and reserve garlic. Return dressing to refrigerator.

Heat over low heat in a large skillet

2 tablespoons salad or olive oil

Add the clove of garlic from the dressing and

1 clove garlic, cut in halves

Meanwhile, stack and, if desired, trim crusts from

2 slices toasted bread

Cut bread into ½-in. cubes. Add to skillet and move gently with a spoon over medium heat until all sides of cubes are well coated and browned. Remove from heat.

Rub the salad bowl with

1 clove garlic, cut in halves

Remove salad greens from refrigerator and put into bowl. Sprinkle over greens a mixture of

¾ cup grated Parmesan cheese
½ teaspoon dry mustard
½ teaspoon salt
½ teaspoon Accent
¼ teaspoon pepper

Shake the chilled salad dressing and pour over the greens.

Caesar Salad

Break into a small bowl

1 egg

Add to the seasoned greens. Gently turn and toss salad until greens are well coated with dressing and no trace of egg remains. Add the croutons and toss lightly to mix thoroughly. Top with

Anchovy fillets (about 12 to 15)

Serve at once. *6 to 8 servings*

Kidney Bean Salad

Prepare and dice

4 hard-cooked eggs

Meanwhile, drain contents of

1 No. 2 can kidney beans (about 2 cups, drained)

Put beans into a bowl. Add the eggs and toss lightly with

⅓ cup coarsely chopped sweet pickle
¼ cup finely chopped onion
3 tablespoons sweet pickle juice
¼ teaspoon Accent

Blend together

½ cup Mayonnaise (*page 177*)
1 tablespoon sweet pickle liquid

Turn dressing over salad mixture and toss lightly to coat vegetables. Chill in refrigerator until ready to serve.

Serve in crisp lettuce cups. *About 4 servings*

Hot Potato Salad

△ Garden Potato Salad

Follow ▲ Recipe; increase potatoes to 6. Prepare 2 **hard-cooked eggs.** Dice the eggs and add to potatoes. Decrease celery to ½ cup and add ½ cup diced, pared **cucumber** and ¼ cup chopped **onion.** Mix with potatoes and eggs. Add and blend until vegetables are well coated ¼ cup **French Dressing** (*page 176*). Omit shrimp, olives, pickle relish and ketchup. Decrease total amount of Mayonnaise to ¾ cup and blend in with potato mixture shortly before serving. To serve, sprinkle with **paprika.**

▲ Louisiana Potato Salad

MRS. HARVEY SPARKS, KENT, WASH.

Wash and cook (*page 149*) 20 to 30 min.

4 medium-size (about 1⅓ lbs.) potatoes

Drain potatoes. To dry potatoes, shake pan over low heat. Set aside to cool.

Peel potatoes; cut into cubes and toss with

1 cup chopped celery (*page 6*)
¼ cup chopped green pepper (*page 6*)
½ cup Mayonnaise (*page 177*)

and a mixture of

1½ teaspoons salt
½ teaspoon Accent
⅛ teaspoon pepper

Cover and set aside in refrigerator to chill.

Drain, remove black vein, coarsely chop and chill in refrigerator contents of

2 5-oz. cans shrimp (about 1½ cups, drained)

(Or prepare 1 lb. fresh shrimp with shells, see Cooked Shrimp, *page 126*.)

Shortly before serving, cut into thin slices

6 stuffed olives

Mix together

½ cup Mayonnaise
2 tablespoons sweet pickle relish
2 tablespoons ketchup

Gently blend potato mixture, shrimp, olives and dressing together, tossing lightly to coat vegetables and shrimp. *4 to 6 servings*

Hot Potato Salad

Wash and cook (*page 149*) 20 to 30 min.

6 medium-size (about 2 lbs.) potatoes

Drain potatoes. To dry potatoes, shake pan over low heat. Peel potatoes, cut into ¼-in. slices, put in a bowl and toss lightly with

1 cup (about 2 medium-size) finely chopped onion (*page 6*)
3 tablespoons finely chopped parsley

and a mixture of

1½ teaspoons Accent
1¼ teaspoons salt
¼ teaspoon pepper

Set aside.

Combine in a small saucepan and heat to boiling

⅔ cup vinegar
⅓ cup water
1½ teaspoons sugar

Beat slightly

1 egg

Continue beating while gradually adding the vinegar mixture. Add gradually, while beating constantly

⅓ cup salad oil

Pour dressing over potato mixture and toss lightly to coat evenly. Turn salad into a large skillet and put over low heat for 10 to 15 min., or until potatoes are heated. Keep mixture moving gently with spoon. Transfer to warm serving dish and garnish. *About 6 servings*

▲ Creamy Cole Slaw

Put a large bowl into refrigerator to chill.

Blend together thoroughly

½ cup Mayonnaise (*page 177*)
¼ cup thick sour cream
1 tablespoon lemon juice

and a mixture of

2 teaspoons celery seed
1 teaspoon sugar
¼ teaspoon salt
⅛ teaspoon Accent
Few grains pepper

Place in refrigerator to chill.

Wash and finely shred or chop

¾ lb. cabbage (about 3 cups, shredded)

Put cabbage into the bowl, cover and place in refrigerator to chill.

Shortly before serving time, remove cabbage from refrigerator and pour over enough chilled dressing to moisten. Toss lightly to blend.

Wash, quarter, core and thinly slice

3 apples

Gently toss apple slices with the cabbage. Add more dressing if desired. *About 6 servings*

△ Pineapple Cole Slaw

Follow ▲ Recipe. Omit celery seed. Substitute drained contents of 1 9-oz. can **pineapple tidbits** (about ⅔ cup drained) for apples.

Penny Salad

CLAUDE E. METZ, MORENCI, MICH.

An economy salad with a luxury flavor.

Rinse, shred and put into a large bowl

1 lb. cabbage (about 4 cups, shredded)

Cover and place in refrigerator to chill.

Blend together and set in refrigerator to chill

¾ cup Mayonnaise (*page 177*)
¼ cup sugar
2 tablespoons vinegar
¼ teaspoon salt
¼ teaspoon Accent
Few grains pepper

Coarsely chop and set aside

1 cup (about 5 oz.) unsalted peanuts, without skins

Shortly before serving, remove cabbage from refrigerator. Pour the chilled dressing over the cabbage. Toss lightly until cabbage is well coated. Mix in the nuts and serve immediately. *About 8 servings*

Red Cabbage-Almond Slaw

Wash and finely shred or chop

¾ lb. red cabbage (about 3 cups, shredded)

Put cabbage into a bowl, cover and place in refrigerator to chill.

Prepare and set aside

½ to 1 cup (about 3 to 5 oz.) whole, toasted, blanched almonds (*page 5*) or coarsely chopped toasted almonds

Drain thoroughly, reserving sirup, contents of

1 9-oz. can pineapple tidbits (about ⅔ cup, drained)

Blend together 1 to 2 tablespoons of the reserved pineapple sirup and

⅓ to ½ cup Cooked Salad Dressing (*page 177*)

Place in refrigerator to chill.

Shortly before serving time, remove cabbage from refrigerator and mix lightly with the almonds and drained pineapple tidbits. Pour over cabbage mixture enough chilled dressing to moisten. Toss lightly to blend. Add more dressing if desired. *About 6 servings*

Tuna Salad Mold

Tuna Salad Mold

Set out a 1-qt. mold (fish-shaped, if desired). Set out a large bowl.

Pour into a small bowl

½ cup cold water

Sprinkle evenly over cold water

2 tablespoons (2 env.) unflavored gelatin

Let stand 5 min. to soften.

Meanwhile, heat until very hot

1 cup quick chicken broth (*page 7*)

Add softened gelatin, stirring until dissolved.

Grate and set aside

2 oz. Cheddar cheese (about ½ cup, grated)

Put into the large bowl

1 cup Mayonnaise (*page 177*)

Add gelatin mixture gradually, stirring constantly. Thoroughly blend in the cheese and

2 tablespoons lemon juice
1 tablespoon minced onion
½ teaspoon Worcestershire sauce
½ teaspoon Accent
⅛ teaspoon salt
⅛ teaspoon pepper

Chill (*page 6*) until mixture begins to gel (gets slightly thicker).

Lightly oil the mold with salad or cooking oil (not olive oil). Set aside to drain.

Meanwhile, blanch (*page 5*), sliver, toast (*page 6*) and set aside

½ cup (about 3 oz.) almonds

Slice and set aside enough olives to yield

½ cup sliced stuffed olives

Drain and flake (*page 6*) contents of

1 7-oz. can tuna (about 1 cup, flaked)

Gently fold the slivered almonds, sliced olives and flaked tuna into the thickened gelatin mixture, reserving one slice of olive if using a fish-shaped mold. Turn mixture into mold. Chill in refrigerator until firm.

Unmold (*page 6*) onto a chilled serving plate. If mold is fish-shaped, place reserved olive slice on "head" of fish for the "eye". Garnish with crisp **lettuce leaves.** *About 8 servings*

Favorite Crab Meat Mold

MRS. WILLIAM HOWLAND
SOUTH DUXBURY, MASS.

Lightly oil a 1-qt. ring mold with salad or cooking oil (not olive oil). Set aside to drain.

Pour into a small cup or custard cup

¼ cup cold water

Sprinkle evenly over cold water

1 tablespoon (1 env.) unflavored gelatin

Let stand about 5 min. to soften.

Meanwhile, drain, remove and discard bony tissue and separate contents of

1 6½-oz. can crab meat (about 1 cup, drained)

Prepare and mix with the drained crab meat

½ cup chopped celery (*page 6*)
½ cup peeled, chopped cucumber
2 tablespoons minced parsley
2 tablespoons minced stuffed olives

Set crab meat mixture aside.

Put into a bowl

¾ cup Mayonnaise (*page 177*)

Dissolve gelatin completely by placing over very hot water. Stir the dissolved gelatin and add gradually, stirring constantly, to the Mayonnaise. Thoroughly blend in

1 tablespoon lemon juice

and a mixture of

½ teaspoon salt
½ teaspoon paprika
¼ teaspoon Accent

Blend into crab-meat mixture. Turn into the mold. Chill in refrigerator until firm.

Unmold (*page 6*) onto chilled serving plate. Serve with **mayonnaise.** *About 8 servings*

Red 'n' White Salad Mold

MRS. W. P. BRILL, WOODSTOCK, VA.

Lightly oil a 3-qt. mold with salad or cooking oil (not olive oil). Set aside to drain.

For Cranberry Layer—Pour into a small cup or custard cup

¼ cup cold water

Sprinkle evenly over cold water

1 tablespoon (1 env.) unflavored gelatin

Let stand about 5 min. to soften.

Blend together in a large bowl

4 cups (2 1-lb. cans) whole cranberry sauce
1 cup (1 9-oz. can) crushed pineapple
½ cup (about 2 oz.) chopped walnuts

Dissolve gelatin completely by placing over very hot water. When gelatin is dissolved, stir it and blend into cranberry mixture. Turn mixture into the prepared mold. Chill (*page 6*) until gelatin mixture is slightly set.

Red 'n' White Salad Mold

For Chicken Layer—Set out

2 cups cubed cooked chicken
1 cup finely chopped celery (*page 6*)
¼ cup finely chopped parsley

Pour into a small cup or custard cup

¼ cup cold water

Sprinkle evenly over the water

1 tablespoon (1 env.) unflavored gelatin

Let stand about 5 min. to soften.

Blend together until smooth

1 cup Mayonnaise (*page 177*)
½ cup undiluted evaporated milk
1 teaspoon Accent
½ teaspoon salt
⅛ teaspoon pepper

Dissolve gelatin completely by placing over very hot water. When gelatin is dissolved, stir it and blend into the mayonnaise mixture. Fold in (*page 6*) the chicken, celery and parsley.

When first layer in mold is of proper consistency, immediately turn chicken mixture onto first layer. (Both layers should be of almost same consistency to avoid separation of layers when unmolded.) Place in refrigerator and chill until firm.

Unmold (*page 6*) onto chilled serving plate. If desired, serve with additional **mayonnaise.**

About 12 servings

Southwestern Salad Bowl

Creamy avocado slices, juicy grapefruit sections and onion rings—mmmm! A perfect pick-up for days when the mercury soars. The citrus fancier may add slices of orange.

Set out a salad bowl.

Wash, discarding bruised leaves, and thoroughly dry (enough to line the salad bowl)

Bibb lettuce or leaf lettuce

With a sharp knife, cut away peel and white membrane from

1 large grapefruit

Remove sections by cutting on either side of dividing membranes; remove section by section, over a bowl to save the juice. Set aside.

Rinse, peel, cut into halves and remove and discard pit from

1 large avocado

Cut into slices and add to bowl containing the grapefruit juice. Toss avocado slices gently to cover with juice (this helps to prevent discoloring).

Arrange the slices of avocado alternately with grapefruit sections on the lettuce. Cover and place in refrigerator until ready to serve.

Just before serving, arrange over grapefruit and avocado sections

7 or 8 thin onion rings (thinly slice onion, *page 6*; separate into rings)

Serve with

French Dressing (*page 176*)

4 to 6 servings

Frozen Fruit Salad

Set refrigerator control at coldest operating temperature. Put a bowl and a rotary beater into refrigerator to chill. Set out a 1½-qt. mold, a large refrigerator tray or 3 1-pt. round freezer-type containers.

Coarsely chop and set aside

½ cup (about 2½ oz.) salted, toasted, blanched almonds (*page 5*)

Set aside to drain, reserving sirup, contents of

1 No. 2 can crushed pineapple (about 1½ cups, drained)

Cut into quarters and set aside to drain

½ cup maraschino cherries

(To avoid pink-tinted salad, drain thoroughly.)

Cut (*page 6*) into slivers and set aside

½ cup (about 3 oz.) pitted dates

Cut into eighths and set aside

24 (6 oz.) marshmallows

Combine in a bowl 3 tablespoons of the reserved pineapple sirup and

8 oz. cream cheese, softened

Beat until smooth and fluffy. Blend in

¼ cup mayonnaise

Gently mix in the pineapple, cherries, dates, almonds and marshmallows.

Using chilled bowl and beater, beat until cream is of medium consistency (piles softly)

1 cup chilled whipping cream

Gently fold (*page 6*) whipped cream into the fruit and cheese mixture. Turn into mold, tray or freezer-type containers and freeze (2 to 4 hrs.). *About 8 to 10 servings*

▲ Cider Salad

MRS. JOE A. GENGLER, LE MARS, IOWA

Lightly oil with salad or cooking oil (not olive oil) a 1-qt. fancy mold. Set aside to drain.

Pour into a small bowl
½ cup cold water
Sprinkle evenly over cold water
2 tablespoons (2 env.) unflavored gelatin
Let gelatin stand about 5 min. to soften.

Heat until very hot
2 cups apple cider
¼ teaspoon salt
Remove from heat and immediately add softened gelatin, stirring until gelatin is completely dissolved. Spoon a small amount of the gelatin mixture into mold. Chill in refrigerator until partially set. Cool remaining mixture; chill (*page 164*) until slightly thicker than consistency of thick, unbeaten egg white.

Just before gelatin is of desired consistency, prepare
2 cups (about 2 medium-size) diced apple (do not pare)
¼ cup (about 1 oz.) chopped walnuts
1 tablespoon finely chopped parsley
When gelatin is of desired consistency, blend in the apples, walnuts and parsley. Turn into the mold. Chill in refrigerator until firm.

Unmold (*page 164*) onto chilled serving plate. Garnish with
Curly endive

About 6 servings

△ Apple-Jack Salad

Follow ▲ Recipe. Decrease cider to 1¾ cups. Add ¼ cup **apple brandy** to gelatin after it has cooled but before chilling it.

Cider Salad

Sparkling Salad Mold

RUTH GOSERUD, ST. PAUL, MINN.

Set out a 1-qt. fancy mold.

Empty into a bowl contents of
1 pkg. lime-flavored gelatin
Add and stir until the gelatin is completely dissolved
1 cup very hot water
Blend in contents of
1 7-oz. bottle lemon-lime-flavored carbonated beverage
Chill (*page 164*) until slightly thicker than the consistency of thick, unbeaten egg white.

Meanwhile, lightly oil the mold with salad or cooking oil (not olive oil). Set aside to drain.

When gelatin has desired consistency, blend in
1 cup thick, sweetened applesauce
Turn mixture into mold. Chill until firm.

Unmold (*page 164*) onto chilled serving platter. Arrange around sides of mold
Galax leaves
Frosted grapes
Mint sprigs

About 6 servings

▲ Tomato Aspic

Lightly oil a 1-qt. ring mold with salad or cooking oil (not olive oil). Set aside to drain.

Pour into a saucepan

4 cups tomato juice

Add to tomato juice

⅓ cup chopped celery leaves
⅓ cup chopped onion
2½ tablespoons sugar
1¼ teaspoons salt
½ teaspoon Accent
½ bay leaf
3 peppercorns

Simmer, uncovered, 10 min.

Meanwhile, pour into a small bowl

½ cup cold water

Sprinkle evenly over cold water

2 tablespoons (2 env.) unflavored gelatin

Let stand about 5 min. to soften.

Remove tomato-juice mixture from the heat. Strain liquid into a large bowl. Immediately add the gelatin to tomato-juice mixture and stir until gelatin is completely dissolved.

Add and stir well

2½ tablespoons vinegar

Pour tomato-juice mixture into mold. Cool and place in refrigerator to chill until firm.

To serve, unmold (*page 164*) onto a chilled serving plate. *About 8 servings*

△ Low-Calorie Luncheon Platter

Follow ▲ Recipe. Substitute 6 individual ring molds for the 1-qt. mold. Pour ⅔ cup of the tomato-juice mixture into each mold. Chill in refrigerator until firm. Arrange 7 crisp **lettuce cups** on a large chilled salad platter. Unmold one aspic ring into each cup. Garnish each ring with **parsley.** Spoon **cottage cheese** into the remaining lettuce cup and sprinkle with chopped **chives.** Quarter 3 **hard-cooked eggs;** pile into center of platter.

Tomato Aspic with Tuna Salad

△ Tomato Aspic with Tuna Salad

Follow ▲ Recipe. Unmold the aspic ring onto a chilled plate. Surround ring with **leaf lettuce.** With a sharp knife, cut away peel and white membrane from 1 chilled **grapefruit.** Remove sections by cutting on either side of dividing membranes; remove section by section, over a small bowl to save the juice. Set sections aside. Rinse, peel, cut into halves and remove and discard pit from 1 chilled **avocado.** Cut avocado halves into crosswise slices. Brush with **grapefruit juice.** Arrange avocado slices and grapefruit sections around the aspic ring (see photo). Pile **Tuna Salad** (*page 175*) into center of ring and serve.

Curried Tuna-Tomato Salad

MRS. HUGH W. GLADDEN, DETROIT, MICH.

Set in refrigerator to chill

4 medium-size (about 1⅓ lbs.) tomatoes (for Tomato Flowers, Shells or slices)

Prepare

Curried Tuna Salad

While salad is chilling, prepare Tomato Flowers or Tomato Shells. Spoon tuna mixture onto center of flowers or fill shells with the tuna mixture. Or spoon tuna salad onto thick tomato slices. Serve on crisp greens.

For Curried Tuna Salad—Drain, flake (*page 6*) and set aside contents of

1 7-oz. can tuna (about 1 cup, flaked)

Blend together

¼ cup mayonnaise
½ teaspoon curry powder
½ teaspoon Accent

Prepare

1 cup (about 1 medium-size) chopped apple
½ cup diced celery (*page 6*)

Lightly toss the apple and celery with the mayonnaise mixture. Add the tuna. Mix gently and thoroughly. Chill in refrigerator.

For Tomato Flowers—Rinse and cut a slice from tops of the tomatoes. Start at top of tomato and cut through peel and pulp to center. Make 6 equally spaced cuts down to ½ in. from bottom. Pull pieces back to form petals.

For Tomato Shells—Rinse and cut a slice from tops of the chilled tomatoes. Remove pulp from tomatoes with a spoon. Invert the tomato shells and set aside to drain.

4 servings

▲ Salmon-Vegetable Salad

Drain, flake (*page 6*) and turn into a bowl the contents of

1 7¾-oz. can salmon (about 1 cup, flaked)

Prepare

½ cup grated carrot
⅓ cup chopped celery

Toss salmon and vegetables lightly with

⅔ to 1 cup cooked peas
¼ cup chopped sweet pickle
6 ripe olives, pitted and chopped

and a mixture of

½ teaspoon salt
¼ teaspoon Accent
⅛ teaspoon pepper

Add and toss lightly until vegetables are well coated with a mixture of

¼ cup French dressing
1 tablespoon lemon juice

Set in refrigerator to chill at least 1 hr.

Before serving, add and gently toss with

¾ cup Mayonnaise (*page 177*)

Serve on crisp salad greens.

About 6 servings

△ Tuna Salad

Follow ▲ Recipe. Omit carrots and peas. Increase celery to ½ cup.

Shrimp Salad with Herbs

MRS. MARTIN LARSGAARD
DICKINSON, N. DAK.

A touch of herb genius gives you a new recipe for your repertory of exciting shrimp dishes.

Set out a large bowl.

Blend together and set in refrigerator to chill

¾ cup Mayonnaise (*page 177*)
2 tablespoons tarragon vinegar
2 tablespoons cream
2 tablespoons finely chopped parsley
2 tablespoons minced onion

and a mixture of

½ teaspoon celery seed
½ teaspoon basil
½ teaspoon salt
½ teaspoon Accent
¼ teaspoon pepper

Drain, remove black vein, and coarsely chop contents of

2 5-oz. cans shrimp (about 1½ cups, drained)

(Or prepare 1 lb. fresh shrimp with shells, see Cooked Shrimp, *page 126*).

Prepare

2 cups (about ½ lb.) shredded cabbage
1 cup chopped celery (*page 6*)

Combine the shrimp, cabbage and celery in the bowl. Cover and set in refrigerator to chill.

Shortly before serving, add the dressing to the salad. Toss lightly to mix thoroughly.

Serve at once on lettuce. *About 8 servings*

▲ Chicken Salad

Prepare and put into a large bowl
3 cups cubed cooked chicken (stewed or roasted)
1 cup diced celery (*page 6*)
Toss lightly and mix in, in order
½ teaspoon salt
½ teaspoon Accent
½ cup Cooked Salad Dressing (*page 177*)
Chill in refrigerator until ready to serve.

Serve in
Crisp lettuce cups; or spoon into cavities of 3 medium-size chilled avocados, cut into halves and pitted
Garnish with
Capers, olives or water cress

About 6 servings

△ Elegant Chicken Salad

Follow ▲ Recipe. Mix with the chicken and celery ½ cup small **seedless grapes** (or halved and seeded green grapes) and ¼ cup moist shredded **coconut,** cut. Just before serving, mix in ½ cup **pecans** or blanched **almonds,** toasted (*page 5*). Whip (*page 7*) ¼ cup chilled **whipping cream.** Blend into dressing.

△ Turkey Salad

Follow ▲ Recipe. Substitute 3 cups cubed cooked **turkey** for chicken.

▲ French Dressing

Secret formula for successful salads is the tang and zest of this French Dressing.

Combine in a 1-pt. screw-top jar
¾ cup salad oil
¼ cup lemon juice or vinegar
1 tablespoon sugar
¾ teaspoon salt
½ teaspoon Accent
¼ teaspoon pepper
¼ teaspoon paprika
¼ teaspoon dry mustard
Cover jar tightly and shake vigorously. Store covered in refrigerator.

Shake well before using. *About 1 cup dressing*

△ Garlic French Dressing

Follow ▲ Recipe. Cut into halves 1 clove **garlic** (*page 6*); add to completed dressing. To season well, chill dressing about 12 hours before using. Remove garlic before serving.

△ Honey French Dressing

Follow ▲ Recipe; use lemon juice. Blend in ½ cup **honey** and ¼ teaspoon grated **lemon peel** (*page 5*). For added flavor, add ½ teaspoon **celery seed.**

△ Roquefort French Dressing

Follow ▲ Recipe. Add ½ cup (about 2 oz.) crumbled **Roquefort** or **Blue cheese.**

Cooked Salad Dressing

Mix thoroughly in the top of a double boiler

- **¼ cup sugar**
- **1 tablespoon flour**
- **½ teaspoon dry mustard**
- **½ teaspoon salt**
- **¼ teaspoon Accent**
- **⅛ teaspoon pepper**

Blend in gradually

- **1 cup water**

Place over direct heat. Stirring gently and constantly, bring mixture to boiling. Cook 1 to 2 min. longer. Stir in

- **¼ cup vinegar**

Vigorously stir about 3 tablespoons hot mixture into

- **4 egg yolks, slightly beaten**

Immediately blend egg-yolk mixture into mixture in top of double boiler. Place over simmering water and cook 3 to 5 min. Stir slowly to keep mixture cooking evenly. Remove from heat and stir in

- **2 tablespoons butter or margarine**

Cool. Store salad dressing in tightly covered jar in refrigerator.

Before using, thin to desired consistency with sweet cream, fruit juice or vinegar.

About 1½ cups salad dressing

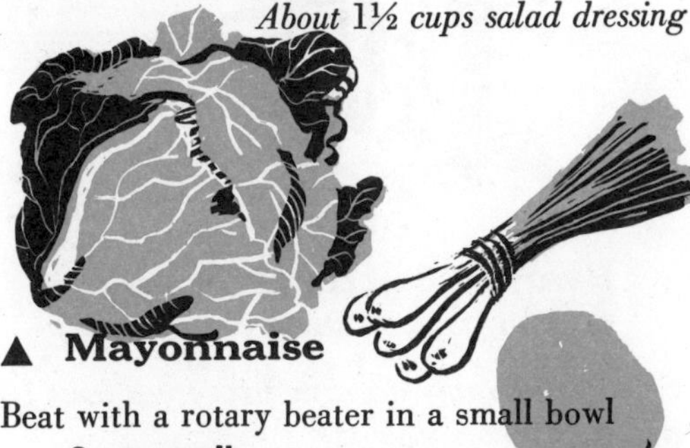

▲ Mayonnaise

Beat with a rotary beater in a small bowl

- **2 egg yolks**
- **1 tablespoon lemon juice**
- **1½ teaspoons salt**
- **1 teaspoon sugar**
- **½ teaspoon Accent**
- **½ teaspoon dry mustard**
- **½ teaspoon paprika**

Add, 1 teaspoon at a time at first

- **½ cup salad oil**

Beating vigorously after each addition, gradually increase amount of addition. Alternately beat in (in very small amounts)

- **½ cup salad oil**
- **1 tablespoon lemon juice**

(If Mayonnaise separates because oil has been added too rapidly, beat it slowly and thoroughly into 1 egg yolk.)

Store Mayonnaise covered in refrigerator.

About 1½ cups Mayonnaise

Note: Mayonnaise may be thinned with a small amount of **cream** before serving. For a special touch, fold in **whipped cream** (*page* 7).

△ Thousand Island Dressing

Follow ▲ Recipe. To ½ cup Mayonnaise add 1 or 2 **hard-cooked eggs** (chilled), sieved or finely chopped, 2 tablespoons **chili sauce,** 2 tablespoons finely chopped **scallions** (with tops), 2 tablespoons chopped **sweet pickle,** 1 tablespoon chopped **green olives,** and ½ teaspoon **paprika.**

△ Russian Dressing

Follow ▲ Recipe. To ½ cup Mayonnaise add 3 tablespoons **chili sauce,** 1 tablespoon minced **onion** and ½ teaspoon **prepared horse-radish.**

Cosmopolitan Dressing

MRS. H. A. LEWICKI, JR., CONCORD, CALIF.

Blend together until smooth and creamy

- **5 oz. (1 jar) process cheese spread with Blue cheese**
- **3 oz. (1 pkg.) cream cheese, softened**
- **1 cup thick sour cream**
- **¼ cup sherry**
- **1 tablespoon grated onion**
- **½ teaspoon salt**
- **¼ teaspoon paprika**
- **⅛ teaspoon Accent**

Store dressing covered in refrigerator.

About 2 cups dressing

Fluffy Citrus Salad Dressing

This delicate fruit dressing is at its flavorsome best when served with a plate of chilled California orange slices, grapefruit sections, avocado slices and whole berries.

Put a bowl and rotary beater into refrigerator to chill.

Mix together
3 tablespoons honey
2 to 3 teaspoons lemon, lime or orange juice
Using chilled bowl and beater, whip (*page 7*)
½ cup chilled whipping cream
Beat honey mixture into whipped cream with final few strokes. *1¼ cups salad dressing*

Pineapple Salad Dressing

Sift together in the top of a double boiler
½ cup sugar
1 tablespoon cornstarch
⅛ teaspoon salt
Stir in
½ cup unsweetened pineapple juice
Stirring gently and constantly, bring rapidly to boiling over direct heat. Cook 3 min. Place over simmering water.

Vigorously stir about 3 tablespoons hot mixture into
2 egg yolks, slightly beaten
Immediately blend into mixture in double-boiler top, stirring constantly. Cook over simmering water 3 to 5 min. Stir slowly to keep mixture cooking evenly. Remove double boiler from heat.

Beat until frothy
2 egg whites
Add gradually, beating well after each addition
2 tablespoons sugar
Beat until rounded peaks are formed. Gently blend egg whites into pineapple mixture.

Add gradually, stirring constantly
1 cup lukewarm, unsweetened pineapple juice
Cook over simmering water until thick and smooth, stirring constantly (about 10 min.). Remove from heat and blend in
2 tablespoons butter or margarine
Cool and set in refrigerator to chill.

Before serving, whip (*page 7*)
¾ cup chilled whipping cream
Carefully blend whipped cream into pineapple mixture. *About 4 cups dressing*

Fluffy Citrus Salad Dressing

Peanut Butter Dressing

ETTA DEVINE, FARMINGTON, N. MEX.

Serve this creamy dressing with fresh fruit for a quick and tasty salad.

Cream together until well mixed
½ cup peanut butter
2 tablespoons sugar
Add gradually, mixing well
6 tablespoons cream or undiluted evaporated milk
Beat until smooth and creamy. Store covered in refrigerator. *¾ cup dressing*

Melbourne Salad Dressing

A piquant dressing for salad greens.

Combine in a screw-top jar
- **⅔ cup lemon juice**
- **¼ cup olive oil**
- **2 tablespoons Worcestershire sauce**
- **¼ cup sugar**

Cover jar tightly and shake well. Store covered in refrigerator. Shake dressing well before serving. Serve icy cold.

About 1¼ cups dressing

Blue Cheese Salad Dressing

Gourmet's choice for tossed green salad.

Mix in a small bowl
- **½ cup cream**
- **1 teaspoon prepared mustard**
- **¾ teaspoon paprika**
- **½ teaspoon Worcestershire sauce**
- **¼ teaspoon salt**
- **⅛ teaspoon coarsely ground pepper**
- **2 or 3 drops tabasco sauce**

Add, about 1 teaspoon at a time, while beating constantly with a rotary beater
- **¾ cup salad oil or olive oil**

Continue beating while adding gradually
- **2 tablespoons wine vinegar or cider vinegar**

Add to dressing
- **1 cup (about 4 oz.) crumbled Blue cheese**

Blend only until mixed. Store dressing in a screw-top jar in refrigerator. Shake well before using. *About 2 cups dressing*

Ida's Favorite Dressing

IDA GLESSNER, GROVE CITY, PA.

Put through fine blade of food chopper
- **1 medium-size green pepper (*page 6*)**
- **1 medium-size onion (*page 6*)**

Combine in a 1-pt. screw-top jar with
- **6 tablespoons orange juice**
- **¼ cup salad oil**
- **3 tablespoons lemon juice**
- **2 tablespoons vinegar**
- **2 tablespoons sugar**
- **½ teaspoon Accent**
- **½ teaspoon salt**
- **¼ teaspoon pepper**
- **1 clove garlic (*page 6*), cut in halves**

Cover jar tightly and shake well. Store covered in refrigerator. Shake well before using.

About 1½ cups dressing

Note: The longer garlic remains in salad dressing, the stronger the flavor will be.

Salad Dressing Supreme

MRS. BRYANT PERKINS, HULLS COVE, ME.

A spirited and unusual combination.

Combine in a 1-qt. screw-top jar
- **1½ cups olive oil**
- **1¼ cups (10½- to 11-oz. can) condensed tomato soup**
- **½ cup vinegar**
- **5 tablespoons honey**
- **2 tablespoons tarragon vinegar**
- **1 tablespoon Worcestershire sauce**
- **1 tablespoon dry mustard**
- **2 teaspoons salt**
- **1 teaspoon paprika**
- **¼ teaspoon Accent**
- **1 clove garlic (*page 6*), cut in halves**
- **2 or 3 drops tabasco sauce**

Cover tightly and shake well. Store covered in refrigerator. Shake well before using.

About 3⅔ cups dressing

Note: The longer garlic remains in salad dressing, the stronger the flavor will be.

The Art of Sauce Making

Sauces enhance the appearance and flavor of food and add to its nutritive value. They should offer pleasing contrasts in color, flavor and consistency to the dishes they accompany. In most cases they should be thin enough to flow but thick enough not to saturate food.

Sauces for Meat, Poultry, Fish and Vegetables—Basic sauces for these are few in number, but their variations are almost limitless. Wherever spices, herbs, seasonings and a few basic ingredients are available, the art of sauce making is open to amateur and professional alike.

Foremost among the basic sauces and keystone of the whole art is white sauce. This is the indispensable base for innumerable sauces and is frequently used in other food preparation as well—in cream soups, casserole dishes, croquettes or soufflés. Four main groups are made from the basic sauce by varying the type of liquid used or by browning the flour. White sauce, as the name implies, is made with milk or cream. Spices, seasonings and condiments add their piquant flavor to many variations of white sauce. A second group is created by the substitution of meat or vegetable stock or water for milk; an example is gravy. When the flour is browned before liquid is added the resulting sauce is a brown sauce. The fourth group of sauces results from the substitution of tomato juice or purée for milk.

For a smooth sauce always blend flour or cornstarch with a cold liquid or with melted fat, or cream the fat thoroughly with the flour before adding hot liquids.

Frequently gravy lumps because hot liquid is added to the fat-flour mixture, causing the starch particles to become sticky and clump together. Therefore only warm or cold liquid rather than hot liquid should be used to avoid lumping.

An easy way to blend flour and liquid for gravy is to put the required amount of cold liquid in a screw-top jar, sprinkle the flour OVER the liquid and shake the mixture to blend. This mixture is also used to thicken liquids for stews. Sauces made with flour or cornstarch must be cooked rapidly and thoroughly to overcome the raw starch taste.

When adding whole eggs or egg yolks to a sauce, always stir a little of the hot sauce into the slightly beaten eggs; immediately blend into the remaining hot sauce. Cook 3 to 5 min., stirring slowly to keep the mixture cooking evenly. Temperature of the mixture should not drop before adding the eggs, to insure an adequately thickened sauce.

Cheese is a protein food and so it is toughened by high heat. Slightly cool a hot sauce before adding grated cheese (add all at one time and stir until blended). If all the cheese does not melt, heat sauce over simmering water and stir.

Dessert Sauces—Create an enticing dessert dish by combining a sweet sauce with any of these: ice cream, sherbet, parfait, mousse, fruit, pudding, pancakes, cookies, cake, or cake bits.

The special-flavor sauces, such as chocolate and butterscotch, and hard sauce do not normally separate and so they can be stored, tightly covered, in the refrigerator for over a month. Harmless mold may form, but it can be skimmed off and the sauce used. The high sugar content of sweet sauces prevents other spoilage organisms from developing.

▲ Medium White Sauce I

Melt in a saucepan over low heat

2 tablespoons butter or margarine

Blend in a mixture of

2 tablespoons flour
¼ teaspoon salt
¼ teaspoon Accent
Few grains pepper

Heat until mixture bubbles. Remove from heat. Add gradually, stirring in

1 cup milk or a mixture of ½ cup undiluted evaporated milk and ½ cup water

Cook rapidly, stirring constantly, until sauce thickens. Cook 1 to 2 min. longer.

Use sauce for gravies, scalloped and creamed dishes, for topping cooked vegetables, fish, eggs and meat. *About 1 cup sauce*

△ Thin White Sauce

Follow ▲ Recipe, using 1 tablespoon flour and 1 tablespoon butter or margarine. Use as base for cream soups.

△ Thick White Sauce

Follow ▲ Recipe, using 3 to 4 tablespoons flour and 3 to 4 tablespoons butter or margarine. Use for preparation of soufflés and croquettes.

△ Mushroom Sauce

Follow ▲ Recipe. Clean and slice (*page 6*) ½ lb. **mushrooms.** Heat in a skillet ¼ cup **butter** or **margarine.** Add mushrooms and 1 tablespoon minced **onion.** Cook slowly, moving and turning with a spoon until mushrooms are tender. Do not brown. Stir into sauce. (Or ½ cup, 4-oz. can, drained mushrooms may be substituted for fresh mushrooms, and mushroom liquid may be used for part of milk.)

△ Cheese Sauce

Follow ▲ Recipe. Blend in ¼ teaspoon **dry mustard** and a few grains **cayenne pepper** with flour and seasonings. Cool sauce slightly. Add all at one time ¼ cup (1 oz.) grated sharp **Cheddar cheese.** Stir sauce rapidly until the cheese is melted and well blended.

△ Mock Hollandaise Sauce

Follow ▲ Recipe, preparing sauce in a double-boiler top and using **chicken stock** (a clear canned chicken soup may be used). When sauce is thickened, vigorously stir about 3 tablespoons of hot mixture into 2 **egg yolks,** slightly beaten. Immediately blend into sauce; cook over simmering water 3 to 5 min. Stir slowly to keep mixture cooking evenly. Stir in 1 tablespoon **lemon juice** and 2 tablespoons **butter** or **margarine.**

Medium White Sauce II

Pour into a saucepan

1 cup water

Sprinkle over top of water, a mixture of

⅓ cup instant nonfat dry milk solids
2 tablespoons flour
¼ teaspoon salt
¼ teaspoon Accent
Few grains pepper

Beat slowly with rotary beater just until blended. Cook over medium heat, stirring constantly. When sauce begins to thicken, stir in

2 tablespoons butter or margarine

Continue cooking, stirring constantly, until sauce thickens. Cook 1 to 2 min. longer.

About 1 cup sauce

Note: This sauce may be used as the base for any variation of **Medium White Sauce I** (*on this page*).

Hollandaise Sauce: Using a wire whisk, beat egg yolks and cream in the top of a small double boiler.

Hollandaise Sauce

In the top of a small double boiler, beat with a wire whisk until thickened and light-colored

2 egg yolks
2 tablespoons cream

Blend in

¼ teaspoon salt
Few grains cayenne pepper

Place top of double boiler over hot (not boiling) water. (Bottom of double-boiler top should not touch the water.) Add gradually, beating constantly

2 tablespoons lemon juice or tarragon vinegar

Cook over low heat, beating constantly with whisk until sauce is consistency of thick cream. Remove double boiler from heat, leaving top in place.

Add, beating constantly, ½ teaspoon at a time

½ cup butter or margarine

Beat with whisk until butter is thoroughly melted and blended into mixture.

Serve immediately. If necessary, this sauce may be kept warm 15 to 30 min. by setting over hot water. Cover tightly. Stir the sauce occasionally. *1 cup sauce*

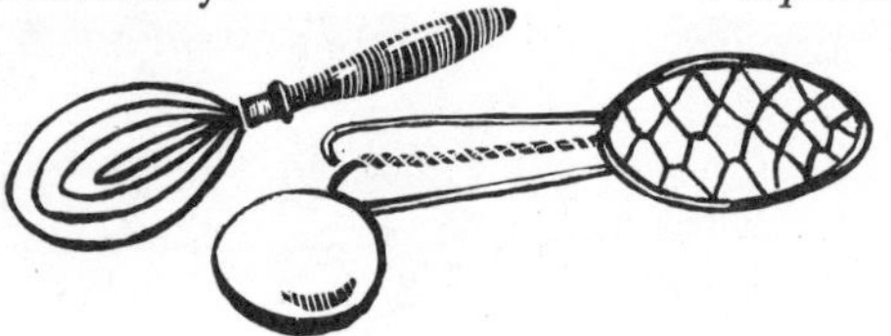

Béarnaise Sauce

JO ELLYN MEADOR, SCOTIA, CALIF.

A sprightly Hollandaise-type sauce.

Set out a small double boiler and a saucepan.

Prepare and set aside

1 tablespoon chopped chives
1 tablespoon chopped parsley
1 tablespoon chopped fresh tarragon leaves*

Combine in the saucepan

¼ cup white wine vinegar
4 fresh tarragon leaves, minced*
2 sprigs parsley, finely chopped
1 teaspoon chopped chives
3 whole peppercorns, bruised

Boil until only two tablespoons of liquid remain. Set aside.

In the top of the double boiler, beat with a wire whisk until thickened and light-colored

3 egg yolks

Blend in

½ teaspoon salt

Place top of double boiler over hot (not boiling) water. (Bottom of double-boiler top should not touch the water.)

Add, beating constantly with the whisk until butter is melted and blended into mixture

1 tablespoon softened butter

Strain the hot, seasoned vinegar mixture into the egg-yolk mixture, beating constantly. Cook over low heat, beating constantly with whisk until sauce is the consistency of light cream.

Remove double boiler from heat, leaving top in place. Add, beating constantly, one tablespoon at a time

¾ cup softened butter

Beat with whisk until butter is thoroughly melted and blended into mixture. Blend in the chopped fresh herbs.

Serve immediately with broiled fish or with any dark meat. *About 1½ cups sauce*

*If the fresh tarragon leaves are not available, substitute **tarragon vinegar** for wine vinegar.

Quick Tomato Sauce

Heat in a saucepan over low heat
1 tablespoon butter or margarine
Blend in
1 tablespoon flour
½ teaspoon onion salt
Few grains cayenne pepper
Heat until mixture bubbles. Remove from heat. Add gradually, stirring constantly
1 cup (8-oz. can) tomato sauce
¼ cup hot water
1 teaspoon Worcestershire sauce
Return to heat and bring rapidly to boiling, stirring constantly, until sauce thickens. Cook 1 to 2 min. longer. Serve sauce hot.

About 1 cup sauce

Creamy Mustard Sauce

A perfect sauce to serve with ham or with cauliflower, asparagus, green beans or broccoli.

Set out
1 cup cream or undiluted evaporated milk
Scald (*page* 7) ¾ cup of the cream or evaporated milk in top of double-boiler. Set remaining ¼ cup aside.

Sift together into a small saucepan
¼ cup sugar
2 tablespoons dry mustard
2 teaspoons cornstarch
½ teaspoon salt
Blend in the ¼ cup reserved cream or evaporated milk. Gradually add the scalded cream or milk, stirring constantly.

Stirring gently and constantly, bring cornstarch mixture rapidly to boiling over direct heat and cook for 3 min.

Wash double-boiler top to remove scum.

Pour mixture into double-boiler top and place over simmering water. Cover and cook 10 to 12 min., stirring occasionally.

Remove cover and vigorously stir about 3 tablespoons of this hot mixture into
1 egg yolk, slightly beaten
Immediately blend into mixture in double boiler. Cook over simmering water 3 to 5 min. Stir slowly to keep mixture cooking evenly. Remove from heat. Add gradually, stirring constantly
¼ cup vinegar
Serve hot over vegetables or meat.

About 1¼ cups sauce

Zippy Mustard Sauce

MRS. FAROL E. RILEY, ULYSSES, KANS.

A zesty sauce that will add a sharp, tangy flavor to hot or cold ham.

Combine in top of double boiler
⅓ cup firmly packed brown sugar
2 teaspoons flour
1 teaspoon prepared mustard
Blend in
⅓ cup vinegar
Add gradually, stirring constantly
⅓ cup water
Stirring gently and constantly, bring mixture rapidly to boiling over direct heat and cook for 3 min.

Remove from heat and vigorously stir about 3 tablespoons of hot mixture into
2 egg yolks, slightly beaten
Immediately blend into mixture in double boiler. Cook over hot water 3 to 5 min. Stir slowly to keep mixture cooking evenly.

Remove from heat and stir in
1 tablespoon butter or margarine
Serve hot or cold with ham.

About 1 cup sauce

Note: For a milder sauce, use 3 tablespoons vinegar and ½ cup water.

▲ Horse-radish Sour Cream Sauce

The tang of sour cream lends distinction.

Blend together
1 cup thick sour cream
⅓ cup prepared horse-radish
1 tablespoon grated lemon peel (*page 5*)
¾ teaspoon salt
⅛ teaspoon white pepper
Chill in refrigerator until ready to serve.

Serve with ham or fish. *About 1⅓ cups sauce*

△ Sour Cream Cucumber Sauce

Follow ▲ Recipe. Decrease sour cream to ½ cup; blend in ½ cup **Mayonnaise** (*page 177*). Decrease horse-radish to 2 teaspoons. Blend in 1 medium-size **cucumber,** pared and chopped.

Sour Cream Cucumber Sauce with broiled fish

△ Apple Sour Cream Sauce

Follow ▲ Recipe. Add to the sauce before chilling 1 medium-size **red apple,** chopped.

Tartar Sauce

Combine in a small bowl
1 cup Mayonnaise (*page 177*)
3 tablespoons chopped sweet pickle
3 tablespoons chopped green olives
2 tablespoons drained capers
2 teaspoons minced onion
Stir until well blended. Store in a tightly covered jar in refrigerator and use as needed.
About 1½ cups sauce

Shrimp Remoulade Sauce

MRS. ERIC GUSTAFSON, CLEBURNE, TEXAS

Combine in a large bowl
3 cups Mayonnaise (*page 177*)
⅓ cup minced green onion (*page 6*)
3 tablespoons drained capers
3½ teaspoons Worcestershire sauce
3½ teaspoons prepared horse-radish
1 tablespoon finely chopped parsley
1 clove garlic (*page 6*), minced; or crushed in a garlic press
Few drops tabasco sauce
Stir until well blended. Store the sauce in a tightly covered container in refrigerator.

Serve cold. *About 3¾ cups sauce*

Zippy Cocktail Sauce with shrimp

▲ Creamy Sea Food Cocktail Sauce

MRS. NEIL DAMMARELL
MOUNTAIN HOME, IDAHO

Put a small bowl and rotary beater into refrigerator to chill.

Blend thoroughly in a mixing bowl
- **1 cup ketchup or chili sauce**
- **½ cup Mayonnaise (*page 177*)**
- **1 tablespoon lemon juice**
- **1 tablespoon prepared horse-radish**
- **1 teaspoon minced onion**
- **1 teaspoon Worcestershire sauce**
- **¼ teaspoon Accent**
- **⅛ teaspoon salt**

Beat in the chilled bowl with chilled rotary beater until cream is of medium consistency (piles softly)
- **½ cup chilled whipping cream**

Fold (*page 6*) whipped cream into mayonnaise mixture. Chill at least 1 hr. before serving.

2½ cups sauce

△ Zippy Cocktail Sauce

Follow ▲ Recipe. Omit Mayonnaise and whipping cream. Blend in a few drops of **tabasco sauce.** *About 1¼ cups sauce*

"Dee-lish" Sauce for Fish

BARBARA FORD, DANBURY, N. H.

Brings out the best in food from the sea.

Dice enough cucumber to yield
- **½ cup diced cucumber**

Add to the cucumber
- **1 tablespoon diced pimiento**
- **1 teaspoon minced onion**

Set aside.

Blend together in a bowl
- **½ cup Mayonnaise (*page 177*)**
- **½ cup thick sour cream**
- **½ cup chopped firm ripe tomato**
- **½ teaspoon salt**
- **¼ teaspoon Accent**

Blend in vegetable mixture. Chill at least 1 hr.

Serve sauce with a salmon loaf or mold or with any fish. *About 2 cups sauce*

Lemon Butter Sauce

Good for basting as well as serving with cooked meat and fish.

Combine in a small saucepan and stir over low heat until butter is melted and ingredients are thoroughly heated
- **1 cup butter**
- **2 tablespoons lemon juice**
- **¼ teaspoon salt**
- **¼ teaspoon paprika**
- **⅛ teaspoon pepper**

About 1 cup sauce

Maître d'Hôtel Butter

Gives a master's touch to sea food or vegetables.

Cream together until thoroughly blended
- **½ cup softened butter**
- **2 tablespoons lemon juice**
- **2 teaspoons chopped parsley**
- **¼ teaspoon salt**
- **⅛ teaspoon pepper**

Serve with fish. *About ½ cup sauce*

Spaghetti Sauce

Barbecue Sauce Mexicano

AMELIE M. KINZER, VAN NUYS, CALIF.

A mild, flavorful barbecue sauce.

Heat in a saucepan over low heat

½ cup butter

Add and cook slowly until onion is transparent, keeping mixture moving with a spoon

1 large onion (*page 6*), finely chopped
2 cloves garlic (*page 6*), minced; or crushed in a garlic press

Blend in, and simmer gently for 5 to 10 min. to heat thoroughly and blend flavors

1¼ cups (10½- to 11-oz. can) condensed tomato soup
½ cup water
½ cup lime juice
2 teaspoons dry mustard
2 teaspoons chili powder
1 teaspoon salt
¼ teaspoon crushed cumin seeds
1 large bay leaf

Remove bay leaf before serving. Use as basting sauce for barbecued meat or serve hot over sliced leftover meat. *About 3½ cups sauce*

Spaghetti Sauce

HELEN F. WELLS, SAN JOSE, CALIF.

Set out a large, heavy skillet having a tight-fitting cover.

Finely chop and mix together

2 large onions (*page 6*)
1 large green pepper (*page 6*)

Heat in the skillet

2 tablespoons fat

Add the vegetables and cook, moving mixture with a spoon, until onion is transparent.

Add and cook over medium heat until browned, breaking into small pieces with fork or spoon

1 lb. ground round steak

Meanwhile, blend together

2½ cups (No. 2 can) tomatoes
1¼ cups (12-oz. bottle) chili sauce
1 cup (8-oz. can) tomato sauce
¾ cup (6 oz. can) tomato paste
2 tablespoons brown sugar
2 tablespoons Worcestershire sauce
2 tablespoons vinegar
1 tablespoon prepared mustard
2 large cloves garlic (*page 6*), minced; or crushed in a garlic press
1 bay leaf

and a mixture of

2 tablespoons oregano
2 teaspoons cumin
2 teaspoons thyme
1 teaspoon basil
1 teaspoon cloves
1 teaspoon salt
½ teaspoon pepper
¼ to ½ teaspoon crushed red peppers

Set aside.

Heat in a small saucepan over low heat

2 tablespoons butter or margarine

Add and cook over medium heat, turning and keeping mushrooms moving with a spoon until they are lightly browned, contents of

1 8-oz. can whole mushrooms, drained

Add the mushrooms and tomatoes to meat and bring to a full rolling boil; stir constantly. Reduce heat.

Brown Roux or Paste

Used for thickening brown sauces, this paste can be made in advance and kept in the refrigerator until needed.

Melt in a heavy saucepan or skillet

1 cup fat or meat drippings

Blend in

1½ cups flour

Place over low heat. Stir constantly to distribute heat evenly. The roux is cooked when the mixture acquires a light brown color.

Cool; store covered in refrigerator.

About 2 cups roux

▲ Brown Gravy

A cook is known by the character of her gravies.

Method 1—Remove roasted meat or poultry from roasting pan. Leaving brown residue in pan, pour into bowl

Drippings

Allow fat to rise to surface; skim off fat and reserve. Remaining drippings are meat juices which should be used as part of liquid in gravy.

Measure into roasting pan

3 tablespoons fat

Blend in until smooth

3 tablespoons reserved flour
½ teaspoon Accent
¼ teaspoon salt
⅛ teaspoon pepper

Stirring constantly, heat until mixture bubbles. Brown slightly if desired. Remove from heat and slowly blend in, stirring constantly and vigorously

2 cups liquid, warm or cool (drippings, water, quick meat broth, *page 7*, or milk)

Return to heat and cook rapidly, stirring constantly, until sauce thickens. Cook 1 to 2 min. longer. While stirring, scrape bottom and sides of pan to blend in brown residue.

Serve hot with meat or poultry.

6 to 8 servings

Note: Other **fats** may be substituted if pan drippings are not available.

Method 2—Bring to boiling

2 cups chicken or meat broth (from which the fat has been skimmed)

Drippings from roasted meats may be substituted for part of broth; if necessary, add milk or water to drippings to make 2 cups liquid.

Meanwhile, put into a 1-pt. screw-top jar

½ cup water

Sprinkle evenly over water

¼ cup flour

Cover jar tightly; shake until flour and water are well blended. Stirring broth or liquid constantly, slowly pour one half of the flour-water mixture into broth. Bring to boiling. Gradually add only what is needed of remaining flour-water mixture for consistency desired; bring to boiling after each addition.

Season with

¼ teaspoon salt
⅛ teaspoon pepper
⅛ teaspoon Accent

Cook gravy 3 to 5 min. longer.

△ Giblet Gravy

Follow Method 1 or 2 of ▲ Recipe. Use **chicken** or **giblet broth.** Add chopped cooked **giblets** to gravy; bring to boiling to thoroughly heat giblets.

Giblet Gravy with Roast Chicken (page 94)

Golden Gravy

Set out a large skillet.

Prepare

1 cup quick chicken broth (*page 7*; use 2 bouillon cubes)

Stir in

½ teaspoon Worcestershire sauce
½ teaspoon Accent
⅛ teaspoon salt

Set aside to cool slightly.

Heat in the skillet over low heat

3 tablespoons fat

Blend in

3 tablespoons flour
¼ to ½ teaspoon dry mustard
⅛ teaspoon freshly ground pepper

Stirring constantly, heat until mixture bubbles and browns slightly. Remove from heat and slowly add seasoned chicken broth, stirring constantly and vigorously. Thoroughly blend in

1 cup milk

Return to heat and cook rapidly, stirring constantly, until gravy thickens. Cook gravy 1 to 2 min. longer.

Serve with meat, or heat slices of leftover meat or poultry in the gravy.

About 2 cups gravy

Norwegian Wine Gravy

MRS. CARL F. ERICKSON, SPENARD, ALASKA

For a special taste treat try this piquant gravy.

Heat in a small saucepan over low heat

2 tablespoons butter or margarine

Add and cook slowly over medium heat, stirring occasionally

1 small onion (*page 6*), minced

Cook until onion is transparent.

Blend in

2 tablespoons flour
½ teaspoon dry mustard
⅛ teaspoon pepper

Heat until the mixture bubbles and is lightly browned, stirring constantly.

Remove from the heat; add gradually, stirring constantly

2 cups meat stock or quick meat broth (*page 7*)
¼ cup sherry
1 anchovy, minced

Simmer 5 min. Strain gravy and serve hot over slices of cold roast beef.

About 2½ cups sauce

Tomato Sauce

Combine in a saucepan and simmer 10 to 12 min., stirring occasionally

2½ cups (No. 2 can) cooked or canned tomatoes
2 tablespoons chopped onion
2 teaspoons sugar
½ teaspoon salt
½ teaspoon Accent
⅛ teaspoon pepper

Force through a sieve to remove tomato seeds and onion pieces. Set aside.

Heat in a skillet

2 tablespoons butter or margarine

Blend in

2 tablespoons flour

Heat until mixture bubbles. Remove from heat and gradually add the tomato mixture, stirring constantly. Blend in

½ teaspoon Worcestershire sauce

Return to heat and cook, stirring gently and constantly, until mixture thickens. Cook 1 to 2 min. longer.

Serve with vegetables, meats, fish or omelets.

About 2 cups sauce

Eggnog Sauce

Put a bowl and rotary beater into refrigerator to chill.

Beat until thick and lemon-colored
2 egg yolks
Add alternately, beating until well blended after each addition
¾ cup sifted confectioners' sugar
3 tablespoons brandy
Set aside.

Using the chilled bowl and rotary beater, beat until cream stands in peaks when beater is lifted slowly upright
½ cup chilled whipping cream
Fold (*page 6*) the egg-yolk mixture into the whipped cream.

Serve immediately. *About 1½ cups sauce*

Note: Sauce may be kept in refrigerator up to ½ hr. without separation. If necessary, beat only to blend mixture before serving.

▲ Vanilla Sauce

Old stand-by with dozens of uses.

Sift together into a saucepan
1 cup sugar
2 tablespoons cornstarch
¼ teaspoon salt
Add gradually, stirring constantly
2 cups boiling water
Continue to stir; bring to boiling and simmer 5 min.

Remove from heat and blend in
¼ cup butter or margarine
2 teaspoons vanilla extract
Serve sauce hot on **Old-Fashioned English Plum Pudding** (*page 276*).

About 2 cups sauce

△ Lemon Sauce

Follow ▲ Recipe. Substitute 3 tablespoons **lemon juice** and 2 teaspoons grated **lemon peel** (*page 5*) for vanilla extract.

△ Brandy Sauce

Follow △ Recipe, decreasing lemon juice to 1 tablespoon. Stir in 3 tablespoons **brandy.**

Creamy Orange Custard Sauce

Scald (*page 7*) in top of double boiler
2 cups milk or cream
Meanwhile, beat slightly
4 egg yolks
Blend into egg yolks
⅓ cup sugar
⅛ teaspoon salt
Stirring constantly, add scalded milk gradually to egg-yolk mixture.

Wash double-boiler top to remove scum.

Strain mixture into double-boiler top. Cook over simmering water, stirring constantly and rapidly until mixture coats a silver spoon. Remove from heat and from simmering water at once.

Cool slightly and blend in
¼ cup frozen orange juice concentrate, undiluted but thawed slightly
2 tablespoons butter or margarine
⅛ teaspoon mace
Cover and set sauce aside to cool to lukewarm. Stir, then chill sauce in refrigerator.

Serve sauce with chiffon, sponge or angel-food cake; fruit, fresh or cooked; or puddings.

About 2½ cups sauce

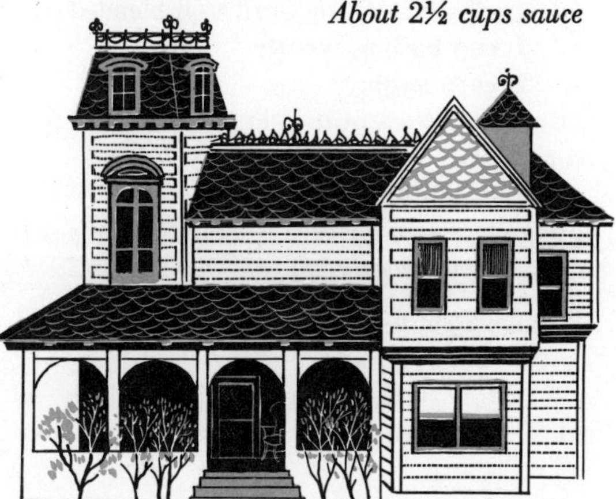

Fudge Sauce Café with Ice Cream and Cake

Cocoa Sirup

Mix together thoroughly
2 cups sugar
1 cup cocoa
¼ teaspoon salt
Add gradually, stirring to make a paste
½ cup water
Stirring constantly, blend in
2 cups boiling water
Boil, stirring gently, for 6 min.

Remove from heat. Cool. Store in covered jar in refrigerator until needed.

About 4 cups sirup

Chocolate Sirup

Melt *(page 6)*
6 sq. (6 oz.) chocolate
Add gradually, stirring until well blended
1 cup boiling water
2 cups sugar
Place over direct heat. Add gradually, stirring constantly
1½ cups boiling water
Bring chocolate mixture to boiling; boil for 6 min., stirring gently.

Remove from heat. Blend in
¼ teaspoon salt
Cool. Store in tightly covered jar in refrigerator until needed.

About 3½ cups sirup

Fudge Sauce Café

Double the mocha pleasure of Fudge Sauce Café by serving with steaming hot coffee.

Mix together in a small, heavy saucepan
½ cup sugar
½ cup double-strength coffee beverage (*page 7*)
2 sq. (2 oz.) chocolate, broken in pieces
1 tablespoon cream
⅛ teaspoon salt
Place over low heat. Cook, stirring constantly, until sauce becomes slightly thickened.

Remove from heat and blend in
1 tablespoon butter or margarine
½ teaspoon vanilla extract
Serve sauce warm or cool.

About 1 cup sauce

▲ Chocolate Miracle Sauce

Cook in double-boiler top 5 min. or until smooth
5 sq. (5 oz.) chocolate
1½ cups sugar
1½ cups water
¼ teaspoon salt
Add and stir in
1⅓ cups (15-oz. can) sweetened condensed milk
Cook over hot water until mixture coats a silver spoon.

About 3 cups sauce

△ Miracle Semi-Sweet Sauce

Follow ▲ Recipe. Substitute 1 pkg. (6 oz.) **semi-sweet chocolate pieces** for chocolate.

Coconut-Praline Sauce

MRS. RAY GARRISON, BOWLING GREEN, KY.

Heat in a saucepan over low heat

1/3 cup butter or margarine

Add and stir frequently until golden brown

1 cup moist shredded coconut, cut

With slotted spoon, remove coconut to dish.

Add to the butter in the saucepan

1/2 cup firmly packed brown sugar
2 tablespoons dark corn sirup
1/8 teaspoon salt

Cook over low heat, stirring constantly, until mixture bubbles vigorously. Remove saucepan from heat.

Add gradually, stirring constantly

3/4 cup undiluted evaporated milk

Return to heat and stir constantly until thoroughly heated.

Remove from heat. Stir in coconut and

1/2 teaspoon vanilla extract

Serve warm or cold on ice cream, or on unfrosted white or chocolate cake squares.

About 2 cups sauce

Luscious Butterscotch Sauce

Put in a small, heavy saucepan

1 cup firmly packed light brown sugar
1/3 cup butter
1/3 cup cream
Few grains salt

Stir over low heat until sugar is dissolved and butter is melted. Increase heat to medium and bring mixture to boiling, stirring occasionally. Boil 5 min. without stirring. Remove from heat and beat sauce about 1 min.

Serve warm over ice cream or unfrosted cake squares. *About 1¼ cups sauce*

▲ Vanilla Hard Sauce

Best-of-all sauce for warm, spicy desserts.

Cream together until butter is softened

1/3 cup butter or margarine
1 teaspoon vanilla extract

Add gradually, creaming until fluffy after each addition

1 cup sifted confectioners' sugar
Few grains salt

Beat in about

1 teaspoon cream or undiluted evaporated milk

Pile sauce lightly into serving bowl. Chill until cold but not hard.

Serve with warm pudding or warm gingerbread or spice cake. *About 2/3 cup sauce*

△ Brandy Hard Sauce

Follow ▲ Recipe. Substitute 2 tablespoons **brandy** for vanilla; beat in after adding salt. Omit cream. Increase sugar if necessary.

Orange Hard Sauce

JEWEL GRAHAM, AMES, IOWA

Especially good with spice cake or gingerbread.

Measure

3 cups sifted confectioners' sugar

Set aside.

Set out to thaw slightly contents of

1 6-oz. can (3/4 cup) frozen orange juice concentrate

Cream until softened

1/2 cup butter or margarine

Beating until smooth after each addition, alternately add the sugar in fourths, the liquid in thirds to the creamed butter.

Add gradually, beating until well blended

1½ cups (about 6½ oz.) non-fat dry milk solids

Continue beating until smooth and creamy.

About 3 cups sauce

The Art of Cakemaking

When a little girl makes her first sally into the kitchen to cook, she does not want to cook an egg, to make French toast, or fry a hamburger. She wants to bake a cake! And though her reach may exceed her grasp, her instincts are leading her in the right direction, for cakemaking is the most womanly of all the household arts. And of all the creations that emanate from the kitchen, none bears a clearer seal of femininity than a cake. All women know that in cakemaking they find expression for many creative impulses, combining form and color and texture to contrast or complement. Women love to bake cakes. And the measure of their devotion and talent may be judged by this collection of some of their masterworks.

TYPES—Basically, cakes are divided into two groups—with and without fat. Actually there are many cakes that are on the borderline of these two main classifications.

Butter-type (shortening) Cakes—These cakes contain a fat (butter, margarine, hydrogenated vegetable shortening, all-purpose shortening or lard) and a chemical leavening agent (baking powder or baking soda). Methods of mixing are: *Conventional*—fat creamed with flavoring extract and then sugar, beaten eggs or egg yolks beaten into creamed mixture and dry and liquid ingredients alternately added and beaten in; egg whites, if used, are beaten and folded in last. *Conventional sponge*—same as conventional except part of sugar beaten with egg whites to make a meringue and folded in last. *Quick-method* (*quick-mix, one-bowl*)—used only when recipe has been developed for the method; dry ingredients and shortening in bowl, eggs and liquid added according to directions; beaten with wooden spoon or electric mixer for specified time.

Chiffon Cakes—These cakes contain a cooking (salad) oil and baking powder. They have the lightness of sponge cake and richness of butter cake.

Sponge-type Cakes—True sponge cakes do not contain any fat, baking powder or baking soda; they are leavened by air and steam. Others may contain a small amount of butter or baking powder. *Angel food cakes* are made with egg whites only and *sponge cakes* with egg yolks or whole eggs.

STORING CAKES—Cakes, except fruitcakes, are at their best when served the same day they are made. But if they are stored properly, most cakes will remain fresh and delicious for a few days.

Plain or frosted cakes—Store in a cake keeper or invert a large, deep bowl over cake on a plate.

Cream filled or whipped cream frosted and filled cakes—Assemble shortly before serving. Always keep frosted cake in refrigerator until ready to serve. Cake may become soggy if kept in refrigerator longer than one hour. Immediately refrigerate any leftover cake.

Fruitcakes—When cake is completely cooled wrap tightly in aluminum foil or moisture-vapor-proof material and store in a cool place to age for several weeks before serving. If desired, once or twice a week, using a pastry brush, paint cake with rum, brandy or other liqueur, or fruit juice; rewrap and store again.

When a Cake Lacks Perfection

A cake may have . . .	BUTTER-TYPE CAKES *Because of . . .*	SPONGE-TYPE CAKES
A hard top crust	Temperature too high Overbaking	Temperature too high Overbaking
A sticky top crust	Too much sugar Insufficient baking	Too much sugar Insufficient baking
A humped or cracked top	Too much flour or too little liquid Overmixing Batter not spread evenly in pan Temperature too high	Too much flour or sugar Temperature too high
One side higher	Batter not spread evenly Uneven pan Pan too close to side of oven Oven rack or range not level Uneven oven heat	Uneven pan Oven rack or range not level
A soggy streak or layer at bottom	Too much liquid Underbeaten eggs Shortening too soft Undermixing Insufficient baking	Too many eggs or egg yolks Underbeaten egg yolks Undermixing
Fallen	Too much sugar, liquid, leavening or shortening Too little flour Temperature too low Insufficient baking	Too much sugar Overbeaten egg whites Underbeaten egg yolks Use of greased pan Insufficient baking
Coarse grain	Use of all-purpose flour instead of cake flour Too much leavening Shortening too soft Insufficient creaming Undermixing Temperature too low	Use of all-purpose flour instead of cake flour Omitting cream of tartar (angel food) Undermixing
Tough crumb	Too much flour Too many eggs Too little sugar or shortening Overmixing Temperature too high	Too little sugar Overbeaten egg whites Underbeaten egg yolks Omitting cream of tartar (angel food) Overmixing Temperature too high Overbaking
A heavy, compact quality	Too much liquid or shortening Too many eggs Too little leavening or flour Overmixing Temperature too high	Overbeaten egg whites Underbeaten egg yolks Overmixing
Crumbled or fallen apart	Too much sugar, leavening or shortening Undermixing Improper pan treatment Improper cooling	
Fallen out of pan before completely cooled		Too much sugar Use of greased pan Insufficient baking

A Check List for Successful Cakemaking

(See For These Recipes—What To Use, How To Do It, and Oven Temperatures on *pages 4-7.*)

√ **Read recipe** carefully.

√ **Assemble** all ingredients and utensils.

√ **Have all ingredients** at room temperature unless recipe specifies otherwise.

√ **Select pans** of proper kind and size. Measure inside, from rim to rim.

√ **Use standard measuring** cups and spoons. Use liquid measuring cups (rim above 1-cup line) for liquids. Use nested or dry measuring cups (1-cup line even with top) for dry ingredients.

√ **Check liquid measurements** at eye level.

√ **Level dry measurements** with straight-edged knife or spatula.

√ **Preheat oven** 12 to 20 min. at required temperature. Leave oven door open first 2 min.

√ **Place oven rack** so top of product will be almost at center of oven. Stagger pans so no pan is directly over another and they do not touch each other or walls of oven. Place single pan so that the center of product is as near to the center of the oven as possible.

√ **Prepare pan**—For cakes *with shortening* and for cake rolls, grease bottom of pan only; line with waxed paper cut to fit bottom of pan only; grease waxed paper. For cakes *without shortening* (sponge-type), do not grease or line pan. If recipe directs "Set out pan," do not grease or line pan.

√ **Sift all flour** except whole-grain types before measuring. Spoon lightly into measuring cup; do not jar. Level with straight-edged knife or spatula.

√ **Cream shortening** (alone or with flavorings) by stirring, rubbing or beating with spoon or electric mixer until softened. Add sugar in small amounts; cream after each addition until all graininess disappears and mixture is light and fluffy. Thorough creaming helps to insure a fine-grained cake.

√ **Beat whole eggs** until thick and piled softly when recipe calls for well-beaten eggs.

√ **Beat egg whites** as follows: *Frothy*—entire mass forms bubbles; *Rounded peaks*—peaks turn over slightly when beater is slowly lifted upright; *Stiff peaks*—peaks remain standing when beater is slowly lifted upright.

√ **Beat egg yolks** until thick and lemon-colored when recipe calls for well-beaten yolks.

√ **When dry and liquid ingredients** are added to cake batters, add alternately, beginning and ending with dry. Add dry ingredients in fourths, liquid in thirds. After each addition, beat only until smooth. Finally beat only until batter is smooth (do not overbeat). Scrape spoon or beater and bottom and sides of bowl during mixing.

If using an electric mixer, beat the mixture at a low speed when alternately adding the dry and liquid ingredients.

√ **Fill cake pans** one-half to two-thirds full.

√ **Tap bottom of cake pan** sharply with hand to release air bubbles before placing in oven.

√ **Test cake** when minimum baking time is up. Touch lightly at center; if it springs back, cake is done. Or insert a cake tester or wooden pick in center; if it comes out clean, cake is done.

√ **Cool butter-type cakes** 10 min. in pan on cooling rack after removing from oven.

√ **Remove butter-type cakes** from pan after cooling. Run spatula gently around sides of pan. Cover with cooling rack. Invert and remove pan. Turn cake right side up immediately after peeling off waxed paper. Cool cake completely before frosting.

√ **Cool sponge-type cakes**—After removing tubed cake from oven, immediately invert pan on end of tube and let hang in pan until completely cooled. If cake is higher than tube, invert between two cooling racks so top of cake does not touch any surface. Invert other types of cake pans so opposite edges of pan rest on edges of two cooling racks; let cake hang in pan until completely cooled.

√ **Remove sponge-type cakes** from pan when completely cooled. Cut around tube with paring knife to loosen cake. Loosen sides with spatula and gently remove cake.

√ **Fill layer cakes**—Spread filling or frosting over top of bottom layer. Cover with the second layer. Repeat procedure if more layers are used. If necessary, hold layers in position with wooden picks; remove when filling is set.

√ **Frost filled layer cakes**—Frost sides first, working rapidly. See that frosting touches plate all around bottom, leaving no gaps. Pile remaining frosting on top of cake and spread lightly.

▲ Angel Food Cake

Set out a 10-in. tubed pan.

Measure and pour into a large bowl
1½ cups (about 12) egg whites
Allow to stand at room temperature at least 1 hr. before beating to insure greater volume.

Meanwhile, sift together
1 cup sifted cake flour
½ cup sugar
Set aside.

Add to egg whites
½ teaspoon salt
Beat with wire whisk, hand rotary beater or electric mixer until frothy. Beat in
1½ teaspoons cream of tartar
Continue beating just until rounded peaks are formed and egg whites do not slide when bowl is partially inverted.

Gently sprinkle over surface of egg whites and fold in (*page 6*), 2 tablespoons at a time
¾ cup sugar
Blend in
1 teaspoon vanilla extract
½ teaspoon almond extract
Sift about 4 tablespoons of flour mixture over surface of meringue (egg-white mixture); fold gently together. Repeat until all of the flour mixture is folded in.

Carefully slide batter into pan, turning pan as batter is poured. Cut through batter with knife or spatula to break large air bubbles.

Bake at 350°F about 45 min., or until cake surface springs back when lightly touched.

Immediately invert pan on end of tube; cool and remove from pan as directed for sponge-type cakes (*page 194*). *One 10-in. tubed cake*

△ Cocoa Angel Food Cake

Follow ▲ Recipe. Decrease cake flour to ⅔ cup. Sift ⅓ cup **cocoa** with cake flour and sugar. Increase vanilla extract to 1½ teaspoons. Omit almond extract.

Mock Angel Food Cake

MRS. ALFRED BRINGE, HOLMEN, WIS.

Set out a 13x9½x2-in. cake pan.

Measure and pour into a large bowl
¾ cup (about 6) egg whites
Allow to stand at room temperature at least 1 hr. before beating to insure greater volume.

Sift together into a bowl
2 cups sifted cake flour
2 cups sugar
1 teaspoon baking powder
Add gradually, stirring in
1 cup boiling water
Stir until well blended (mixture will be a smooth paste). Set aside.

Add to egg whites
½ teaspoon salt
Beat with wire whisk, hand rotary beater or electric mixer until frothy. Beat in
½ teaspoon cream of tartar
Continue beating until rounded peaks are formed and egg whites do not slide when bowl is partially inverted.

Carefully spread beaten egg whites over flour-water mixture and gently fold (*page 6*) together. Fold in with a minimum number of strokes
1 teaspoon vanilla extract
½ teaspoon almond extract
Turn batter into pan.

Bake at 350°F 35 to 40 min. or until cake surface springs back when lightly touched.

Cool and remove from pan as directed for sponge-type cakes (*page 194*).
One 13x9-in. cake

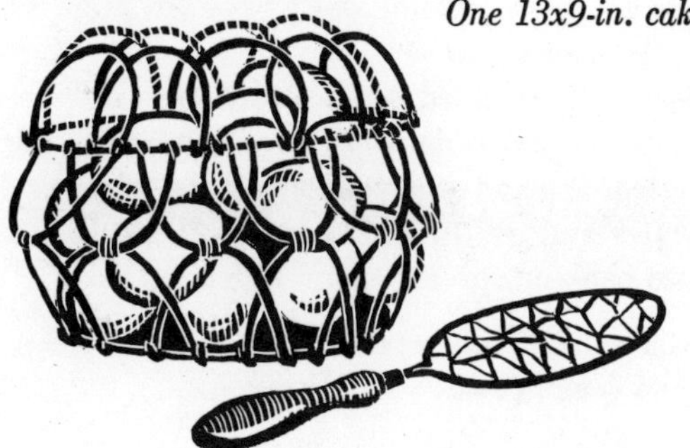

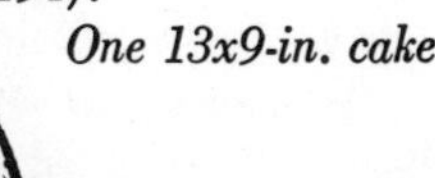

Ice Cream Cake Roll

▲ Lincoln Log

Prepare (*page 194*) 15½x10½x1-in. jelly roll pan.

Sift together and set aside
- **¾ cup sifted cake flour**
- **5 tablespoons cocoa**
- **¼ teaspoon salt**

Beat until very thick and lemon-colored
- **4 egg yolks**
- **½ cup sugar**
- **¼ cup water**
- **1½ teaspoons vanilla extract**

Sift one fourth of the dry ingredients at a time over egg-yolk mixture; fold (*page 6*) until just blended after each addition. Set aside.

Using clean beater, beat until frothy
- **4 egg whites**

Add and beat slightly
- **½ teaspoon cream of tartar**

Add gradually, beating well after each addition
- **½ cup sugar**

Beat until rounded peaks are formed and egg whites do not slide when bowl is partially inverted. Spread egg-yolk mixture over egg whites and gently fold together. Turn batter into pan and spread evenly to edges.

Bake at 325°F about 30 min., or until cake tests done (*page 194*).

Meanwhile, sift onto a clean towel
- **Confectioners' sugar**

Turn cake onto towel. Remove paper; cut off any crisp edges. Begin rolling nearest edge. Using towel as guide, tightly grasp nearest edge of towel and quickly pull it over beyond opposite edge. Cake will roll itself as you pull. Wrap in towel and set on cooling rack.

Meanwhile, prepare
- **Sweetened Whipped Cream (*page 223*) or any of the variations for Sweetened Whipped Cream**
- **Brown Velvet Frosting (*page 214*)**

Carefully unroll cooled cake and spread with filling. Carefully reroll. Trim ends diagonally.

Frost sides, ends and top with Brown Velvet Frosting. Gently draw tines of a fork lengthwise through frosting to make a pattern simulating bark of log.

Chill the cake roll in refrigerator until serving time. (To avoid sogginess, chill roll no longer than 1 hr.)

Garnish top of log with
- **Maraschino cherries with stems**

Or surround base of log with cherries and top each serving with a cherry. With a sharp knife, cut roll into crosswise diagonal slices.

About 8 servings

△ Ice Cream Cake Roll

Follow ▲ Recipe. Substitute 1-qt. of **vanilla ice cream** for cream filling. Omit Brown Velvet Frosting. When ready to serve, carefully unroll cooled cake. Spoon ice cream over cake and smooth with spoon. Reroll and sift 2 tablespoons **confectioners' sugar** over top.

△ Light Sponge Cake Roll

Follow ▲ Recipe. Increase cake flour to 1 cup. Omit cocoa. Bake at 350°F 20 to 25 min., or until cake tests done (*page 194*). Substitute **Seven-Minute Chocolate Frosting** (one-half recipe, *page 218*) for the Brown Velvet Frosting. Omit marking frosted roll with fork.

▲ Holiday Roll

Follow ▲ Recipe or Recipe; omit filling and frosting. When baked, rolled and cooled, unroll cake and spread with one half of Holiday Filling. Reroll and spread top and sides with filling. Garnish with **maraschino cherry halves** and chopped **candied citron.**

For Holiday Filling—Prepare **Sweetened Whipped Cream** (double recipe, *page 223*). Carefully fold in (*page 6*) ⅔ cup well-drained, chopped **maraschino cherries,** ¼ cup (about 2 oz.) **candied citron,** cut in pieces (*page 6*), and ½ cup (about 2 oz.) chopped, toasted, blanched **almonds** (*page 5*).

Golden Sponge Cake

MRS. DWAYNE BURAK, GLADSTONE, MICH.

Set out a 10-in. tubed pan.

Sift together and set aside
- **1¾ cups sifted cake flour**
- **2 teaspoons baking powder**
- **¼ teaspoon salt**

Measure and pour into a large bowl
- **1 cup (about 12) egg yolks**

Add gradually to egg yolks and beat until thick and lemon-colored
- **½ cup orange juice**
- **¼ cup hot water**

Beat in
- **1 tablespoon grated orange peel (page 5)**
- **1 teaspoon orange extract**

Add gradually, beating well after each addition
- **1¼ cups sugar**

Gently fold in (*page 6*) dry ingredients in fourths until just blended.

Carefully turn batter into pan.

Bake at 325°F 60 to 65 min., or until cake surface springs back when lightly touched.

Immediately invert pan on end of tube; cool and remove from pan as directed for sponge-type cakes (*page 194*). *One 10-in. tubed cake*

▲ Cocoa Sponge Cake

Set out a 9-in. tubed pan.

Sift together and set aside
- **¾ cup sifted cake flour**
- **¼ cup cocoa**

Combine and beat until very thick and lemon-colored (3 to 4 min. with electric mixer on medium-high speed)
- **5 egg yolks**
- **½ cup sugar**
- **2 tablespoons lemon or orange juice**
- **1 teaspoon grated lemon or orange peel (page 5)**
- **1 teaspoon vanilla extract**

Set aside.

Using clean beater, beat until frothy
- **5 egg whites**
- **½ teaspoon salt**

Add gradually, beating well after each addition
- **½ cup sugar**

Continue beating until rounded peaks are formed and whites do not slide when bowl is partially inverted. Spread the egg-yolk mixture over beaten egg whites and gently fold (*page 6*) together. Fold in dry ingredients, sifting in about one fourth at a time. Fold after each addition. Turn batter into pan.

Bake at 325°F 60 to 65 min., or until cake surface springs back when lightly touched.

Immediately invert pan on end of tube; cool and remove from pan as directed for sponge-type cakes (*page 194*). *One 9-in. tubed cake*

△ True Sponge Cake

Follow ▲ Recipe; increase cake flour to 1 cup and omit cocoa.

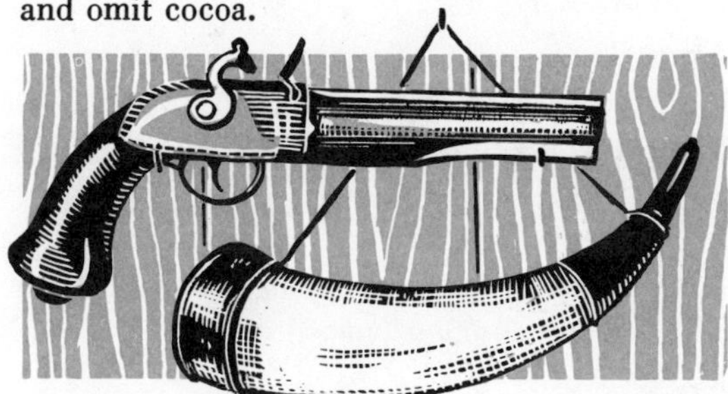

Banana-Pecan Chiffon Cake

Banana-Pecan Chiffon Cake

Set out a 10-in. tubed pan.

Measure and pour into a large bowl

1 cup (7 to 8) egg whites

Allow to stand at room temperature at least 1 hr. before beating to insure greater volume.

Put into a small bowl

5 egg yolks

Reserve remaining 2 or 3 egg yolks for use in other food preparation.

Chop finely and set aside

1 cup (about 4 oz.) pecans

Peel and force through sieve or food mill enough bananas to yield

1 cup sieved banana (2 to 3 bananas with brown-flecked peel)

Stir in until well blended

1 tablespoon lemon juice

Set aside.

Sift together into a bowl

2¼ cups sifted cake flour
1 cup sugar
1 tablespoon baking powder
¾ teaspoon salt

Make a well in center of dry ingredients and add

½ cup cooking (salad) oil

Add in order the 5 egg yolks and the sieved banana mixture. Beat until smooth. Set aside.

Using clean beater, beat the egg whites until frothy. Beat in

½ teaspoon cream of tartar

Add gradually, beating well after each addition

½ cup sugar

Beat until rounded peaks are formed and meringue (egg-white-sugar mixture) does not slide when bowl is partially inverted.

Slowly pour egg-yolk mixture over entire surface of meringue, then sprinkle pecans over surface of egg-yolk mixture. Gently fold (*page 6*) pecans, egg-yolk mixture, and meringue together until just blended. *Do not stir.* Carefully pour batter into pan, rotating pan as you pour in the batter.

Bake at 325°F 55 min., then at 350°F 10 to 15 min., or until cake surface springs back when lightly touched.

Immediately invert pan on end of tube; cool and remove from pan as directed for sponge-type cakes (*page 194*). *One 10-in. tubed cake*

Lemon Chiffon Cake

MRS. L. A. KING, JACKSONVILLE, N. C.

Frost the cake as suggested in the recipe or split when cold and fill and frost as layer cake.

Set out a 10-in. tubed pan.

Measure and pour into a large bowl

6 (about ¾ cup) egg whites

Allow to stand at room temperature at least 1 hr. before beating to insure greater volume.

Put into a small bowl

6 egg yolks

Sift together into a bowl

2¼ cups sifted cake flour
1 cup sugar
1 tablespoon baking powder
1 teaspoon salt

Make a well in center of dry ingredients; add

½ cup cooking (salad) oil

Add in order the 6 egg yolks and

¾ cup water
1 tablespoon lemon juice
1 teaspoon grated lemon peel (*page 5*)

Beat until smooth. Set aside.

Using clean beater, beat the egg whites until frothy. Beat in

½ teaspoon cream of tartar

Add gradually, beating well after each addition

½ cup sugar

Beat until rounded peaks are formed and meringue (egg-white-sugar mixture) does not slide when bowl is partially inverted. Slowly pour egg-yolk mixture over entire surface of meringue. Gently fold (*page 6*) together until just blended. *Do not stir.* Carefully pour batter into pan.

Bake at 325°F 55 min., then at 350°F 10 to 15 min., or until cake surface springs back when lightly touched.

Immediately invert pan on end of tube; cool and remove from pan as directed for sponge-type cakes (*page 194*).

Frost sides and top with

Lemon Butter Frosting (double recipe, *page 214*)

One 10-in. tubed cake

Sweetheart Cake

Set out three heart-shaped layer cake pans.

Prepare

Lemon Chiffon Cake (*page 198*)

Turn batter into pans.

Bake at 325°F 35 to 40 min., or until cake surface springs back when lightly touched.

Cool and remove from pans as directed for sponge-type cakes (*page 194*).

Prepare

Butter Cream Frosting (*page 214*)

When cake is completely cooled, fill the layers with the frosting.

Prepare

Sweetened Whipped Cream (double recipe, *page 223*)

Reserve 1 cup of the whipped cream for decoration. Spread top and sides of cake with a thin layer of the remaining cream.

Tint reserved portion a delicate pink with

1 or 2 drops red food coloring

Decorate, using a pastry bag and a No. 27 star tube (see photo).

Chill well before serving.

One heart-shaped layer cake

Sweetheart Cake

Pound Cake

Prepare (*page 194*) a 9½x5¼x2¾-in. loaf pan.

Sift together and set aside

2½ cups sifted cake flour
¾ teaspoon baking powder
¼ teaspoon salt
¼ teaspoon mace

Cream together until butter is softened

1 cup butter
2 teaspoons grated lemon peel (*page 5*)
1½ teaspoons vanilla extract
½ teaspoon almond extract

Add gradually, creaming until fluffy after each addition

1 cup plus 2 tablespoons sugar

Add in thirds, beating well after each addition

4 eggs, well beaten

Blend in dry ingredients in fourths. After each addition, beat only until smooth. Finally beat only until batter is smooth (do not overbeat).

Turn batter into pan. With spatula, draw batter from center toward edges of pan.

Bake at 325°F 1 hr. 10 min., or until cake tests done (*page 194*).

Cool; remove from pan as directed (*page 340*).

One 9x5-in. loaf cake

Note: Pound cake may be used as a base for Baked Alaska. Bake batter in a deep 9-in. sq. pan about 50 min. When cool, split into two layers. For round Alaska, trim corners.

Spice Cake, Basic Butter Frosting (page 214)

▲ Two-Egg Cake

Prepare (*page 194*) a 9x9x2-in. pan or two 8-in. round layer cake pans.

Sift together and set aside

1⅔ cups sifted cake flour
2 teaspoons baking powder
½ teaspoon salt

Cream together until shortening is softened

½ cup shortening
1 teaspoon vanilla extract

Add gradually, creaming until fluffy after each addition

1 cup sugar

Add in thirds, beating well after each addition

2 eggs, well beaten

Measure

½ cup milk

Beating only until smooth after each addition, alternately add dry ingredients in fourths, milk in thirds, to creamed mixture. Finally beat only until smooth (do not overbeat). Turn batter into pans.

Bake square cake at 350°F 35 to 45 min.; bake layers at 375°F 25 to 30 min., or until cake tests done (*page 194*).

Cool; remove from pans as directed (*page 194*).

Two 8-in. round layers or one 9-in. square cake

△ Spice Cake

Follow ▲ Recipe. Sift 1 teaspoon **cinnamon,** ¼ teaspoon **cloves** and ¼ teaspoon **nutmeg** with dry ingredients. Bake in square pan, layer or muffin pans. Frost top of cake with **Basic Butter Frosting** (*page 214*). To serve, cut into 2-in. squares.

△ Two-Egg Cupcakes

Follow ▲ Recipe; use 12 to 15 muffin-pan wells instead of 9x9x2-in. pan. Line with paper baking cups or grease bottom of wells. Fill each only two-thirds full. Bake at 375°F 20 to 25 min., or until cakes test done (*page 194*). Cool as directed (*page 194*). Frost with any favorite frosting. Decorate if desired.

Golden Honey Cake

(*See photo on page 217*)

Prepare (*page 194*) two 8-in. round layer cake pans.

Sift together into a large bowl

2 cups sifted cake flour
⅔ cup sugar
2 teaspoons baking powder
1 teaspoon salt
¼ teaspoon baking soda

Set out

¾ cup buttermilk or sour milk (*page 5*)

Add one half of milk to dry ingredients with

½ cup honey
½ cup hydrogenated vegetable shortening or all-purpose shortening
1 teaspoon vanilla extract

Stir only enough to moisten dry ingredients. Beat 200 strokes, or 2 min. on electric mixer on medium speed. Scrape sides of bowl several times during beating.

Add remaining milk and

4 egg yolks (about ⅓ cup), unbeaten

Beat 200 strokes, or 2 min. on electric mixer. Scrape sides of bowl several times. Turn into cake pans.

Bake at 350°F about 30 min., or until cake tests done (*page 194*).

Cool; remove from pans as directed (*page 194*).

Meanwhile, prepare

Honey-Chocolate Frosting (*page 217*)

Fill and frost (*page 213*) cake.

One 8-in. round layer cake

Golden Orange Crunch Cake

A golden beauty with its own baked-in topping.

Set out a 9-in. tubed pan.

For Crunch Topping—Chop finely

1½ cups (about 6 oz.) walnuts

Melt in a small saucepan over low heat

⅓ cup butter

Mix thoroughly the nuts, melted butter and

¾ cup fine, dry bread crumbs (about 2 slices bread)
½ cup firmly packed brown sugar
¼ teaspoon cinnamon
¼ teaspoon salt

Using the back of a spoon, press nut mixture very firmly into an even layer on bottom and sides of the tubed pan. Set aside.

For Cake—Sift together and set aside

3 cups sifted flour
1 tablespoon baking powder
½ teaspoon salt

Cream together until butter is softened

¾ cup butter
1 tablespoon grated orange peel (*page 5*)

Add gradually, creaming until fluffy after each addition

1¼ cups sugar

Add in thirds, beating well after each addition

3 eggs, well beaten

Measure and combine

½ cup undiluted evaporated milk
¼ cup orange juice

Beating only until smooth after each addition, alternately add dry ingredients in fourths, liquid in thirds, to creamed mixture. Finally beat only until smooth (do not overbeat). Turn batter into pan.

Bake at 375°F 55 to 60 min., or until cake tests done (*page 194*).

Remove cake from oven and place on a cooling rack. Allow cake to cool in pan 30 min. Cover with cake plate, carefully invert and remove pan. Cool thoroughly before cutting.

One 9-in. tubed cake

▲ Valentine Cake

Prepare (*page 194*) two 9-in. heart-shaped or round layer cake pans.

Sift together and set aside
3 cups sifted cake flour
1 tablespoon baking powder
½ teaspoon salt
Cream together until softened
1 cup butter or margarine
1 tablespoon vanilla extract
Add gradually, creaming until fluffy after each addition
1 cup sugar
Set aside.

Beat until frothy
6 egg whites
Add gradually, beating well after each addition
¾ cup sugar
Beat until rounded peaks are formed.

Measure
½ cup water
½ cup milk
Beating only until smooth after each addition, alternately add dry ingredients in fourths, liquid in thirds, to creamed mixture. Finally beat only until smooth (but do not overbeat). Spread beaten egg whites over batter and gently fold (*page 6*) together. Turn into pans.

Bake at 350°F 30 to 35 min., or until cake tests done (*page 194*).

Cool; remove from pans as directed (*page 194*).

Prepare
Creamy Cherry Filling (*page 222*)
Seven-Minute Frosting (*page 218*)
White Velvet Frosting (one-third recipe, *page 214*)
Place one cake layer on cake plate and spread filling over top. Place other layer over filling. Frost (*page 213*) with Seven-Minute Frosting.

Tint White Velvet Frosting desired color by blending in one or more drops **red food coloring.** Force frosting through pastry bag and No. 3 stem decorating tube to write on cake.

Valentine Cake

To Make Nosegays—Place small red **gumdrops** on wooden picks. Make soft folds in paper doilies from center to edge. Poke wooden picks down through center of doily and tie in place with red ribbon. Place nosegays on plate around cake. Make one nosegay without ribbon and place it on top of cake.

One 9-in. heart-shaped or round layer cake

Note: If round cake layers are used, heart-shaped layers can be made by cutting around a waxed-paper pattern with a knife.

△ Christmas Tree Cake

Prepare three 9-in. round cake layer pans.

Follow ▲ Recipe, making one and one-half times recipe. Do not prepare filling and Seven-Minute Frosting. Prepare **White Velvet Frosting** (double recipe, *page 214*). Place one third of frosting in a small bowl and tint by blending in one or more drops **green food coloring.**

Frost (*page 213*) two cake layers with untinted two-thirds of frosting. Cut third layer into a tree-shape by cutting around a tree-shaped waxed-paper pattern with a knife. Frost tree-shaped layer with the tinted frosting and place on top of other two cake layers. Decorate tree with **red cinnamon candies.**

▲ Happy Memories Cake

WILMA SCHULTZ, STOCKTON, KANS.

Prepare (*page 194*) a 13x9½x2-in. cake pan.

Sift together into a large bowl

2¼ cups sifted cake flour
1½ cups sugar
3½ teaspoons baking powder
¾ teaspoon salt

Set out

1 cup milk

Add one half of milk to dry ingredients with

½ cup hydrogenated vegetable shortening or all-purpose shortening
1½ teaspoons vanilla extract

Stir only enough to moisten dry ingredients.

Beat 200 strokes, or 2 min. on electric mixer. Scrape the sides of bowl several times during beating.

Add remaining milk and

4 egg whites, unbeaten

Beat 200 strokes, or 2 min. on electric mixer. Scrape the sides of bowl several times. Pour batter into pan.

Combine and mix thoroughly

1½ cups firmly packed dark brown sugar
½ cup cream

Pour brown-sugar-cream mixture over batter.

Sprinkle top with

1 cup (4 oz.) moist shredded coconut, cut

Bake at 350°F 30 to 35 min., or until cake tests done (*page 194*).

Using a spatula, loosen cake from sides of pan and invert immediately on serving plate. Let pan rest over cake a few seconds so sirup will drain onto cake. Remove pan, peel off waxed paper and serve warm or cold.

One 13x9-in. cake

△ Upside-Down Cupcakes

Line with paper baking cups 18 2½-in. muffin-pan wells.

Follow ▲ Recipe. Fill cups one-half full. Spoon one tablespoon of the brown-sugar mixture over each and sprinkle with coconut.

Bake at 350°F 20 to 25 min., or until cakes test done (*page 194*). Remove from cups and serve upside down.

Poppy Seed Cake

Prepare (*page 194*) two 8-in. round layer cake pans.

Mix together and let soak for 2 hours

½ cup (about 2½ oz.) poppy seeds
¾ cup milk

Sift together and set aside

2¼ cups sifted cake flour
2 teaspoons baking powder
½ teaspoon salt

Cream together until butter is softened

¾ cup butter
1 teaspoon vanilla extract

Add gradually, creaming until fluffy after each addition

1½ cups sugar

Beating only until smooth after each addition, alternately add dry ingredients in fourths, poppy seed-milk mixture in thirds, to creamed mixture. Finally beat only until smooth (do not overbeat).

Beat until rounded peaks are formed and egg whites do not slide when bowl is partially inverted

4 egg whites

Carefully spread beaten egg whites over batter and gently fold (*page 6*) together. Turn batter into pans.

Bake at 350°F 30 to 35 min., or until cake tests done (*page 194*).

Cool; remove from pans as directed (*page 194*). When cake is completely cooled, prepare

White Mountain Frosting (*page 219*)

Fill and frost (*page 213*) cake.

Sprinkle top of cake with **poppy seeds.**

One 8-in. round layer cake

Elegant Loaf Cake

Prepare (*page 194*) a 9½x5¼x2¾-in. loaf pan.

Coarsely chop and set aside
½ cup (about 2 oz.) walnuts

Chop very finely and set aside
1 cup (about 4 oz.) walnuts
¾ cup (about 6 oz.) candied cherries (*page 6*)
2 oz. (about ¼ cup, chopped) candied citron (*page 6*)

Sift together and set aside
2 cups sifted cake flour
2½ teaspoons baking powder
¾ teaspoon salt

Cream together until shortening is softened
⅔ cup shortening
1 teaspoon almond extract
½ teaspoon vanilla extract

Add gradually, creaming until fluffy after each addition
½ cup sugar

Add in thirds, beating well after each addition
2 egg yolks, well beaten

Measure
⅔ cup milk

Beating only until smooth after each addition, alternately add dry ingredients in fourths, milk in thirds, to creamed mixture. Finally beat only until smooth (do not overbeat). Stir in chopped cherries, citron and the cup of finely chopped nuts.

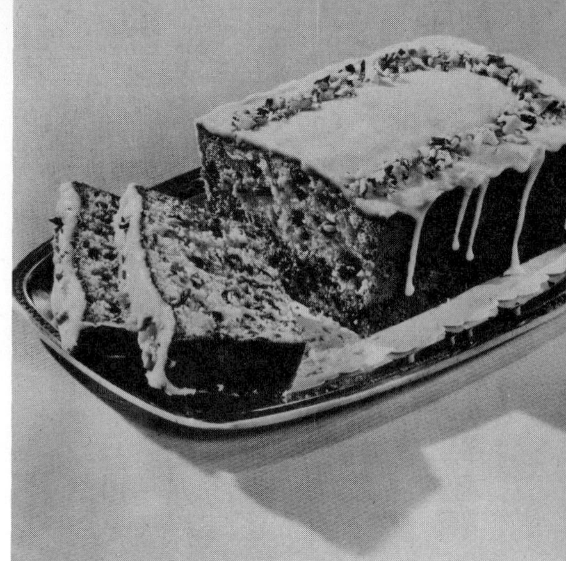

Elegant Loaf Cake with Glossy Vanilla Icing (page 220)

Beat until frothy
4 egg whites

Add gradually, beating well after each addition
¼ cup sugar

Beat until rounded peaks are formed. Spread beaten egg whites over batter and gently fold (*page 6*) together. Turn batter into pan.
Bake at 350°F 1 hr. 10 min., or until cake tests done (*page 194*).

Cool; remove from pan as directed (*page 194*).

Prepare
Glossy Vanilla Icing (*page 220*)

Top cake with icing and decorate with the coarsely chopped nuts. *One 9x5-in. loaf cake*

▲ Shower Cake

Prepare (*page 194*) two 9-in. round layer cake pans. Set a bowl and a rotary beater in refrigerator to chill.

Prepare and set in refrigerator to chill
Black Walnut Filling (*page 222*)
Set out
1½ cups sugar
Sift ½ cup of the sugar with
2 cups sifted cake flour
1 tablespoon baking powder
½ teaspoon salt
Set mixture aside.

Using chilled bowl and beater, whip (*page 7*)
1 cup chilled whipping cream
Beat in ¼ cup of the sugar. Set in refrigerator while beating egg whites.

Using clean beater, beat until frothy
4 egg whites
Add gradually the remaining ¾ cup sugar, beating well after each addition. Beat until rounded peaks are formed. Fold (*page 6*) the whipped cream and the beaten egg whites together with
¾ teaspoon almond extract
Measure
½ cup water
Folding only until blended after each addition, alternately add dry ingredients in fourths, water in thirds, to whipped cream mixture. Finally fold only until blended.

Shower Cake

Turn batter into pans.

Bake at 350°F 30 min., or until cake tests done (*page 194*).

Cool and remove from pans as directed (*page 194*). Cool completely and fill with the Black Walnut Filling.

Frost sides and top of cake with
Seven-Minute Frosting (*page 218*) or
White Mountain Frosting (*page 219*)
Reserve ½ cup frosting for decorating.

For Shower Decoration—If necessary, add 1 to 2 tablespoons sifted **confectioners' sugar** to the reserved frosting to give it a decorating-frosting consistency. Blend in **red food coloring,** a drop at a time, until frosting is a delicate pink color. Set frosting aside. To make umbrella, cut a piece of heavy aluminum foil into a wedge shape, 4 in. wide at base and 4 in. long. Curve wedge to form umbrella top (see photo). Using a spatula, spread pink frosting over both sides of umbrella, using lengthwise strokes on the outside to simulate umbrella spokes. Allow frosting to set on umbrella, keeping curved position.

At one side of the frosted cake form the shaft and curved handle of the umbrella by forcing remaining pink frosting through a pastry bag and No. 2 decorating tube. Make the shaft about 4 in. long. Using same decorating tube form small droplets over top of cake (see photo). Set umbrella top in place.

One 9-in. round layer cake

△ Meltaway Whipped Cream Cake

(*See photo on page 218*)

Follow ▲ Recipe. Omit Pineapple Cream Filling. Sift the 1½ cups of sugar and 8 tablespoons **cocoa** with the dry ingredients. Do not add sugar to whipped cream and egg whites. Decrease egg whites to 3; substitute 2 teaspoons **vanilla extract** for almond extract and ½ cup **milk** for water.

Chocolate Drum Cake

Prepare (*page 194*) two 9-in. round layer cake pans.

Melt (*page 6*) and set aside to cool

3 sq. (3 oz.) chocolate

Sift together and set aside

2½ cups sifted cake flour
1 teaspoon baking soda
¾ teaspoon salt

Cream together until lard is softened

¾ cup lard
2 teaspoons vanilla extract

Add gradually, creaming until fluffy after each addition

2 cups sugar

Add in thirds, beating thoroughly after each addition

5 egg yolks, well beaten

Blend in the cooled chocolate.

Measure

1 cup buttermilk or sour milk (*page 5*)

Beating only until smooth after each addition, alternately add dry ingredients in fourths, buttermilk or sour milk in thirds, to creamed mixture. Finally beat only until smooth (do not overbeat).

Beat until rounded peaks are formed

5 egg whites

Carefully spread egg whites over batter and gently fold (*page 6*) together. Turn batter into pans.

Bake at 375°F 30 to 35 min., or until cake tests done (*page 194*).

Cool; remove from pans as directed (*page 194*).

When cake is cooled, prepare

White Mountain Frosting (*page 219*)

Fill and frost (*page 213*) cake.

To Decorate as a Drum—Place round peppermint candies around top edge of cake to form rim of "drum". On sides of cake place peppermint candy sticks diagonally, extending sticks from top to bottom of cake.

One 9-in. round layer cake

Chocolate Cake

BEULAH RANDALL, PITTSFIELD, MAINE

Prepare (*page 194*) two 8-in. round layer cake pans.

Mix in a saucepan

½ cup sugar
½ cup cocoa
½ cup double-strength coffee beverage (*page 7*)

Bring to boiling. Boil 1 min., stirring constantly. Set aside to cool.

Melt and set aside to cool

½ cup shortening

Sift together and set aside

2 cups sifted flour
1 teaspoon baking soda
½ teaspoon salt

Beat until thick and piled softly

2 eggs

Add gradually, beating well after each addition

1 cup sugar

Stir in the cocoa mixture and the shortening.

Measure

1 cup buttermilk or sour milk (*page 5*)

Beating only until smooth after each addition, alternately add dry ingredients in fourths, buttermilk in thirds, to egg mixture. Finally beat only until smooth (do not overbeat).

Turn batter into pans.

Bake at 350°F 25 to 30 min., or until cake tests done (*page 194*).

Cool; remove from pans as directed (*page 194*).

Two 8-in round layers

▲ Sour-Cream Chocolate Cake

Prepare (*page 194*) two 8-in. round layer cake pans or one 9x9x2-in. cake pan.

Combine and set over simmering water

3 sq. (3 oz.) chocolate
½ cup double-strength coffee beverage (*page 7*)

When chocolate is melted, blend thoroughly.

Set aside to cool.

Sift together and set aside

2 cups sifted cake flour
1½ teaspoons baking soda
½ teaspoon salt

Combine and beat until well blended

1½ cups sugar
1 cup thick sour cream
2½ teaspoons vanilla extract

Add in thirds, beating well after each addition

2 eggs, well beaten

Beat in the chocolate mixture. Add dry ingredients in thirds, beating only until batter is smooth after each addition. Finally beat only until smooth (do not overbeat). Turn batter into pans.

Bake layers at 350°F 35 min.; bake square cake at 350°F 40 to 45 min., or until cake tests done (*page 194*).

Cool; remove from pans as directed (*page 194*).

Meanwhile, prepare

Bittersweet Velvet Frosting (page 215)

Frost (*page 213*) cake. Garnish (see photo) with

Walnut halves

One 8-in. round layer cake
or one 9-in. square cake

△ Black Walnut Chocolate Cake

Follow ▲ Recipe. Stir in ⅔ cup (2⅓ oz.) chopped **black walnuts** with final strokes.

Sour-Cream Chocolate Cake with Bittersweet Velvet Frosting (page 215)

Chocolate Potato Cake

Prepare (*page 194*) two 9-in. round layer cake pans.

Set out

1 cup mashed potato

Melt (*page 6*) and set aside to cool

1 sq. (1 oz.) chocolate

Sift together and set aside

2 cups sifted cake flour
2 teaspoons baking powder
½ teaspoon salt

Blend together

1 cup hydrogenated vegetable shortening or all-purpose shortening
2 teaspoons grated lemon peel (page 5)

Add gradually, creaming until fluffy after each addition

2 cups sugar

Add in thirds, beating well after each addition

4 eggs, well beaten

Stir in the cooled chocolate.

Blend potatoes with

½ cup milk

Beating only until smooth after each addition, alternately add dry ingredients in fourths, potato mixture in thirds, to creamed mixture. Finally beat only until smooth (do not overbeat). Turn batter into pans.

Bake at 350°F 40 to 45 min., or until cake tests done (*page 194*).

Cool; remove from pans as directed (*page 194*).

Two 9-in. round layers

Note: Grated **raw potatoes** may be substituted for the cooked ones; grate them just after adding the eggs to the creamed mixture.

Maple Sirup Cake

Prepare (*page 194*) three 8-in. round layer cake pans.

For Cake—Sift together and set aside

2⅔ cups sifted cake flour
1 tablespoon baking powder
¾ teaspoon salt

Cream until softened

¾ cup shortening

Add gradually, creaming until fluffy after each addition

⅔ cup firmly packed light brown sugar

Set mixture aside.

Add in thirds, beating thoroughly after each addition

7 egg yolks, well beaten

Measure and blend together

⅔ cup milk
⅔ cup maple sirup

Beating only until smooth after each addition, alternately add dry ingredients in fourths, liquid in thirds, to creamed mixture. Finally beat only until smooth (do not overbeat).

Turn batter into pans.

Bake at 350°F 45 to 50 min., or until cake tests done (*page 194*).

Cool; remove from pans as directed (*page 194*).

For Jam Filling—When cake layers are completely cooled, set out

⅔ cup raspberry jam

Spread one half of the jam over top of bottom cake layer. Cover with second cake layer; spread top of second layer with remaining jam. Cover with third layer.

For Frosting—Prepare

Maple Frosting (*page 220*)

Frost (*page 213*) sides and top of cake.

One 8-in. round layer cake

Burnt Sugar Cake

Prepare (*page 194*) a 9x9x2-in. cake pan.

For Burnt Sugar Sirup—Melt in a heavy, light-colored skillet (a black skillet makes it difficult to see the color of the sirup) over low heat

2 cups sugar

With back of wooden spoon, gently keep sugar moving toward center of skillet until it is melted. Heat to a rich brown, until foam appears. Remove from heat and add gradually, a very small amount at a time

1½ cups boiling water

Cook until bubbles are the size of dimes (about 5 min.). Set aside to cool completely.

Note: Burnt Sugar Sirup may be stored in a tightly covered jar for future use.

For Cake—Sift together

2½ cups sifted cake flour
2½ teaspoons baking powder
½ teaspoon salt

Set aside.

Cream together until shortening is softened

½ cup shortening
1 teaspoon vanilla extract

Add gradually, creaming until fluffy after each addition

½ cup sugar

Add in thirds, beating well after each addition

2 egg yolks, well beaten

Mix together

½ cup water
½ cup Burnt Sugar Sirup (part of remainder to be used for Burnt Sugar Frosting)

Beating only until smooth after each addition, alternately add dry ingredients in fourths, liquid in thirds, to creamed mixture. Finally beat only until smooth (do not overbeat).

Beat until frothy

2 egg whites

Add gradually, beating thoroughly after each addition

¼ cup sugar

Beat until rounded peaks are formed. Spread beaten egg whites over batter and gently fold (*page 6*) together. Turn batter into pan.

Bake at 350°F 35 to 40 min., or until cake tests done (*page 194*).

Cool; remove from pan as directed (*page 194*).

When cake is completely cool, prepare

Burnt Sugar Frosting (*page 215*)

Frost sides and top of cake. Sprinkle top with

Chopped toasted pecans

One 9-in. square cake

Note: For a square layer cake, double recipe.

Burnt Sugar Cake with Burnt Sugar Frosting (page 215)

Cocoa Date-Nut Cake

KAY CALHOUN, SITKA, ALASKA

This unusual cake comes from a homestead in Alaska where numerous chores and limited facilities make short cuts in baking important.

Prepare (*page 194*) a 9x9x2-in. cake pan.

Coarsely chop

1 cup (about 7 oz.) pitted dates
½ cup (about 2 oz.) walnuts

Combine the chopped dates and nuts with

1 cup boiling water

Set aside to cool.

Sift together into a large bowl

2 cups sifted flour
1 cup sugar
3 tablespoons cocoa
1 teaspoon baking soda
⅛ teaspoon salt

Make a well in center of dry ingredients and add all at one time, the date-nut mixture and

1 cup mayonnaise
1 teaspoon vanilla extract

Beat only until batter is blended (do not overbeat). Turn batter into pan.

Bake at 375°F 45 min., or until cake tests done (*page 194*).

Cool; remove from pan as directed (*page 194*).

One 9-in. square cake

Cleveland Cake

(Crumb Cake)

MRS. WILL W. COTTINGHAM, ROLLA, MO.

Prepare (*page 194*) a 13x9½x2-in. cake pan.

Coarsely chop and set aside
1 cup (about 4 oz.) walnuts
Sift together into a large bowl
3 cups sifted flour
2 cups sugar
Cut in with pastry blender or two knives until pieces are the size of small peas
1 cup butter
Measure 1 cup of the crumb mixture and set aside.

To remaining crumb mixture in bowl, stir in until well blended, a mixture of
2 tablespoons cinnamon
1 tablespoon cocoa
1 teaspoon nutmeg
1 teaspoon baking soda
½ teaspoon baking powder
¼ teaspoon salt
¼ teaspoon cloves
Mix in walnuts and
1 cup (about 5 oz.) seedless raisins
Make a well in center of dry ingredients and add all at one time
2 cups buttermilk or sour milk (page 5)
Beat until just blended.

Turn batter into pan and sprinkle top with the reserved crumb mixture.

Bake at 350°F 1 hr., or until cake tests done (*page 194*).

Cool; remove from pan as directed (*page 194*).

18 to 24 servings

Graham Cracker Cake

MRS. L. E. COX, Jr., GREENEVILLE, TENN.

A truly superior cake, but a bit temperamental. It may choose to dip slightly toward the center on the day you bake it. The flavor, however, is dependable—and thoroughly delicious.

Prepare (*page 194*) a 9x9x2-in. cake pan.

Crush (*page 6*)
25 graham crackers (or enough to yield 2 cups crumbs)
Turn crumbs into a bowl. Stir in
2 teaspoons baking powder
Set aside.

Cut into short lengths and set aside
1 cup (4 oz.) moist shredded coconut
Cream together until butter is softened
½ cup butter
1 teaspoon vanilla extract
Add gradually, creaming until fluffy after each addition
1 cup sugar
Add in thirds, beating well after each addition
3 eggs, well beaten
Stir in the graham mixture and the coconut.

Turn batter into pan. With spatula, draw batter from center toward edges of pan.

Bake at 350°F 40 to 45 min., or until cake tests done (*page 194*).

Cool; remove from pan as directed (*page 194*).

One 9-in. square cake

Ambrosia White Fruitcake

MRS. E. C. MEREDITH, VICKSBURG, MISS.

Prepare (*page 194*) 10-in. tubed pan.

Put in a large bowl
- **1 cup sifted flour**

Chop and combine with flour
- **½ lb. candied pineapple (about 1⅔ cups, chopped)**
- **½ lb. candied cherries (about 1⅔ cups, chopped)**
- **½ lb. pecans (about 2 cups, chopped)**

Add and set aside
- **5 oz. (about 1 cup) golden raisins**
- **4 oz. (about 1 cup) moist shredded coconut, cut**

Sift together and set aside
- **2 cups sifted flour**
- **1 teaspoon baking powder**

Cream together until butter is softened
- **1 cup butter**
- **1 tablespoon vanilla extract**

Add gradually, creaming until fluffy after each addition
- **2 cups sugar**

Measure
- **½ cup unsweetened pineapple juice**

Beating only until smooth after each addition, alternately add dry ingredients in fourths, liquid in thirds, to creamed mixture. Finally beat only until smooth (do not overbeat). Pour batter over the fruit-coconut mixture and mix thoroughly.

Beat until rounded peaks are formed and egg whites do not slide when bowl is partially inverted
- **8 egg whites**

Carefully spread beaten egg whites over batter and fold (*page 6*) together.

Place a shallow pan containing 2 cups water on bottom rack of oven during baking time. Turn batter into pan, spreading evenly.

Bake at 275°F about 4 hrs., or until cake tests done (*page 194*) with cake tester.

Cool completely, remove from pan and store (*page 192*). Once or twice a week, using a pastry brush, paint cake with rum and store again.

About 4½ lbs. fruitcake

Christmas Fruitcake

MRS. CLIFFORD MAREK, BLOOMER, WIS.

Prepare (*page 194*) two 8-in. round layer cake pans.

Combine in a 2-qt. saucepan, bring to boiling and cook over low heat 10 min., stirring occasionally
- **1 cup (about 7 oz.) pitted dates**
- **1 cup (about 5 oz.) seedless raisins**
- **1 cup plus 2 tablespoons water**
- **1 cup sugar**
- **½ cup hydrogenated vegetable shortening or all-purpose shortening**
- **1 teaspoon cinnamon**
- **1 teaspoon cloves**

Remove from heat and set aside to cool.

Meanwhile, mix together in a large bowl and set aside
- **½ cup sifted flour**
- **4 oz. (about ¾ cup) whole Brazil nuts**
- **2 oz. (about ½ cup) walnut halves**
- **½ lb. (about 1½ cups) whole candied cherries**

Sift together
- **2 cups sifted flour**
- **½ teaspoon baking soda**
- **½ teaspoon salt**

Beating only until blended after each addition, add dry ingredients in thirds to cooked fruit mixture. Finally beat only until blended (do not overbeat). Pour batter over nut-cherry mixture and mix thoroughly.

Place a shallow pan containing 2 cups water on bottom rack of oven during baking time. Turn batter into pans, spreading to edges.

Bake at 325°F 1 hr., or until cake tests done. Cool completely, remove from pans and store (*page 192*). Once or twice a week, using a pastry brush, paint cakes with brandy or sherry, and store again. *About 3¼ lbs. fruitcake*

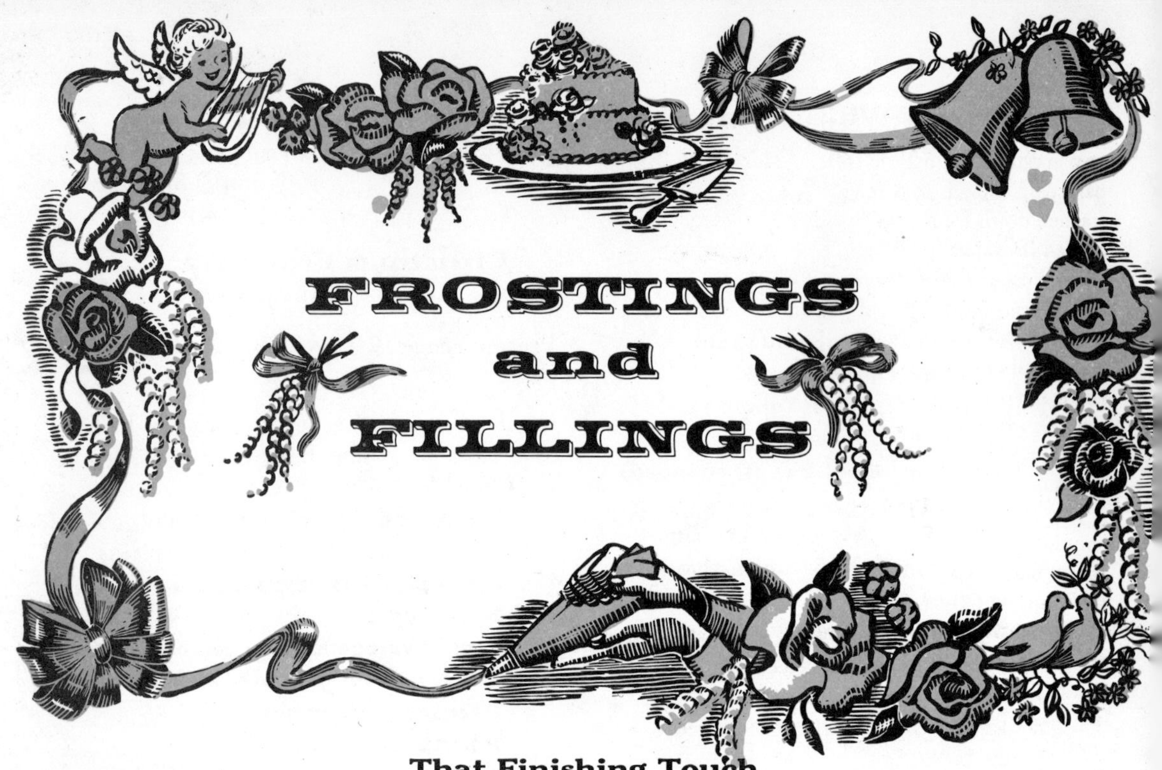

That Finishing Touch

A cake without frosting may be laden with virtues and be a fine creation. Yet somehow, cake seems to come into its glory only when it is decked in a sculptured or swirled coat of sweetness. Frostings may be plain or fancy, chocolate brown or pale as dawn, delicately laced with essence of fruits or flecked with fragments of nuts or candy. They may be prepared in many ways, but they are always designed for delight.

SUGAR, in some form, is the main ingredient in cooked and uncooked frostings. As used in these recipes, *sugar* refers to granulated beet or cane sugar.
Confectioners' or powdered sugar is granulated sugar crushed and screened to a desired fineness. It usually contains a small amount of cornstarch to prevent caking. Generally, confectioners' sugar is finer than powdered sugar although there are no set standard terms in the sugar industry. Uncooked frostings prepared with the finer confectioners' sugar remain softer longer than those prepared with a coarser powdered sugar. The reason—the smaller the particle size the greater the total surface area, thus the greater amount of moisture held.
Brown sugar is a soft sugar that contains three to four per cent moisture. It ranges in color from yellow to dark brown. The intensity of molasses flavor increases as the color deepens. Brown sugar adds color and flavor as well as sweetening to the finished product.
Maple sugar is the solid product that is left after evaporation of maple sap or maple sirup.
Corn sirup, made from cornstarch, is commonly marketed in two forms, white and dark. Dark corn sirup is used in products where the darker color and distinctive flavor are desirable.
Molasses is the sirup remaining when most of the sugar has crystallized from cane sirup.
Maple sirup is made from the sap of the sugar maple tree.
Honey is the nectar of plants gathered, modified and stored in the comb by honey bees. Extracted or strained honey is used in cooking.

COOKED FROSTINGS—Seven-minute, white mountain and fudge frostings are the basic cooked frostings. Special flavorings and other ingredients are added to create any number of frostings.

These frostings are easy to make successfully if certain techniques and rules are followed.

All the sugar crystals must be dissolved before cooking starts to prevent unwanted graininess in the frosting. The steam formed during the first 5 minutes of cooking period, while the saucepan is covered and the mixture boiling, helps to dissolve any crystals that may have formed on the sides of pan. Any crystals that form during cooking may be washed down from sides of pan with a pastry brush dipped in water.

Separate egg whites very carefully from egg yolks. Any trace of egg yolk in the whites will cut down the volume of beaten egg whites and the quality of the frosting. Beat egg whites when they are at room temperature for the greatest volume.

Use a candy thermometer for accurate temperature readings. The cold water tests may be used if a thermometer is not available.

The saucepan used for cooking a sirup or frosting should be large enough to allow contents to boil freely without running over. If a cover is needed, it should be tight-fitting.

The double boiler should be large enough for the amount of frosting to be beaten.

Use clean spoons for each process-stirring, testing and beating. Otherwise undissolved sugar crystals may get into the finished frosting and cause it to become grainy.

When the humidity is high, cook frostings 2 to 4 degrees higher so frosting will hold its shape.

Seven-Minute Frosting—All the ingredients (except flavoring extracts) are combined in the top of a double boiler. As soon as the double-boiler top is set over simmering water the mixture should immediately be beaten. Beating should continue until the frosting holds stiff peaks. Move a rotary beater throughout the mixture while beating for thorough blending. Extract is blended in last.

White Mountain Frosting—A hot sugar sirup is cooked to a given temperature and then poured in a steady fine stream into stiffly beaten egg whites while beating constantly. If using a hand rotary beater, turn it over on its side and beat mixture with one hand while pouring sirup with the other. If the frosting is slow to thicken, let it stand for several minutes; if too firm, blend in hot water, a few drops at a time, until it is of spreading consistency.

Fudge Frosting—The frosting is cooked to a given temperature and beaten, when the mixture has cooled sufficiently (bottom of the pan should feel just comfortably warm), until it becomes creamy and begins to lose its gloss. If it hardens too quickly, beat in about one tablespoon of hot milk or water. It is important to use *clean* spoons each time the frosting is stirred, beaten or tested; this helps to avoid graininess.

UNCOOKED FROSTINGS—Often the uncooked confectioners' sugar frosting is called butter frosting. For a smooth frosting, sift confectioners' sugar before using and add in small amounts to the creamed mixture, beating well after each addition. From a few basic frostings, many variations result with the addition of flavorings, nuts and fruits.

TO FILL AND FROST—Cool cake completely before frosting. Brush loose crumbs off cake. Cover cardboard, cut ½ inch larger than cake, with aluminum foil. Arrange cake or bottom cake layer on covered cardboard. For ease and convenience, put cake on a stand so cake can be turned while frosting. Use a flexible spatula to frost cake.

Tubed, Loaf, Sheet and Square Cake—Place cake on cake plate. Frost sides first, working rapidly. See that frosting touches plate, covering cardboard all around bottom, leaving no gaps. Pile remaining frosting on top of cake and spread lightly.

Layer Cake—Place cake layer, bottom side up, on cake plate. Spread filling or frosting over top of layer. Cover with the second layer, bottom side down, fitting it so that cake is even. (Repeat procedure if more layers are used with top layer, bottom side down.) If necessary, hold layers in position with wooden picks or metal skewers; remove when filling is set. Frost sides of cake first, working rapidly. See that frosting touches plate all around bottom, leaving no gaps. Pile remaining frosting on top of cake and spread lightly.

Decorating—Use pastry bag and decorating tubes.

WHEN YOU COOK SIRUPS—A candy thermometer is an accurate guide to correct stage of cooking. Hang thermometer on pan so bulb does not touch side or bottom of pan.

Sirup Stages and Temperatures

Thread (230°F to 234°F)—Spins 2-in. thread when allowed to drop from fork or spoon.

Soft Ball (234°F to 240°F)—Forms a soft ball in very cold water; flattens when taken from water.

Firm Ball (244°F to 248°F)—Forms a firm ball in very cold water; does not flatten in fingers.

Hard Ball (250°F to 266°F)—Forms a ball which is pliable but holds its shape in very cold water.

Soft Crack (270°F to 290°F)—Forms threads which are hard but not brittle in very cold water.

Hard Crack (300°F to 310°F)—Forms threads which are hard and brittle in very cold water.

Decorating Frosting

Easy to use for many interesting decorations.

Cream together until softened
2 tablespoons butter or margarine
½ teaspoon vanilla extract
Thoroughly blend in, in order
1½ cups sifted confectioners' sugar
1 tablespoon warm cream
Tint as desired, with about
1 drop food coloring
Use for decorating cakes, cup cakes and petits fours. *About 1½ cups frosting*

▲ Basic Butter Frosting

(*See photo on page 200*)

Cream together until butter is softened
¼ cup butter
1 teaspoon vanilla extract
Add gradually, beating well after each addition
2 cups sifted confectioners' sugar
Stir in and beat to spreading consistency
1 tablespoon milk or cream
Enough to frost sides and tops of two 8-in. cake layers or 24 cupcakes

△ Lemon Butter Frosting

Follow ▲ Recipe. Substitute **lemon juice** for milk. If desired, add a few drops of **yellow food coloring.**

△ Mocha Butter Frosting

Follow ▲ Recipe. Add and beat in 1 teaspoon **concentrated soluble coffee** with the confectioners' sugar.

△ Chocolate Butter Frosting

Follow ▲ Recipe. Melt (*page 6*) 2 sq. (2 oz.) **chocolate.** Cool; stir in with milk or cream.

Butter Cream Frosting

Cream together until softened
½ cup butter or margarine
½ teaspoon almond extract
Add gradually, beating well after each addition
5 cups sifted confectioners' sugar
Mix in (enough for spreading consistency)
4 to 5 tablespoons milk or cream
Tint with **green food coloring** if desired.
Enough to generously frost sides and tops of three 9-in. round cake layers

▲ White Velvet Frosting

Cream together until softened
¼ cup butter or margarine
1½ teaspoons vanilla extract
⅛ teaspoon salt
Add gradually, beating until smooth after each addition
3 cups sifted confectioners' sugar
Blend in
1 egg yolk
Add slowly to blended mixture
3 tablespoons milk or cream
Beat until frosting is of spreading consistency.
Enough to frost sides and tops of two 8- or 9-in. round cake layers

△ Brown Velvet Frosting

Follow ▲ Recipe. Melt (*page 6*) and cool 2 sq. (2 oz.) **chocolate;** mix in after addition of egg yolk.

Bittersweet Velvet Frosting

(*See photo on page 207*)

Melt (*page 6*) together and stir until smooth

4 sq. (4 oz.) chocolate
3 tablespoons butter or margarine

Remove from heat and add, beating well

2¼ cups sifted confectioners' sugar
½ cup rich milk or cream
1 teaspoon vanilla extract

Enough to frost sides and tops of two 8-in. round cake layers

Burnt Sugar Frosting

(*See photo on page 209*)

Cream together until softened

¼ cup butter or margarine
1 teaspoon vanilla extract

Blend in and beat until thoroughly blended

2 cups sifted confectioners' sugar
5 tablespoons Burnt Sugar Sirup (*page 208*)
1½ tablespoons cream
Few grains salt

Enough to frost sides and top of one 9-in. square cake layer

▲ Cream Cheese-Cocoa Frosting

Blend together

3 oz. (1 pkg.) cream cheese, softened
½ teaspoon vanilla extract

Sift together and add gradually

1 cup confectioners' sugar
3 tablespoons cocoa

Beat well after each addition.

Mix in (enough for spreading consistency)

Milk or cream

Enough to frost one 8- or 9-in. round cake layer

△ Cream Cheese-Chocolate Frosting

Follow ▲ Recipe. Melt (*page 6*) and cool 1 sq. (1 oz.) **chocolate;** mix in after sugar.

Cream Cheese-Lemon Frosting

Blend together

3 oz. (1 pkg.) cream cheese, softened
2 teaspoons lemon juice
½ teaspoon grated lemon peel (*page 5*)

Add gradually, beating well after each addition

2½ cups sifted confectioners' sugar

If frosting is too stiff to spread, add

Several drops milk or cream

Enough to frost sides and top of one 8-in. square cake

Caramel Mocha Frosting

MRS. ELSTON CHITTENDEN
SPRINGFIELD, MO.

Sift together and set aside

3½ cups sifted confectioners' sugar
2 teaspoons cocoa

Cream together until softened

½ cup butter or margarine
1 tablespoon vanilla extract

Add dry ingredients gradually, beating until smooth after each addition.

Blend in

1 egg yolk

Add slowly to blended mixture

3 tablespoons double-strength coffee beverage (*page 7*)

Beat until frosting is of spreading consistency.

Enough to frost sides and tops of three 9-in. round cake layers

Peanut Mocha Frosting

LONACE E. GEARHART, SAN DIEGO, CALIF.

Blend thoroughly

1 tablespoon peanut butter
½ teaspoon vanilla extract

Beat in until thoroughly blended

3 cups sifted confectioners' sugar
¼ cup double-strength coffee beverage (*page 7*)

Enough to frost sides and tops of two 8-in. round cake layers or one 9-in. square cake layer

▲ Mocha Cocoa Frosting

Sift together

3 cups confectioners' sugar
½ cup cocoa

Make a well in center.

Add and beat until smooth

½ cup butter or margarine, softened
3 tablespoons double-strength coffee beverage (*page 7*)

Add and beat well

2 egg yolks or 1 whole egg

Enough to frost sides and tops of two 9-in. cake layers

△ Cocoa Cream Frosting

Follow ▲ Recipe. Substitute for coffee, ¼ cup **cream** or top **milk.**

△ Toasted Almond Chip Frosting

Follow ▲ Recipe. Sprinkle 1 cup (about 5½ oz.) sliced, toasted **almonds** (*page 6*) on top and sides of frosted cake.

△ Sunshine Chocolate Frosting

Follow ▲ Recipe. Substitute for coffee, 1 or 2 tablespoons **lemon juice** or **orange juice** with 1 teaspoon grated **peel** (*page 5*).

Banana Frosting

MRS. JAMES T. MOORE, SAN ANGELO, TEXAS

Peel and force through a sieve or food mill enough banana to yield

½ cup sieved banana (1 banana with brown-flecked peel)

Stir in

½ teaspoon lemon juice

Cream until softened

¼ cup butter

Measure

3½ cups sifted confectioners' sugar

Add sugar and sieved banana alternately to creamed butter, beating thoroughly after each addition. Finally beat until frosting is of spreading consistency.

Enough to frost sides and tops of two 9-in. round cake layers

▲ Confectioners' Sugar Frosting

Combine

1 cup sifted confectioners' sugar
½ teaspoon vanilla extract

Add

Milk or cream

(Use just enough milk or cream to make a frosting that will hold its shape when forced through a pastry bag and tube.)

About 1 cup frosting

Note: Mixture may be tinted by stirring in one or more drops of **food coloring.**

△ Confectioners' Sugar Glaze

Follow ▲ Recipe. Thin frosting to spreading consistency with additional milk or cream (about 2 tablespoons). Or substitute **water** for milk or cream. Drizzle glaze over hot breads, sweet rolls or coffee cake.

Fudge Glaze

Rich and glossy—black beauty elegance.

Melt (*page 6*) together and set aside

2 sq. (2 oz.) chocolate
3 tablespoons butter or margarine

Heat

¼ cup cream

Mix in

1¼ cups sifted confectioners' sugar
⅛ teaspoon salt

Vigorously stir in the melted chocolate mixture until frosting is smooth.

Enough to glaze top of one 9-in. cake layer

Honey-Chocolate Frosting

A frosting with a hint of honey in it to give it an intriguingly "different" flavor.

Combine in top of double boiler and place over simmering water

½ cup sugar
2 sq. (2 oz.) chocolate, cut in pieces
⅓ cup honey
¼ cup cream or rich milk
¼ cup butter or margarine
⅛ teaspoon salt

When chocolate is melted, blend well with rotary beater.

Vigorously stir about 3 tablespoons of the hot mixture into

2 egg yolks, slightly beaten

Immediately blend into the mixture in top of double boiler.

Cook over simmering water, stirring constantly. When slightly thickened (about 2 min.), remove from heat; place pan in bowl of ice and water and beat frosting until of spreading consistency.

Enough to frost sides and tops of two 8-in. round cake layers

Honey-Chocolate Frosting on Golden Honey Cake (page 201)

▲ Seven-Minute Frosting

Combine and mix well in top of a double boiler

- **1½ cups sugar**
- **⅓ cup water**
- **1 tablespoon white corn sirup**
- **⅛ teaspoon salt**
- **2 egg whites, unbeaten**

Place over simmering water and immediately beat with rotary beater 7 to 10 min., or until mixture holds stiff peaks.

Remove from heat and blend in

- **1 teaspoon vanilla extract**

Enough to frost sides and tops of two 9-in. cake layers

Note: Mixture may be tinted by gently stirring in one or more drops of **food coloring.**

Seven-Minute Frosting on Meltaway Whipped Cream Cake (page 205)

△ Green Valley Frosting

Follow ▲ Recipe; substitute a few drops **peppermint extract** for vanilla extract. Blend in about 2 drops **green food coloring.**

△ Seven-Minute Pistachio Frosting

Follow ▲ Recipe; substitute ½ to 1 teaspoon **pistachio extract** for vanilla extract. Blend in 1 or 2 drops **green food coloring.** If desired, sprinkle ½ cup (about 2 oz.) chopped salted **pistachio nuts** evenly over top of frosted cake in any desired pattern.

△ Seven-Minute Peppermint Frosting

Follow ▲ Recipe. Fold in (*page 6*) ½ cup finely crushed **peppermint-stick candy** and about 2 drops **red food coloring.**

△ Seven-Minute Chocolate Frosting

Melt (*page 6*) 3 sq. (3 oz.) **chocolate** and set aside to cool. Follow ▲ Recipe. Blend in chocolate when mixture holds stiff peaks.

Fluffy White Frosting

MRS. A. E. SEASTROM, HOPEDALE, MASS.

Set out a candy thermometer and a 1-qt. saucepan having a tight-fitting cover.

Combine in the saucepan

1½ cups sugar
½ cup water

Place over low heat, stirring until sugar is dissolved. Cover saucepan and bring to boiling.

Boil 5 min. to help dissolve any crystals that may have formed on sides of pan. Uncover saucepan and put candy thermometer in place (*page 213*). Continue cooking without stirring until mixture reaches 230°F (thread stage, *page 213*; remove from heat while testing).

Using pastry brush dipped in water, wash down crystals from sides of saucepan from time to time during cooking.

Meanwhile, beat until frothy

2 egg whites

Add

½ teaspoon cream of tartar

Beat until stiff (but not dry) peaks are formed.

Continue beating egg whites while pouring the hot sirup over them in a steady thin stream. (Do not scrape sirup from bottom and sides of pan.) After all the sirup is added, continue beating, 2 to 3 min., or until frosting is very thick and forms rounded peaks (holds shape). Fold in (*page 6*) with minimum number of strokes

½ teaspoon lemon extract

Enough to frost sides and tops of three 8-in. round cake layers

White Mountain Frosting

Set out a candy thermometer and a medium-size saucepan having a tight-fitting cover.

Combine in the saucepan

2 cups sugar
¾ cup water
2 tablespoons white corn sirup
⅛ teaspoon salt

Place over low heat, stirring gently until sugar is dissolved. Cover saucepan and bring to boiling. Boil 5 min. to help dissolve any crystals that may have formed on sides of pan.

Uncover saucepan and put candy thermometer in place (*page 213*). Continue cooking, without stirring, until mixture reaches 244°F (firm ball stage, *page 213*; remove from heat while testing). Using pastry brush dipped in water, wash down crystals from sides of saucepan from time to time during cooking.

Beat until stiff (but not dry) peaks are formed

½ cup (about 4) egg whites

Continue beating egg whites while pouring the hot sirup over them in a steady thin stream. (Do not scrape sirup from bottom and sides of pan.) After all the hot sirup is added, continue beating 2 to 3 min., or until frosting is very thick and forms rounded peaks (holds shape). Fold in (*page 6*) with minimum number of strokes

2 teaspoons vanilla extract
½ teaspoon almond extract
¼ teaspoon orange extract

Frost (*page 213*) cake immediately.

Enough to frost sides and tops of two 8- or 9-in. round cake layers

▲ Glossy Vanilla Icing

(*See photo on page 204*)

Cook in top of double boiler over simmering water, stirring until shortening is melted

¼ cup sugar
¼ cup cream
1½ teaspoons white corn sirup
2 teaspoons butter or margarine

Remove from heat; gradually blend in, in order

1½ cups sifted confectioners' sugar
1¼ teaspoons vanilla extract

If frosting is too stiff to spread, blend in

Several drops cream

With spatula, spread frosting on top of cake, allowing some frosting to trickle down the sides of the cake. *Enough to frost top of one 9x5-in. loaf cake*

△ Glossy Rum Frosting

Follow ▲ Recipe. Substitute ¾ teaspoon **rum extract** for vanilla extract.

Broiler Fudge Frosting

Have ready a hot cake in an 8-in. square pan.

Coarsely chop and set aside

½ cup (about 2 oz.) nuts

Cream until fluffy

2 tablespoons butter or margarine, softened
½ cup firmly packed brown sugar
2 tablespoons cocoa

Blend in until smooth

2 tablespoons cream

Stir in the chopped nuts. Spread lightly over the cake.

Set temperature control of range at Broil.

Place cake in broiler with top of frosting about 4 in. from source of heat. Broil about 1 min. or until frosting bubbles. Watch closely to avoid scorching. *Enough to frost top of one 8-in. square cake*

Quick Fudge Frosting

Heat in double-boiler top over simmering water

1 pkg. (6 oz.) semi-sweet chocolate pieces
⅔ cup (one-half 15-oz. can) sweetened condensed milk
1 tablespoon water

Stir until chocolate is melted and mixture is smooth. Remove from heat; cool in pan of ice and water. *Enough to frost sides and top of one 8-in. square cake*

Maple Frosting

Set out a candy thermometer and a 1-qt. saucepan having a tight-fitting cover.

Combine in the saucepan

¾ cup maple sirup
½ cup sugar

Place over low heat, stirring until sugar is dissolved. Cover saucepan and bring to boiling. Boil 5 min. to help dissolve any crystals that may have formed on sides of pan. Uncover saucepan and put candy thermometer in place (*page 213*). Continue cooking without stirring until mixture reaches 230°F (thread stage, *page 213*; remove from heat while testing).

Using pastry brush dipped in water, wash down crystals from sides of saucepan from time to time during cooking.

Beat until stiff (but not dry) peaks are formed

1 egg white
Few grains salt

Continue beating egg white while pouring the hot sirup over it in a thin steady stream. (Do not scrape sirup from bottom and sides of pan.) After all the sirup is added, continue beating 2 to 3 min., or until frosting is very thick and forms rounded peaks (holds shape). Fold in (*page 6*) with minimum strokes

1 teaspoon vanilla extract

Enough to frost sides and tops of two 8-in. square cake layers or three 8-in. round cake layers

Marshmallow Chocolate Filling

Melt over simmering water

32 marshmallows (about ½ lb.), cut in quarters (*page 6*)

1 sq. (1 oz.) chocolate

Meanwhile, prepare and set aside

¼ cup (about 1 oz.) chopped seedless raisins

¼ cup (about 1 oz.) chopped nuts

½ teaspoon grated orange or lemon peel (*page 5*)

Remove melted marshmallows and chocolate from heat and stir in

1 tablespoon cream

Blend in the raisins, nuts and grated peel. Stir until filling is of spreading consistency.

(Omit chocolate if white filling is desired.)

Enough filling for one 8- or 9-in. cake layer

Lemon Filling

Combine in double-boiler top and beat slightly with rotary beater

3 egg whites

1 cup sugar

3 tablespoons lemon juice

1 teaspoon grated lemon peel (*page 5*)

Place over simmering water. Cook about 5 min., or until thickened, stirring constantly.

Vigorously stir about 3 tablespoons of hot mixture into

3 egg yolks, slightly beaten

Immediately blend into mixture in double boiler. Cook over simmering water 10 min.; stir slowly to keep mixture cooking evenly. Remove from heat and cool thoroughly before using.

About 1 cup filling

Orange Filling

Mix together in top of double boiler

½ cup sugar

2½ tablespoons cornstarch

⅛ teaspoon salt

Add gradually, stirring in

½ cup water

½ cup orange juice

Stirring gently and constantly, bring rapidly to boiling over direct heat and cook for 3 min. Cover and cook over simmering water 12 min., stirring three or four times.

Vigorously stir about 2 tablespoons hot mixture into

1 egg yolk, slightly beaten

Immediately blend into mixture in double boiler. Cook over simmering water 3 to 5 min., stirring slowly and constantly to keep mixture cooking evenly.

Remove from heat and blend in

1 tablespoon lemon juice

1 tablespoon grated orange peel (*page 5*)

2 teaspoons butter or margarine

Cool filling before spreading on the cake.

About 1 cup filling

Uncooked Orange Filling

Mix together and set aside

¾ cup orange juice

½ cup sugar

1 tablespoon grated orange peel (*page 5*)

Beat until frothy

2 egg whites

Add gradually, beating thoroughly after each addition

¼ cup sugar

Beat until stiff (but not dry) peaks are formed (peaks remain standing when beater is slowly lifted upright).

Gently fold (*page 6*) orange mixture into beaten egg whites.

About 1 cup filling

▲ Creamy Vanilla Filling

Excellent as is and adaptable in endless ways. Just add chopped nuts, coconut or crushed fruit.

Set out

1½ cups cream

Scald (*page 7*) in top of double boiler 1 cup of the cream; reserve remainder.

Meanwhile, sift together into a small saucepan

⅓ to ½ cup sugar
2½ tablespoons flour
¼ teaspoon salt

Blend in the reserved cream; add gradually, stirring in, the scalded cream. Bring rapidly to boiling over direct heat, stirring gently and constantly; cook 3 min. Remove from heat.

Wash the double-boiler top to remove scum; pour cream mixture into it and place over simmering water. Cover and cook about 5 to 7 min., stirring three or four times.

Vigorously stir about 3 tablespoons of the mixture into

3 egg yolks, slightly beaten

Immediately blend into mixture in double boiler. Cook over simmering water 3 to 5 min., stirring slowly and constantly to keep mixture cooking evenly.

Remove from heat and blend in

1 tablespoon butter or margarine
2 teaspoons vanilla extract
¼ teaspoon almond extract

Cover, cool slightly and chill in refrigerator.

About 1½ cups filling

△ Creamy Cherry Filling

Follow ▲ Recipe. Substitute 1 to 2 tablespoons **maraschino-cherry sirup** for almond extract. Fold ½ cup chopped **maraschino cherries.**

△ Black-Walnut Cream Filling

Follow ▲ Recipe. Blend in ¾ cup (about 3 oz.) coarsely chopped **black walnuts.**

Chocolate Filling

Melt (*page 6*) and set aside to cool

2 sq. (2 oz.) chocolate

Bring just to boiling

¾ cup hot water

Sift together into top of a double boiler

1 cup sugar
¼ cup cornstarch
½ teaspoon salt

Stir in and blend well

¼ cup cold water

Gradually add the boiling water. Stirring gently and constantly bring mixture rapidly to boiling over direct heat, and cook 3 min. Place over simmering water; cover and cook 12 min., stirring three or four times.

Remove from heat; stir in melted chocolate and

¼ cup butter or margarine
2 teaspoons vanilla extract

Cool filling slightly.

About 1 cup filling

▲ Sweetened Whipped Cream

Place a rotary beater and a 1-qt. bowl in refrigerator to chill.

Using the chilled bowl and beater, beat until soft peaks are formed when beater is slowly lifted upright

1 cup chilled whipping cream

Beat into whipped cream with final few strokes until blended

3 tablespoons sifted confectioners' sugar
1 teaspoon vanilla extract

Set in refrigerator if not used immediately.

About 2 cups whipped cream

Note: Mixture may be tinted by gently stirring in one or more drops of **food coloring.**

△ Mocha Whipped Cream

Follow ▲ Recipe. Sift 1 teaspoon **concentrated soluble coffee** with the sugar.

△ Dutch Cocoa Whipped Cream

Follow ▲ Recipe. Sift 3 tablespoons **Dutch process cocoa** with the sugar.

△ Rum Whipped Cream

Follow ▲ Recipe. Substitute 1 to 1½ tablespoons **rum** for vanilla extract.

△ Almond Whipped Cream

Blanch (*page 5*), sliver and toast (*page 6*) ½ cup (about 3 oz.) **almonds** and set aside. Follow ▲ Recipe; substitute ¼ teaspoon **almond extract** for vanilla extract.

Fold (*page 6*) the almonds into the whipped cream after blending in the sugar and extract.

Coffee Whipped Cream

Place a rotary beater and a bowl in refrigerator to chill.

Pour into a small cup or custard cup

2 tablespoons cold double- or triple-strength coffee beverage (*page 7*)

Sprinkle evenly over cold coffee

1 teaspoon unflavored gelatin

Let stand about 5 min. to soften. Dissolve gelatin completely by placing over hot water.

Using the chilled bowl and rotary beater, beat only until frothy

1 cup chilled whipping cream

Stir cooled gelatin. *Very* gradually add gelatin to cream and continue to beat after each addition until cream is of medium consistency (piles softly). Work quickly. When all gelatin has been added, beat into whipped cream with final few strokes until blended

⅓ cup sifted confectioners' sugar

Beat until cream stands in peaks when beater is slowly lifted upright.

Filling for 24 Miniature Puffs

Note: The use of gelatin in the whipped cream helps to stabilize the cream or to hold its volume and shape. Therefore, when the stabilized whipped cream is used to decorate molds or used as a filling or frosting, it should hold its shape for hours, if necessary.

The Art of Cookie Making

Surely there is a special place in heaven for the unknown person—probably a grandmother—who created the first cookies! The perfect small treat, cookies are for the eager hands of children and for the child in all of us that never grows up. On these pages are gathered treasured recipes for cookies for all occasions, including the daily, never-ending occasion when some member of the family has a little empty spot and seeks the cookie jar for wherewithal to fill it.

THE PERFECT COOKIE should have good flavor, tender crumb unless the variety is a hard cookie, soft or crisp texture depending upon variety of cookie, uniform color and uniform shape depending upon type of cookie.

TYPES—Cookies are classified in many ways—by the texture of the baked cookie (soft or crisp), the consistency of batter or dough (soft or stiff), the richness of cookie (plain or rich), or by the method used in shaping the cookie.

Bar—Dough is baked in a four-sided pan and cut into bars or squares after baking.

Refrigerator (*icebox*)—Dough is pressed into a cookie mold or shaped into a thick roll or bar, chilled and kept in refrigerator ready to be cut into thin slices with a sharp, thin knife and baked.

Drop—Dough is dropped from a teaspoon onto a lightly greased cookie sheet.

Molded—Dough is shaped by hand.

Pressed—Dough is soft enough to go through a cookie press but stiff enough to hold a shape.

Rolled—Dough is rolled to desired thickness on a lightly floured surface and cut into various shapes with a cookie cutter.

INGREDIENTS—Each ingredient has its own role to play in the cookie batter or dough.

Flour—Generally all-purpose; major ingredient in all batter and dough products; when combined with moisture gives structure to baked products.

Sugar—Contributes sweetness and flavor. As sugar is increased in proportion to flour it tends to increase browning and crispness. Liquid forms of sweetening (honey, sugar sirup, maple sirup and molasses) may supply liquid.

Fat—Increases tenderness, gives flavor and aids in browning.

Liquid—From melted (caramelized) sugar, liquid, sweetenings, melted or liquid fat or eggs is often sufficient. Milk, buttermilk, sweet or sour cream, fruit juices or water are liquids used, but in a small proportion to flour because cookie batters and doughs are meant to be fairly stiff.

Eggs—May or may not be used; increase fineness of texture, add flavor and color, act to bind the ingredients together and sometimes leaven the batter or dough, especially beaten egg whites. Too large a proportion of eggs can make the texture tough; when large number of eggs is used, amount of fat should be increased to counteract toughening effect of eggs.

Leavening Agents—In some cases, no leavening ingredient is needed. Often both baking powder and baking soda are used together. *Air*—may be the only leavening when beaten into egg whites as in ladyfingers and meringue-type cookies. *Baking powder*—may be the sole leavening agent. *Baking soda*—used to neutralize acid foods such as molasses, buttermilk, sour cream, fruit juices and dried fruits. When baking soda is not used to neutralize the acid ingredient in cookies, it nevertheless tends to tenderize the cookies. Some cookies with no baking soda or an insufficient amount tend to have light-colored centers and browned edges.

Other Ingredients—Various flavoring extracts, spices, nuts, fruits in several forms, citrus peels, cereals, chocolate, cocoa, candies, mincemeat and coconut are used alone or in suitable combinations for the various cookies. Wheat germ, when added, increases food value and imparts a pleasing nut-like flavor and crispness. Avoid chunky pieces in the cookie dough when using a cookie press.

A Check List for Successful Cookie Making

(See For These Recipes—What To Use, How To Do It and Oven Temperatures on *pages 4-7.*)

√ **Read** recipe carefully.

√ **Assemble** all ingredients and utensils.

√ **Have all ingredients** at room temperature unless recipe specifies otherwise.

√ **Select pans** of proper kind and size. Measure inside, from rim to rim.

√ **Lightly grease** cookie sheets or pan. If recipe states "set out cookie sheets or pan," do not grease cookie sheets or pan.

√ **Use standard measuring cups and spoons.** Use liquid measuring cups (rim above 1-cup line) for liquids. Use nested or dry measuring cups (1-cup line even with top) for dry ingredients. *Check liquid* measurements at eye level. *Level dry* measurements with straight-edged knife or spatula.

√ **Preheat oven** 12 to 20 min. at required temperature. Leave oven door open first 2 min.

√ **Place oven rack** so top of product will be almost at center of oven. Stagger pans so no pan or cookie sheet is directly over another and they do not touch each other or walls of oven. Place single pan so that center of product is as near center of oven as possible.

√ **Sift all flour** except whole-grain types before measuring. Spoon lightly into measuring cup. Do not jar. Level with straight-edged knife or spatula.

√ **Cream shortening** (alone or with flavorings) by stirring, rubbing or beating with spoon or electric mixer until softened. Add sugar in small amounts; cream after each addition until all graininess disappears and mixture is light and fluffy.

√ **Beat whole eggs** until thick and piled softly when recipe calls for well-beaten eggs.

√ **Beat egg whites** as follows: *Frothy*—entire mass forms bubbles; *Rounded peaks*—peaks turn over slightly when beater is slowly lifted upright; *Stiff peaks*—peaks remain standing when beater is slowly lifted upright.

√ **Beat egg yolks** until thick and lemon-colored when recipe calls for well-beaten yolks.

√ **When dry and liquid ingredients** are added to batters, add alternately, beginning and ending with dry. Add dry ingredients in fourths, liquid in thirds. After each addition, mix only until well blended. Finally mix only until batter is well blended (do not overmix). Scrape spoon or beater and bottom and sides of bowl during mixing. If using an electric mixer, beat at a low speed when alternately adding dry and liquid ingredients.

√ **Apply baking tests** when minimum baking time is up. Thin, crisp cookies are baked to an even, delicate brown. Drop and soft, thicker cookies are done when almost no imprint remains when lightly touched with finger tip. Some bar cookies test done when a wooden pick or cake tester comes out clean when inserted in center.

√ **Remove cookies** from pans as they come from the oven, unless otherwise directed. Set on cooling racks to cool.

√ **Store cookies** when cool in a cookie jar, canister or casserole having a cover.

√ **Pack cookies** for mailing, wrapped (separately if possible) in moisture-vapor-proof material, in sturdy container lined with extra wrapping material. Used crumpled waxed paper, popcorn or shredded packing material to fill extra space.

▲ Marbled Brownies

For Cheese Mixture—Cream until softened
1½ tablespoons butter or margarine
Add gradually, creaming until fluffy after each addition
3 tablespoons sugar
Blend in, in order
2 teaspoons cornstarch
⅔ cup dry cottage cheese
1 egg, well beaten
1 tablespoon milk
½ teaspoon vanilla extract
⅛ teaspoon salt
Set aside.

For Brownie Dough—Grease and set aside a 9x9x2-in. pan.

Melt (*page 6*) and set aside to cool
2 sq. (2 oz.) chocolate
Sift together
1 cup sifted cake flour
½ teaspoon baking powder
½ teaspoon salt
Set aside.

Chop and mix with dry ingredients
1 cup (about 4 oz.) nuts
Cream together until softened
½ cup butter or margarine
½ teaspoon vanilla extract
Add gradually, creaming until fluffy after each addition
1 cup sugar
Add in thirds, beating thoroughly after each addition
2 eggs, well beaten
Stir in the chocolate. Blend in dry ingredients in fourths.

Spread one half of dough in pan. Spread cheese mixture over chocolate layer. Spread remaining dough over cheese mixture. Draw spoon through layers until marbled effect is produced.

Bake at 375°F 40 to 45 min., or until wooden pick inserted in center comes out clean. Remove pan to cooling rack; cool in pan and cut into squares. *16 brownies*

Fudge Brownies with Basic Butter Frosting (page 214)

△ Fudge Brownies

(*See photo on page 238*)

Follow ▲ Recipe for dough. Omit cheese mixture. Frost with any **butter-type frosting.**

Double-Decker Brownies

CLAUDE E. METZ, MORENCI, MICH.

An innovation in brownie-making that makes these popular favorites doubly appealing.

Grease and set aside two 9x9x2-in. pans.

Finely chop
1 cup (about 4 oz.) pecans
Mix with pecans and set aside
1 pkg. (6 oz.) semi-sweet chocolate pieces
Grind enough dates to yield
½ cup (3½ oz.) ground dates
Set aside.

Sift together
¾ cup sifted flour
5 tablespoons cocoa
½ teaspoon salt
Set aside.

Cream together

½ cup shortening

1 teaspoon vanilla extract

Add gradually, creaming until fluffy after each addition

1 cup sugar

Add in thirds, beating thoroughly after each addition

3 eggs, well beaten

Mixing until well blended after each addition, add dry ingredients in fourths to creamed mixture. Blend in the ground dates. Turn one half of the batter into each pan, spreading evenly. Sprinkle one half of the pecan mixture over batter. Set aside.

Melt

⅓ cup shortening

Blend into melted shortening

1 cup firmly packed brown sugar

Set sugar mixture aside to cool.

Sift together and set aside

1 cup sifted flour

½ teaspoon baking powder

½ teaspoon baking soda

½ teaspoon salt

Add to sugar mixture, beating thoroughly

1 egg, well beaten

1 teaspoon vanilla extract

Mixing until well blended after each addition, add dry ingredients in fourths. Spread one half of this batter evenly over the batter in each pan.

Bake at 350°F about 30 min., or until wooden pick inserted in center comes out clean. Remove pans to cooling racks. Cut into bars while still warm; cool completely in pan.

4 doz. brownies

Raspberry Squares

MRS. A. E. MARTINSON
DETROIT LAKES, MINN.

Set out an 8x8x2-in. pan.

Chop and set aside

2 cups (about 8 oz.) moist, shredded coconut

Measure and set aside

½ cup raspberry jam

Sift together and set aside

1 cup sifted flour

1 teaspoon baking powder

Cream until softened

½ cup butter or margarine

Add gradually, beating thoroughly after each addition

1 egg, well beaten

Blend in

1 tablespoon milk

Mixing until well blended after each addition, add dry ingredients in fourths to creamed mixture. Spread batter evenly in the pan and cover with the raspberry jam. Set aside.

Melt and set aside to cool

¼ cup butter or margarine

Beat until thick and piled softly

1 egg

1 teaspoon vanilla extract

Add gradually, beating thoroughly after each addition

1 cup sugar

Blend in the cooled butter and chopped coconut. Spread over cookie batter in the pan.

Bake at 350°F 30 min., or until golden brown.

Remove pan to cooling rack. When completely cooled, cut into 2-in. squares. *16 cookies*

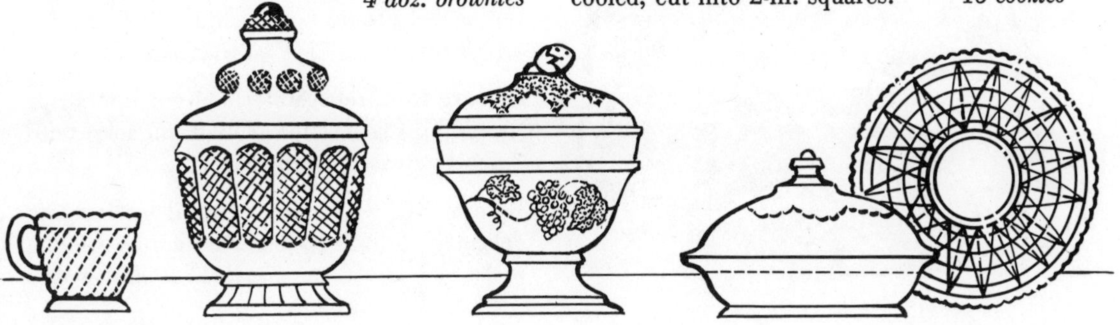

Grandma's Crisscross Cookies

DOROTHY HJORTH, LONG BEACH, CALIF.

Set out a 15½x10½x1-in. jelly roll pan.

Sift together

3 cups sifted flour
½ cup sugar

Cut in with a pastry blender or two knives until pieces are the size of small peas

1 cup butter

Beat until thick and lemon-colored

3 egg yolks

Blend egg yolks into flour mixture. Mix in

½ cup orange juice

Chill in refrigerator 2 to 3 hrs.

Pat three-fourths of the dough evenly over bottom of pan. Spread evenly over dough about

1 cup strawberry or apricot jam

Roll out remaining dough ¼ in. thick. Cut into strips ½ in. wide and 4 to 5 in. long. With hands, roll and stretch dough into long, pencil-thin strips. Cut to desired lengths. Place strips over jam-covered dough forming a crisscross pattern.

Bake at 300°F 40 min. Remove pan to cooling rack; cool completely. Cut the baked dough into 2½x1-in. strips. *About 5 doz. cookies*

French Nut Sticks

EMILY EWING, EASTON, MD.

Lightly grease a 15½x10½x1-in. jelly roll pan.

Measure and set aside

3 cups sifted cake flour

Cream together until butter is softened

¾ cup butter
1 teaspoon vanilla extract

Add gradually, beating until fluffy after each addition

1 cup sugar

Add in thirds, beating thoroughly after each addition

2 eggs, well beaten

Mixing until well blended after each addition, add dry ingredients in fourths to creamed mixture. Turn dough into pan, spreading evenly. Spread evenly over dough

1 cup (12-oz. jar) apricot preserves

Bake at 350°F 15 min., or until edges of dough are lightly browned. Set aside on cooling rack; do not remove from pan.

Finely chop

1 cup (about 4 oz.) pecans

Set aside.

Beat until frothy

2 egg whites
⅛ teaspoon salt

Add gradually, beating thoroughly after each addition, a mixture of

1 cup sugar
1 tablespoon flour

Continue beating until rounded peaks are formed and egg whites do not slide when bowl is partially inverted. Fold in (*page 6*) the chopped pecans. Spread meringue evenly over the cooled cookie layer. Chill in refrigerator 2 to 3 hrs.

Remove from refrigerator and cut into strips 2½x½-in. Place strips about ½ in. apart onto 2 lightly greased baking sheets.

Bake at 375°F 15 min., or until meringue is delicately browned. Remove bars to cooling racks. *About 10 doz. cookies*

▲ Refrigerator Cookies
(Basic Chocolate and Vanilla Doughs)

Melt (*page 6*) and set aside to cool
2 sq. (2 oz.) chocolate
Sift together and set aside
3 cups sifted flour
2 teaspoons baking powder
½ teaspoon salt
Cream together
1 cup shortening
2 teaspoons vanilla extract
Add gradually, creaming until fluffy after each addition
1 cup sugar
Add in thirds, beating thoroughly after each addition
2 eggs, well beaten
Mixing until well blended after each addition, add dry ingredients in fourths to creamed mixture.

Divide dough into two equal portions. Stir into one portion of the dough the melted chocolate and
1 tablespoon milk
Wrap each half of dough in waxed paper and chill in refrigerator until easy to handle.

Shape each dough into 2 rolls, 1½ in. in diameter. Wrap each roll in waxed paper and chill several hours or overnight.

Set out cookie sheets.

Remove rolls from refrigerator as needed. Cut into ⅛-in. slices. Place them 1½ in. apart on the cookie sheets.

Bake at 400°F 5 to 9 min. Remove to cooling racks. *10 doz. cookies*

△ Pinwheels

Follow ▲ Recipe. After chilling dough enough to handle, divide each dough into three portions. Roll one third of the chocolate and one third of the white dough into rectangles about 8x6x⅛-in. Place rolled chocolate dough on top of white dough and roll up tightly into a roll. Repeat process, forming two more rolls. Wrap each roll in waxed paper and chill in refrigerator several hours or overnight. Proceed as in ▲ Recipe.

△ Stripers

Follow ▲ Recipe. After chilling dough enough to handle, divide each dough into six portions. Roll two portions of the chocolate dough into rectangles about 6x2x¼-in. Roll two portions of the white dough to the same size. Line a shallow pan with waxed paper. Stack layers in pan, alternating colors and brushing each layer with slightly beaten **egg white** before putting on the next layer. Repeat process with remaining portions of dough, forming two additional stacks. Wrap waxed paper around each block of dough. Chill several hours or overnight.

Remove blocks from refrigerator as needed. Remove from pan and unwrap. Cut into slices ¼ in. thick and place 1½ in. apart on the cookie sheets. Bake as in ▲ Recipe.

▲ Date Swirls

CLAUDE E. METZ, MORENCI, MICH.

For Filling—Combine in a saucepan and cook over low heat until thickened (about 5 min.)

- **3 cups (about 1¼ lb.) chopped pitted dates**
- **¾ cup sugar**
- **¾ cup water**

Remove from heat. Blend in

- **½ cup (about 2 oz.) chopped nuts**
- **4 teaspoons lemon juice**

Set aside to cool.

For Cookies—Sift together and set aside

- **4 cups sifted flour**
- **1½ teaspoons salt**
- **1 teaspoon baking soda**

Cream together until softened

- **½ cup butter**
- **½ cup shortening**

Add gradually, creaming until fluffy after each addition

- **2 cups firmly packed brown sugar**

Add gradually, beating thoroughly after each addition

- **1 egg, well beaten**

Mixing until well blended after each addition, add dry ingredients in fourths to creamed mixture. After the third addition, blend in

- **2 tablespoons milk**

Chill in refrigerator until easy to handle.

Divide dough into halves. Roll out one portion ¼ in. thick. Spread with one half of the cooled filling. Roll up like a jelly roll. Repeat with second portion of dough. Cut rolls into halves crosswise, forming four short rolls.

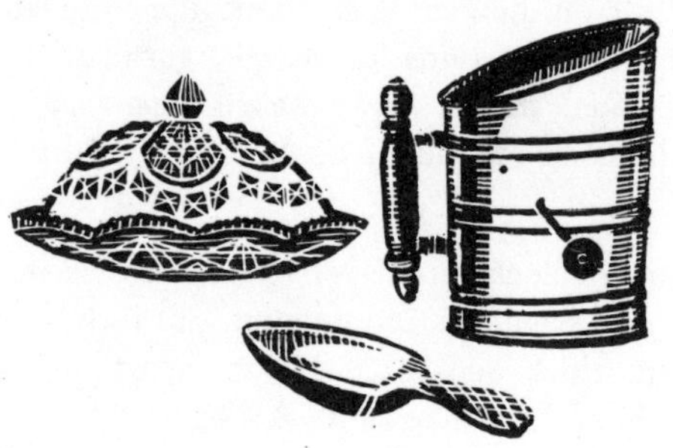

Wrap each in waxed paper. Chill in refrigerator several hours or overnight.

Lightly grease cookie sheets.

Remove rolls from refrigerator as needed. Cut into thin slices and place about 2 in. apart on the cookie sheets.

Bake at 400°F 10 to 15 min. Remove to cooling racks. *About 6 doz. cookies*

△ Butterscotch Refrigerator Cookies

Follow ▲ Recipe; omit date filling. Cream 1½ teaspoons **vanilla extract** and 3 drops **walnut extract** with the shortening. Decrease flour to 3 cups. Add 1 cup chopped **walnuts** to dough before chilling. Form dough into five rolls about 1½ in. in diameter. Bake on *ungreased* cookie sheets at 375°F 10 min.

About 12 doz. cookies

French Pain d'Amande

MRS. GLENA E. WILSON, MADISON, OHIO

A French grandmother taught her grandchild how to make these cookies a half-century ago. They are traditional Christmas cookies in Aniche, France.

Finely chop and set aside

- **½ cup (about 3 oz.) blanched almonds (*page 5*)**

Sift together and set aside

- **2 cups sifted flour**
- **¼ teaspoon baking soda**
- **¼ teaspoon cinnamon**

Cream until softened

- **½ cup butter**

Add gradually, creaming until fluffy after each addition

- **1 cup plus 2 tablespoons firmly packed brown sugar**

Add gradually, beating thoroughly after each addition

- **1 egg, well beaten**

Mixing until well blended after each addition,

add dry ingredients in fourths to creamed mixture. Blend in the chopped almonds. Chill dough in refrigerator until easy to handle.

Shape into short rolls about 2 in. in diameter. Wrap each roll in waxed paper. Chill in refrigerator several hours or overnight.

Set out cookie sheets.

Remove rolls from refrigerator as needed. Cut into ⅛-in. slices and place about 1 in. apart on the cookie sheets.

Bake at 375°F 10 min. Remove to cooling racks. *About 7 doz. cookies*

▲ Krispie Oatmeal Cookies

MRS. FRANK YOUNG, TOPEKA, KANS.

Coarsely chop and set aside

½ cup (about 2 oz.) nuts

Sift together and set aside

1½ cups sifted flour
1 teaspoon baking soda
1 teaspoon salt

Cream together

1 cup shortening
1 teaspoon vanilla extract

Add gradually, creaming until fluffy after each addition

1 cup sugar
1 cup firmly packed brown sugar

Add in thirds, beating thoroughly after each addition

2 eggs, well beaten

Mixing until well blended after each addition, add dry ingredients in fourths to creamed mixture. Blend in the nuts and

2 cups uncooked rolled oats
½ cup semi-sweet chocolate pieces or raisins

Form into 4 rolls about 2 in. in diameter, chilling dough first if necessary. Wrap each roll in waxed paper. Chill in refrigerator several hours or overnight.

Set out cookie sheets.

Remove rolls from refrigerator as needed. Cut into thin slices and place about 1 in. apart on the cookie sheets.

Bake at 375°F 10 to 12 min. Remove to cooling racks. *About 8½ doz. cookies*

△ Oatmeal Drops

Follow ▲ Recipe. Omit forming rolls and chilling dough. Drop by teaspoonfuls 2 in. apart onto *lightly greased* cookie sheets. Garnish with pieces of **dates** or **nuts.**

Oatmeal Drops

Perky Cookies

(*See photo on page 238*)

MRS. FRED H. LARSON, VILLANOVA, PA.

Set out cookie sheets.

Finely chop and set aside
1 cup (about 4 oz.) pecans
Put into a small dish and set aside
½ cup sugar
Sift together and set aside
2¼ cups sifted flour
1 teaspoon cinnamon
1 teaspoon ground cardamom seed
½ teaspoon baking soda
Cream together until softened
1¼ cups butter or margarine
½ teaspoon vanilla extract
Add gradually, beating until fluffy after each addition
1 cup firmly packed brown sugar
Beat until thick and piled softly
1 egg
1 egg yolk
Add in thirds to creamed mixture, beating thoroughly after each addition. Mixing well after each addition, blend in the dry ingredients in fourths. Shape into balls 1 in. in diameter. Set aside.

Beat until frothy
1 egg white
Dip balls into egg white, then in nuts and finally in sugar. Flatten each cookie slightly. Place 1½ in. apart on cookie sheets.

Bake at 350°F 15 to 18 min.

About 5 doz. cookies

Berlinerkranser

MRS. PEARL CARLETON, EMILY, MINN.

Traditional to Christmas, but always a favorite.

Lightly grease cookie sheets.

Sift together into a large bowl
4 cups sifted flour
½ teaspoon baking soda
Cut in with a pastry blender or two knives until pieces are size of small peas
1 cup butter
Set aside.

Beat until thick and lemon-colored
4 egg yolks
Add gradually, beating well after each addition
1 cup sugar
Blend into the egg mixture
½ cup thick sour cream
1 teaspoon vanilla or almond extract
Blending lightly after each addition, add the liquid mixture in thirds to the flour mixture. Chill dough until firm enough to roll.

Break off small pieces of dough. Roll with hands on a lightly floured surface into rolls about 6 in. long and ¼ in. thick. Form into wreaths or bowknots, or twist into pretzels. Brush top of each cookie with
Egg white, slightly beaten
Dip each cookie in
Crushed loaf sugar
Bake at 350°F until firm and very lightly browned (about 10 min.).

About 8 doz. cookies

▲ Buttery Nut Cookies

CLAUDE E. METZ, MORENCI, MICH.

From a proud husband comes his wife's Christmas specialty—a cookie "rich as candy."

Set out cookie sheets.

Melt and set aside to cool
2 cups butter
Finely chop and set aside
2 cups (about 8 oz.) walnuts
Measure and set aside
4 cups sifted flour
Mix until well blended, the cooled butter and
1 cup firmly packed brown sugar
4 teaspoons vanilla extract
Measure
½ cup milk
Mixing until well blended after each addition, alternately add flour in fourths, milk in thirds, to butter mixture. Blend in the walnuts. Place in refrigerator to chill slightly.

Form into balls about 1 in. in diameter; roll in
½ cup sugar
Place balls about 2 in. apart on cookie sheets. Using the tines of a fork, flatten each ball, making a crisscross design.

Bake at 400°F 10 to 12 min. Remove to cooling racks. *About 11 doz. cookies*

△ Pecan Crispies

Follow ▲ Recipe. Substitute 2 cups finely chopped **pecans** for the walnuts.

Chocolate Snowflake Cookies

MRS. W. L. ISBELL, BROOKSTON, IND.

A delightful surprise awaits you when you open the oven door.

Melt (*page 6*) together
2 sq. (2 oz.) chocolate
¼ cup shortening
Add, stirring until sugar is dissolved
1 cup sugar
Set aside to cool.

Coarsely chop
1 cup (about 4 oz.) nuts
Set aside.

Sift together
1 cup sifted flour
1 teaspoon baking powder
¼ teaspoon salt
Set aside.

Add in thirds to the cooled chocolate mixture, beating thoroughly after each addition
2 eggs, well beaten
1 teaspoon vanilla extract
Quickly blend in dry ingredients. Stir in the chopped nuts. Chill dough about 3 hrs.

Lightly grease cookie sheets.

Dampen hands slightly and roll small pieces of dough between palms to form balls about 1 in. in diameter. Roll balls in
Sifted confectioners' sugar
Place 2 in. apart on the cookie sheets.

Bake at 400°F 10 to 12 min. Remove to cooling racks. *About 4 doz. cookies*

▲ Plain and Fancy Sugar Cookies

Sift together and set aside
2 cups sifted flour
1½ teaspoons baking powder
½ teaspoon salt
Cream together until softened
½ cup butter or margarine
1 teaspoon vanilla extract
Add gradually, creaming until fluffy after each addition
¾ cup sugar
Add in thirds, beating thoroughly after each addition
2 eggs, well beaten
Mixing until well blended after each addition, add dry ingredients gradually to the creamed mixture. Chill thoroughly in refrigerator.

Lightly grease cookie sheets.

Roll dough ¼ to ⅛ in. thick on lightly floured surface. Using floured cookie cutter, cut dough into desired shapes. Sprinkle cookies with
Sugar or colored sugar
Place cookies on cookie sheets.

Bake at 375°F 10 to 12 min. Immediately remove to cooling racks. *2 to 3 doz. cookies*

△ Ginger Cookies

Follow ▲ Recipe. Reduce baking powder to ½ teaspoon. Sift ¼ teaspoon **baking soda,** 1½ teaspoons **ginger,** ½ teaspoon **cinnamon** and ¼ teaspoon **allspice** with the flour mixture. Decrease sugar to ½ cup and blend 6 tablespoons **molasses** into creamed mixture. Omit vanilla extract.

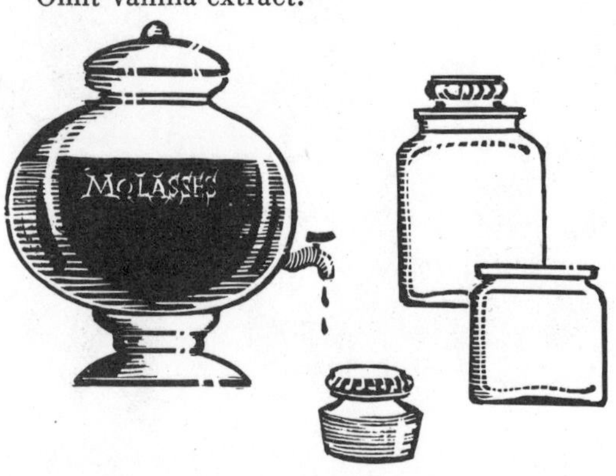

Plain and Fancy Sugar Cookies

△ Chocolate Sugar Cookies

Follow ▲ Recipe. Melt (*page 6*) 2 sq. (2 oz.) **chocolate** and set aside to cool. Blend in after addition of eggs.

Scotch Shortbread

MRS. E. W. SCHENCK, JANESVILLE, WISC.

Set out cookie sheets.

Sift together and set aside
2 cups sifted flour
¼ teaspoon baking powder
¼ teaspoon salt
Cream together until butter is softened
1 cup butter
1 teaspoon vanilla extract
Add gradually, creaming until fluffy
½ cup sifted confectioners' sugar
Mixing until well blended after each addition, add dry ingredients in fourths to creamed mixture. Chill dough until stiff enough to roll easily (at least ½ hr.).

Roll dough ¼ in. thick on a lightly floured surface. Cut into 3-in. rounds; lightly mark each round to indicate 6 wedge-shaped pieces which can be easily broken apart after baking.

Or cut dough into fancy shapes. Place on cookie sheets and prick with a fork.

Bake at 350°F 20 min. or until delicately browned. Remove cookies to cooling racks.

About 2 doz. rounds

For Bars or Squares—Press the chilled dough to a depth of about ¼ in. onto a 14x10-in. cookie sheet with a ½-in. rim on three sides. (Having one side open facilitates removal of bars from sheet.) Prick with a fork. Bake at 350°F 25 min. Remove to cooling rack; do not remove from sheet. Immediately cut into 2-in. squares, or into bars about 2x1-in. Remove cookies from sheet when completely cooled.

Christmas Cookies

MRS. VICTOR PFLIEGER, MENASHA, WIS.

Political differences between a German baker and civil authorities in his country brought this recipe and an old iron nut grater to America four generations ago. The grater is still being used by his descendants.

Lightly grease cookie sheets.

Grate (*page 5*) but do not combine

3 cups (about 1 lb.) blanched almonds (about 7½ cups, grated)

3½ cups (about 1 lb.) hazelnuts (about 6 cups, grated)

Set nuts aside.

Beat until thick and piled softly

4 eggs

Add gradually, beating thoroughly after each addition

2½ cups sugar

Beat for 15 min., or until very light. Beat in

2 teaspoons grated lemon peel (*page 5*)

Pour one half of the batter into a second bowl and set aside.

Add the almonds to the batter in the first bowl, mixing thoroughly to form a stiff dough.

Lightly sprinkle pastry cloth with

Sifted confectioners' sugar

Using palm of hand, shape dough, one teaspoonful at a time, into rounds about ¼ in. thick. Bring the opposite sides together and overlap at center. Place on cookie sheets.

To batter in second bowl, add the hazelnuts, mixing thoroughly to form a stiff dough. Using a rolling pin, roll dough about ¼ in. thick on the pastry cloth. Cut dough with diamond-shaped cookie cutter and place on the cookie sheets.

Bake at 350°F 10 to 12 min. Remove to cooling racks. *About 4 doz. cookies*

Flaky Nut or Mexican Sugarless Cookies

MRS. DEL LANPHEAR, WOODLAND, WASH.

The flavor of these cookies improves with age. The recipe came to this country through the pen-pal correspondence of two schoolgirls.

Set out cookie sheets.

Finely chop and set aside

½ cup (about 2 oz.) nuts

Sift together into a 1-qt. bowl

1 cup sifted flour

1 teaspoon baking powder

Cut in with pastry blender or two knives until pieces are size of small peas

¼ cup butter

¼ cup shortening

Add gradually, mixing well after each addition

1 egg, well beaten

Blend in the nuts.

Roll dough ⅛ in. thick on lightly floured surface. Cut into desired shapes with floured cookie cutter. Place cookies about 1 in. apart on cookie sheets.

Bake at 375°F 12 to 15 min. Remove to cooling racks and immediately sift over cookies

Confectioners' sugar

Cool completely. *About 5 doz. small cookies*

Date-Nut Cookies

EDITH L. SULLIVAN, WASHINGTON, D.C.

Spicy nuggets that recall happy memories of childhood visits to Grandmother's house.

Lightly grease cookie sheets.

Prepare, combine and set aside

1¼ cups (about 8 oz.) coarsely chopped dates
½ cup (about 2 oz.) chopped nuts

Sift together and set aside

2 cups sifted flour
1¼ teaspoons baking powder
½ teaspoon baking soda
¼ teaspoon cinnamon
¼ teaspoon cloves
¼ teaspoon nutmeg
⅛ teaspoon salt

Cream together until shortening is softened

¼ cup butter or margarine
¼ cup lard
¼ teaspoon vanilla extract

Add gradually, creaming until fluffy after each addition

½ cup sugar
¼ cup firmly packed brown sugar

Add gradually, beating thoroughly after each addition

1 egg, well beaten

Mixing until well blended after each addition, add dry ingredients in fourths to creamed mixture. Blend in the nuts and dates, reserving ¼ cup of the mixture for topping. Drop by teaspoonfuls 2 in. apart on cookie sheets. Top each cookie with a piece of **date** or **nut.**

Bake at 350°F 12 min. Remove to cooling racks.

About 6 doz. cookies

French Cookies

DOROTHY J. MARCUSSEN, RIVERTON, ILL.

During the Civil War a wounded prisoner in a hospital near Gettysburg tasted cookies brought by a compassionate visitor and he asked for the recipe for his own mother. These cookies became a family favorite.

Lightly grease cookie sheets.

Prepare and set aside to cool

1 cup double-strength coffee beverage (*page 7*)

Coarsely chop and set aside

1 cup (about 4 oz.) nuts

Measure and set aside

2 cups dark seedless raisins

Sift together and set aside

3 cups sifted flour
1 teaspoon baking soda
1 teaspoon allspice
1 teaspoon cinnamon
1 teaspoon nutmeg

Cream thoroughly

⅔ cup shortening

Add gradually, creaming until fluffy after each addition

2 cups firmly packed brown sugar

Add in thirds, beating thoroughly after each addition

2 eggs, well beaten

Mixing until well blended after each addition, alternately add dry ingredients in fourths, cooled coffee in thirds, to creamed mixture. Stir in the raisins and nuts. Drop by teaspoonfuls about 2 in. apart onto cookie sheets.

Bake at 375°F about 12 min. Remove to cooling racks.

About 6 doz. 2-in. cookies

Frosted Orange Drops

MRS. H. S. NAGLER, ONTARIO, CALIF.

Lightly grease cookie sheets.

Sift together and set aside
1⅓ cups sifted flour
¼ teaspoon baking powder
¼ teaspoon baking soda
⅛ teaspoon salt
Measure and set aside
¼ cup orange juice
Cream together
¼ cup shortening
2 teaspoons grated orange peel (*page 5*)
Add gradually, creaming until fluffy after each addition
⅔ cup firmly packed brown sugar
Add gradually, beating thoroughly after each addition
1 egg, well beaten
Mixing until well blended after each addition, alternately add dry ingredients and juice to creamed mixture, beginning and ending with dry. Drop by teaspoonfuls 2 in. apart onto cookie sheet.

Bake at 375°F 12 to 15 min. Remove to cooling racks. When cool, frost with
Confectioners' Sugar Glaze (*page 217*)

About 8 doz. small cookies

"Go To School" Cookies

MRS. VIRGIL W. MILLER
PRINCETON, W. VA.

A favorite from kindergarten to college.

Melt (*page 6*) and set aside to cool
2 sq. (2 oz.) chocolate
Coarsely chop and set aside
¾ cup (about 3 oz.) nuts
Sift together and set aside
1½ cups sifted flour
½ teaspoon salt
½ teaspoon baking powder
¼ teaspoon baking soda
Cream together
½ cup shortening
½ teaspoon vanilla extract
Add gradually, creaming until fluffy after each addition
1 cup firmly packed brown sugar
Blend in the melted chocolate. Add gradually, beating thoroughly after each addition
1 egg, well beaten
Measure
½ cup milk
Mixing until well blended after each addition, alternately add dry ingredients in fourths, milk in thirds, to the creamed mixture. Stir in the chopped nuts.

Drop by teaspoonfuls 2 in. apart on cookie sheets.

Bake at 350°F 12 to 15 min. Remove to cooling racks. Frost when cool.

For Frosting—Melt (*page 6*) and set aside to cool
1 sq. (1 oz.) chocolate
Cream together until softened
¼ cup butter or margarine
½ teaspoon vanilla extract
Add alternately, creaming until smooth after each addition
2 cups sifted confectioners' sugar
¼ cup hot water
Put one third of the frosting into another bowl. Add, blending in, the chocolate and
1 tablespoon hot water
Spread cookies with the white frosting. Top each with a small amount of chocolate frosting. Allow frosting to become firm before storing cookies.

About 2 doz. cookies

Lemon Sugar Wafers, Fudge Brownies, Perky Cookies and strawberry ice cream

Gingersnaps

Lightly grease cookie sheets.

Sift together and set aside

2 cups sifted flour
2 teaspoons concentrated soluble coffee
1 teaspoon baking soda
1 teaspoon cinnamon
½ teaspoon ginger
¼ teaspoon cloves
½ teaspoon salt

Cream

¾ cup shortening

Add gradually, creaming until fluffy after each addition

1 cup firmly packed brown sugar

Add in thirds, beating thoroughly after each addition

2 eggs, well beaten

Blend in

¼ cup molasses

Mixing until well blended after each addition, add dry ingredients in fourths to creamed mixture. Drop by teaspoonfuls about 2 in. apart onto the cookie sheets. (These cookies will puff up, spread, then flatten.)

Bake at 350°F 10 to 12 min. Remove to cooling racks. *About 7 doz. cookies*

Lemon Sugar Wafers

The kind of delicate cookie that is the perfect accompaniment for ice cream, cooling beverages, or a spot of afternoon tea.

Lightly grease cookie sheets.

Set out about

¼ cup broken walnut meats

Sift together and set aside

3 cups sifted flour
1½ teaspoons baking powder
1 teaspoon salt

Cream together until softened

1 cup butter or margarine
2 teaspoons grated lemon peel (page 5)
1 teaspoon lemon extract
1 teaspoon vanilla extract

Add gradually, creaming until fluffy after each addition

1½ cups sugar

Beat together thoroughly

1 egg
1 egg yolk
3 tablespoons cream or undiluted evaporated milk

Add egg mixture in thirds to creamed mixture, beating thoroughly after each addition. Mixing until well blended after each addition, add dry ingredients in fourths to creamed mixture.

Drop by teaspoonfuls 1½ in. apart onto cookie sheets. Flatten slightly with spatula or back of spoon. Top each cookie with a walnut piece.

Bake at 400°F 8 to 10 min., or until cookies are very lightly browned. Remove immediately to cooling racks. *About 5 doz. cookies*

Apple Bandits

MRS. ROSS ANDERSON, TAHLEQUAH, OKLA.

For Dough—Sift together and set aside

2 cups sifted flour
½ teaspoon cinnamon
¼ teaspoon baking soda

Cream

½ cup shortening

Add gradually, creaming until fluffy after each addition

1 cup firmly packed brown sugar

Add in thirds, beating thoroughly after each addition

2 eggs, slightly beaten

Mixing until well blended after each addition, add dry ingredients in fourths to creamed mixture. Chill thoroughly.

Meanwhile, prepare filling.

For Filling—Wash, quarter, core, chop and drain (do not pare) enough red apples to yield

2 cups chopped apples (2 to 3 medium-size)

Mix together and blend with the apples

1 cup firmly packed brown sugar
1 cup bran flakes
1 tablespoon melted butter or margarine
½ teaspoon cinnamon
⅛ teaspoon salt

Set mixture aside.

Lightly grease cookie sheets.

Place chilled dough on a lightly floured surface and roll into a 12x7-in. rectangle about ½ in. thick. Spread filling evenly over dough. Starting at wide side, roll dough quickly and carefully. Press edges to seal. Using a sharp, floured knife, cut roll into slices ¼ to ½ in. thick. Place slices on cookie sheets.

Bake at 350°F 30 min., or until lightly browned. *About 2 doz. cookies*

Kipfeln

MRS. CLYDE M. NORTH, BALTIMORE, MD.

A rich butter cookie from Austria-Hungary.

For Pastry—Sift together into a bowl

2 cups sifted flour
½ teaspoon salt

Cut in with pastry blender or two knives until pieces are the size of small peas

½ cup butter

Beat until thick and lemon-colored

2 egg yolks
1 tablespoon cream

Add gradually to flour-butter mixture, blending ingredients with a fork. Gather dough into a ball. Work with hands, squeezing dough until well blended. Form into balls ¾ in. in diameter. Chill in refrigerator about 1 hr.

Meanwhile, prepare filling.

For Filling—Finely grind and set aside

1 cup (about 4 oz.) pecans

Beat until frothy

2 egg whites
1 teaspoon vanilla extract
½ teaspoon salt

Add gradually, beating thoroughly after each addition

1 cup sifted confectioners' sugar

Continue beating until rounded peaks are formed and egg whites do not slide when bowl is partially inverted. Fold in (*page 6*) the ground pecans and

1 tablespoon melted butter

Set filling aside.

To Form Kipfeln—Put one ball of dough at a time on a lightly floured surface and roll into a paper-thin round. Place about 1½ teaspoons filling onto center of each round. Fold pastry over filling, overlapping edges at center. Pinch ends to seal and curve cookies into crescents. Place Kipfeln 1 in. apart on the cookie sheets.

Bake at 375°F 15 min., or until lightly browned. Remove to cooling racks.

About 3½ doz. cookies

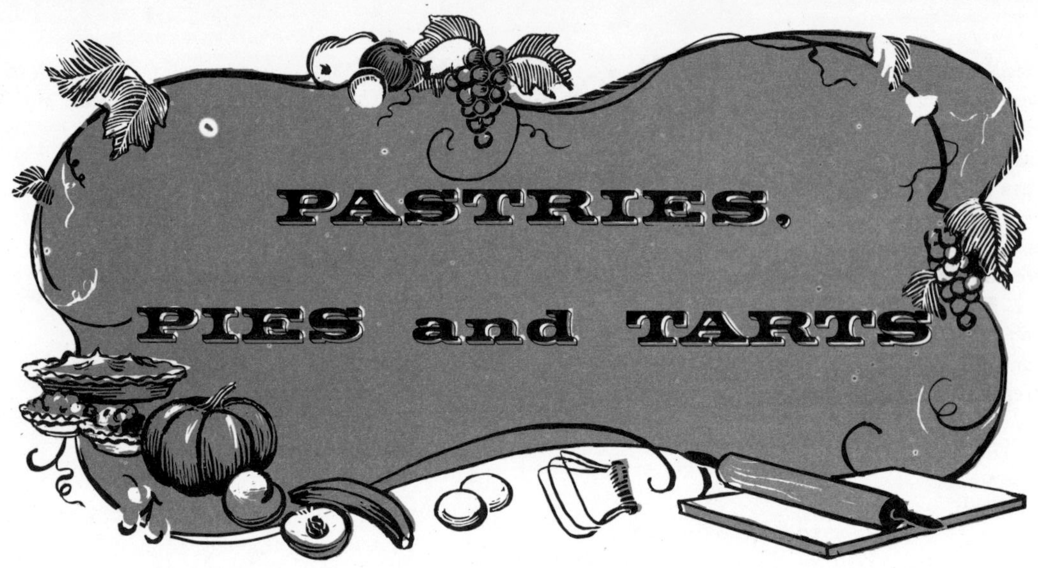

A Check List for Successful Pie Making

(See For These Recipes—What To Use, How To Do It and Oven Temperatures on *pages* 4-7.)

√ **Read** recipe carefully.

√ **Assemble** all ingredients and utensils—*A pastry blender* cuts shortening into flour evenly and quickly; *a pastry canvas and a stockinet-covered rolling pin* prevent sticking and rolling in extra flour.

√ **Select pie pans** of proper size. Measure inside, from rim to rim.

√ **Use standard** measuring cups and spoons. Use liquid measuring cups (rim above 1-cup line) for liquids. Use nested or dry measuring cups (1-cup line even with top) for dry ingredients. Check liquid measurements at eye level. Level dry measurements with straight-edged knife or spatula.

√ **Preheat oven** 12 to 20 min. at required temperature. Leave oven door open first 2 min.

√ **Place oven rack** so top of pie will be almost at center of oven. Stagger pie pans so no pan is directly over another and they do not touch each other or walls of oven. Place single pan so that center of pie is as near center of oven as possible.

FOR PASTRY

√ **Cut** any of the shortenings, such as lard, hydrogenated vegetable shortening, all-purpose shortening and/or butter or margarine, into a mixture of flour and salt with a pastry blender or two knives until the particles are the size of small peas. (Use cooking or salad oil for pastry making only with recipes specifically developed for oil.)

√ **Use cold water** to aid in producing a more tender pastry. (Hot water may be used in making pastry if specific recipe is followed. Usually shortening and hot water are blended together.)

√ **Add only enough water** to hold pastry dough together. An excess tends to cause shrinkage and a less tender pastry. Toss lightly with a fork after each addition of water; work quickly and only until dough holds together. Do not overmix.

√ **Shape pastry dough** (for a 1-crust pie) into a smooth ball and flatten slightly on a lightly floured surface. If preparing double the amount of dough, cut dough into halves and shape one portion at a time. Overhandling dough toughens pastry.

√ **Chill pastry dough** in refrigerator before rolling if the room is warm. This will aid in ensuring a more tender pastry.

√ **Roll pastry dough** from center to edge with fewest number of strokes possible, shaping it round and of same thickness throughout. Test thickness of dough by pressing dough with finger; it should make only a slight dent. Fold into halves or quarters before transferring to pie pan. Gently unfold and fit loosely to pan.

√ **Prevent shrinkage** of pastry by loosely fitting pastry to bottom and sides of pan, being certain not to stretch dough. Be careful not to tear pastry; mend cracks by pressing pastry together or by patching with another piece of pastry. Cracks or tears in bottom crust permit filling to soak through crust and cause pie to stick to pan.

√ **For an attractive edge** on a 1-crust pie allow about ½ in. of pastry to extend beyond edge of pan after trimming excess pastry and just before fluting. Fold this overhanging pastry under, allowing it to rest on pie pan and extend just to edge of pan; flute.

√ **Flute edge of pastry** by pressing index finger on edge of pastry, then pinch pastry with thumb and index finger of other hand. Lift fingers and repeat procedure to flute around entire edge.

√ **Prick pastry shell** *thoroughly* with a fork before baking to prevent buckling and large blisters from forming. If any blisters do appear during the first few minutes of baking, prick them. Omit all pricking if filling is to be baked in shell.

√ **Moisten edge** of bottom crust of 2-crust pie with water after trimming it even with edge of pie pan. Gently press edges of bottom and top crust together for a tight seal. Fold extra pastry of top crust under edge of bottom crust; then flute or press edges together with a fork.

√ **Make enough slits** in top crust of a 2-crust pie to allow steam to escape.

FOR SOFT MERINGUES AND FILLINGS

√ **Add sugar** gradually for soft meringue, beginning in early stage (frothy) of beating egg whites. This lessens the tendency toward formation of sirup beads and meringue's leaking. Beating in the sugar instead of folding it in gives a more stable meringue. Beat meringue until rounded peaks are formed. Generally 2 tablespoons sugar per egg white is the proportion used for soft meringues. Too much sugar tends to produce beading and results in a meringue with sticky crust; too little sugar results in a less tender meringue that is less fluffy in appearance and flat in taste.

√ **Seal meringue** to edge of crust to help prevent meringue from shrinking.

√ **Bake meringue-topped** pie at 350°F 10 to 15 min., or until meringue is delicately browned. A baking temperature that is too high or a baking time that is too long results in a shrunken, tough meringue that sticks to the knife when cut.

√ **Beat whole eggs** until thick and piled softly when recipe calls for well-beaten eggs.

√ **Beat egg whites** as follows: *Frothy*—entire mass forms bubbles; *Rounded peaks*—peaks turn over slightly when beater is slowly lifted upright; *Stiff peaks*—peaks remain standing when beater is slowly lifted upright.

√ **Beat egg yolks** until thick and lemon-colored when recipe calls for well-beaten egg yolks.

√ **Prevent soaking of crust** of custard pie by: 1) scalding milk before adding to the other ingredients because this shortens the time for the custard to set during baking; 2) baking pastry shell and custard separately, then slipping custard into shell (see Slipped Custard Pie, *page 249*).

√ **Cook cream filling** by vigorously stirring about 3 tablespoons of hot filling mixture into beaten egg yolks and immediately blending into mixture in top of double boiler. This method blends egg yolks evenly into the hot mixture without lowering the temperature. For maximum thickening power of the egg the temperature of the mixture must not be lowered. *Help prevent the filling from becoming thin and runny* after standing a short time (when it was once of serving consistency) by cooking the mixture 3 to 5 min. over simmering water after the egg yolks have been blended into the mixture.

√ **Fillings** containing a high-acid fruit or fruit juice (such as lemon, lime, or strawberry) usually require more cornstarch or flour than other fillings because of the thinning effect of the acid of the fruit or fruit juice upon starch when subjected to heat. For example, lemon fillings should call for the lemon juice to be blended in after the mixture has been cooked and removed from heat; this ensures a filling which should not thin.

√ **Cool cream filling** by covering cooked filling and cooling slightly, stirring occasionally to prevent film from forming; cool to lukewarm in refrigerator. (Cooling filling before turning into cooled pastry shell helps prevent soaking of crust.) Turn filling into baked and cooled pastry shell and chill in refrigerator until ready to serve.

√ **Thoroughly mix** fruit and sugar-flour mixture for fruit-filled pie to prevent hard sugar lumps in baked pie and produce even thickening.

√ **Baking of fruit pies** at two temperatures helps to prevent soaking of crust; higher temperature sets crust, lower temperature finishes baking pie.

√ **Keep** cooled custard-type, cream, whipped cream topped and filled pies in refrigerator until ready to serve; return any leftover pie to refrigerator. DO NOT ALLOW TO STAND AT ROOM TEMPERATURE because these pies spoil easily and have been known to cause food poisoning if not adequately refrigerated.

▲ Pastry for 1-Crust Pie

Set out an 8- or 9-in. pie pan.

Sift together into a bowl
1 cup sifted flour
½ teaspoon salt

Cut in with pastry blender or two knives until pieces are size of small peas
⅓ cup lard, hydrogenated vegetable shortening or all-purpose shortening

Sprinkle gradually over mixture, a teaspoon at a time, about
2½ tablespoons cold water

Mix lightly with a fork after each addition. Add only enough water to hold pastry together. Work quickly; do not overhandle. Shape into a ball and flatten on a lightly floured surface.

Roll from center to edge into a round about ⅛ in. thick and about 1 in. larger than over-all size of pan. With knife or spatula, loosen pastry from surface whenever sticking occurs; lift pastry and sprinkle flour underneath.

Loosen one half from board with spatula and fold over other half. Loosen remaining part and fold in quarters. Gently lay pastry in pan and unfold it, fitting it to the pan so that it is not stretched.

Trim edge with scissors or sharp knife so pastry extends about ½ in. beyond edge of pie pan. Fold extra pastry under at edge and flute (*page 241*) or press with a fork. Thoroughly prick bottom and sides of pastry shell with a fork. (Omit pricking if filling is to be baked in shell.)

Bake at 450°F 10 to 15 min., or until crust is light golden brown.

Cool on cooling rack.

One 8- or 9-in. pastry shell

△ Pastry for 2-Crust Pie

Double ▲ Recipe. Divide pastry into halves and shape each into a ball. Roll each ball as in ▲ Recipe. For top crust, roll out one ball of pastry and cut 1 in. larger than pie pan. Slit pastry with knife in several places to allow steam to escape during baking. Gently fold in half and set aside while rolling bottom crust.

Roll second ball of pastry and gently fit pastry into pie pan; avoid stretching. Trim pastry with scissors or sharp knife around edge of pan. Do not prick.

Fill as directed in specific recipe.

Moisten edge with water for a tight seal. Carefully arrange top crust over filling. Gently press edges to seal. Fold extra top pastry under bottom pastry. Flute (*page 241*) or press edges together with a fork.

Bake as directed in specific recipes.

◬ Pastry for 1-Crust 10-in. Pie

Follow ▲ Recipe. Increase flour to 1⅓ cups, shortening to ½ cup, salt to ¾ teaspoon, and water to about 3 tablespoons.

◬ Pastry for Lattice-Top Pie

Prepare pastry as in △ Recipe. Divide pastry into halves and shape into two balls. Follow directions in ▲ Recipe for rolling pastry. Roll one pastry ball for bottom crust; fit gently into pie pan.

Roll the second pastry ball into a rectangle about ⅛ in. thick and at least 10 in. long. Cut pastry with a sharp knife or pastry wheel into strips that are about ½ in. wide.

Fill pastry shell as directed in specific recipe.

To Make a Lattice Top—Cross two strips over the pie at the center. Working out from center to edge of pie, add the remaining strips one at a time, weaving the strips under and over each other in crisscross fashion; leave about 1 in. between the strips. Trim the strips even with the edge of the pastry. Moisten the edge of pastry shell with water for a tight seal. Fold edge of bottom crust over ends of strips. Flute (*page 241*) or press edges together with a fork.

Bake as directed in specific recipe.

△ Pastry for Little Pies and Tarts

Prepare ▲ Recipe. Roll pastry ⅛ in. thick and cut about ½ in. larger than over-all size of pans. Carefully fit rounds into pans without stretching. Fold excess pastry under at edge and flute (*page 241*) or press with a fork. Prick bottom and sides of shell with fork. (Omit pricking if filling is to be baked in shell.)

Bake at 450°F 8 to 10 min., or until light golden brown.

Cool on cooling rack. Carefully remove from pans. *Three 6-in. pies, six 3½-in. tarts or nine 1½-in. tarts*

△ Pastry for Rose-Petal Tarts

Double ▲ Recipe. Roll pastry ⅛ in. thick. Cut pastry into rounds, using 2½-in. round cutter. Place one pastry round in bottom of each 2¾-in. muffin-pan well. Fit 5 pastry rounds around inside of each well, overlapping edges. Press overlapping edges together. Prick bottom and sides well with fork.

Bake at 450°F 8 to 10 min., or until light golden brown.

Cool on cooling rack. Carefully remove from pans. *Six 2¾-in. tarts*

△ Braided-Edge Pastry Shell

Set out a 10-in. pie pan.

Double ▲ Recipe. Shape two-thirds of the pastry into a ball and flatten on a lightly floured surface. Roll and fit into pie pan as in ▲ Recipe. Trim edge with scissors or a sharp knife so that pastry comes just to edge of pie pan. Set aside.

Shape remaining pastry into a ball and flatten on the lightly floured surface. Roll from center into a rectangle about 14 in. long and ⅛ in. thick. Cut into 9 lengthwise strips about ¼ in. wide. With strips on board, carefully braid three strips loosely. Repeat braiding twice for remaining strips.

Brush rim of pastry shell with water and place the three braids on rim. Join by overlapping and pressing ends of braids together.

Bake at 450°F 10 to 15 min., or until crust is light golden brown.

Cool on cooling rack.

△ Cheese Pastry for 1-Crust Pie

Follow ▲ Recipe; cut in ½ cup (2 oz.) grated **Cheddar cheese** with the lard or shortening.

△ Cheese Pastry for 2-Crust Pie

Follow △ Recipe; cut in 1 cup (4 oz.) grated **Cheddar cheese** with the lard or shortening.

△ Pastry Topping

Follow ▲ Recipe for preparing pastry. Roll dough to about ⅛-in. thickness and about 1 in. larger than over-all size of casserole or baking dish top. Cut a simple design near center of pastry to allow steam to escape during baking. Moisten rim of casserole with cold water.

Loosen pastry and place loosely over mixture in casserole; unfold. Trim edge so pastry extends about ¾ in. beyond edge of casserole. Fold extra pastry under at edge and gently press edges to seal to moistened rim of casserole. Flute (*page 241*) or press with a fork.

Bake as directed in specific recipe.

Perfect Pastry Mix

Sift together into a large bowl

6 cups sifted flour
1 tablespoon salt

Cut in with pastry blender or two knives until pieces are size of small peas

2 cups (1 lb.) lard, hydrogenated vegetable shortening or all-purpose shortening

Store in covered bowl or container in refrigerator and use as needed. This mix will keep at least 1 month. *Six 9-in. or eight 8-in. pie shells*

Before measuring for recipe, lighten mix by tossing with fork. Lightly pile mix into measuring cup. Level with spatula.

For 1-Crust Pies—Use 1 cup pastry mix with 2 to 3 tablespoons water for 8-in. pie shells. Use 1¼ cups mix with 2 to 3 tablespoons water for 9-in. pie shells. Proceed as in **Pastry for 1-Crust Pie** (*page 242*).

For 2-Crust Pies—Use 2 cups pastry mix with 3 to 5 tablespoons water for 8-in. 2-crust pie. Use 2¼ cups pastry mix with 3 to 5 tablespoons water for 9-in. 2-crust pie. Proceed as in **Pastry for 2-Crust Pie** (*page 242*).

Graham Cracker Tart Shells: **Using a spoon press crumb mixture firmly onto bottoms and sides.**

▲ Graham Cracker Pie Shell

Set out an 8- or 9-in. pie pan.

Crush (*page 6*)

16 to 18 graham crackers (or enough to yield 1⅓ cups crumbs)

Turn crumbs into a medium-size bowl. Stir in

¼ cup sugar

Using a fork or pastry blender, blend in evenly

¼ cup butter or margarine, softened

Using back of spoon, press crumb mixture very firmly into an even layer on bottom and sides of the pie pan. Level edges of pie shell.

Bake at 375°F 8 min. Cool thoroughly before filling. *One 8- or 9-in. pie shell*

△ Graham Cracker 10-in. Pie Shell

Follow ▲ Recipe. Increase crumbs to 1⅔ cups, sugar to 5 tablespoons, and butter to 5 tablespoons.

△ Graham Cracker Tart Shells

Follow ▲ Recipe. Line 8 2½-in. muffin-pan wells with paper baking cups. Using back of spoon, press crumb mixture firmly into even layers on bottom and sides of the paper cups. Bake. Cool thoroughly on cooling rack; remove paper baking cups.

▲ Cookie Crumb Pie Shell

Follow ▲ Recipe. Substitute 1⅓ cups **cookie crumbs** (about twenty-four 2⅛-in. cookies such as vanilla or chocolate wafers) for graham cracker crumbs. Omit sugar. Bake at 325°F 10 min.

▲ Coffee-Flavored Crumb Pie Shell

Follow ▲ Recipe. Use either **vanilla** or **chocolate wafers.** Stir into crumbs 2 teaspoons **concentrated soluble coffee.**

▲ Zwieback Crumb Pie Shell

Follow ▲ Recipe. Substitute 1⅓ cups **zwieback crumbs** (about eighteen 3½x1⅛-in. zwieback) for graham cracker crumbs.

Crispy Crumb Pie Shell

MRS. J. W. STEPHENS, PATAGONIA, ARIZ.

A shortage of graham crackers and a knack for experiment led to the discovery of this family-favorite pie crust. The sweetness of the shell makes it a perfect foil for fillings with a tart flavor, such as lemon or lime.

Set out a 9- or 10-in. pie pan.

Crush (*page 6*)

2⅓ cups pre-sweetened corn flakes (or enough to yield 1 cup, crushed)
6 graham crackers (or enough to yield ½ cup, crushed)

Mix the crumbs together.

Add gradually, stirring in with a fork.

¼ cup butter or margarine, melted

Using back of spoon, press crumb mixture very firmly into an even layer on bottom and sides of pie pan. Level edges of pie shell.

Bake at 375°F 8 min.

Cool thoroughly before filling.

One 9- or 10-in. pie shell

Choco-Coconut Pie Shell

An intriguingly different kind of pie shell.

Set out an 8- or 9-in. pie pan.

Melt in the top of a double boiler over simmering water

2 sq. (2 oz.) chocolate
3 tablespoons butter or margarine
1 teaspoon vanilla extract

Blend ingredients well and remove from simmering water. Add, stirring constantly

¼ cup sweetened condensed milk

Blend in well, in order

½ cup sifted confectioners' sugar
2 cups (8 oz.) moist shredded coconut, cut

Press coconut mixture firmly into an even layer onto bottom and on sides of pie pan. Wrap in waxed paper, aluminum foil or moisture-vapor-proof material. Chill in refrigerator about 1 hr., or until firm.

One 8- or 9-in. pie shell

Spice Pastry for 1-Crust Pie

Set out an 8- or 9-in. pie pan.

Sift together

1 cup sifted flour
2 tablespoons sugar
½ teaspoon salt
¼ teaspoon cinnamon
⅛ teaspoon ginger
⅛ teaspoon cloves

Cut in with pastry blender or two knives until pieces are size of small peas

⅓ cup lard, hydrogenated vegetable shortening or all-purpose shortening

Sprinkle gradually over mixture, a teaspoon at a time, about

2½ tablespoons orange juice

Mix lightly with fork after each addition. Add only enough orange juice to hold pastry together. Work quickly and do not overhandle. Shape into a ball and flatten on a lightly floured surface. Proceed as in **Pastry for 1-Crust Pie** (*page 242*).

One 8- or 9-in. pastry shell

Meringue

Meringue Shell

Lightly grease a 9-in. pie pan.

Beat until frothy
4 egg whites
Add and beat slightly
½ teaspoon cream of tartar
Add gradually, beating well after each addition
1 cup sugar
Continue beating until stiff (but not dry) peaks are formed and egg whites do not slide when bowl is partially inverted.

Spread a 1-in. layer of meringue on bottom of pie pan. Pile remaining meringue around edge of pan and swirl with a spatula to form the sides of the shell.

Bake at 250°F about 2¼ hrs., or until meringue is dry. (The door of the oven of some ranges will have to be partially open to maintain low temperature.) To assure even drying of meringue turn pan occasionally. Remove from oven; cool completely on cooling rack. (If the meringue shell is to be stored, keep it in an air-tight container so that the meringue will not absorb moisture and become soft.)

The meringue shell should be crisp and dry and have a very fine texture.

One 9-in. pie shell

▲ Meringue I

Beat until frothy
3 egg whites
⅛ teaspoon salt
Add gradually, beating well after each addition
6 tablespoons sugar
Continue to beat until rounded peaks are formed. Pile meringue lightly over pie filling, sealing meringue to edge of crust.

Bake at 350°F 10 to 15 min., or until meringue is delicately browned. Cool pie on cooling rack.

△ Meringue II

Follow ▲ Recipe. Decrease egg whites to 2 and sugar to ¼ cup.

Toasted Coconut

Set out a large, shallow baking pan.

Cut into short lengths and spread over bottom of the pan
½ cup (2 oz.) moist shredded coconut
Set pan in 350°F oven for 10 to 15 min., or until coconut is lightly toasted.

One-half cup Toasted Coconut

Jiffy Lemon or Lime Pie

Prepare, bake and set aside to cool
Pastry for 1-Crust Pie (*page 242*; use 8-in. pie pan)
Blend just until well mixed
1⅓ cups (1 15-oz. can) sweetened condensed milk
⅔ cup lemon or lime juice
1½ teaspoons grated lemon or lime peel (*page 5*)
3 egg yolks, slightly beaten
1 or 2 drops yellow or green food coloring
Pour into pastry shell. Complete pie with
Meringue II
Cool on cooling rack.

One 8-in pie

Lemon Meringue Pie

Prepare, bake and set aside to cool

Pastry for 1-Crust Pie (*page 242*; use 9-in. pie pan)

Sift together into top of double boiler

1½ cups sugar
⅓ cup cornstarch
⅛ teaspoon salt

Blend in

½ cup cold water

Add gradually and stir in

1 cup boiling water

Stirring gently and constantly, bring cornstarch mixture rapidly to boiling over direct heat and cook 3 min. Place over simmering water. Cover and cook about 12 min., stirring three or four times.

Vigorously stir about 3 tablespoons of hot mixture into

3 egg yolks, slightly beaten

Immediately blend into mixture in double boiler. Cook over simmering water 3 to 5 min. Stir slowly to keep mixture cooking evenly. Remove from simmering water. Blend in

2 tablespoons butter or margarine
¼ cup lemon juice
1½ tablespoons grated lemon peel (*page 5*)

Cover and cool slightly, stirring occasionally; cool to lukewarm in refrigerater. Turn filling into the cooled pastry shell.

Complete pie with

Meringue I (*page 246*)

Cool on cooling rack. *One 9-in. pie*

Black Raspberry Cream Pie

MRS. T. J. VANDERVELDT, ASTORIA, ORE.

This is quite literally "like the pies that Mother used to make"—an old-time favorite.

Prepare, bake and set aside to cool

Pastry for 1-Crust Pie (*page 242*; use 8-in. pie pan)

Scald (*page* 7) in top of double boiler

1½ cups milk

Meanwhile, sift together into a saucepan

⅔ cup sugar
¼ cup sifted flour
¼ teaspoon salt

Add, stirring well

¼ cup cold milk

Add gradually and stir in the scalded milk. Stirring gently and constantly, bring rapidly to boiling over direct heat and cook 3 min.

Wash double-boiler top to remove scum.

Pour mixture into double-boiler top and place over simmering water. Cover and cook about 5 to 7 min., stirring three or four times.

Vigorously stir about 3 tablespoons of hot mixture into

3 egg yolks, slightly beaten

Immediately blend into mixture in double boiler. Cook over simmering water 3 to 5 min. Stir slowly to keep mixture cooking evenly. Remove from simmering water.

Blend in

2 tablespoons butter
1 tablespoon lemon juice

Cover and cool slightly, stirring occasionally; cool to lukewarm in refrigerator.

Meanwhile, drain thoroughly the contents of

2 1-lb. cans (about 2 cups, drained) black raspberries

(Reserve sirup for use in other food preparation.) Turn well-drained berries into pastry shell. Turn lukewarm filling over berries.

Complete pie with

Meringue II (*page 246*)

One 8-in. pie

Banana Cream Pie

▲ De Luxe Cream Pie or Tarts

Prepare, bake and set aside to cool

Pastry for 1-Crust Pie (*page 242*; use 8-in. pie pan) or Pastry for Little Pies and Tarts (*page 243*; use 3½-in. tart pans)

Scald (*page* 7) in top of double boiler

1½ cups milk

Meanwhile, sift together into a saucepan

⅔ cup sugar
¼ cup sifted flour
¼ teaspoon salt

Add, stirring well

½ cup cold milk

Add gradually and stir in the scalded milk. Stirring gently and constantly, bring rapidly to boiling over direct heat and cook 3 min.

Wash double-boiler top to remove scum.

Pour mixture into double-boiler top and place over simmering water. Cover and cook about 5 to 7 min., stirring three or four times.

Vigorously stir about 3 tablespoons of hot mixture into

3 egg yolks, slightly beaten

Immediately blend into mixture in double boiler. Cook over simmering water 3 to 5 min. Stir slowly to keep mixture cooking evenly. Remove from simmering water. Blend in

2 tablespoons butter or margarine
2 teaspoons vanilla extract

Cover and cool slightly, stirring occasionally; cool to lukewarm in refrigerator. Turn into the pastry shell or spoon into the tart shells. Chill in refrigerator. *One 8-in. pie or six 3½-in. tarts*

△ Banana Cream Pie or Tarts

Follow ▲ Recipe. Set out 3 **bananas** with brown-flecked peel. For pie, peel 2 of the bananas; cut into crosswise slices and arrange over bottom of pastry shell. Turn lukewarm filling over banana slices. Chill in refrigerator. Before serving, peel remaining banana and draw tines of a fork lengthwise over entire surface of banana; cut into crosswise slices. Arrange slices in a ring on top of pie. Garnish with **whipped cream** and a **maraschino cherry.** For tarts, put about 10 slices and about ⅓ cup of filling into each tart shell.

△ Lemon Cream Pie or Tarts

Follow ▲ Recipe. Increase sugar to ¾ cup and flour to 6 tablespoons. Omit vanilla extract; add ¼ cup **lemon juice** and 2 teaspoons grated **lemon peel** (*page 5*) with the butter. Tint to desired color by blending in 5 or 6 drops **yellow food coloring.**

△ Lime Cream Pie or Tarts

Follow △ Recipe. Substitute ¾ cup **lime juice** for lemon juice and ½ teaspoon grated **lime peel** for lemon peel. Tint by blending in 3 or 4 drops **green food coloring.**

△ Butterscotch Cream Pie or Tarts

Follow ▲ Recipe. Decrease sugar to ⅓ cup and add ⅓ cup firmly packed **brown sugar.** Increase butter to 3 tablespoons.

△ Cocoa Cream Pie

Follow ▲ Recipe. Sift ½ cup **cocoa** with dry ingredients.

▲ Custard Pie

Take insurance against the possibility of a soggy crust by using the slipped version.

Prepare (do not bake) and set aside

Pastry for 1-Crust Pie (*page 242*; use 8-in. pie pan)

***To Prepare Custard*—**Scald (*page 7*)

1½ cups milk
¾ cup cream

Beat slightly

4 eggs

Add and beat just until blended

½ cup sugar
½ teaspoon nutmeg
¼ teaspoon salt

Blend in the scalded milk and cream and

1 teaspoon vanilla extract

Strain mixture into the pastry shell.

***To Complete Pie*—**Bake at 450°F 10 min. Reduce heat to 350°F and bake 15 to 20 min. longer, or until a silver knife comes out clean when inserted halfway between center and edge of filling.

Cool on cooling rack. Place in refrigerator until ready to serve. *One 8-in. pie*

△ Slipped Custard Pie

Follow ▲ Recipe for amounts of ingredients.

Prepare, bake and set pastry shell aside to cool. Heat water for boiling water bath (*page 6*). Lightly butter a second 8-in pie pan.

Prepare custard and strain into the buttered pan. Bake in boiling water bath at 325°F 25 to 30 min., or until custard tests done. Set aside to cool.

When custard is cool, run tip of knife around edge of pie pan; hold the pan level and shake gently to loosen custard. Hold pan at a slight angle and slip the custard carefully into the pastry shell. Work quickly to avoid breaking the custard. Set aside for a few minutes to allow custard to settle.

Buttermilk Custard Pie

OPAL A. BLASDEL, LA JUNTA, COLO.

Prepare (do not bake) and set aside

Pastry for 1-Crust Pie (*page 242*; use 9-in. pie pan)

Melt and set aside to cool

3 tablespoons butter

Beat slightly

3 egg yolks

Blend in a mixture of

⅔ cup sugar
2 tablespoons flour
⅛ teaspoon salt

Stir in the melted butter and

1⅔ cups buttermilk
1½ teaspoons vanilla extract

Beat until rounded peaks are formed

3 egg whites

Spread over buttermilk mixture and fold (*page 6*) together. Turn into pastry shell.

Bake at 450°F 10 min. Reduce heat to 350°F and bake 20 to 25 min. longer, or until a silver knife comes out clean when inserted halfway between center and edge of filling.

Cool on cooling rack. *One 9-in. pie*

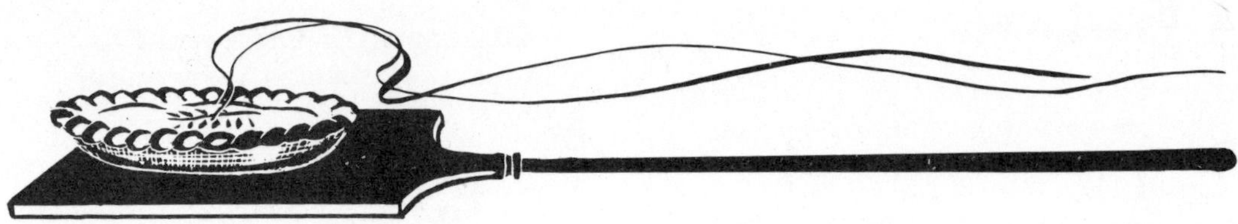

Peanut-Butter Custard Pie

NORMA SCHMID, KIMBERLY, IDAHO

The nut-like sweetness of this unusual pie makes it a delightfully different treat.

Prepare (do not bake) and set aside
Pastry for 1-Crust Pie (*page 242*; use 9-in. pie pan)
Cream together until blended
1 cup peanut butter
1 teaspoon vanilla extract
Add gradually, creaming until fluffy after each addition
1½ cups sugar
½ teaspoon salt
Add in thirds, beating thoroughly after each addition
2 eggs, well beaten
Blend in
1½ cups milk
Turn into the pastry shell.

Bake at 450°F 10 min. Reduce heat to 350°F and bake 20 to 25 min. longer, or until a silver knife comes out clean when inserted halfway between center and edge of filling.

Cool on cooling rack. *One 9-in. pie*

Pumpkin Pie with Edam cheese

▲ Pumpkin Pie

Prepare, bake 10 min. and set aside to cool
Pastry for 1-Crust Pie (*page 242*; use 9-in. pie pan)
Mix together
2 cups (1 1-lb. can) canned pumpkin
and a mixture of
⅔ cup firmly packed dark brown sugar
1 teaspoon cinnamon
½ teaspoon ginger
½ teaspoon nutmeg
½ teaspoon salt
⅛ teaspoon cloves
Blend together and add, mixing until smooth
2 eggs, slightly beaten
1 cup cream
Pour into the pastry shell.

Bake at 350°F 50 to 60 min., or until a silver knife comes out clean when inserted halfway between center and edge of filling.

Cool on cooling rack.

Serve with
Edam cheese or Sweetened Whipped Cream (*page 223*)

One 9-in. pie

△ Southern Pumpkin Pecan Pie

MRS. E. E. McKAY, MT. VERNON, ILL.

Follow ▲ Recipe. Blend 1 cup firmly packed **brown sugar** with ¼ cup **butter,** softened. Remove pie from oven and spoon mixture evenly over top. Top with ½ cup (about 2 oz.) **pecans.**

Set temperature control of range at Broil. Set pie on broiler rack and place in broiler with top of pie 3 in. from source of heat. Broil 1 min., or until butter mixture bubbles. Watch closely to avoid scorching.

▲ Pecan-Topped Pumpkin Tarts

Follow ▲ Recipe; substitute **Pastry for Little Pies and Tarts** (one and one-third recipe, *page 243*; use 8 3½-in. tart pans) for Pastry for 1-Crust Pie. Do not bake. Pour about ½ cup filling into each shell. Bake at 450°F 10 min. Reduce heat to 350°F and bake 10 min. Quickly arrange coated pecan halves over tops. Return to oven; bake at 350°F 10 min. longer, or until a silver knife comes out clean when inserted halfway between center and edge. Remove from oven; cool on cooling rack.

For Coated Pecans—Melt in a small skillet over low heat ¼ cup **butter.** Add 1½ cups (about 6 oz.) **pecan halves;** move and turn pecans gently with a spoon until thoroughly coated with butter. Remove pecans and mix lightly with ¼ cup firmly packed **brown sugar.**

Sour Cream-Raisin Pie

Prepare (do not bake) and set aside

Pastry for 1-Crust Pie (*page 242*; use 9-in. pie pan)

Mix together

½ cup sugar
2 tablespoons flour
½ teaspoon cinnamon
¼ teaspoon nutmeg
¼ teaspoon salt

Blend together

1 egg, well beaten
1½ cups thick sour cream

Add dry ingredients to the sour-cream mixture and blend thoroughly. Mix in

1½ cups (about 7 oz.) seedless raisins

Turn into the pastry shell.

Bake at 450°F 10 min. Reduce heat to 350°F and bake 20 to 25 min. longer, or until a silver knife comes out clean when inserted halfway between center and edge of filling. Place on cooling rack to cool slightly.

Serve slightly warm. *One 9-in. pie*

Pecan Pie

Pecan Pie

GLENELLEN STEVENSON, BERKELEY, CAL.

A dark rich sweet pie that does honor to the superb flavor of the native American pecan.

Prepare (do not bake) and set aside

Pastry for 1-Crust Pie (*page 242*; use 9-in. pie pan)

Set out

½ cup (about 2 oz.) pecan halves
½ cup (about 2 oz.) chopped pecans

Cream together until butter is softened

3 tablespoons butter
1 teaspoon vanilla extract

Add gradually, creaming until fluffy after each addition

¾ cup sugar

Add in thirds, blending well after each addition

3 eggs, well beaten

Thoroughly blend in the chopped pecans and

1 cup dark corn sirup
⅛ teaspoon salt

Turn into the pastry shell.

Bake at 450°F 10 min. Arrange pecan halves on top of pie filling. Reduce heat to 350°F and bake 30 to 35 min. longer, or until a silver knife comes out clean when inserted halfway between center and edge of filling.

Cool on cooling rack. *One 9-in. pie*

Eggnog Chiffon Pie

Prepare, bake and set aside to cool

Pastry for 1-Crust 10-in. Pie (*page 242*)

Place a bowl and rotary beater in refrigerator to chill.

Pour into a small cup or custard cup

¼ cup cold water

Sprinkle evenly over cold water

1 tablespoon (1 env.) unflavored gelatin

Let stand about 5 min. to soften.

Mix in top of double boiler and heat over simmering water until scalded (*page 7*)

1½ cups milk
5 tablespoons sugar
½ teaspoon salt

Vigorously stir 3 tablespoons hot mixture into

4 egg yolks, slightly beaten

Immediately blend into mixture in double boiler. Stirring constantly, cook over simmering water until mixture coats a silver spoon. Immediately remove from heat and stir in softened gelatin, stirring until gelatin is completely dissolved. Cool; chill (*page 6*) until mixture begins to gel (gets slightly thicker).

When gelatin mixture is of desired consistency, using chilled bowl and beater, beat until cream is of medium consistency (piles softly)

1 cup chilled whipping cream

Set in refrigerator while beating egg whites. Using clean beater, beat until frothy

2 egg whites

Add gradually, beating well after each addition, a mixture of

¼ cup sugar
½ teaspoon nutmeg

Beat until rounded peaks are formed. Spread egg whites and whipped cream over gelatin mixture and gently fold (*page 6*) with

2 tablespoons rum
2 teaspoons vanilla extract

Turn into pastry shell. Sprinkle over top

½ teaspoon nutmeg

Chill in refrigerator until firm.

One 10-in. pie

Tropical Chiffon Pie

Prepare, bake and set aside to cool

Pastry for 1-Crust Pie (*page 242*; use 9-in. pie pan)

Pour into a small cup or custard cup

2 tablespoons cold water
2 tablespoons lemon juice

Sprinkle evenly over liquid

1 tablespoon (1 env.) unflavored gelatin

Let stand about 5 min. to soften.

Set out

1¼ cups orange juice

Heat ¾ cup of the orange juice until very hot. Remove from heat and immediately stir in gelatin, stirring until gelatin is completely dissolved. Add, stirring until dissolved

⅓ cup sugar
¼ teaspoon salt

Stir in the reserved ½ cup orange juice and

¼ teaspoon grated orange peel (*page 5*)

Cool mixture; chill (*page 6*) until mixture is slightly thicker than consistency of thick, unbeaten egg white.

Put a bowl and rotary beater into refrigerator to chill.

When gelatin is of desired consistency, wash, cut into halves, remove pit and peel from

1 large, ripe avocado

Force through sieve or food mill enough to yield 1 cup of sieved avocado; blend into the gelatin mixture.

Using the chilled bowl and beater, beat until cream is of medium consistency (piles softly)

1 cup chilled whipping cream

Spread over gelatin mixture and fold (*page 6*) together. Turn mixture into the pastry shell. Chill in refrigerator until firm. *One 9-in. pie*

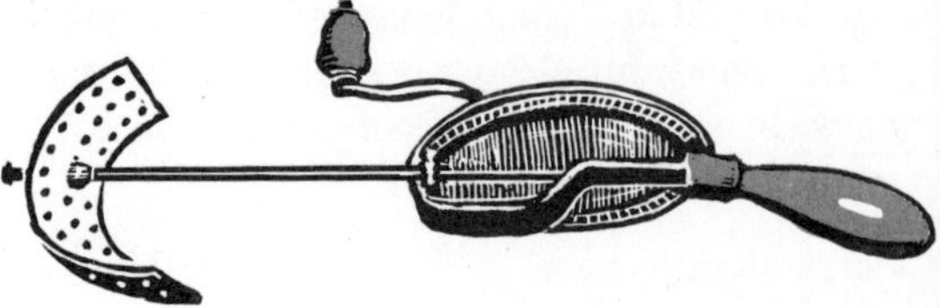

Lemon Cloud Pie

Refreshing as only lemon can be, this light-as-air pie is a welcome dessert at any time.

Prepare, bake and set aside to cool
Pastry for 1-Crust Pie (*page 242*; use 9-in. pie pan)
Mix together in top of double boiler
½ cup sugar
1 tablespoon (1 env.) unflavored gelatin
¼ teaspoon salt
Set aside.

Mix together
5 egg yolks, slightly beaten
½ cup water
½ cup lemon juice
½ teaspoon vanilla extract
Add gradually to gelatin mixture, stirring constantly, and mix well. Cook over simmering water, stirring constantly, until gelatin is dissolved and mixture is slightly thickened. Remove from simmering water and stir in
1 teaspoon grated lemon peel (*page 5*)
Cool mixture; chill (*page 6*) until mixture begins to gel (gets slightly thicker).

When gelatin mixture is of desired consistency, beat until frothy
5 egg whites
Add gradually, beating well after each addition
½ cup sugar
Beat until rounded peaks are formed. Spread over gelatin mixture and gently fold (*page 6*) together. Turn mixture into the pastry shell. Chill in refrigerator until firm.

If desired, serve with **Sweetened Whipped Cream** (*page 223*). *One 9-in. pie*

Orange Chiffon Pie

Prepare, bake and set aside to cool
Graham Cracker Pie Shell (*page 244*, use 9-in. pie pan; reserve 2 to 4 tablespoons of the crumb mixture for topping)
Pour into a small cup or custard cup
2 tablespoons cold water
2 tablespoons lemon juice
Sprinkle evenly over liquid
1 tablespoon (1 env.) unflavored gelatin
Let stand about 5 min. to soften.

Blend together in top of double boiler
4 egg yolks, slightly beaten
⅔ cup sugar
½ cup orange juice
¼ teaspoon salt
Cook over simmering water, stirring constantly until mixture thickens. Remove from heat and stir in softened gelatin and
2 teaspoons grated orange peel (*page 5*)
Stir until gelatin is completely dissolved. Cool mixture; chill (*page 6*) until mixture begins to gel (gets slightly thicker).

When gelatin is of desired consistency, beat until frothy
4 egg whites
Add gradually, beating well after each addition
½ cup sugar
Continue beating until rounded peaks are formed. Spread over gelatin mixture and gently fold (*page 6*) together. Turn into pie shell. Sprinkle the reserved crumbs over filling. Chill in refrigerator until firm.

One 9-in. pie

▲ Cocoa Chiffon Pie

Prepare, bake and set aside to cool

Pastry for 1-Crust Pie (*page 242;* use 8-in. pie pan)

Pour into a small cup or custard cup

¼ cup cold water

Sprinkle evenly over cold water

1 tablespoon (1 env.) unflavored gelatin

Let stand about 5 min. to soften.

Mix thoroughly in top of double boiler

⅓ cup sugar
⅓ cup cocoa
¼ teaspoon salt

Gradually blend in

⅔ cup milk

Stir over medium heat until sugar is dissolved. Bring mixture to boiling. Cook about 3 min. Vigorously stir about 3 tablespoons of hot mixture into

4 egg yolks, slightly beaten

Immediately blend into mixture in double boiler. Stirring constantly, cook over simmering water until mixture is slightly thickened.

Remove from heat and stir in softened gelatin, stirring until gelatin is completely dissolved. Blend in

1 teaspoon vanilla extract

Cool mixture; chill (*page 6*) until mixture begins to gel (gets slightly thicker).

When mixture is of desired consistency, beat until frothy

4 egg whites

Add gradually, beating well after each addition

⅓ cup sugar

Beat until rounded peaks are formed. Spread over gelatin mixture and gently fold (*page 6*) together. Turn into cooled pastry shell. Chill thoroughly in refrigerator.

Spread over top of pie and swirl with a spatula

Sweetened Whipped Cream (*page 223*)

One 8-in. pie

△ Chocolate Chiffon Pie

Follow ▲ Recipe. Substitute 2 sq. (2 oz.) **chocolate,** grated, for cocoa. Increase each of the sugar measurements to ½ cup.

Coconut Chiffon Pie

Prepare, bake and set aside to cool

Pastry for 1-Crust Pie (*page 242;* use 9-in. pie pan)

Set out

1 cup (4 oz.) moist shredded coconut, cut

Pour into a small cup or custard cup

¼ cup cold water

Sprinkle evenly over cold water

1 tablespoon (1 env.) unflavored gelatin

Let stand about 5 min. to soften.

Meanwhile, mix together in the top of a double boiler

4 egg yolks, slightly beaten
1 cup milk
½ cup sugar
¼ teaspoon salt

Cook over simmering water, stirring constantly until mixture coats a silver spoon. Remove from simmering water and stir in softened gelatin, stirring until gelatin is completely dissolved. Blend in ¾ cup of the coconut (reserve ¼ cup for garnish) and

1½ teaspoons vanilla extract

Cool mixture; chill (*page 6*) until mixture begins to gel (gets slightly thicker).

Meanwhile, spread evenly in cooled pastry shell and set aside

½ cup jellied cranberry sauce

When gelatin is of desired consistency, beat until frothy

4 egg whites

Add gradually, beating well after each addition

¼ cup sugar

Beat until rounded peaks are formed. Spread over gelatin mixture and gently fold (*page 6*) together. Turn into pastry shell. Sprinkle with the reserved coconut. Chill until firm.

Garnish just before serving with a few stars or other shapes cut from

Jellied cranberry sauce, cut into slices ¼ in. thick

One 9-in. pie

▲ Coffee-Nog Pie

For a double-mocha dessert treat—coffee in the pie and coffee with the pie.

Prepare, bake and set aside to cool

Pastry for 1-Crust 10-in. Pie (*page 242*)

Put a bowl and rotary beater into refrigerator to chill. Set out a double boiler.

Pour into a small bowl

½ cup cold water

Sprinkle evenly over cold water

2 tablespoons (2 env.) unflavored gelatin

Let stand about 5 min. to soften.

Meanwhile, prepare

2 cups double-strength coffee beverage (*page 7*)

Pour into top of the double boiler; add

⅔ cup sugar

½ teaspoon nutmeg

Stir over medium heat until sugar is dissolved. Bring mixture to boiling. Vigorously stir about 3 tablespoons hot coffee mixture into

3 egg yolks, slightly beaten

Immediately blend into mixture in double boiler. Stirring constantly, cook over simmering water until mixture is slightly thickened.

Coffee-Nog Pie and hot coffee

Remove from heat and stir in softened gelatin, stirring until gelatin is completely dissolved. Cool mixture; chill (*page 6*) until mixture begins to gel (gets slightly thicker).

When gelatin mixture is of desired consistency, beat, using chilled bowl and beater, until cream is of medium consistency (piles softly)

1 cup chilled whipping cream

Set in refrigerator while beating egg whites.

Using clean beater, beat until rounded peaks are formed

3 egg whites

Spread egg whites and whipped cream over gelatin mixture and gently fold (*page 6*) with

1½ teaspoons vanilla extract

Turn into cooled pastry shell. Chill in refrigerator until firm.

Top with chocolate curls made by pulling across a shredder

½ sq. (½ oz.) chocolate

Place in refrigerator until thoroughly chilled.

One 10-in. pie

△ Coffee-Nog Pie with Almonds

Follow ▲ Recipe. Fold in 1 cup (about 5½ oz.) salted, toasted **almonds** (*page 6*) with the vanilla extract.

▲ American Glory Apple-Cheese Pie

Prepare and set aside
Cheese Pastry for 2-Crust Pie (*page 243*; use 9-in. pie pan)
Crush (*page 6*) and set aside
4 or 5 graham crackers (or enough to yield 1/3 cup crumbs)
Grate and set aside
4 oz. Cheddar cheese (about 1 cup, grated)
Wash, quarter, core, pare and thinly slice
6 to 8 medium-size apples (about 6 cups, sliced)
Sprinkle evenly over apples
2 teaspoons lemon juice
Toss gently with apples a mixture of
3/4 cup sugar
2 tablespoons flour
1/2 teaspoon cinnamon
1/2 teaspoon nutmeg
1/8 teaspoon salt

Sprinkle graham cracker crumbs evenly over bottom of pastry shell. Spoon one third of apple mixture over bottom of the pastry shell. Top with one half of the grated cheese. Beginning with apples, repeat layers and end with apples. Slightly heap the last layer of apples in the center. Dot with
2 tablespoons butter or margarine

Complete as in **Pastry for 2-Crust Pie** (*page 242*).

Bake at 450°F 10 min. Reduce heat to 350°F and bake about 40 min. longer, or until crust is light golden brown.

Serve warm or cold. *One 9-in. pie*

△ Favorite-Treat Apple Pie

Follow ▲ Recipe. Substitute **Pastry for 2-Crust Pie** (*page 242*) for Cheese Pastry. Omit graham cracker crumbs and cheese from filling. Increase lemon juice to 1 tablespoon and cinnamon to 1 teaspoon. Serve with slices of sharp Cheddar cheese.

Favorite-Treat Apple Pie

▲ Cherry Pie

Prepare (do not bake) and set aside

Pastry for 1-Crust Pie (*page 242*; use 9-in. pie pan)

Sort, rinse, drain, and remove and discard the stems and pits from enough cherries to yield

4 cups pitted, fresh, sour red cherries

Toss gently with a mixture of

1½ cups sugar
5 tablespoons flour
⅛ teaspoon salt

Turn cherry mixture into pastry shell, heaping slightly at center. Sprinkle with

¼ teaspoon almond extract

Dot with

2 tablespoons butter or margarine

Bake at 450°F 10 min. Reduce heat to 375°F and bake about 45 min. longer.

Remove to cooling rack and allow to cool thoroughly.

Prepare

Vanilla Hard Sauce (double recipe, *page 191*; substitute 1 teaspoon almond extract for the 2 teaspoons vanilla extract)

When pie is cool, force hard sauce through pastry bag and No. 27 star decorating tube, forming a crisscross design over top of pie. At points where lines cross, make small rosettes with same decorating tube. *One 9-in. pie*

Note: If pie filling is not completely cool when lattice design is formed on it, hard sauce will melt slightly. This alters the appearance but does not affect the flavor.

△ Sweet Cherry Pie

Follow ▲ Recipe. Substitute **dark, sweet cherries** for sour cherries. Decrease sugar to 1 cup. Bake at 450°F 10 min., at 350°F 40 min.

Cranberry Lattice Pie

Lustrous cranberries have been American favorites since the days of early New England.

Prepare and set aside

Pastry for Lattice-Top Pie (*page 242*; use 9-in. pie pan)

Sort, rinse and drain

4 cups (1 lb.) cranberries

Set aside.

Mix together in a medium-size saucepan

2¼ cups sugar
¼ cup orange juice
2 tablespoons water
¼ teaspoon salt

Stir over medium heat until sugar is dissolved. Increase heat and bring mixture to boiling; add cranberries. Cook slowly 3 to 4 min., or just until skins of cranberries begin to pop.

Mix together

2 tablespoons cold water
1 tablespoon cornstarch

Blend thoroughly to a smooth paste. Gradually add cornstarch mixture to hot cranberries while stirring constantly. Bring rapidly to boiling, stirring constantly; cook 3 min. Remove from heat. Blend in

2½ tablespoons butter or margarine
1 teaspoon grated lemon peel (*page 5*)
1 teaspoon grated orange peel

Set cranberry filling aside to cool.

When filling is cool, brush pastry shell with

Melted butter or margarine

Pour cooled filling into pastry shell.

Complete as in Pastry for Lattice-Top Pie.

Bake at 450°F 10 min. Reduce heat to 350°F and bake about 20 min. longer, or until pastry is light golden brown.

Serve warm or cold. *One 9-in. pie*

Grape Arbor Pie

Prepare and set aside
Pastry for Lattice-Top Pie (*page 242*; use 8-in. pie pan)
Rinse and stem enough grapes to yield
3 cups Concord grapes
Slip skins from grapes. Chop skins; set aside.

Put the pulp in a small saucepan and bring to boiling; reduce heat and simmer 5 min., or until seeds are loosened. Drain pulp, reserving juice. Force the pulp through a fine sieve or food mill to remove the seeds. Discard seeds. Add the chopped grape skins to pulp. Set aside.

Sift together into a medium-size saucepan
1 cup sugar
3 tablespoons cornstarch
¼ teaspoon salt
Gradually add the reserved grape juice, stirring mixture well. Stirring gently and constantly, bring cornstarch mixture rapidly to boiling over direct heat; cook 3 min. Remove from heat. Stir in the pulp and skins with
1 tablespoon lemon juice
1 tablespoon orange juice
2 teaspoons grated orange peel (*page 5*)
Turn grape filling into pastry shell.

Complete as in Pastry for Lattice-Top Pie.

Bake at 450°F 10 min. Reduce heat to 350°F and bake 20 to 25 min. longer, or until pastry is light golden brown.

Cool on cooling rack. *One 8-in. pie*

Peach Pie

Peach Pie

If you count golden peach pie among life's blessings, you may thank the Spanish colonists who brought the peach tree to the New World.

Prepare and set aside
Pastry for 2-Crust Pie (*page 242*; use 9-in. pie pan)
Rinse and plunge into boiling water
12 medium-size (about 3 lbs.) firm, ripe peaches
Plunge peaches into cold water. Gently slip off skins. Cut peaches into halves; remove and discard pits. Slice peaches into a bowl and sprinkle with
1 teaspoon lemon juice
Gently toss with slices a mixture of
1¼ cups sugar
3 tablespoons quick-cooking tapioca
1 teaspoon grated lemon peel (*page 5*)
¼ teaspoon salt
Turn peach mixture into pastry shell, heaping slightly at center. Dot with
2 tablespoons butter or margarine
Complete as in Pastry for 2-Crust Pie.

Bake at 450°F 10 min. Reduce heat to 350°F and bake about 40 min. longer, or until crust is light golden brown.

Serve warm. *One 9-in. pie*

French Apricot Tart

Prepare, bake and set aside to cool
Pastry for 1-Crust Pie (*page 242*; use 9-in. pie or tart pan)
Drain, reserving sirup, contents of
2 No. 2½ cans peeled, whole apricots
Carefully remove and discard pits, leaving apricots intact.

Combine in a small saucepan 1 tablespoon of the reserved apricot sirup and
¼ cup strawberry or other red jelly
2 drops red food coloring
Heat slowly, stirring occasionally, until jelly is melted and ingredients are well blended. Set glaze aside to cool slightly.

(Remaining apricot sirup may be reserved for use in other food preparation.)

Spread carefully over bottom of pastry shell
1 cup apricot preserve
Place the whole apricots on preserve. Spoon glaze over apricots. Set aside in refrigerator to chill. This allows glaze to thicken slightly before serving. *One 9-in. pie*

Blueberry Pie

Prepare and set aside
Pastry for 2-Crust Pie (*page 242*; use 8-in. pie pan)
Sort, rinse and drain thoroughly
4 cups fresh blueberries
Sprinkle over the blueberries
4 teaspoons lemon juice
Toss gently with a mixture of
¾ cup sugar
¼ cup sifted flour
1 teaspoon grated lemon peel (*page 5*)
½ teaspoon cinnamon
¼ teaspoon nutmeg
⅛ teaspoon salt
Turn blueberry mixture into pastry shell, heaping slightly at center. Dot with
2 tablespoons butter or margarine
Complete as in Pastry for 2-Crust Pie.

Bake at 450°F 10 min. Reduce heat to 350°F and bake 30 to 35 min. longer, or until crust is light golden brown.

Cool on cooling rack. *One 8-in. pie*

Luscious Blueberry Pie

Prepare, bake and set aside to cool
Pastry for 1-Crust Pie (*page 242*; use 9-in. pie pan)
Drain, reserving sirup, contents of
2 No. 2 cans blueberries (about 2½ cups, drained)
Set aside.

Put into a saucepan
3 tablespoons cornstarch
Add gradually and stir in 1 cup of the reserved blueberry sirup. Mix well and bring rapidly to boiling, stirring constantly until mixture is thick and clear. When clear, stir in
6 tablespoons sugar
Remove from heat and mix in
2 tablespoons lemon juice
1½ tablespoons butter or margarine
⅛ teaspoon salt
Gently mix in the blueberries. Cover and set aside to cool.

Spoon filling into pastry shell. If desired, serve with **vanilla ice cream.** *One 9-in. pie*

Blueberry Pie

▲ Black Bottom Pie I

To be frank about it, there's a bit of making goes into this stunning pie. But the minutes are well-spent, and you'll find your reward in blissful faces and calls for more.

Prepare, bake and set aside to cool
Braided-Edge Pastry Shell (*page 243*)
Melt (*page 6*) and set aside to cool
1½ sq. (1½ oz.) chocolate

For Custard Filling—Scald (*page 7*) in top of double boiler
1½ cups milk
Meanwhile, pour into a small cup or custard cup
¼ cup cold water
Sprinkle evenly over cold water
1 tablespoon (1 env.) unflavored gelatin
Let stand about 5 min. to soften.

Sift together into a saucepan
½ cup sugar
4 teaspoons cornstarch
Add and blend in well
½ cup cold milk
Stir scalded milk into cornstarch mixture. Bring rapidly to boiling over direct heat, stirring gently and constantly. Cook 3 min.

Wash double-boiler top to remove scum.

Pour cornstarch mixture into double-boiler top. Vigorously stir about 3 tablespoons of hot mixture into
4 egg yolks, slightly beaten
Immediately blend into mixture in double boiler, stirring constantly. Cook, stirring constantly, over simmering water 3 to 5 min., or until mixture thickens and coats a silver spoon. Immediately remove from heat. Remove 1 cup cooked filling from double boiler and set aside to use in Chocolate Filling. Add softened gelatin to mixture in double boiler and stir until gelatin is completely dissolved. Set aside to cool until mixture sets slightly. If it becomes too stiff upon standing, soften mixture over simmering water and cool again.

For Chocolate Filling—Stir melted chocolate into the reserved filling with
2 teaspoons vanilla extract
Cool completely. Pour into pie shell and spread evenly over bottom. Chill in refrigerator until set.

To Complete Pie—Beat until frothy
4 egg whites
¼ teaspoon salt
Add and beat slightly
¼ teaspoon cream of tartar
Add gradually, beating well after each addition
½ cup sugar
Continue beating until rounded peaks are formed. Spread over gelatin mixture and gently fold (*page 6*) together. Blend in
1 tablespoon rum extract
Pour over set Chocolate Filling in pastry shell. Chill in refrigerator until firm.

Put a small bowl and rotary beater in refrigerator to chill.

About 30 min. before serving, using chilled bowl and beater, whip (*page 7*)
1 cup chilled whipping cream
Using a spatula, spread whipped cream over pie and swirl for decorative effect. Top with chocolate curls made by pulling across a shredder
½ sq. (½ oz.) chocolate
Chill in refrigerator until ready to serve.

One 10-in. pie

△ Black Bottom Pie II

Follow ▲ Recipe. Substitute 1 pkg. (6 oz.) **semi-sweet chocolate pieces** for chocolate, reserving about ¼ cup for topping. Omit whipped cream. Arrange reserved semi-sweet chocolate pieces over top of chilled pie.

Chocolate-Rum Angel Pie

Prepare, bake and set aside to cool
Meringue Shell (*page 246*)
Put a bowl and a rotary beater into refrigerator to chill.

Melt (*page 6*) and set aside to cool
4 oz. sweet chocolate
Using the chilled bowl and beater, beat until cream is of medium consistency (piles softly)
1 cup chilled whipping cream
Blend into the cooled chocolate
3 tablespoons rum
Spread the chocolate mixture over the whipped cream and gently fold (*page 6*) together. Turn into cooled meringue shell.

Place in refrigerator until thoroughly chilled.

One 9-in. pie

▲ Lemon Angel Pie

Prepare, bake and set aside to cool
Meringue Shell (*page 246*)
Spoon into a small cup or custard cup
4 teaspoons cold water
Sprinkle evenly over cold water
1 teaspoon unflavored gelatin
Set aside to soften.

Beat until thick and piled softly
4 egg yolks
2 eggs
Add gradually, beating constantly
1 cup sugar

Mix together
⅓ cup lemon juice
⅓ cup water
2 tablespoons grated lemon peel (*page 5*)
Add gradually to egg-yolk mixture, stirring until well blended. Pour into top of double boiler and place over simmering water. Cook, stirring constantly, until thick.

Remove from simmering water. Immediately stir in softened gelatin, stirring until gelatin is completely disolved. Cool mixture; chill (*page 6*) until mixture is partially set.

When mixture is of desired consistency, spoon into meringue shell. Place in refrigerator to chill just until mixture is set.

Put a bowl and a rotary beater into refrigerator to chill.

A few minutes before serving, using the chilled bowl and beater, whip (*page 7*)
1 cup chilled whipping cream
Spread over top and swirl with a spatula.

One 9-in. pie

△ Orange Angel Pie

Follow ▲ Recipe. Substitute ⅓ cup **orange juice** and 2 tablespoons grated **orange peel** for lemon juice and grated lemon peel.

△ Pineapple Angel Pie

Follow ▲ Recipe. Omit lemon peel and the ⅓ cup water. Reduce lemon juice to 2 tablespoons and mix with ⅔ cup **pineapple juice.**

△ Raspberry Angel Pie

Follow ▲ Recipe. Omit lemon peel and the ⅓ cup water. Reduce lemon juice to 1 tablespoon and sugar to ½ cup. Drain, reserving sirup, contents of 1 1-lb. can (about 1¼ cups, drained) **red raspberries.** Mix ⅔ cup of the **raspberry sirup** with the tablespoon of lemon juice. Fold the raspberries into the whipped cream before spreading over pie.

Almond-Mallow Pie

MRS. CLARENCE FARKE, ARMOUR, S. DAK.

Prepare, bake and set aside to cool
Cookie Crumb Pie Shell (*page 245;* use vanilla wafers and 8-in. pie pan)
Put a bowl and a rotary beater into refrigerator to chill.

Coarsely chop
½ cup (about 3 oz.) blanched, toasted almonds (*page 6*)
Set aside.

Combine in top of a double boiler
16 (¼ lb.) marshmallows, cut into quarters (*page 6*)
4 oz. milk chocolate
½ cup milk
Heat over simmering water, stirring frequently, until marshmallows and chocolate are melted. Remove from heat. Stir in the almonds; let stand until cool but not set. When mixture is cool, using the chilled bowl and beater, beat until cream is of medium consistency (piles softly)
1 cup chilled whipping cream
Blend in with final few strokes
¼ teaspoon almond extract
Spread over cooled chocolate and fold (*page 6*) together. Turn into pie shell. Chill in refrigerator until firm. *One 8-in. pie*

Chocolate Dream Pie

MRS. A. E. MARTINSON
DETROIT LAKES, MINN.

Prepare, bake and set aside to cool
Cookie Crumb Pie Shell (*page 245;* use vanilla wafers and 9-in. pie pan)
Put a bowl and a rotary beater into refrigerator to chill.

Chop and set aside
1 cup (about 4 oz.) walnuts
Melt (*page 6*) and set aside to cool
2 sq. (2 oz.) chocolate
Cream until softened
½ cup butter
Add gradually, creaming until fluffy after each addition
1 cup sifted confectioners' sugar
Add, one at a time, beating well after each addition
3 egg yolks
Blend in the cooled chocolate and the walnuts. Turn mixture into pie shell; chill in refrigerator until firm.

To serve, whip (*page 7*), using the chilled bowl and beater
1 cup chilled whipping cream
Spread over top of pie and swirl with spatula.

Serve immediately. *One 9-in. pie*

Chocolate Mint Pie

A flash of mint for perfect taste satisfaction.

Prepare, bake and set aside to cool
Cookie Crumb Pie Shell (*page 245;* use vanilla wafers and 9-in. pie pan)
Melt (*page 6*) and set aside to cool
1 sq. (1 oz.) chocolate
Cream until softened
½ cup butter or margarine
Add gradually, creaming until fluffy after each addition
¾ cup sugar
Blend in the cooled chocolate and
2 or 3 drops peppermint extract
Add, one at a time, beating about 5 min. after each addition
2 eggs, unbeaten
Turn filling into pie shell. Chill 2 or 3 hrs.

Spread over top of pie and swirl with a spatula
Sweetened Whipped Cream (*page 223*)
Top with chocolate curls made by pulling across a shredder
½ sq. (½ oz.) chocolate
Serve at once. *One 9-in. pie*

Red Raspberry Mallow Pie

JUNE HANSON, BAILEYS HARBOR, WIS.

Prepare, bake and set aside to cool

Cookie Crumb Pie Shell (*page 245;* use vanilla wafers and 9-in. pie pan)

Put into refrigerator to chill a bowl, rotary beater and

1½ cups whipping cream

Sort, rinse and drain thoroughly

2 cups fresh red raspberries (or 2 1-lb. pkgs. frozen red raspberries, thawed and drained)

Set ¼ cup of the berries aside for topping.

Combine in the top of a double boiler

32 (½ lb.) marshmallows, cut into quarters (*page 6*)

½ cup milk

Heat over simmering water, stirring frequently, until marshmallows are melted. Set aside to cool slightly.

When mixture is slightly cooled, chill in refrigerator until mixture becomes thicker.

Using the chilled bowl and beater, beat 1 cup of the chilled whipping cream until cream is of medium consistency (piles softly). Blend in with final few strokes

1 teaspoon vanilla extract

¼ teaspoon salt

Blend the whipped cream and 1¾ cups raspberries into the marshmallow mixture. Turn into pie shell. Chill in refrigerator until firm.

Put a clean bowl and beater into refrigerator.

Just before serving, using the chilled bowl and beater, whip (*page* 7) the ½ cup chilled whipping cream. Fold (*page 6*) the ¼ cup of reserved berries into the whipped cream. Pile in mounds around top of pie. *One 9-in. pie*

Strawberry Chiffon Pie

A wonderful way to use the first strawberries.

Prepare, bake and set aside to cool

Graham Cracker Pie Shell (*page 244;* use 9-in. pie pan)

Put a bowl and rotary beater into refrigerator to chill.

Sort, rinse, drain, hull, cut into thin slices and put into a medium-size bowl

2 cups fresh, ripe strawberries

Mix with the strawberries

1 cup sugar

Cover bowl and allow strawberries to stand until sugar has dissolved and sirup formed.

Pour into a small cup or custard cup

¼ cup cold water

Sprinkle evenly over cold water

1 tablespoon (1 env.) unflavored gelatin

Let stand about 5 min. to soften.

When strawberry sirup has formed, drain strawberries, reserving sirup. If necessary, add to reserved strawberry sirup

Water (enough to make 1 cup liquid)

Heat the sirup until very hot. Remove from heat and immediately add the softened gelatin, stirring until gelatin is completely dissolved. Blend into gelatin mixture

2 tablespoons lemon juice

Cool mixture; chill (*page 6*) until mixture is slightly thicker than consistency of thick, unbeaten egg white.

Meanwhile, pour into the chilled bowl

½ cup icy cold water

Sprinkle evenly over water

½ cup instant nonfat dry milk solids

Using the chilled beater, beat until mixture stands in peaks when beater is slowly lifted upright. When gelatin mixture is of desired consistency, spread the whipped nonfat dry milk solids over the gelatin mixture. Add the drained strawberries and gently fold (*page 6*) together. Turn into prepared pie shell and chill in refrigerator until firm. *One 9-in. pie*

Butter Tarts

MRS. F. W. BASHAM, RIVERSIDE, CALIF.

Prepare (do not bake) and set aside

Pastry for Little Pies and Tarts (*page 243*; use 10 2¾-in. muffin-pan wells)

Melt and set aside to cool

½ cup butter

Beat slightly

2 eggs

Add gradually, mixing thoroughly

2 cups firmly packed brown sugar

Stir in the melted butter and

1 teaspoon vanilla extract
1⅓ cups (about 7 oz.) currants

Spoon filling into tarts shells, allowing about ¼ cup for each tart.

Bake at 350°F 35 min., or until filling is golden brown.

Cool in muffin-pan wells on rack. *10 tarts*

Cherry Rose-Petal Tarts

Prepare, bake and set aside to cool

Pastry for Rose-Petal Tarts (*page 243*)

Drain, reserving sirup, contents of

2 No. 2 cans pitted, sour red cherries (about 4 cups, drained)

Put into a saucepan

3 tablespoons cornstarch

Add gradually and stir in 1 cup of the reserved cherry sirup. Mix well and bring rapidly to boiling, stirring constantly; cook until mixture is thick and clear. When clear, stir in

¾ cup sugar

Remove from heat and mix in

1 teaspoon lemon juice
½ teaspoon almond extract
¼ teaspoon salt

(For brighter color, stir in a few drops of red food coloring.) Gently mix in the cherries. Cover and set aside to cool.

Spoon cooled filling into Rose-Petal Tart shells. *6 tarts*

▲ Lime Chiffon Tarts

These attractive dainties of pale shimmering green lend special grace to the tea table or to the dessert course of a luncheon.

Prepare, bake and set aside to cool

12 Graham Cracker Tart Shells (one and one-half times recipe, *page 244*)

Pour into a small cup or custard cup

¼ cup cold water

Sprinkle evenly over cold water

1 tablespoon (1 env.) unflavored gelatin

Let stand about 5 min. to soften.

Meanwhile, mix together in top of a double boiler

4 egg yolks, slightly beaten
⅔ cup sugar
½ cup lime juice
¼ teaspoon salt

Cherry Rose-Petal Tarts

Lime Chiffon Tarts

Set over simmering water and cook, stirring constantly, until mixture thickens.

Remove from simmering water and stir in softened gelatin and

2 teaspoons grated lime peel (*page 5*)

Stir until gelatin is dissolved completely. Tint to desired color by blending in

1 or 2 drops green food coloring

Cool mixture; chill (*page 6*) until mixture begins to gel (gets slightly thicker).

When mixture is of desired consistency, beat until frothy

4 egg whites

Add gradually, beating thoroughly after each addition

½ cup sugar

Beat until rounded peaks are formed. Spread over gelatin mixture and gently fold (*page 6*) together. Spoon into tart shells and chill in refrigerator just until firm.

If desired, serve with

Sweetened Whipped Cream (*page 223*)

12 tarts

△ Lemon Chiffon Tarts

Follow ▲ Recipe; substitute ½ cup **lemon juice** for lime juice and 2 teaspoons grated **lemon peel** for lime peel. Omit food coloring.

Blushing Pear Tarts

Lovely to look at and luscious to taste.

Prepare, bake and set aside to cool

Pastry for Little Pies and Tarts (*page 243*; use 3½-in. tart pans)

Prepare filling for

De Luxe Cream Pie or Tarts (one-half recipe, *page 248*)

While cream filling is cooling, drain, reserving sirup, contents of

1 1-lb. can pear halves (about 6 halves)

Sift together into top of double boiler

⅓ cup sugar
1½ tablespoons cornstarch
⅛ teaspoon salt

Add and blend well

2 tablespoons cold water

Heat 1 cup of the reserved pear sirup until very hot; gradually add to cornstarch mixture, stirring constantly. Stirring gently and constantly, bring mixture rapidly to boiling over direct heat and cook 3 min. Place over simmering water. Cover and cook about 12 min., stirring three or four times. Remove from heat and blend in

2 teaspoons lemon juice
1½ teaspoons butter or margarine
⅛ teaspoon grated lemon peel (*page 5*)
2 or 3 drops yellow food coloring
1 or 2 drops red food coloring

Set glaze aside to cool slightly.

Spoon about 3 tablespoons of the cooled cream filling into each tart shell. Place a pear half, rounded side up, in each tart shell. Put into a small cup or custard cup

Few drops red food coloring

Apply blush to rounded side of pears with a small amount of the food coloring. Spoon the lukewarm glaze evenly over pear halves. Set aside until glaze is completely cool.

While glaze is cooling, prepare

Toasted Coconut (*page 246*)

Sprinkle the coconut around edge of the tarts.

6 tarts

Individual Pumpkin Pies

Prepare (do not bake)

Pastry for Little Pies and Tarts (one and one-half times recipe, *page 243*; use 8 4½-in. pie pans)

Set aside in refrigerator.

Mix together

2 cups (1-lb. can) canned pumpkin

and a mixture of

⅔ cup firmly packed light brown sugar
1 teaspoon mace
¾ teaspoon ginger
¾ teaspoon nutmeg
½ teaspoon cinnamon
½ teaspoon salt

Blend together and add, mixing until smooth

2 eggs, slightly beaten
1 cup cream
1 cup milk

Pour about ½ cup filling into each pastry shell. Sprinkle tops with

Nutmeg

Bake at 450°F 10 min. Reduce heat to 350°F and bake 20 min. longer, or until a silver knife comes out clean when inserted halfway between center and edge of filling.

Cool completely on cooling rack.

Using a cookie cutter or waxed-paper pattern and knife, cut turkeys or other shapes from

Thin slices process American cheese

Garnish pies with cutouts. *8 individual pies*

Individual Pumpkin Pies with cheese cutouts

▲ Little Princess Fried Pies

Prepare and shape into 2 balls (do not roll)

Cheese Pastry for 2-Crust Pie (*page 243*, double recipe; no pie pan will be needed)

Set out a 2-qt. saucepan, having a tight-fitting cover, and a heavy 10-in. skillet.

Wash, quarter, core, pare and coarsely dice

6 medium-size (about 2 lbs.) cooking apples (about 6 cups diced)

Put apples into saucepan with

⅓ cup hot water

Cover and simmer, stirring occasionally, 5 to 10 min., or until apples are just tender when pierced with a fork. Drain thoroughly.

While apples are cooking, mix together

1 cup (about 4 oz.) grated Cheddar cheese
½ to ⅔ cup sugar (depending upon tartness of apples)
1½ teaspoons cinnamon
½ teaspoon nutmeg

Set aside.

Add to the drained, cooked apples

2 tablespoons butter
4 teaspoons lemon juice

Blend in the cheese mixture. Stir only enough to mix ingredients evenly. Set aside.

Flatten one ball of the pastry on a lightly floured surface. Follow directions in **Pastry for 1-Crust Pie** (*page 242*) for rolling pastry.

Cut out 6-in. rounds, using a saucer or waxed-paper pattern as a guide. Spoon about 4 tablespoons of the apple filling onto one half of each round. Moisten the edge of one half of the round with water to help form a tight seal.

Fold the other half of the round over the filling. Press edges together with a fork. Be certain that the seal is tight to avoid leakage of filling. Repeat this process with the remaining ball of pastry. Set pies aside.

Melt in the skillet over medium heat

3 to 4 tablespoons lard, hydrogenated vegetable shortening or all-purpose shortening

Carefully place the pies, as many as will fit uncrowded, into the skillet. Fry pies on one side 8 to 10 min., or until golden brown. Turn and fry until other side is golden brown. Add more shortening to skillet if necessary to keep pies from sticking.

Serve pies warm with slices of sharp **cheese,** a dip of **ice cream** or a mound of **whipped cream;** or sift **confectioners' sugar** over top.

12 to 14 pies

△ Fried Pies à la Roberta

Follow ▲ Recipe. Substitute **Pastry for 2-Crust Pie** (*page 242*) for cheese pastry. Omit cheese in filling.

Deep-Fried Peach Pies

▲ Deep-Fried Peach Pies

Set out a deep saucepan or automatic deep-fryer (*page 7*) and heat fat to 375°F.

Drain contents of

1 No. 2½ can (about 2½ cups, drained) sliced peaches

Prepare and shape into 2 balls

Pastry for 2-Crust Pie (*page 242*; no pie pan will be needed)

Flatten one ball of the pastry on a lightly floured surface. Follow directions in **Pastry for 1-Crust Pie** (*page 242*) for rolling pastry.

Using a 3½-in. cookie cutter, cut out pastry rounds. Place 3 peach slices onto each round. Moisten the edge of one half of the round with water to help form a tight seal. Fold the other half of the round over the filling. Press edges together with a fork. Be certain that the seal is tight to avoid leakage of filling. Repeat this process with the remaining ball of pastry.

Lower pies into hot fat. Deep-fry only as many as will float uncrowded one layer deep in fat. Deep-fry about 3 min., or until golden brown. Turn pies as they rise to surface and several times during cooking (do not pierce). Remove with a slotted spoon. Drain over fat for a few seconds before removing to absorbent paper.

Serve warm; sprinkle with

Confectioners' sugar

About 15 pies

△ Deep-Fried Apple Pies

Follow ▲ Recipe; omit peaches. Wash, quarter, core, pare and thinly slice 3 to 4 medium-size tart **apples** (about 3 cups, sliced). Put apples into a saucepan having a tight-fitting cover; add ½ cup **water** and 1 teaspoon **lemon juice.** Cook, covered, over low heat about 15 min., or until tender.

Meanwhile, mix together ¼ cup **sugar,** ½ teaspoon **cinnamon** and ⅛ teaspoon **nutmeg.**

Remove apples from heat and drain; add sugar mixture, blending thoroughly. Place about 2 tablespoons apple mixture onto each pastry round. Dot with **butter.** Proceed as in ▲ Recipe.

Dessert is the course of the meal that almost everyone enjoys, that children never have to learn to like nor have to be coaxed to eat. But there is more reason than just its popularity for making a practice of ending the meal with dessert. It is often quite important nutritionally, contributing a significant share of the day's food requirements. Furthermore, the course which ends the meal seems to have a definite satiety value, perhaps more psychological than physical; that is, it gives a sense that the meal is now complete.

PIES, CAKES AND COOKIES—These desserts are so important that each has a section elsewhere.

GELATIN DESSERTS—These may range from plain fruit-flavored gelatin through elaborate refrigerator desserts with gelatin; but the techniques are all similar to those described on *page 164.*

FRUIT DESSERTS—Fresh fruits in season, with a dash of liqueur, sugar and cream or a topping, if desired, and unelaborated stewed, frozen or canned fruits, are probably the lightest and easiest to prepare of all desserts. They are also suitable choices to follow an otherwise hearty meal.

PUDDINGS—Baked, steamed or top-of-the-range puddings are usually thickened with flour or cornstarch, or with starchy cereals such as tapioca, rice and corn meal.

Starches and the above-mentioned starchy cereals thicken liquids because the starch granules, as they are heated in the liquid, gradually swell and absorb moisture. The extent of thickening, of course, depends primarily upon the proportion of starch to liquid. Thickening continues as the mixture cools. To make such mixtures smooth, the starch granules should be separated before hot liquid is added: blend until smooth with a little cold liquid after mixing the sugar in the recipe with the starch; help keep granules separated as they thicken by constantly stirring while cooking—this also insures uniform heating. Starch mixtures must be brought to boiling and cooked long enough to destroy the raw starch flavor.

CUSTARDS are mixtures of sweetened and flavored milk and eggs. Custard may be cooked in the oven, without stirring, or with constant stirring on top of the range. Thickening is due to the coagulation of the egg proteins on heating.

Baked Custard—The custard mixture thickens in the form of a "gel" in which the coagulated egg protein encloses and holds the liquid. As in all forms of egg cookery, custards should be baked at a low temperature, because too high a temperature (or too long baking) will cause the protein to toughen and squeeze out liquid, producing "weeping." A useful method of shortening baking time is to scald the milk before stirring it into the slightly beaten eggs. To insure uniform temperature throughout the mixture, custards are usually baked in a boiling water bath. A baked custard is done when a silver knife inserted halfway between the center and edge of custard comes out clean.

Stirred Custard—The custard mixture is cooked over simmering water with constant stirring until it is just thick enough to coat a silver spoon. The custard may not yet appear sufficiently thickened, but it becomes somewhat thicker on cooling. Curdling may occur in a fraction of a second when the mixture is nearing the proper consistency if the cooking is too rapid (that is, if the water under the custard is boiling rather than just simmering) or is continued too long.

SOUFFLÉS—This baked product is made light and fluffy by the addition of beaten egg whites. For maximum volume and easy folding into mixture, beat egg whites until they form rounded peaks and do not slide when bowl is partially inverted.

A baked soufflé may be left in the oven for a short time with the heat turned off if it cannot be served immediately. As a soufflé cools it tends to shrink and fall because the volume of air decreases. An underbaked soufflé will fall rapidly; a soufflé baked until done and cooled slowly will fall slowly upon removal from the oven.

TORTES—These are cake-like desserts, made light with eggs and often rich with nuts; white bread crumbs, cracker crumbs or grated nuts sometimes take the place of flour. Tortes differ in texture from cakes, but are handled in much the same way (See A Check List For Successful Cakemaking, *page 194;* cool tortes 15 min. in pans).

REFRIGERATOR DESSERTS are mixtures that may or may not have gelatin; they must be chilled in refrigerator until firm enough to serve. An example is a rich dessert in a ladyfinger-lined spring-form pan, chilled several hours or overnight.

FROZEN DESSERTS—This term takes in a number of different types of mixtures that can be frozen—in the refrigerator or in an ice-cream freezer. Some frozen desserts should be agitated during freezing to break up large ice crystals while they are forming. The smaller the ice crystals in the frozen dessert, the smoother and creamier-seeming will be the texture of the dessert. Therefore, when the dessert is frozen to a mushy consistency it should be removed from the refrigerator and beaten or stirred until smooth. The whipped cream used in mousses prevents formation of large ice crystals by incorporating air into the mixture. Any substance, such as gelatin, eggs, flour, cornstarch and rennet, which increases the viscosity (resistance to pouring) of the mixture tends to separate the crystals and prevent them from growing.

Stirring (agitation) during freezing process—*American ice cream*—mixture of cream, sugar and flavoring. Cream that can be whipped is highly desirable since the incorporation of air during whipping gives a smooth texture to the ice cream. Whipping also distributes the fat evenly, creating added smoothness as the mixture becomes frozen. Because heavy cream is expensive, recipes have been developed which call for substitution of thin cream, evaporated milk, or milk thickened with gelatin, flour, eggs or marshmallows for part or all of the heavy cream. *French ice cream*—a rich mixture of eggs, cream, sugar and flavorings; virtually a frozen custard. *Philadelphia ice cream*—uncooked mixture of cream, sugar and flavorings; never with gelatin or other binder added. *Frozen custard*—mixture with a custard base; also a frozen product, in the wholesale and retail trade, too low in butterfat content to be legally called ice cream. *Water ices*—fruit juice which is diluted and sweetened with sugar, sirup or honey; has rather coarse texture, melts easily. *Granites*—water ices frozen with little stirring; rough and icy in texture. *Frappé*—water ice frozen to a mushy consistency. *Sherbet*—water ice (the base of which may be fruit juice, fruit pulp or crushed pulp) with beaten egg white or gelatin added—this decreases the size of crystals and gives a smoother product; milk sherbet uses milk as part of liquid in the water ice. *Sorbet*—sherbet made of several kinds of fruit. *Coupe*—frozen cup usually composed of fruit and ice cream and attractively garnished with whipped cream, candied fruits and peels, chopped nuts, mint leaves or fresh fruit; originally served in a special glass similar to the "champagne coupe."

Little or no stirring during freezing process—The following are ice creams made of heavy cream with or without eggs: *Parfait*—made by pouring a hot thick sirup over beaten egg whites or beaten egg yolks, adding flavoring and folding in whipped cream. *Biscuit*—parfait or similar mixture, partially frozen, then packed in small individual paper cases and frozen until firm. *Bombe*—two or more frozen mixtures packed in a melon-shaped or round mold and refrozen. *Mousse*—sweetened and flavored whipped cream; may contain gelatin for firmness.

▲ Banana Fritters

A deep saucepan or automatic deep-fryer for deep-frying will be needed.

Peel, cut into 1½-in. crosswise pieces and put into a bowl
4 firm bananas with all-yellow peel
Gently toss banana pieces with a mixture of
3 tablespoons confectioners' sugar
2 tablespoons lemon juice
1½ tablespoons rum or kirsch
Cover bowl and allow banana pieces to marinate 45 min. to 1 hr., turning occasionally.

Fill deep saucepan with fat and heat to 365°F (*page 7*).

Sift together into a bowl and set aside
1⅓ cups sifted flour
2 tablespoons sugar
1 teaspoon baking powder
½ teaspoon salt
Melt and set aside to cool
1 tablespoon shortening
Drain banana pieces and set aside, reserving liquid for fritter batter.

Beat until thick and lemon-colored
2 egg yolks
Beat in until blended, the melted shortening, the reserved liquid from bananas and
⅔ cup milk
1 teaspoon vanilla extract
Make a well in center of dry ingredients. Pour in liquid mixture all at one time and blend just until batter is smooth.

Beat until rounded peaks are formed
2 egg whites
Spread beaten egg whites over batter and gently fold (*page 6*) together.

Coat banana pieces by rolling in shallow pan containing
¼ cup flour
Using a large fork or slotted spoon, dip banana pieces into batter and coat evenly. Drain excess batter from banana pieces before deep-frying. Deep-fry only as many fritters at one time as will float uncrowded one layer deep in the heated fat. Turn fritters with tongs or a fork as they rise to surface of fat and frequently thereafter (do not pierce). Deep-fry 2 to 3 min., or until golden brown.

Lift out with slotted spoon and drain fritters over fat for a few seconds before removing to absorbent paper.

Sift over fritters
Confectioners' sugar
Serve immediately. *About 6 servings*

△ Strawberry Fritters

Follow ▲ Recipe; substitute for bananas 1 qt. large firm **strawberries,** rinsed and hulled. Do not marinate strawberries. Add the rum to the batter; omit lemon juice. Increase the confectioners' sugar to ½ cup and roll the strawberries in it (instead of in flour) before dipping into the batter. Increase flour in batter to 1½ cups.

Casserole Cottage-Cheese Cake

A delicate concoction that can be served warm.

Butter a shallow 1½-qt. casserole.

Crush (*page 6*)
12 vanilla wafers (or enough to yield ½ cup crumbs)
Turn crumbs into a bowl. Add gradually, stirring in with a fork
3 tablespoons butter or margarine, melted
With back of spoon, press crumb mixture very firmly in an even layer on bottom of casserole.

Bake at 325°F 5 min. Remove from oven and set aside to cool.

Sift together and set aside
⅓ cup sugar
3 tablespoons flour
¼ teaspoon salt
Force through a sieve or a food mill into a bowl and set aside
1½ cups cream-style cottage cheese
Beat until thick and lemon-colored
4 egg yolks
Combine egg yolks with the cottage cheese and
½ cup cream or undiluted evaporated milk
1 teaspoon lemon juice
½ teaspoon grated lemon peel (*page 5*)
½ teaspoon vanilla extract
Blend thoroughly. Stir in the dry ingredients.

Beat until rounded peaks are formed
4 egg whites
Spread beaten egg whites over cheese mixture and gently fold (*page 6*) together.

Turn into the casserole and sprinkle with
Nutmeg
Bake at 325°F 1 to 1½ hrs., or until a silver knife inserted halfway between center and edge of casserole comes out clean.

Serve warm. If desired, serve with **Sweetened Whipped Cream** (*page 223*). *4 to 6 servings*

Luscious Lemon Cheese Cake

Butter the bottom and sides of a 9-in. spring-form pan.

For Crust—Crush (*page 6*)
24 slices (6 oz.) zwieback (or enough to yield 2⅔ cups crumbs)
Turn crumbs into a bowl. Stir in
½ cup sifted confectioners' sugar
1½ teaspoons grated lemon peel (*page 5*)
Using a fork, evenly blend with
½ cup butter or margarine, softened
Turn into spring-form pan, reserving ¾ cup for topping. Using fingers or back of spoon, press crumbs very firmly into an even layer on bottom and sides of pan to rim; set aside.

For Filling—Combine and beat until smooth and fluffy
2½ lbs. cream cheese, softened
1¾ cups sugar (add gradually)
3 tablespoons flour
1½ teaspoons grated lemon peel
½ teaspoon vanilla extract
Add in thirds, beating well after each addition, a mixture of
5 eggs, slightly beaten
2 egg yolks
Blend in
¼ cup heavy cream
Turn into pan. Spread evenly. Sprinkle reserved crumb mixture over top.

Bake at 250°F 1 hr. Turn off heat. Let stand in oven 1 hr. longer. Remove to cooling rack to cool completely (4 to 6 hrs.).

Chill in refrigerator several hours or overnight. *16 to 20 servings*

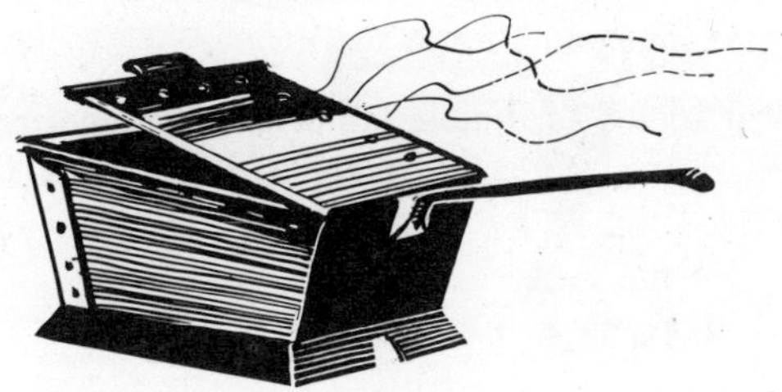

Lemon Soufflé

MRS. DALE RILEY, CLARKSBURG, W. VA.

Butter bottom of a 2-qt. casserole. Heat water for boiling water bath (*page 6*).

Mix thoroughly in a saucepan
- **½ cup sugar**
- **4½ teaspoons cornstarch**

Add gradually, stirring in
- **1½ cups milk**

Set over direct heat and bring rapidly to boiling, stirring constantly; cook 3 min. longer. Cool slightly.

Beat until thick and lemon-colored
- **3 egg yolks**
- **2 tablespoons plus 1 teaspoon lemon juice**
- **1 tablespoon grated lemon peel (*page 5*)**

Stirring vigorously to blend, pour sauce slowly into egg-yolk mixture. Cool to lukewarm.

Beat until frothy
- **3 egg whites**

Add gradually, beating well after each addition
- **¼ cup sugar**

Beat until rounded peaks are formed.

Spread egg-yolk mixture over beaten egg whites and carefully fold (*page 6*) together.

Bake in boiling water bath at 350°F 1 hr. or until a silver knife, inserted halfway between center and edge, comes out clean.

Serve immediately. *8 servings*

Chocolate Soufflé

MRS. JAMES C. FAHL, WASHINGTON, D. C.

Butter bottom of a 1½-qt. casserole. Heat water for boiling water bath (*page 6*).

Heat in top of double boiler over simmering water until chocolate is melted and milk is scalded (*page 7*)
- **½ cup milk**
- **2 sq. (2 oz.) chocolate**

Chocolate Soufflé

Blend with rotary beater and set aside.

Mix together
- **⅓ cup sugar**
- **3 tablespoons flour**

Add gradually, stirring in
- **½ cup cold milk**
- **2 tablespoons water**

Add to mixture in double boiler. Cook over simmering water until thickened, stirring constantly. Continue cooking 5 to 7 min., stirring occasionally.

Meanwhile, beat until thick and lemon-colored
- **4 egg yolks**

Remove about 3 tablespoons chocolate mixture and stir vigorously into beaten egg yolks. Immediately blend into mixture in double boiler and cook 3 to 5 min., stirring constantly. Remove from heat and blend in
- **2 tablespoons butter or margarine**
- **1 teaspoon vanilla extract**

Set aside.

Beat until rounded peaks are formed
- **4 egg whites**

Fold (*page 6*) chocolate mixture quickly into beaten egg whites. Turn into casserole.

Bake in boiling water bath at 325°F 1 hr. and 10 min., or until a silver knife, inserted halfway between center and edge, comes out clean.

Serve immediately. *6 servings*

Creamy Rice Pudding

Creamy Rice Pudding

Prepare

Perfection Boiled Rice (one-fourth recipe, *page 147*)

Meanwhile, set out

2 cups milk

Scald (*page* 7) in top of double boiler 1½ cups of the milk; reserve remainder. Sift together into a mixing bowl

⅔ cup sugar
1 tablespoon flour
¼ teaspoon salt

Blend in the reserved milk; gradually add the scalded milk, stirring constantly.

Wash double-boiler top to remove scum.

Pour mixture into double-boiler top and set over direct heat. Stirring gently and constantly, bring rapidly to boiling and cook 2 min. Set over simmering water.

Cover and cook about 5 to 7 min., stirring occasionally. Vigorously stir about 3 tablespoons of the hot mixture into

3 egg yolks, slightly beaten

Immediately blend into mixture in double boiler. Cook over simmering water 3 to 5 min., stirring slowly and constantly to keep mixture cooking evenly.

Fluff rice with a fork and stir into hot mixture. Remove from heat.

Stir in

½ cup seedless raisins
2 tablespoons butter or margarine
1 teaspoon vanilla extract

Cover and set pudding aside to cool slightly, stirring occasionally.

Serve in sherbet glasses. Sprinkle pudding with a mixture of

1 teaspoon nutmeg
1 teaspoon cinnamon

About 6 servings

▲ Soft Custard

Scald (*page* 7) in top of double boiler

2 cups milk

Beat slightly

3 eggs

Add and beat just until blended

¼ cup sugar
⅛ teaspoon salt

Stirring constantly, gradually add scalded milk to the egg mixture.

Wash double-boiler top to remove scum.

Strain mixture into double-boiler top and place over simmering water, stirring constantly and rapidly until mixture coats a silver spoon.

Remove from simmering water at once. Cool to lukewarm over cold water. Blend in

2 teaspoons vanilla extract

Pour into 4 sherbet glasses and immediately chill in refrigerator.

Coarsely chop

¼ cup (about 1 oz.) nuts

Sprinkle 1 tablespoon of the nuts over each serving. *4 servings*

Baked Custard

Caramel-Glazed Custard

▲ Baked Custard

Heat water for boiling water bath (*page 6*). Set out 4 heat-resistant custard cups.

Scald (*page 7*) in top of double boiler

2 cups milk

Beat slightly

3 eggs

Add and beat just until blended

¼ cup sugar

⅛ teaspoon salt

Stirring constantly, gradually add scalded milk to egg mixture. Strain mixture.

Blend in

2 teaspoons vanilla extract

Pour immediately into custard cups and sprinkle each serving with

Nutmeg

Bake in boiling water bath at 325°F 30 to 45 min., or until a silver knife comes out clean when inserted halfway between center and edge of custard.

Serve warm or chilled. *4 servings*

△ Caramel-Glazed Custard

Set out 5 heat-resistant custard cups.

To Prepare Caramel Glaze—Put ¼ cup **sugar** in a small light-colored heavy skillet. Stir over low heat until sugar is melted and becomes a golden brown sirup. Remove from heat and quickly drizzle on bottom and sides of each custard cup. For a thin, even glaze, twirl custard cup while pouring. Set aside while preparing custard.

Follow ▲ Recipe. Pour custard over sirup in custard cups. Bake in boiling water bath at 325°F 30 to 35 min., or until custard tests done. Remove carefully from boiling water bath. Set on a cooling rack until lukewarm. Chill thoroughly in refrigerator.

When ready to serve, unmold by running a knife around inside edge of custard cups; invert onto chilled serving dishes. The top will be caramel coated and the excess coating will run down the sides to form a sauce at the base of the custard mixture.

Lemon Cake-Top Pudding

MRS. VERNON SHEAN, ROCK ISLAND, ILL.

Grease a 2-qt. casserole. Heat water for boiling water bath (*page 6*).

Melt and set aside to cool
2 tablespoons butter
Sift into a large bowl
1 cup sugar
½ cup sifted flour
½ teaspoon baking powder
¼ teaspoon salt
Beat until thick and lemon-colored
3 egg yolks
¼ cup lemon juice
2 teaspoons grated lemon peel (page 5)
Stir into the egg-yolk mixture the melted butter and
1½ cups milk
Stir mixture into dry ingredients.

Beat until frothy
3 egg whites
Add gradually, beating well after each addition
½ cup sugar
Spread beaten egg whites over batter and gently fold (*page 6*) together. Turn batter into casserole.

Bake in boiling water bath at 350°F 50 min., or until a cake tester or wooden pick inserted in center of casserole comes out clean.

6 to 8 servings

Date-Nut Indian Pudding

▲ Indian Pudding

Butter a 1½-qt. casserole.

Scald (*page 7*) in top of double boiler
3 cups milk
Remove from heat. Stirring constantly, gradually add milk to a mixture of
½ cup yellow corn meal
¼ cup sugar
1 teaspoon salt
1 teaspoon cinnamon
½ teaspoon ginger
Wash double-boiler top to remove scum.

Vigorously stir about 3 tablespoons hot mixture into a mixture of
1 egg, well beaten
½ cup molasses
Immediately blend the molasses mixture into the corn meal mixture. Cook over simmering water about 20 min., or until very thick, stirring constantly. Blend in
2 tablespoons butter or margarine
Turn into casserole. Carefully pour over top
1 cup cold milk
Bake at 300°F 2½ to 3 hrs., or until a silver knife comes out clean when inserted halfway between center and edge of casserole.

Serve warm with **Vanilla Hard Sauce** (*page 191*) or **Sweetened Whipped Cream** (*page 223*) or **vanilla ice cream.** *About 6 servings*

△ Date-Nut Indian Pudding

Follow ▲ Recipe. Blend in with the butter ½ cup chopped **nuts** and ¼ cup cut **dates.**

Old-Fashioned English Plum Pudding with Vanilla Hard Sauce

Old-Fashioned English Plum Pudding

MRS. R. M. HERKENRATT
NORTHFIELD, MINN.

Prize-winning story of a favorite recipe:

"In our family this pudding has always meant Christmas!

"Each year Father made a special trip to town for nuts and fruit. The family, having procured the other ingredients, would then gather in the kitchen. My brother, sister, and I each held one corner of the sack, Mother took the flour sifter and Father held the key corner to evenly flour the pudding-sack.

"Then we lowered it into the mixing bowl and Mother spooned in the mixture. We each carefully brought in our corners for Father to take, tie and lower the pudding into boiling water. Three hours later Father would gently lift out the pudding with the aid of a clothes stick, letting it drip over a pan. After the dripping stopped Mother would slip a big platter under the pudding, while Father cut the string and peeled the sack. We would all vow it was the best-looking pudding ever."

Here is a streamlined version of the recipe.

Grease a 2-qt. mold or two 1-qt. molds.

Coarsely chop

1 cup (about 4 oz.) walnuts
¾ cup (about 4 oz.) blanched almonds (*page 5*)

Mix the chopped nuts with

½ lb. (about 1¼ cups) diced, assorted candied fruits
2 cups (about 10 oz.) seedless raisins
2 cups fine, dry bread crumbs (*page 4*)

Set aside.

Break apart, discarding membrane which coats it, finely chop and set aside

6 oz. suet (about 1½ cups, chopped)

Sift together in a large bowl

2 cups plus 2 tablespoons sifted flour
2 tablespoons sugar
½ teaspoon baking soda
½ teaspoon salt
1½ teaspoons cinnamon
1¼ teaspoons nutmeg
¾ teaspoon cloves
Few grains allspice

Blend in

½ cup plus 2 tablespoons firmly packed brown sugar

Blend the fruit-nut mixture and the suet into the dry ingredients. Set aside.

Blend together thoroughly

- **4 eggs, slightly beaten**
- **½ cup molasses**
- **½ cup milk**
- **¼ cup double-strength coffee beverage (*page 7*)**

Add liquid ingredients to dry ingredients, mixing until well blended. Turn batter into mold, filling about two-thirds full.

Cover mold tightly with greased lid or tie on aluminum foil, parchment paper or 2 layers of waxed paper. Place on trivet or rack in steamer or deep kettle with tight-fitting cover. Pour boiling water into bottom of steamer (enough to continue boiling throughout entire steaming period, if possible). If necessary, quickly add more boiling water during cooking period. Tightly cover steamer and steam 3 hrs. Keep water boiling at all times.

Remove pudding from steamer and immediately loosen edges of pudding with spatula. Unmold onto serving plate.

Serve with

Vanilla Hard Sauce (*page 191*)

About 16 servings

Note: If pudding is to be stored several days, unmold onto cooling rack. Let stand until cold. Wrap in aluminum foil or moisture-vapor-proof material and store in cool place. Steam thoroughly before serving (1 to 2 hrs.).

To Flame a Plum Pudding—Heat **brandy** in a small saucepan. Ignite brandy with match and pour over top of pudding. Serve when flaming stops.

Steamed Chocolate Pudding

Grease a 1½-qt. mold.

Melt (*page 6*) and set aside to cool

- **3 sq. (3 oz.) chocolate**

Sift together and set aside

- **1½ cups sifted flour**
- **1½ teaspoons baking powder**
- **½ teaspoon salt**

Cream together until shortening is softened

- **⅔ cup shortening**
- **1½ teaspoons vanilla extract**

Add gradually, creaming until fluffy after each addition

- **¾ cup sugar**

Add in thirds, beating well after each addition

- **2 eggs, well beaten**

Blend in chocolate.

Measure

- **¾ cup milk**

Beating only until blended after each addition, alternately add dry ingredients in fourths, milk in thirds, to creamed mixture. Finally beat only until blended (do not overbeat). Turn batter into mold.

Cover mold tightly with greased lid or tie on aluminum foil, parchment paper or 2 layers of waxed paper. Place on trivet or rack in steamer or deep kettle with tight-fitting cover. Pour boiling water into bottom of steamer (enough to continue boiling throughout entire steaming period if possible). If necessary, quickly add more boiling water during cooking period. Tightly cover steamer and steam 1½ hrs. Keep water boiling at all times.

Remove pudding from steamer and immediately loosen edges of pudding with a spatula. Unmold onto serving plate.

If desired, garnish pudding with

- **¼ cup (about 1½ oz.) seedless raisins**
- **4 pecan halves**
- **4 candied cherries**

Serve hot with **Sweetened Whipped Cream** (*page 223*).

6 to 8 servings

Cream Puffs: Beat mixture with wooden spoon until it leaves sides of saucepan and forms a ball.

Drop dough by tablespoonfuls onto a lightly greased baking sheet. Allow room for expansion.

Fill shells with Mocha Whipped Cream. Frost with Coffee Glaze. Serve with cups of steaming coffee.

▲ Cream Puffs

A coffee duet—cream puffs with a mocha glaze and an elegant coffee-whipped-cream filling.

For Cream Puffs or Choux Paste—Bring to a rolling boil

1 cup hot water
½ cup butter
1 tablespoon sugar
½ teaspoon salt

Add, all at one time

1 cup sifted flour

Beat vigorously with a wooden spoon until mixture leaves sides of pan and forms a smooth ball. Remove from heat. Quickly beat in, one at a time, beating until smooth after each addition

4 eggs

Continue beating until thick and smooth.

Dough may be shaped and baked at once, or wrapped in waxed paper and stored in refrigerator overnight. *1 doz. large or 4 doz. miniature puffs or éclairs*

For Coffee-Glazed Cream Puffs—Form small puffs. Force dough through a pastry bag or drop by tablespoonfuls 2 in. apart onto lightly greased baking sheet. Bake at 450°F 15 min. Reduce heat to 350°F; bake 5 min. longer, or until golden in color. Remove to racks to cool. To serve, cut off tops and fill shells with **Coffee** or **Mocha Whipped Cream** (*page 223*). Replace tops and frost with Coffee Glaze.

For Coffee Glaze—Measure into a bowl

3¾ cups sifted confectioners' sugar

Add and mix thoroughly

¼ cup plus 2 tablespoons warm triple-strength coffee beverage (*page 7*)
1½ teaspoons rum extract

For Gourmet Cream Puffs—Form and bake large puffs. Increase baking time at 350°F to 20 to 25 min. Fill shells with **Sweetened Whipped Cream** (three times recipe, *page 223*). Replace tops, pressing down gently until ruffles of whipped cream are formed. Frost with **Chocolate Glaze** (*page 279*).

△ Éclairs

Follow ▲ Recipe for Cream Puffs, forming dough into 4½x1-in. oblongs. When cool, cut small opening at one end and force filling through a pastry bag and a No. 6 decorating tube into éclair. Fill with **Creamy Vanilla Filling** (*page 222*). Frost with Coffee or Chocolate Glaze.

For Chocolate Glaze (cooked)—Melt (*page 6*) 2 sq. (2 oz.) **chocolate.** Mix in heavy saucepan with 1½ cups sifted **confectioners' sugar,** 2 teaspoons **dark corn sirup,** 2 tablespoons **cream,** 1 tablespoon plus 1 teaspoon **boiling water** and 2 teaspoons **butter.** Place over low heat and stir constantly until butter melts. Remove from heat and add 1 teaspoon **vanilla extract.** Cool slightly.

For Chocolate Glaze (uncooked)—Melt (*page 6*) 3 sq. (3 oz.) **chocolate.** Blend 3 cups **confectioners' sugar** into 2 **egg whites.** Add the chocolate and 1½ teaspoons **vanilla extract.** Mix until smooth.

Savoy Meringues

Heaped with ice cream, fruit or cream filling, these snowy meringues make an elegant dessert.

Line a baking sheet with unglazed paper.

Beat until frothy
2 egg whites
Add and beat slightly
1 teaspoon vanilla extract
½ teaspoon cream of tartar
¼ teaspoon salt
Add gradually, beating well after each addition
½ cup sugar
Beat until stiff (but not dry) peaks are formed and egg whites do not slide when bowl is partially inverted.

Drop 6 large or 18 small mounds from spoon onto baking sheet, allowing 2 in. between mounds. Using back of spoon, form meringue into shells or nests.

Savoy Meringues

Sprinkle over meringue shells
Sifted confectioners' sugar (about ½ teaspoon each for larger shells)
Bake at 250°F about 1 hr., or until meringue is dry to touch. (The oven door of some ranges may have to be propped open partially to maintain low temperature.) With a spatula carefully remove meringues at once and turn upside down onto same paperlined pan. (If meringues are difficult to remove from paper, raise paper from baking sheet. Lightly moisten underside of paper directly under each meringue; carefully remove shells at once with a spatula. Re-line baking sheet with dry paper.)

Return to oven 5 min. to complete drying. Cool completely on cooling rack. Meringues should be crisp, dry, and very fine textured. (Store meringues in an air-tight container so that they will not absorb moisture and soften.)

Prepare filling for
Lemon Cream Pie or Lime Cream Pie (*page 248*)
Fill meringue shells with the filling. Top with
Fresh, ripe strawberries
About 6 large or 18 small meringue shells

Note: Meringue shells may also be filled with **ice cream, sherbet** or **fruit;** garnish with **fruit, whipped cream,** chopped **nuts** or **fruit** flavored with any one or any combination of **kirsch, curaçao, Cointreau, brandy** or **rum.**

▲ Blancmange

Set out

2 cups milk

Scald (*page* 7) in top of double boiler 1½ cups of the milk; reserve remainder.

Meanwhile, sift together into a saucepan

⅓ cup sugar
3 tablespoons cornstarch
⅛ teaspoon salt

Blend in the reserved milk; gradually add the scalded milk, stirring constantly. Bring rapidly to boiling over direct heat, stirring gently and constantly; cook 3 min. Remove from heat.

Wash double-boiler top to remove scum.

Pour mixture into double-boiler top; set over simmering water. Cover and cook about 12 min., stirring three or four times.

Lightly oil a 1-qt. mold with salad or cooking oil (not olive oil); set aside to drain.

Remove cornstarch mixture from simmering water. Cool slightly.

Beat until rounded peaks are formed

4 egg whites

Blend into cornstarch mixture

1 teaspoon vanilla extract

Spread beaten egg whites over mixture and fold (*page* 6) together. Turn into prepared mold and chill until firm.

When ready to serve, unmold onto chilled serving plate. Serve with

Crushed fresh strawberries

4 to 6 servings

△ Coconut Blancmange

Follow ▲ Recipe. Blend in 1 cup finely chopped, moist shredded **coconut** with vanilla extract.

△ Fruit Blancmange

Follow ▲ Recipe. Blend in 1 cup well-drained, canned or sweetened fresh **fruit** with vanilla extract.

Blancmange

Trifle

Set out a shallow 2-qt. casserole. Chill a small bowl and rotary beater in refrigerator.

Cut into 1-in. pieces

Day-old pound cake (enough to line bottom of casserole)

Arrange over bottom of casserole. Pour over

½ cup brandy or rum

Cover and set aside.

Pour into a small cup or custard cup

¼ cup cold water

Sprinkle evenly over cold water

1 tablespoon (1 env.) unflavored gelatin

Let stand 5 min. to soften.

Meanwhile, scald (*page* 7) in the top of a double boiler

1½ cups milk

Beat slightly

5 egg yolks

Blend in

¼ cup sugar

Add gradually and blend in the scalded milk.

Wash double-boiler top to remove scum.

Return mixture to double-boiler top. Cook over simmering water, stirring constantly and rapidly until mixture coats a silver spoon.

Remove from heat and immediately stir in softened gelatin until gelatin is completely

dissolved. Cool; chill (*page 6*) until mixture begins to gel (gets slightly thicker).

When gelatin mixture is of desired consistency, prepare whipped cream. Using the chilled bowl and beater, beat until cream is of medium consistency (piles softly)

¼ cup chilled whipping cream

Set in refrigerator while beating egg whites.

Using clean beater, beat until frothy

3 egg whites

Add gradually, beating well after each addition

¼ cup sugar

Beat until rounded peaks are formed.

Spread egg whites and whipped cream over gelatin mixture and gently fold (*page 6*) together. Turn into the casserole. Chill in refrigerator until firm.

When ready to serve, garnish (see photo) with

Candied cherry
Slivered blanched almonds
Pieces of angelica

Prepare

Sweetened Whipped Cream (one-half recipe, *page 223*)

Force through pastry bag and No. 27 star decorating tube, forming a border around Trifle. *About 12 servings*

Trifle

Angel's Delight

MRS. FRANK J. CORDERA, BENLD, ILL.

Line bottom and sides of a 9½x5¼x2¾-in. loaf pan with waxed paper.

Melt (*page 6*) and set aside to cool

1 pkg. (6 oz.) semi-sweet chocolate pieces

Coarsely chop and set aside

1 cup (about 4 oz.) walnuts or pecans

Tear into small pieces enough angel food cake to yield

4 cups angel food cake pieces

Beat until thick and lemon-colored

4 egg yolks
6 tablespoons sugar

Stirring vigorously to blend, add melted chocolate to the egg-yolk mixture. Stir in the chopped nuts.

Beat until rounded peaks are formed

4 egg whites

Spread beaten egg whites over chocolate mixture and gently fold (*page 6*) together.

Put about 1 cup of the cake pieces in the loaf pan. Cover with about one fourth of the chocolate mixture. Repeat, ending with chocolate mixture.

Chill in refrigerator until firm (at least 4 hrs.).

When ready to serve, invert onto chilled serving plate; remove waxed paper. If desired, garnish with **whipped cream** and **maraschino cherries.**

Serve immediately. *8 to 10 servings*

Nesselrode Pudding

AMY S. BOYD, LAKE CHARLES, LA.

American version of a European creation.

Set out a 9½x5¼x2¾-in. loaf pan. Set refrigerator control at coldest operating temperature. Put a medium-size bowl and a rotary beater into refrigerator to chill.

Set out
1½ doz. ladyfingers (or use sponge cake cut in 4x1½x1-in. pieces)
Line sides of the loaf pan with the ladyfingers and set aside.

Put into a large bowl and beat until very thick and lemon-colored
2 egg yolks
Add gradually, beating well after each addition
½ cup sugar
Add gradually, beating constantly
¼ cup (2 oz.) sherry
Set egg-yolk mixture aside.

Beat until rounded peaks are formed
2 egg whites
Spread beaten egg whites over egg-yolk mixture and gently fold (*page 6*) together.

Meanwhile, using chilled bowl and beater, beat until cream is of medium consistency (piles softly)
1¾ cups chilled whipping cream (beat only half of this amount at a time)
Beat into whipping cream, with final few strokes until blended
¼ cup sifted confectioners' sugar
1 teaspoon vanilla extract
Gently fold together the whipped cream, the egg-yolk mixture and contents of
1 10-oz. jar (about 1¼ cups) Nesselrode mixture
Turn the mixture into the prepared pan.

Place in freezing compartment of refrigerator until firm (about 12 hrs.).

If desired, garnish with **nuts, maraschino cherries** and **whipped cream.**

8 to 10 servings

▲ Favorite Vanilla Ice Cream

These ice cream recipes may be prepared in a dasher-type freezer or in refrigerator.

If using the dasher-type freezer, wash and scald cover, container and dasher of a 2-qt. ice-cream freezer. Chill before using.

If using a refrigerator, set control at coldest operating temperature, and chill a large bowl and a rotary beater and refrigerator trays.

Scald (*page 7*) in top of double boiler
2 cups milk
Combine and then gradually stir into milk
1 cup sugar
1 tablespoon sifted flour
¼ teaspoon salt
Stirring constantly, cook over direct heat 5 min. Remove from heat and vigorously stir about 3 tablespoons of hot mixture into
3 egg yolks, slightly beaten
Immediately stir into hot mixture in top of double boiler. Return to heat and cook over simmering water 10 min., stirring constantly until mixture coats a silver spoon. Remove from heat and cool. Stir in
2 cups cream
2 teaspoons vanilla extract
Chill in refrigerator.

For Dasher-Type Freezer—Fill chilled container two-thirds full with ice-cream mixture. Cover tightly. Set into freezer tub. (For electric freezer, follow manufacturer's directions.) Fill tub with alternate layers of
8 parts crushed ice
1 part rock salt
Turn handle slowly 5 min. Turn rapidly until handle becomes difficult to turn (about 15 min.), adding ice and salt as necessary. Carefully wipe cover and remove dasher. Pack down ice cream and cover with waxed paper. Replace cover; fill dasher opening with cork.

Repack freezer in ice using
4 parts crushed ice
1 part rock salt
Cover with paper or cloth. Let ripen 2 to 3 hrs.

For Mechanical Refrigerator—Pour mixture into refrigerator trays and place in freezing compartment of refrigerator. When mixture becomes mushy, turn into chilled bowl and beat with chilled beater. This helps to form fine crystals and to give a smooth creamy mixture. Return mixture to trays and freeze until firm. *About 1½ qts. ice cream*

△ French Vanilla Ice Cream

Follow ▲ Recipe. Omit flour and increase egg yolks to 5. Substitute 2 cups **heavy cream** for cream.

△ Chocolate Ice Cream

Follow ▲ Recipe. Add 2 sq. (2 oz.) **chocolate** to milk and heat until milk is scalded and chocolate is melted in top of double boiler.

△ Chocolate-Chip Ice Cream

Follow ▲ Recipe. Just before freezing, blend in 2 oz. **semi-sweet chocolate,** grated.

△ Butter-Pecan Ice Cream

Follow ▲ Recipe. Melt in a skillet 3 tablespoons **butter.** Add 1 cup (about 3¾ oz.) chopped **pecans** and heat to golden brown, occasionally moving and turning. Stir into mixture just before freezing.

△ Berry Ice Cream

Follow ▲ Recipe. Just before freezing, blend in 2 cups crushed **strawberries** or **raspberries,** sweetened.

△ Peach Ice Cream

Follow ▲ Recipe. Substitute 1 teaspoon **almond extract** for vanilla extract. Just before freezing, blend in 1 tablespoon **lemon juice** and 1½ cups crushed fresh **peaches,** sweetened.

△ Two-Flavored Brick Ice Cream

Prepare ▲ Recipe and one-half △ Recipe, using refrigerator method. Just before final freezing, form two-flavored ice cream brick by spooning alternate layers of vanilla ice cream and chocolate ice cream into refrigerator trays, starting and ending with vanilla. Return to freezing compartment until firm.

Favorite Vanilla Ice Cream: **When mixture is mushlike, turn it into a chilled bowl.**

Beat with chilled beater for smooth, creamy texture. Return to refrigerator and freeze.

▲ Baked Alaska

Set refrigerator control at coldest operating temperature and chill a 2-qt. mold. Cover a baking sheet with two sheets heavy paper or set out a wooden board.

Line chilled mold with

Chocolate Ice Cream (one-third recipe, *page 283*; or use 1 qt. commercial ice cream)

Pack ice cream firmly against sides of mold.

Fill center of mold, packing firmly, with

Berry Ice Cream (one-half recipe, *page 283*, or 1 qt. commercial ice cream)

Place in freezing compartment of refrigerator until very firm.

Meanwhile, prepare and cool

Pound Cake (*page 200*; see note for round or square Alaska)

Split cake into two layers and trim one layer about ½ in. larger than mold. (Remainder of cake may be frosted, sliced and used as dessert.) Place cake slice on baking sheet or wooden board. Set aside.

Prepare meringue by beating until frothy

5 egg whites
½ teaspoon vanilla extract
¼ teaspoon salt

Add gradually, beating well after each addition

¾ cup sugar

Beat until rounded peaks are formed and egg whites do not slide when the bowl is partially inverted.

Quickly but carefully unmold ice cream. To unmold, loosen top edge of mold with a knife. Wet a clean towel in hot water and wring it almost dry. Invert mold onto center of cake. Wrap hot towel around mold for a few seconds only. (If mold does not loosen, repeat.) Working quickly, completely cover ice cream and cake with meringue, spreading evenly and being careful to completely seal bottom edge. With spatula, quickly swirl meringue into an attractive design and if desired garnish with

Maraschino cherries

Place in 450°F oven for 4 to 5 min., or until meringue is lightly browned.

Using two broad spatulas, quickly slide Baked Alaska onto a chilled serving plate. Slice and serve immediately. *12 to 16 servings*

Note: **Sponge cake** may also be used as a base for Baked Alaska.

△ Baked Alaska Loaf

Follow ▲ Recipe. Substitute a 1-qt. **brick** of **commercial ice cream** for molded ice cream. Prepare **Pound Cake** (loaf, *page 200*) or substitute purchased oblong pound cake. Slice ½-in. layer from bottom of cake and cut layer about ½ in. larger than length and width of brick of ice cream to be used.

Chocolate Funny Cake-Pie

For Pastry—Prepare (do not bake)

Pastry for 1-Crust Pie (*page 242*; use 9-in. pie pan)

Set aside.

For Sauce—Combine in a saucepan

½ cup water
1½ sq. (1½ oz.) chocolate

Put over low heat and stir constantly until chocolate is melted.

Add
⅔ cup sugar
Stirring constantly, bring to boiling; remove from heat and stir in
¼ cup butter or margarine
1½ teaspoons vanilla extract
Set aside.

For Cake—Finely chop and set aside
1 cup (about 4 oz.) walnuts
Sift together into a large bowl
1¼ cups sifted cake flour
¾ cup sugar
1¼ teaspoons baking powder
¼ teaspoon salt
Add to sifted dry ingredients
½ cup milk
¼ cup hydrogenated vegetable shortening or all-purpose shortening
1½ teaspoons vanilla extract
Beat until dry ingredients are just mixed.

Add
1 egg, unbeaten
Beat 200 strokes, or 2 min. on electric mixer on medium speed. Scrape sides of bowl several times during beating.

Add nuts and beat 100 strokes, or 1 min. on electric mixer. Turn batter into pastry shell. Stir sauce and carefully pour over cake batter. (Sauce will sink to bottom.)

Bake at 350°F 50 to 55 min., or until cake tests done (*page 194*).

Serve warm. Top with **whipped cream.**
6 to 8 servings

△ Apple Butter Funny Cake-Pie

ARLETTA WHALEY, OTWELL, IND.

Follow ▲ Recipe; omit sauce and nuts. Sift ½ teaspoon **cinnamon,** ¼ teaspoon **cloves** and ¼ teaspoon **allspice** with dry ingredients. Spread 1 cup **apple butter** evenly over unbaked pastry shell. Turn cake batter into shell.

Strawberry Shortcakes

(See color photo inside back cover)

For Sweetened Crushed Strawberries—Sort, rinse, drain and hull
1 qt. fresh ripe strawberries
Reserve ½ cup strawberries for garnish.

Crush remaining berries slightly. Sprinkle with
1 cup sugar
Cover and set in refrigerator to chill thoroughly. Gently mix fruit occasionally.

For Shortcakes—Prepare
Tender-Rich Rolled Shortcakes (*page 43*)

To Serve—Split shortcakes while hot and spoon one half of the crushed berries over the bottom halves. Cover with top halves and spoon remaining berries over top. Top with
Sweetened Whipped Cream (*page 223*)
Serve immediately. *6 servings*

Note: **Raspberries, blackberries** or **blueberries** may be substituted for strawberries.

Pineapple-Orange Fantasies

MRS. VERNON SHEAN, ROCK ISLAND, ILL.

An inspired combination of orange-flavored pastry and a piquant filling, layered into little towers that are topped with a fluff of meringue, make this prize-winner a truly original and distinguished dessert.

For Pineapple-Orange Filling—Cut into short lengths and set aside

¾ cup (3 oz.) moist, shredded coconut

Drain (reserving sirup in a 1-cup measuring cup for liquids) contents of

1 9-oz. can crushed pineapple (about ¾ cup, drained)

Sift together into top of a double boiler

6 tablespoons flour
⅓ cup sugar

Mix with the reserved pineapple sirup

Cold water (enough to make ½ cup liquid)

Add gradually, stirring into flour mixture with

½ cup orange juice
2 teaspoons lemon juice

Bring mixture rapidly to boiling over direct heat, stirring gently and constantly; cook 3 min. Place over simmering water. Cover and cook 5 to 7 min., stirring three or four times.

Vigorously stir about 3 tablespoons hot mixture into

2 egg yolks, slightly beaten

Immediately blend into mixture in double boiler. Cook over simmering water 3 to 5 min., stirring slowly and constantly to keep mixture cooking evenly. Remove from simmering water and blend in the coconut, crushed pineapple and

2 tablespoons butter

Cover and cool slightly, stirring occasionally. Put filling into refrigerator while preparing Orange Pastry.

For Orange Pastry—Set out baking sheets. Sift together into a bowl

1½ cups sifted flour
½ teaspoon salt

Cut in with pastry blender or two knives until pieces are size of small peas

½ cup hydrogenated vegetable shortening or all-purpose shortening

Blend in with a fork

2 teaspoons grated orange peel (page 5)

Sprinkle gradually over mixture, a teaspoon at a time, about

2½ tablespoons cold water

Mix lightly with fork after each addition. Add only enough water to hold pastry together. Work quickly; do not overhandle. Shape into a ball. Divide into halves. Flatten one half at a time on a lightly floured surface. Roll from center to edge into a round about ⅛ in. thick.

With knife or spatula, loosen pastry from surface wherever sticking occurs; lift pastry slightly and sprinkle flour underneath. Cut with lightly floured 2½-in. round cookie cutter. With spatula, gently lift pastry rounds onto baking sheets.

Bake at 400°F 10 min., or until golden brown.

Carefully remove pastry rounds to cooling racks and set aside to cool.

Meanwhile, prepare Meringue.

For Meringue—Beat until frothy

2 egg whites

Add gradually, beating well after each addition

¼ cup sugar

Continue beating until rounded peaks are formed and egg whites do not slide when bowl is partially inverted. Fold in

½ teaspoon lemon juice

To Assemble Fantasies—Using three Orange Pastry rounds for each serving, spread Pineapple-Orange Filling over two rounds. Spread the third round with meringue. Cover one frosted round with the other and top with the meringue-topped round.

Bake at 400°F 3 to 4 min., or until meringue is delicately browned.

Cool and serve. *About 1 doz. desserts*

Pineapple-Mint Sherbet

RUTH V. POWELL, CADES, TENN.

Set refrigerator control at coldest operating temperature. Put a bowl and a rotary beater and refrigerator trays into refrigerator to chill.

Rinse, drain and bruise
½ cup fresh mint leaves
Combine in a saucepan
2 cups sugar
2 cups water
Set over low heat and stir until sugar is dissolved. Increase heat and bring to boiling.

Remove from heat. Add bruised mint leaves, cover and set aside for 1 hr.

Meanwhile, drain (reserving sirup for use in other food preparation) contents of
1 9-oz. can crushed pineapple (about ⅔ cup, drained)
Peel and force through a sieve or food mill enough bananas to yield
⅔ cup sieved banana (about 2 bananas with brown-flecked peel)
Strain sirup to remove mint leaves. Add and thoroughly blend with sirup, the pineapple, sieved banana and
⅔ cup orange juice
6 tablespoons lemon juice
To tint, stir in, a drop at a time
3 to 4 drops green food coloring
Beat until rounded peaks are formed
2 egg whites
Fold (*page 6*) egg whites into fruit mixture.

Turn sherbet into refrigerator trays. Freeze until mixture is mush-like in consistency.

Turn mixture into chilled bowl and beat thoroughly with chilled beater. Immediately return mixture to refrigerator trays and place in freezing compartment. Freeze until firm.

About 2 qts. sherbet

▲ Lime Ice

Set refrigerator control at coldest operating temperature. Chill a 1-qt. refrigerator tray.

Pour into a small cup or custard cup
¼ cup cold water
Sprinkle evenly over cold water
2 teaspoons unflavored gelatin
Let stand about 5 min. to soften.

Meanwhile, heat until very hot
3 cups water
Remove from heat and immediately stir in softened gelatin until gelatin is completely dissolved. Add, stirring until sugar is dissolved
2 cups sugar
Blend into gelatin mixture
¾ cup lime juice
2 tablespoons lemon juice
2 teaspoons grated lemon peel (*page 5*)
Tint to desired color by mixing in, a drop at a time
Green food coloring (about 4 drops)
Cool. Pour into a refrigerator tray. Place in freezing compartment of refrigerator and freeze until firm (3 to 4 hrs.), stirring 2 or 3 times during freezing.

Serve in chilled sherbet glasses.

About 1 qt. ice

△ Apricot Ice

Follow ▲ Recipe. Decrease hot water to 1½ cups and sugar to 1 cup. Substitute 2 cups **apricot nectar** for lime juice and 2 tablespoons **orange juice** for lemon juice. Omit food coloring.

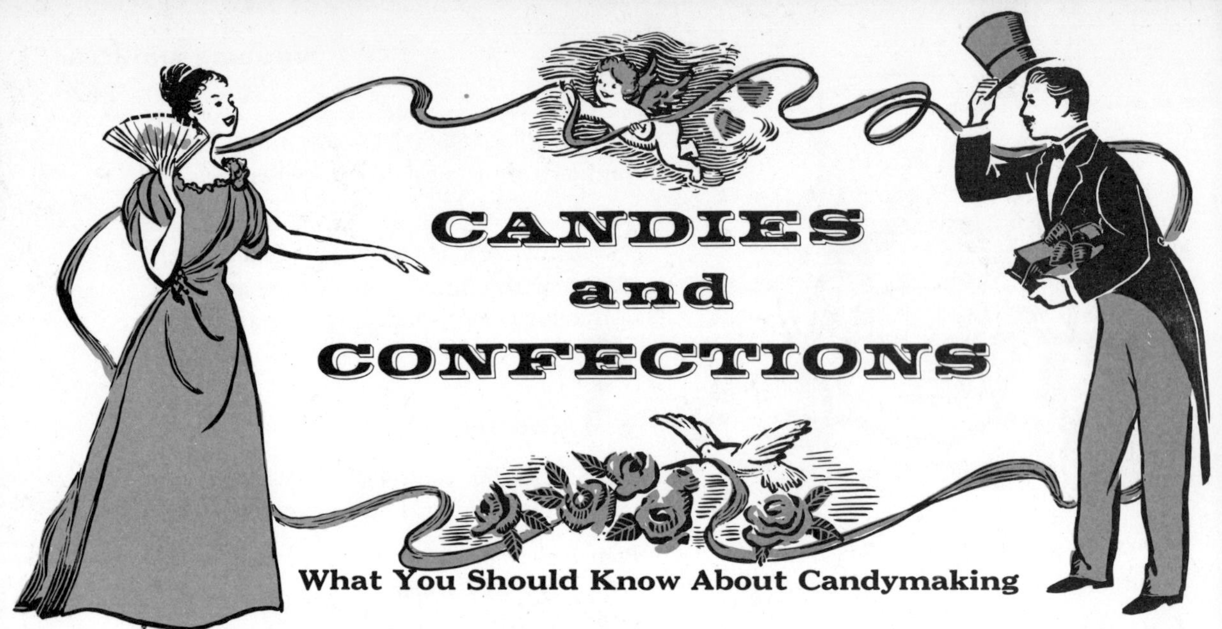

What You Should Know About Candymaking

There is nothing like a box of beautifully made candies for telling some one that you love him—or her. And what promotes good-natured camaraderie more surely than an evening of candymaking in the kitchen? The taffy-pulls and fudgemaking with which young people amused themselves for generations have never wholly passed from our community traditions—and a good thing, too. But candies are more than a casual ministering to the sweet tooth or a means to sociability. At their best they represent a happy blend of art and science, of beauty and delectability that makes candymaking one of the most rewarding of all the household arts.

TYPES—Candies are usually classified as two types—crystalline and noncrystalline.

Crystalline—The outstanding characteristic of standard crystalline candy is that the sugar crystals are so small that the candy at all times feels creamy and velvety to the tongue. Fondant, fudge, panocha, bonbons, pralines, nougat, divinity and kisses are common examples.

To produce great numbers of very tiny crystals and thereby ensure a creamy candy: 1) The sugar must be completely dissolved. 2) The sugar solution must be boiled to a certain temperature and then cooled to a much lower temperature before agitation or beating thereby producing a highly supersaturated solution (a solution holding more dissolved sugar than it ordinarily would at this lower temperature). 3) The sugar crystals in the supersaturated solution must recrystalize in a great number of very tiny crystals. Therefore, when the mixture has cooled to the proper temperature, it must be extensively agitated or beaten at this temperature so many small crystals may form. 4) Ingredients known as interfering substances help to avoid the formation of large crystals. In fudge, these substances are butter, corn sirup and the starch of chocolate or cocoa; in fondant, corn sirup and an acid such as lemon juice, vinegar or cream of tartar are generally used; in divinity, egg protein is the substance.

Noncrystalline—Toffee, peanut brittle, lollipops, butterscotch and caramels are examples of noncrystalline candies. As in making crystalline candies, completely dissolving the sugar crystals is important. The mixture must be cooked to a high enough temperature to produce a highly viscous (resistance of the solution to pouring) solution which upon cooling quickly immediately becomes thicker (as caramels) or solidifies (as lollipops).

Ingredients which help to produce a viscous mixture in caramels are the large quantities of milk solids and fat. In caramels, the cream with corn sirup, or milk solids are classified as interfering substances and help to prevent the formation of sugar crystals. If the total amount of cream or milk is added at the beginning of cooking period of caramels, the milk or cream may curdle. Therefore, cream or milk should be added in more than one addition to avoid curdling.

During pulling of taffies, air bubbles become incorporated causing taffies to become white or, if made with molasses, become much lighter in color.

Baking soda is frequently added to brittles. It neutralizes the acidity; it also gives a porous texture to the brittle because of gas formation.

When You Make Candy or Cook Sirup

MAKE CANDY on a dry, cool day for best results. If it is necessary to make candy on a day when the humidity is high (an excessive amount of moisture in the air), cook the candy two degrees higher than the temperature given in the recipe; this should help to produce a satisfactory product.

A CANDY THERMOMETER is an accurate guide to correct stages of cooking. Test it for accuracy each time before using as the boiling point of water varies from day to day depending upon atmospheric pressure (barometric reading). Stand thermometer in boiling water (3-in. depth) for 10 minutes. It should read 212°F at sea level; if there is any variation, add or subtract the same number of degrees to or from the temperature required for the candy.

If you do not know at what degree water boils in your community, take the average of several successive daily readings (thermometer standing in 3-in. depth of boiling water for 10 minutes). The boiling point of water drops 1°F for each 500 feet of increased altitude. Correct the temperatures given in the sirup stages in accordance with the altitude in your community.

Hang thermometer on pan so it does not touch side or bottom of pan, being certain that the bulb is covered with mixture, not just foam. Check temperature readings at eye level.

Sirup Stages and Temperatures

Thread (230°F to 234°F)—Spins 2-in. thread when allowed to drop from fork or spoon.
Soft Ball (234°F to 240°F)—Forms a soft ball in very cold water; flattens when taken from water.
Firm Ball (244°F to 248°F)—Forms a firm ball in very cold water; does not flatten in fingers.
Hard Ball (250°F to 266°F)—Forms a ball which is pliable yet hard enough to hold its shape in very cold water.
Soft Crack (270°F to 290°F)—Forms threads which are hard but not brittle in very cold water.
Hard Crack (300°F to 310°F)—Forms threads which are hard and brittle in very cold water.

THE SAUCEPAN used for cooking candy should be large enough to allow contents to boil freely without running over. The cover should be tight-fitting, if cover is needed.

PREVENT GRAININESS in candy by completely dissolving all the sugar crystals; stirring and heating the sugar solution will help. If candy is stirred during cooking, stirring must stop before end of cooking period.
Cover saucepan for the first 5 minutes of boiling time, if recipe so directs. The steam formed helps to wash down any crystals that may have remained on the sides of pan.
Wash down crystals from sides of pan during cooking with a pastry brush dipped in water; move candy thermometer to one side and wash down any crystals that may have formed under thermometer.
Use clean spoons for each process—stirring, testing and beating.
Do not move, jar or stir candy during cooling period because any agitation may cause the formation of large, coarse crystals—the result a grainy, sugary candy.
Pour candy, holding saucepan within an inch or so of cooling pan or surface.
Do not scrape bottom and sides of saucepan.

STIR CANDY gently while cooking without splashing sides of pan, if recipe directs that candy be stirred. Move wooden spoon back and forth across bottom of pan with every few strokes.

AN ELECTRIC MIXER is better for beating divinity than beating it by hand because of the time required to beat divinity and the stiffness of the mass at the end of beating.

A MARBLE SLAB is used by professional candymakers because it has a smooth cold surface that cools candies quickly. It is easier to work large quantities of fondant and fudge on a marble slab than to beat them.

Chocolate Fudge

Butter an 8x8x2-in. pan. Set out a candy thermometer.

Put into a heavy 3-qt. saucepan
1⅓ cups milk
4 sq. (4 oz.) chocolate
Stir over low heat until chocolate is melted. Do not allow mixture to boil. Stir in
4 cups sugar
2 tablespoons white corn sirup
½ teaspoon salt
Stir over low heat until sugar is dissolved. Increase heat and bring mixture to boiling. Put candy thermometer in place. Cook, stirring occasionally to prevent scorching, until mixture reaches 234°F (soft ball stage, *page 289*; remove from heat while testing). During cooking, wash crystals (*page 289*) from sides of pan from time to time. Remove from heat.

Set aside until just cool enough to hold pan on hand. Do not jar pan or stir. When cool, add
¼ cup butter or margarine
4 teaspoons vanilla extract
Beat vigorously until mixture loses its gloss. Quickly turn into the buttered pan without scraping bottom and sides of saucepan and spread evenly. Set aside to cool.

When firm, cut into 1½-in. squares.

About 2 doz. pieces of fudge

△ Cocoa Fudge

Follow ▲ Recipe. Omit chocolate. Mix ¾ cup **cocoa** with sugar before adding milk.

△ Tutti-Frutti Fudge

Follow ▲ Recipe. Before turning candy into pan mix in ⅓ cup each: chopped **candied cherries pineapple and raisins.**

△ Marshmallow Fudge

Follow ▲ Recipe. Add 32 (½ lb.) **marshmallows,** cut in quarters (*page 6*), with the butter or margarine.

Chocolate Fudge and Hawaiian Fudge

△ Peanut Butter Fudge

Follow ▲ Recipe. Substitute 6 tablespoons **peanut butter** for butter or margarine.

△ Pecan Fudge

Follow ▲ Recipe. Mix in 2 cups (about 8 oz.) chopped **pecans.**

Hawaiian Fudge

BEATRICE STOCKDALE, GOLDFIELD, IOWA

Butter an 8x8x2-in. pan. Set out a candy thermometer and a heavy 3-qt. saucepan.

Coarsely chop and set aside
1 cup (about 4 oz.) pecans
Drain contents of
1 14-oz. can crushed pineapple
(Reserve pineapple sirup for use in other food preparation.)

Mix in the saucepan the pineapple and
4 cups sugar
1 cup cream
Stir over low heat until sugar is dissolved. Increase heat and bring mixture to boiling. Put candy thermometer in place. Cook, stirring occasionally to prevent scorching, until mixture reaches 234°F (soft ball stage, *page*

289; remove from heat while testing). During cooking, wash crystals (*page 289*) from sides of pan from time to time. Remove from heat.

Set aside until just cool enough to hold pan on hand. Do not jar pan or stir. When cool, add

2 tablespoons butter

2 teaspoons vanilla extract

Beat vigorously until mixture loses its gloss. With a few strokes stir in the chopped pecans. Quickly turn into the buttered pan without scraping bottom and sides of saucepan and spread evenly. Set aside to cool.

When cool, cut into 1½-in. squares.

About 2 doz. pieces of fudge

Note: For extra-smooth, mellow flavor, allow fudge to stand overnight before serving.

Black Walnut-Caramel Fudge

DORA C. BLOSE, ELYSBURG, PA.

The family will love this delectable candy.

Butter an 8x8x2-in. pan. Set out a candy thermometer and a heavy 3-qt. saucepan.

Chop and set aside

2 cups (about 7 oz.) black walnuts

Measure into a large, heavy light-colored skillet (a black skillet makes it difficult to see the color of the sirup)

2 cups sugar

Put the skillet over low heat. With back of wooden spoon, gently keep sugar moving toward center of skillet until it melts. Remove from heat and set aside.

Mix together in the saucepan

4 cups sugar

2 cups milk

Stir over low heat until sugar is dissolved. Increase heat and bring to boiling. Add the melted sugar very slowly, stirring constantly. Put candy thermometer in place. Cook, stirring occasionally to prevent scorching, until mixture reaches 234°F (soft ball stage, *page 289*; remove from heat while testing). During cooking, wash crystals (*page 289*) from sides of pan. Remove from heat.

Set aside until just cool enough to hold pan on hand. Do not jar pan or stir. When cool, add

2 teaspoons vanilla extract

Beat vigorously until mixture loses its gloss. With a few strokes stir in the chopped nuts. Quickly turn into the buttered pan without scraping bottom and sides of saucepan and spread evenly. Set aside to cool.

When cool, cut into 1½-in. squares.

About 2 doz. pieces of fudge

Penuche

(Panocha)

BETHEL OAKLEY, OWENSBORO, KY.

Butter an 8x8x2-in. pan. Set out a candy thermometer.

Coarsely chop and set aside

¾ cup (about 3 oz.) pecans

Mix together in a heavy 2-qt. saucepan

3 cups firmly packed brown sugar

1 cup plus 2 tablespoons milk

¼ teaspoon salt

Stir over low heat until sugar is dissolved. Increase heat and bring mixture to boiling, stirring frequently. Put candy thermometer in place. Cook, stirring occasionally to prevent scorching, until mixture reaches 234°F (soft ball stage, *page 289*; remove from heat while testing). During cooking, wash crystals (*page 289*) from sides of pan. Remove from heat. Set aside until just cool enough to hold pan on hand. Do not jar pan or stir. When cool, add

3 tablespoons butter

1½ teaspoons vanilla extract

Beat vigorously until mixture loses its gloss. With a few strokes stir in the chopped nuts. Quickly turn into the buttered pan without scraping bottom and sides of saucepan and spread evenly. Set aside to cool.

When cool, cut into 1½-in. squares.

About 2 doz. pieces of Penuche

Chocolate Caramels Supreme

Butter an 8x8x2-in. pan. Set out a candy thermometer and a heavy 3-qt. saucepan.

Chop and set aside

⅔ cup (about 3 oz.) nuts

Melt (*page 6*) and set aside to cool

4 sq. (4 oz.) chocolate

Set out

3 cups heavy cream
2 tablespoons butter

Pour 1 cup of the cream into the saucepan and mix in

2 cups sugar
1 cup white corn sirup
¼ teaspoon salt

Stir over low heat until sugar is dissolved. Increase heat and bring mixture to boiling. Put candy thermometer in place. Cook, stirring frequently, until mixture reaches 234°F (soft ball stage, *page 289*; remove from heat while testing). During cooking, wash crystals (*page 289*) from sides of saucepan from time to time. Stirring constantly, gradually add another cup of cream to saucepan, so slowly that boiling will not stop. Continue cooking, stirring frequently, over low heat until mixture reaches 234°F. Stirring constantly, gradually add remaining cream and the butter to mixture so slowly that boiling will not stop.

Stirring frequently, cook to 244°F (firm ball stage, *page 289*; remove from heat while testing). (Consistency of the candy tested in cold water will be the consistency of the caramel. Caramel mixture cooked to 246°F will give a slightly firmer caramel than mixture cooked to 244°F.)

Remove mixture from heat and remove candy thermometer. Immediately add the melted chocolate and nuts to mixture with

1 tablespoon vanilla extract

Stir just until blended. Immediately pour hot mixture into the buttered pan. Do not scrape bottom and sides of saucepan. Set caramel mixture aside on cooling rack in a cool place.

Creamy and Cocoa Taffy

When completely cooled, (several hours or overnight) invert onto a cutting board and remove pan. Working in a cool place, mark candy into 1-in. squares; using a sharp, long-bladed knife, cut candy with a sawing motion. Wrap each caramel tightly in waxed or glassine paper. Store in a covered container in a cool, dry place. *About 5½ doz. caramels*

Note: For **Vanilla Caramels,** omit chocolate.

▲ Creamy Taffy

Butter a large, shallow pan or platter. Set out a candy thermometer.

Mix together in a heavy 2-qt. saucepan

2¼ cups sugar
1½ cups white corn sirup
4 teaspoons vinegar
¼ teaspoon salt

Stir over low heat until sugar is dissolved. Increase heat and bring to boiling, stirring constantly. Add slowly so boiling does not stop

½ cup undiluted evaporated milk

Put candy thermometer in place. Continue cooking, stirring constantly, until mixture reaches 248°F (firm ball stage, *page 289*; remove from heat while testing). During cooking, wash crystals (*page 289*) from sides of saucepan from time to time. Remove from heat and remove thermometer. Immediately pour mixture into the buttered pan without scraping bottom and sides of saucepan.

When mixture is just cool enough to handle, butter hands. Work in a cool place. Pull a small portion of the taffy at a time, using only the tips of the fingers, until candy is white in color and no longer sticky to the touch. Twist pulled strip slightly and place on waxed paper or on a board. Cut with scissors into 1-in. pieces. Wrap in waxed or glassine paper.

Store in a tightly covered container in a cool, dry place. *About 8 doz. pieces of taffy*

△ Brown Sugar Taffy

Follow ▲ Recipe. Substitute 2¼ cups firmly packed **brown sugar** for the sugar.

△ Cocoa Taffy

Follow ▲ Recipe. Mix ⅔ cup **Dutch process cocoa** with the sugar.

Salt Water Taffy

NAOMI CHILDS, TIONESTA, PA.

Butter a large, shallow pan or platter. Set out a candy thermometer.

Mix together in a heavy 2-qt. saucepan

2 cups sugar
1¼ cups white corn sirup
1 cup water

Stir over low heat until sugar is dissolved. Increase heat and bring mixture to boiling. Put candy thermometer in place. Continue cooking, stirring constantly, until mixture reaches 244°F (firm ball stage, *page 289*; remove from heat while testing). During cooking, wash crystals (*page 289*) from sides of saucepan from time to time. Remove from heat and remove thermometer. Immediately blend in

1 tablespoon butter
1½ teaspoons salt

Pour mixture into the buttered pan without scraping bottom and sides of saucepan.

When mixture is just cool enough to handle, butter hands. Work in a cool place. Pull a small portion of the taffy at a time, using only the tips of the fingers, until candy is firm and cool and no longer sticky to the touch. While pulling, work in

Food coloring
Extract

The amounts of food coloring and flavoring will depend on the amount of taffy being pulled and the color and flavor desired. Twist pulled strip slightly and place on waxed paper or on a board. Cut with scissors into 1-in. pieces. Wrap in waxed or glassine paper.

Store in a tightly covered container in a cool, dry place. *About 6 doz. pieces of taffy*

Note: Good flavor and color combinations are **peppermint extract** and **red food coloring; wintergreen** and **green; lemon** and **yellow.** Or use **vanilla extract** and omit coloring.

▲ Coffee Truffle Balls

Set out

⅓ cup butter

10 oz. milk chocolate

Grate (*page 6*) 2 oz. of the chocolate (about ¾ cup, grated). Mix with the grated chocolate

1½ teaspoons concentrated soluble coffee

Set aside in refrigerator.

Place remaining chocolate in the top of a double boiler with

¼ cup heavy cream

Heat over simmering water, stirring occasionally, until chocolate is melted. Remove from simmering water and cool slightly.

Divide the butter into small pieces and stir into the melted chocolate until butter is melted. Add and mix in thoroughly

½ teaspoon concentrated soluble coffee

Chill thoroughly in freezing compartment of refrigerator about 1 hr., or until firm.

When mixture is chilled, spoon about 1 teaspoonful at a time onto the reserved chocolate-coffee mixture. Quickly work with fingers to form a ball and to coat with the chocolate.

About 1½ doz. truffle balls

△ Liqueur Truffle Balls

Follow ▲ Recipe. Omit total amount of concentrated soluble coffee. Blend in with the butter 1½ teaspoons **kirsch** and 1½ teaspoons **curaçao.**

⚠ Rum Truffle Balls

Follow △ Recipe. Substitute 2½ teaspoons **rum** for total amount of liqueurs.

Caramel Popcorn Balls

For Popped Corn—If using an electric popper, follow the manufacturer's directions. Otherwise, for each pan of corn, melt in heavy skillet or saucepan having a tight-fitting cover

1 tablespoon hydrogenated vegetable shortening, all-purpose shortening, lard or cooking oil

Add enough popcorn (about ¼ cup) to just cover bottom of skillet and cover tightly. Shake pan over medium heat until popping stops. Turn corn into a large bowl. Set aside to keep warm. In the same way prepare

3 qts. popped corn

For Sirup—Measure and set aside

⅓ cup undiluted evaporated milk

Mix together in a saucepan

1 cup firmly packed brown sugar

¾ cup white corn sirup

2 teaspoons vinegar

¼ teaspoon salt

Stir over low heat until sugar is dissolved. Increase heat and bring mixture rapidly to boiling without stirring. Put candy thermometer in place. Cook until mixture reaches 280°F, (soft crack stage, *page 289*; remove from heat while testing). During cooking, wash crystals (*page 289*) from sides of pan from time to time.

When temperature has reached 280°F, add the evaporated milk gradually (so that mixture does not stop boiling), while stirring con-

Caramel Popcorn Balls

stantly. Bring caramel mixture to 280°F again, stirring constantly. Remove from heat and remove thermometer. Stir in

1 teaspoon vanilla extract

For Popcorn Balls—Gradually pour hot caramel sirup into center of warm popped corn. With long-handled fork, *quickly* blend to coat corn with sirup. Dot corn with

2 tablespoons butter or margarine

With buttered hands, gather and press into firm balls. *About 1½ doz. 3-in. popcorn balls*

△ Peanut-Popcorn Balls

Follow ▲ Recipe. Mix 1 cup (about 5 oz.) warm, salted, roasted **peanuts** with popped corn before pouring on caramel sirup.

Spiced Nuts

Set out a candy thermometer and a double boiler having a cover. Lay out on a flat surface a long piece of waxed paper.

Set out

4 cups (about 1 lb.) nuts (such as walnuts or pecans)

Mix together in a large bowl and set aside

¼ cup sugar
2 tablespoons cinnamon
½ teaspoon cloves
½ teaspoon nutmeg
½ teaspoon ginger

Mix together in the top of the double boiler

1 cup sugar
¼ cup water
2 tablespoons cinnamon
½ teaspoon cloves
½ teaspoon nutmeg
½ teaspoon ginger

Stir over low heat until sugar is dissolved. Increase heat and bring mixture to boiling. Cover and boil mixture gently for 5 min. Uncover and put candy thermometer in place. Continue cooking without stirring until mixture reaches 238°F (soft ball stage, *page 289*; remove from heat while testing). During cooking, wash crystals (*page 289*) from sides of pan from time to time.

Remove thermometer and place double-boiler top over simmering water. Immediately add the nuts and mix until well coated with the sirup. Turn into the reserved sugar mixture in the bowl. Toss lightly until all nuts are well coated. Turn onto the waxed paper and separate the nuts. Set aside to cool completely.

Store in a tightly covered container in a cool, dry place. *About 4 cups Spiced Nuts*

▲ Caramel-Nut Mallows

Made in a jiffy and consumed in a flash.

Line a baking sheet with waxed paper.

Put into the top of a double boiler

½ lb. vanilla caramels
3 tablespoons hot water

Heat over simmering water, stirring frequently, until caramels are melted.

Meanwhile, finely chop

¾ cup (about 3 oz.) pecans

Set out

32 (½ lb.) marshmallows

Using a fork, dip each marshmallow into the melted caramel and turn until well coated. Roll in the chopped nuts. Place on the waxed paper. Set in a cool place until caramel is firm.

Store in a covered container in a cool, dry place. *32 pieces of candy*

△ Coconut-Chocolate Mallows

Follow ▲ Recipe. Substitute 6 oz. **semi-sweet candymaking chocolate for dipping** for the caramels and water. Partially melt chocolate over simmering water, being careful not to overheat. Remove chocolate from heat and stir until completely melted. Blend in ½ teaspoon **vanilla extract.** Substitute **Toasted Coconut** (double recipe, *page 246*) for the nuts.

Hot and Cold

All over the world people have their favorite beverages. Here in the United States, where many different peoples have made their homes, we have no truly national beverage and incline to many favorites—judging the rightness of a drink by the occasion for which it is intended. But there is almost universal agreement among Americans that the day properly starts with coffee.

COFFEE—Each cup of coffee should be clear and sparkling. It should have a rich coffee flavor without bitterness or off-taste.

Use only fresh coffee—To ensure freshness use coffee within 7 to 10 days after opening.

Store unsealed coffee in a cool place or in the refrigerator in a tightly covered container of airtight material.

Measure coffee and water accurately. (National Coffee Association Standard Measure—2 level measuring tablespoons of coffee to each ¾ standard measuring cup of water.)

Brew coffee at full capacity of coffee maker for best results—never less than three-fourths full.

Use freshly drawn cold water; water preheated or drawn from the hot water faucet may give an undesirable flat taste to the brew.

Serve coffee as soon as possible after brewing; keep coffee hot but do not boil it.

For uniform results, use same timing secured after finding exact time for desired brew.

Never boil coffee beverage; boiling causes complete breakdown of true coffee flavor and aroma.

Thoroughly wash coffee maker and rinse with clear boiling water after each use.

Rinse coffee maker with boiling water before using.

Never re-use coffee grounds.

Wash cloth filters for vacuum-type coffee makers in clear cold water; keep immersed in cold water.

TEA—The brisk, full flavor and bright, clear color of tea are obtained only from a good quality of fresh tea properly brewed.

Choose a tea that suits your taste: *Black*—rich aroma, mild flavor; *Green*—little aroma, pungent flavor; *Oolong*—aroma of black tea, flavor of green; *Flower* (*such as jasmine*)—scented with flowers.

Teas are graded according to leaf size, such as Pekoe and Orange Pekoe (a smaller leaf) of black teas and Gunpowder, smallest leaf of green teas.

Buy the quantity of tea that fits your needs.

Store tea in an airtight container in a cool, dry place to preserve freshness.

Water for making tea should be freshly drawn and brought just to a brisk boil. Prolonged boiling gives water, thus the tea, a flat taste. Water that is alkaline or high in iron may cloud the beverage.

Brew tea 3 to 5 min. to reach desired flavor peak. Strength of beverage is determined not only by length of brewing time, but also by amount of tea used and freshness of leaves.

Heat tea pot or cups with boiling water.

Tea pots made from glass, china, porcelain or other forms of glazed pottery are desirable because the materials do not affect the flavor of the beverage and they tend to retain the heat.

Wash tea pots and tea holders or tea balls with hot soapy water after each use to keep them free from oily deposits and sediment.

MILK—As soon as received, put milk (whole or skimmed), flavored milk drinks, cream and buttermilk into the coldest area of the refrigerator, about 40°F. Store in the original container and wipe container with a clean, damp cloth. Keep milk out of strong light to retain riboflavin, one of milk's important vitamins.

Always keep milk covered—it quickly absorbs the odors of other foods. Return milk to the refrigerator immediately after using.

Always use pasteurized milk to safeguard the family's health. Use milk within two days, keeping it under proper storage, for best flavor and quality. Buttermilk is best when used the same day.

A package of non-fat dry milk solids kept in a cool, dry place spells convenience to the homemaker, especially the instant milk. Reconstitute the solids and use as fluid milk. Increasing the amount of milk solids used in a beverage gives added nutrients—a good way to get extra protein, calcium and the B vitamins.

CHOCOLATE and COCOA BEVERAGE—Preliminary cooking of the chocolate or cocoa mixture before the addition of milk helps to keep the chocolate or cocoa from settling out.

Beating the beverage with a rotary beater forms a froth and prevents a film from forming.

OTHER BEVERAGE FACTS—Add chilled carbonated beverages to mixtures just before serving and mix only enough to blend to retain carbonation.

Fruits used in beverages should be fully ripe, especially when added to a milk drink.

An electric blender is an invaluable aid to beverage preparation. Add liquid to container, then semisolids while motor is running. Add ice cream or cracked ice last.

Beverage Serving Tips

PARTY POINTERS—Beverages served with a flair and a bit of imagination are conversation starters. Here are a few ideas and helps.

For Decorative Punch Bowl—Trim stems of daisies, sweetheart roses or other small flowers to 1 in. Secure flowers around edge of bowl with pieces of cellulose tape. Secure two flowers to ladle handle and one flower to each punch cup handle.

For Frosted Glasses—Rub the edge of each glass with cut surface of lemon, lime or orange. Or brush rim with citrus juice. Dip the rim of each glass in fine granulated or confectioners' sugar. Place glasses in refrigerator to chill. Carefully pour beverage into glasses without touching frosted edges.

Pink Sugar for Pink-Frosted Glasses—Measure ½ cup sugar into a shallow pan. Tint sugar the desired pink color by thoroughly mixing in, one drop at a time, a mixture of red food coloring and water (equal amounts of each). To obtain a more even-colored sugar, put through a fine sieve.

For Fruit Kabobs—Thread onto each stirrer or skewer, in order, a strawberry, lime slice, maraschino cherry, mint leaves, orange wedge, seedless grape and pineapple chunk. Chill.

For Decorative Ice Cubes—Fill ice-cube tray one-third full with water. Place in freezing compartment of refrigerator; remove ice-cube tray when water is partially frozen. Place well-drained maraschino cherry, mint sprig, pineapple chunk, orange wedge, berry, or small piece of fruit and a mint leaf in each cube section. Fill tray with water and freeze.

For Decorative Ice Blocks—Fill a loaf pan or fancy mold one-third full with water. Place in freezing compartment of refrigerator; remove pan or mold when water is partially frozen. Arrange flowers, such as roses or gardenias, or fruits (small whole, pieces or slices) in interesting designs and combinations suitable for the occasion. Fill pan or mold, covering flowers or fruit, with water and freeze. Boiling water before freezing or stirring water as it freezes helps to make the ice clear.

For Sugar Sirup—Mix together in a saucepan 2 cups sugar and 2 cups water; stir over low heat until sugar is dissolved. Cover, bring to boiling and boil 5 min. Cool and store covered in refrigerator. Use to sweeten beverages. *About 2½ cups sirup*

BEVERAGE SERVINGS—Average servings for beverages are: *Hot beverages*, such as coffee, tea, chocolate and cocoa—6-oz. cup; *Cold beverages* with large quantity of ice, such as iced coffee and tea—10- to 12-oz. glass; cold beverages with little or no ice, such as lemonade, ginger ale and milk drinks—8-oz. glass; *Fruit and vegetable juices*—4-oz. serving; *Punch*—3- to 4-oz. punch cup; *Milk*—8-oz. glass or mug.

▲ Drip Coffee

Preheat a drip coffee maker by filling it with boiling water. Drain.

For each standard measuring cup of water, using standard measuring spoons, measure

2 tablespoons drip grind coffee

Place in filter section of drip coffee maker. Do not overload coffee compartment.

Bring to boiling

Freshly drawn water

Measure and pour boiling water into upper container. Cover. Allow all of water to drip through the coffee, keeping coffee maker over low heat 5 to 8 min., or as long as coffee is dripping. Do not let coffee boil at any time. Remove coffee compartment; stir and cover the brew. If not served immediately, place coffee maker over low heat. Stir before serving.

△ Percolated Coffee

Use regular grind coffee. Follow ▲ Recipe for amount to use. Put into strainer basket of coffee maker. Measure freshly drawn cold water into bottom of percolator. Place basket in coffee maker. Cover.

Place over heat. When percolating begins, reduce heat to low so that percolating will be gentle and slow. Timing varies from 5 to 10 min. after percolation starts. It's wise to experiment to determine exact timing for the amount of coffee generally made in your percolator. Larger amounts of coffee require the longer timing.

Remove coffee basket, cover coffee maker and keep coffee hot over low heat. Do not let coffee boil at any time.

△ Steeped Coffee

Use regular grind coffee. Follow ▲ Recipe for amount to use. Put into coffee maker. To clarify coffee, mix in 1 teaspoon slightly beaten **egg** for each 2 tablespoons coffee used. Measure and add freshly drawn cold water.

Bring very slowly to boiling, stirring occasionally. Remove from heat at once. Pour ¼ cup cold water down spout to settle grounds.

Let stand 3 to 5 min. without heat. Strain through a fine strainer into a server which has been preheated with boiling water. If necessary to keep hot, let coffee stand over low heat without boiling.

△ Coffee for Twenty (Steeped)

Thoroughly mix ½ lb. **coffee,** regular grind, with 1 **egg** and crushed **egg shell.** Tie loosely in fine cheesecloth or put into a lightweight muslin bag. Put into a large kettle with 1 gal. freshly drawn cold **water.** Cover tightly.

Place over low heat and bring very slowly to boiling. Boil 3 to 5 min. Taste to test strength. Remove bag when coffee is of desired strength. Cover kettle and let stand 10 to 15 min. over low heat without boiling. *20 servings*

△ Vacuum-Drip Coffee

Use drip or vacuum grind coffee. Follow ▲ Recipe for amount to use.

Specific directions for making vary according to the type of coffee maker used. Usually, freshly drawn cold water is measured and poured into the decanter or lower bowl. Coffee is measured into upper bowl. Cover.

Place coffee maker over moderate to low heat. When all but a small amount of water has risen to upper bowl, remove coffee maker from heat. Remove top bowl when the brew has run into decanter. Cover. Serve immediately or keep hot over very low heat. Do not boil at any time.

Demitasse
(After-Dinner Coffee)

Using 1½ to 2 times the amount of coffee, prepare

Drip Coffee (*page 298*) or any variation

Serve hot in demitasse or after-dinner cups.

Quick Coffee Beverage

For one cup coffee beverage, place 1 teaspoon **concentrated soluble coffee** into a cup. Add boiling **water** and stir until coffee is completely dissolved. Concentrated frozen coffee may be reconstituted with freshly boiling water. Follow directions on container.

Iced Coffee

For stronger flavor pour the hot coffee over coffee ice cubes.

Using double the amount of coffee, prepare

Drip coffee (*page 298*) or any variation

Do not overload coffee compartment. If there is danger of this, use capacity amount of coffee with one-half as much water as for regular-strength coffee.

Fill tall glasses to brim with

Crushed ice or ice cubes

Pour the hot coffee over the ice. Serve with **granulated** or **confectioners' sugar, sugar sirup, cream,** or **whipped cream** (*page 7*) sprinkled with **cinnamon.**

Iced Coffee with sugar sirup and cream

Iced Tea and Fruit Kabobs (page 297)

▲ Tea

Fill teapot with boiling water. When heated thoroughly, pour off water.

Put into pot for each cup of tea to be brewed

1 rounded teaspoon tea or 1 prepared tea bag

Bring to boiling

Freshly drawn water

For each cup of tea, pour into teapot 1 cup of the briskly boiling water. Cover pot and let brew 3 to 5 min.

Remove tea bags or strain tea into a preheated pot or into cups. Serve immediately with any of the following: thin slices or wedges of **lemon, orange** or **lime; lemon, orange** or **lime juice;** whole **cloves;** sprigs of fresh **mint; cream; sugar** or **sugar sirup.**

△ Iced Tea

Prepare tea as in ▲ Recipe. Use 6 tablespoons tea and 6 standard measuring cups of freshly boiling water. Strain and pour hot tea into tall glasses filled with crushed ice or ice cubes. Serve as in ▲ Recipe or serve with **Fruit Kabobs** (*page 297*).

Dressy Tea

GRACE HAWKINSON, GALLUP, N. MEX.

Combine in a 2-qt. saucepan

1 qt. freshly drawn water
½ cup sugar
4 whole cloves
1 stick cinnamon

Set over medium heat and stir until sugar is dissolved. Increase heat and bring mixture to boiling.

Meanwhile, put into a preheated teapot

2 rounded teaspoons tea or 2 prepared tea bags

Pour the spice mixture into the teapot. Cover and let tea brew 3 to 5 min.

Meanwhile, heat until very hot

1 cup orange juice, strained

After tea has brewed required time strain and return to teapot.

Mix in the hot orange juice. Serve hot in preheated cups and garnish with

Thin lemon or orange slices

About 6 servings

Mint Iced Tea

(*See color photo inside back cover*)

MRS. A. E. BOYCE, RIVERDALE, N. DAK.

Rinse and shake excess water from

12 sprigs of mint

Put 8 sprigs of mint into refrigerator to chill. Bruise the 4 remaining sprigs and set aside.

Combine in a 2-qt. saucepan

1 qt. freshly drawn water
1⅓ cups sugar

Stir over low heat until sugar is dissolved. Increase heat and bring to boiling. Boil sirup gently for 5 min.

Put into a preheated teapot the bruised sprigs of mint and

5 tablespoons tea

Pour the sugar sirup into the teapot. Cover pot and let mixture brew 3 to 5 min. Strain mixture and return to teapot with the bruised sprigs of mint. Cover and let stand 10 min. longer. Remove the sprigs of mint. Pour mixture into a pitcher and stir in

1 qt. freshly drawn water
½ cup lemon juice, strained

Sprinkle over the chilled sprigs of mint

Confectioners' sugar

Pour the tea into tall glasses over crushed ice or ice cubes.

Garnish with the sugared sprigs of mint and

Lemon slices

About 8 servings

▲ Hot Cocoa

Mix in a saucepan or top of a double boiler

5 to 6 tablespoons cocoa
5 to 6 tablespoons sugar
¼ teaspoon salt

Blend in slowly

1 cup water

Boil gently 2 min. over direct heat, stirring until slightly thickened.

Reduce heat and stir in

3 cups milk

Heat slowly over direct heat or simmering water until scalding hot; stir occasionally. Remove from heat. Cover and keep hot, if necessary, over hot water.

Just before serving, add

½ teaspoon vanilla extract

Beat with rotary beater until foamy. Serve steaming hot, plain or with **whipped cream** (*page* 7), **marshmallow cream** or **marshmallows.**

6 servings

△ Hot Chocolate

Follow ▲ Recipe. Substitute 2 sq. (2 oz.) **chocolate** for cocoa. Break into pieces and combine with sugar, water and salt. Mix and stir constantly over low heat. When chocolate is melted, increase heat and boil 2 min., stirring constantly. Add milk and continue as in ▲ Recipe.

△ Spicy Chocolate Mocha

Follow △ Recipe. Reduce chocolate to 1½ sq. (1½ oz.). Heat the water to very hot and pour over the chocolate. Increase sugar to ½ cup and add to chocolate mixture with the salt and ¼ cup **concentrated soluble coffee.** Increase milk to 1 qt. Serve with **whipped cream** (*page* 7), and put a **cinnamon stick** for a stirrer into each mug. If desired, sprinkle each serving with **nutmeg.**

Hot Mint Chocolate

FERN E. GREINERT, HORTOMILLE, WIS.

Put in top of a double boiler
20 (about ½ cup) chocolate mint wafers
1 cup milk
⅛ teaspoon salt
Heat over simmering water, stirring constantly until wafers are melted and mixture is well blended. Add, stirring constantly
2 cups milk
1 cup cream
Heat until scalding hot, stirring occasionally. Serve hot, plain or, if desired, with **whipped cream** (*page* 7). *4 to 6 servings*

Spicy Chocolate Mocha

Iced Cocoa or Chocolate

Put a bowl and a rotary beater into refrigerator to chill.

Prepare, using 6 tablespoons sugar in either
Hot Cocoa (*page 300*) or Hot Chocolate (*on this page*)
Cool and put into refrigerator to chill.

Just before serving, using the chilled bowl and beater, whip (*page* 7)
½ cup chilled whipping cream
Stir the chilled beverage and pour over ice in tall glasses. Top each serving with about three tablespoons of the whipped cream.

Sprinkle each serving lightly with
Cinnamon, nutmeg or ginger
6 servings

Tomato Cocktail

(*See photo on page 15*)

Mix together
3 cups chilled tomato juice
1½ tablespoons lemon or lime juice
2 teaspoons sugar
¼ teaspoon salt
¼ teaspoon Accent
9 drops tabasco sauce
Pour into chilled glasses; garnish with
Lemon slices
6 servings

Eggnog: For a holiday punch bowl, prepare double the recipe for Bobbie's Best Eggnog *(on this page)* or use dairy eggnog. Serve with fruitcake and something small but hearty in the way of party sandwiches.

Bobbie's Best Eggnog

MRS. GEORGE CASTLEBERRY
JACKSONVILLE, FLA.

Set out a small bowl and a large bowl. Put a second small bowl, a rotary beater and 4 glasses into refrigerator to chill.

Put into the large bowl and beat until frothy

4 egg whites
¼ teaspoon salt

Add gradually, beating well after each addition

½ cup sugar

Continue beating until rounded peaks are formed and egg whites do not slide when bowl is partially inverted. Set aside.

Put into the small bowl, beat until thick and lemon-colored and set aside

4 egg yolks

Beat, using chilled bowl and beater, until cream is of medium consistency (piles softly)

½ cup chilled whipping cream

With final few strokes beat in

1½ teaspoons vanilla extract

Gently fold (*page 6*) the whipped cream and beaten egg yolks into the egg whites. Put into refrigerator to chill thoroughly.

Top with a generous sprinkling of **nutmeg.**

About 4 servings

Malted Choco-Milk

MRS. W. L. ISBELL, BROOKSTON, INDIANA

Put a bowl and a rotary beater and 4 tall glasses into refrigerator to chill.

Beat until thick and lemon-colored

4 egg yolks

Add to egg yolks and beat until well blended

4 cups cold milk
½ cup chocolate malted milk powder
¼ teaspoon nutmeg

Using chilled bowl and beater, whip (*page 7*)

¼ cup chilled whipping cream

Pour the beverage into the chilled serving glasses and top each serving with about 2 tablespoons of the whipped cream.

Garnish with chocolate curls, made by pulling across a shredder

Semi-sweet chocolate

4 servings

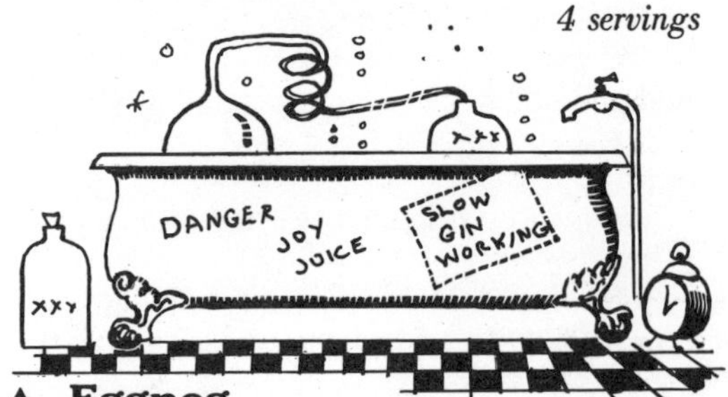

▲ Eggnog

Put into a large bowl and beat until thick and piled softly

3 eggs

Add and beat until well blended

2 cups milk
⅓ cup sugar
1 tablespoon vanilla extract
¼ teaspoon salt

Put into refrigerator to chill thoroughly.

Serve in tall glasses and top with a generous sprinkling of **nutmeg.** *5 to 6 servings*

△ Lemon Eggnog

Follow ▲ Recipe; increase sugar to ½ cup. Omit vanilla extract. Blend in ¼ cup **lemon juice.** Omit nutmeg.

△ Chocolate Eggnog

Follow ▲ Recipe; decrease sugar to ¼ cup. Blend in ⅓ to ½ cup **Chocolate Sirup** (*page 190*). Omit nutmeg.

Pink Fruit Punch

MRS. L. R. SIDDERS, SHATTUCK, OKLA.

A party favorite from Middle America!

A punch bowl and serving cups will be needed.

Put into refrigerator to chill
1 qt. ginger ale
Put into a large bowl
1 qt. water
4 cups unsweetened pineapple juice
1 cup cranberry juice cocktail
1 cup orange juice
⅔ cup lemon juice
½ cup lime juice
Add and stir until sugar is dissolved
1 cup sugar
Chill fruit-juice mixture in refrigerator.

When ready to serve, pour mixture into the punch bowl. Add the ginger ale and stir to blend. Do not fill punch bowl too full so that a Decorative Ice Block (*page 297*) may be floated in the punch. *About 3½ qts. punch*

Party Punch

Set out two large bowls. A punch bowl and serving cups will be needed.

Put into refrigerator to chill
1½ qts. ginger ale
Bring to full rolling boil
5 cups freshly drawn water
Meanwhile, put into one of the bowls
5 tablespoons tea
As soon as water reaches a full boil, pour it over the tea. Brew for 5 min. Strain into the second large bowl. Set aside to cool at room temperature.

When tea is cool, add to it
2½ cups orange juice
1½ cups unsweetened grapefruit juice
⅔ cup lemon juice
¼ cup lime juice
Add and stir until sugar is dissolved
2¼ cups sugar
Chill fruit-juice mixture in refrigerator.

When ready to serve, pour mixture into a Decorative Punch Bowl (*page 297*). Pour in the chilled ginger ale and stir to blend thoroughly. Do not fill punch bowl too full so that a Decorative Ice Block (*page 297*) may be floated in the punch. Serve in Pink-Frosted Punch Cups (*page 297*). *About 3 qts. punch*

Party Punch with Decorative Ice Block, Pink-Frosted Cups

What You Should Know

BEFORE YOU START—Before starting to preserve, assemble and check all equipment. Jars must be free of chips and cracks. When using two-piece metal jar caps, new sealing lids must be used. For other types of jar caps, use new rubber rings. Read carefully beforehand the manufacturer's directions for sealing jars. Read the recipe through and plan the work step by step. Work with quantities that can be easily and quickly handled.

Included in the special equipment needed for pickling and preserving are 2 large sauce pots or kettles (one to be used for sterilizing jars or glasses), long-handled tongs, ladle, slotted spoon, wide-mouthed funnel, colander, coarse sieve or food mill, 1-qt. measures, cheesecloth, food chopper, Mason jars and covers, and jelly glasses and covers.

ABOUT PRESERVING—Select firm fruits only, using a mixture of ripe and slightly under-ripe fruits. The under-ripe fruits contain a large amount of pectin (the substance which makes jelly jell). When making jellies and marmalades, cook the fruit with the peel or skin and core because these contain needed pectin substances. Cook the juice-sugar mixture rapidly; do not simmer. Slow cooking destroys the pectin and produces a tough, gummy product.

All types of preserves, with the possible exception of butters, should be cooked in small amounts. No more than 4 to 6 cups of juice should be cooked at one time when making jelly, and no more than 3 to 4 quarts of fruit for other products.

Jellies are made from the strained fruit juice. A good jelly is clear, sparkling and transparent. It contains neither sediment nor crystals and has the natural color and flavor of fresh fruit. Jelly is firm but tender and holds its shape when turned from the glass.

Jams are made from whole, cut or crushed fruit. The fruit is cooked with sugar until it is tender and the sirup is thick.

Preserves are made from whole or evenly chopped fruit cooked in a sugar sirup. The fruit is tender and transparent, but retains its shape. The sirup will be thick and clear without causing the fruit to shrink and become tough. Shrinking can be avoided by adding the sugar gradually, or by allowing the fruit to remain in the sirup for several hours or overnight to absorb the sirup.

Marmalades are clear, jelly-like and transparent, with small pieces or thin slices of fruit or peel suspended throughout the sirup. Marmalades can be made of almost any firm fruit.

Conserves are a combination of two or more fruits (a citrus fruit is usually included), nuts and raisins. The mixture is cooked until thick and jamlike. Nuts should be added 5 minutes before removing from heat. Longer cooking destroys their flavor.

Butters are made of fruit that has been cooked and put through a coarse sieve or food mill. The fruit is then cooked with sugar until thick enough to spread.

ABOUT PICKLING—The fruits and vegetables to be pickled should be fresh, firm and slightly under-ripe. Sort them for size, using fruits or vegetables of the same size in any one recipe. Cider vinegar's mellow taste and aroma make it better for general pickling than white vinegar, which has a harsher, less fruit-like flavor. However, cider vinegar has a tendency to color white vegetables—such as onions and cauliflower—a reddish-brown. For these light-colored vegetables, a white vinegar is preferred. High-quality, fresh spices are essential for best results. Whole spices are preferred because ground spices tend to lose their flavor in an opened box on the shelf, and may discolor the pickles. Whole spices, when tied together in a spice bag, can easily be removed at the end of the cooking period.

In all pickling, it is important to preserve the crispness of the fresh vegetables. This may be done in a variety of ways. Vegetables may be soaked in a brine (solution of salt and water) overnight, scalded in hot salted water or chilled in iced salted water. A coarse salt should be used for pickling; table salt contains chemicals (added to prevent lumping) and therefore is unsatisfactory.

How To Do It

Sterilize Jars or Glasses—Put a rack or folded dish towel onto bottom of large sauce pot or kettle. Place clean jars or glasses on the rack or towel. Pour boiling water over them and boil 15 min., keeping jars or glasses covered with water at all times; if more water is needed, add boiling water.

Drain Jars or Glasses—Using long-handled tongs, carefully remove one jar or glass at a time and thoroughly drain. Set right side up on cooling rack away from drafts.

Fill and Seal Jars—Immediately after draining jars, pour or ladle mixture to within ½ in. of top. A wide-mouthed funnel will aid in the pouring process. Using a clean, damp cloth or paper towel, remove any food that may be on inside of jar above the surface of the contents or on the mouth of the jar. Be sure sealing edge is free of food particles. Drain the covers; seal jars at once, following cover manufacturer's directions. Cool jars away from drafts. Label; store in a cool, dry place.

Pack Pickles or Fruit in Jars and Seal—Immediately after draining jars, pack pickles or fruit into the jar. Ladle hot liquid to within ½ in. of top. Insert a knife or narrow spatula along the side of the jar at several places to remove any air bubbles. Add additional liquid if needed. With a clean, damp cloth, or paper towel, remove any of the sirup that may be on mouth of jar. Be sure sealing edge is free of food particles. Drain the covers; seal jars at once, following cover manufacturer's directions. Cool jars away from drafts. Label; store in a cool, dry place.

Fill Glasses and Seal with Paraffin—Immediately after draining glasses, pour the mixture to within ½ in. of top. With a clean, damp cloth or a paper towel, remove any particles of food that may be on the inside of glass above surface of mixture.

Immediately pour enough melted paraffin onto top of mixture to make a layer about ⅛ in. thick on each glass. When paraffin has cooled completely, pour enough melted paraffin over first layer to make another layer about ⅛ in. thick. Carefully tilt glasses to distribute paraffin evenly over the top and seal it to edges of the glass. Cool glasses away from drafts. Label and cover glasses; store in a cool, dry place.

Make a Spice Bag—Cut a double thickness of cheesecloth about 9 in. square. Put measured spices in center of the cheesecloth and tie the ends together. Adjust size of cheesecloth to amounts of spices used.

Make a Jelly Bag—Cut a double thickness of cheesecloth about 36 in. long and fold in half. Dip the cloth into hot water and wring well. Put a large strainer or colander over a bowl and lay the cloth in the strainer or colander.

Strain Juice—Pour the cooked fruit carefully into the cheesecloth. Gather the four corners of the cloth together and tie firmly. Allow the juice to drip through the cheesecloth into a bowl. A commercial jelly bag and frame may be used.

A faster method for extracting juice is to force the juice from the bag by pressing the bag against the side of a colander, using a wooden spoon. Pour this juice through a second jelly bag and allow the juice to drip through. This method does not produce as clear a jelly as the first one.

Make a Jelly Test—Dip spoon into boiling liquid; lift it out and tip it to allow mixture to run over edge. At first the sirup will run off in a thin stream. When the last two drops in the spoon run together or "sheet", the mixture should be removed from the heat. Always remove the pan from the heat while testing.

Spiced Grape Jelly and Tender-Rich Buttermilk Biscuits (page 43)

▲ Spiced Grape Jelly

ELIZABETH S. RUDE, HAMBURG, N.J.

Make an extra batch of this spicy, shimmering jelly. It is sure to create a demand for more.

Set out a large, heavy sauce pot or kettle having a cover and eight 8-oz. jelly glasses.

Make a jelly bag (*page 305*).

Rinse, discarding stems and imperfect grapes, drain and put into the sauce pot or kettle

3 lbs. Concord grapes

Crush grapes thoroughly. Blend well and mix thoroughly with crushed grapes

½ cup cider vinegar
2 teaspoons cinnamon
1 teaspoon cloves

Heat to boiling, reduce heat, cover and simmer for 10 min. Remove mixture from heat and strain through jelly bag.

Meanwhile, wash the sauce pot to use later.

Wash and sterilize (*page 305*) jelly glasses.

When juice has strained through jelly bag, melt over simmering water about

½ lb. paraffin

Measure 4 cups of juice into the sauce pot. Put sauce pot over high heat and heat until very hot. Add, stirring until sugar is dissolved

7 cups sugar

Rapidly bring the mixture to boiling and immediately stir in

½ cup bottled fruit pectin

Boil rapidly 1 min., stirring constantly. Remove from heat and skim off any foam.

Immediately fill the drained jelly glasses and cover with paraffin (*page 305*).

About eight 8-oz. glasses jelly

△ Strawberry Jelly

Follow ▲ Recipe. Substitute 2½ qts. rinsed, hulled **strawberries** for grapes. Omit vinegar mixture. Do not cook the berries. Crush berries and put into jelly bag. Force juice through bag by pressing bag against colander with a wooden spoon. Measure 3¾ cups **strawberry juice.** Add ¼ cup strained **lemon juice.** Follow directions for cooking jelly. Increase sugar to 7½ cups and bottled fruit pectin to 1 cup.

△ Red Raspberry Jelly

Follow △ Recipe. Substitute **red raspberries** for strawberries.

▲ Currant Jelly

Set out a large, heavy sauce pot or kettle having a cover, and six 8-oz. jelly glasses. Make a jelly bag (*page 305*).

Rinse, remove leaves (do not remove stems), drain and put into sauce pot or kettle

4 lbs. (about 4 qts.) ripe red currants

Crush currants thoroughly. Add and mix in

1 cup water

Heat to boiling, reduce heat, cover and simmer for 10 min. Remove mixture and strain through jelly bag.

Meanwhile, wash the sauce pot to use later.

Wash and sterilize (*page 305*) jelly glasses.

When juice has strained through jelly bag, melt over simmering water about

¼ lb. paraffin

Measure 4 cups of juice into the sauce pot. Put sauce pot over high heat and heat until very hot. Add

4 cups sugar

Stir until sugar is dissolved. Continue cooking rapidly until sirup responds to jelly test (*page 305*). Remove from heat and skim off any foam.

Immediately fill the drained jelly glasses and cover with paraffin (*page 305*).

About six 8-oz. glasses jelly

△ Grape Jelly

Follow ▲ Recipe. Substitute 3 lbs. **Concord grapes** for currants. Remove stems (do not remove skins); simmer grape-water mixture for 15 min. Use 4 cups grape juice and decrease sugar to 3 cups.

△ Crab Apple Jelly

Follow ▲ Recipe. Omit currants. Rinse, remove stem ends and cut into quarters enough crab apples to yield 3 qts. chopped **crab apples** (do not remove cores or peel). Increase water to 3 cups and cook for 20 min., or until very tender. Decrease sugar to 3 cups.

△ Quince Jelly

Follow ▲ Recipe. Omit currants. Wash well, remove stems and cut into pieces enough to yield 3 qts. diced **quince** (do not remove cores or peel). Increase water to 6 cups and cook for 25 min., or until very tender.

Rosemary Jelly

MRS. HAROLD WHEAT, SAN JOSE, ILL.

Tart Rosemary Jelly is the ideal accompaniment for meat.

Set out a heavy 3-qt. saucepan and four 8-oz. jelly glasses.

Wash and sterilize (*page 305*) jelly glasses.

Measure into a small bowl

2 teaspoons dried rosemary

Pour over the rosemary

1½ cups boiling water

Set aside for 15 min.

Meanwhile, melt over simmering water about

¼ lb. paraffin

Strain rosemary-water mixture into the saucepan and add

3½ cups sugar
2 tablespoons cider vinegar
4 drops red food coloring

Put saucepan over medium heat and stir until sugar is dissolved. Increase heat and bring mixture to boiling. Immediately add

½ cup bottled fruit pectin

Boil rapidly 1 min., stirring constantly. Remove from heat and skim off any foam.

Immediately fill the drained jelly glasses and cover with paraffin (*page 305*).

About four 8-oz. glasses jelly

Blueberry-Lemon Jam

Set out a large, heavy sauce pot or kettle and eight 8-oz. jelly glasses.

Wash and sterilize (*page 305*) jelly glasses.

Melt over simmering water about
½ lb. paraffin
Rinse, drain and put into sauce pot or kettle
4 cups firm, fresh blueberries
Crush berries thoroughly. Add
⅔ cup lemon juice
1½ tablespoons grated lemon peel (*page 5*)
and a mixture of
7 cups sugar
¼ teaspoon salt
¼ teaspoon cloves
Put the sauce pot over medium heat and stir until sugar is dissolved. Bring mixture to boiling and boil rapidly 1 min. without stirring. Remove mixture from heat and blend in
½ cup bottled fruit pectin
Skim off any foam.

Immediately fill the drained jelly glasses and cover with paraffin (*page 305*).

About eight 8-oz. glasses jam

Red Raspberry Jam
(Uncooked)

Set out four 8-oz. jelly glasses.

Sort, rinse, drain and force through coarse sieve or food mill enough raspberries to yield
1½ cups sieved fresh red raspberries (about 3 cups whole berries)
In a medium-size bowl mix the sieved raspberries and
3 cups sugar
Set aside for 20 min.

Meanwhile, wash in hot, sudsy water the jelly glasses and their covers. Rinse with boiling water. Cover and set aside.

Mix thoroughly with the raspberry mixture
¼ cup bottled fruit pectin
Fill jelly glasses (*page 305*) to within ½ in. of top. Cover with a jelly-glass cover, aluminum foil or several thicknesses of waxed paper tied over the top of the glass.

Allow jam to stand at room temperature overnight or until jellied.

Jam must be stored in refrigerator or freezer. It cannot be stored at room temperature.

About four 8-oz. glasses jam

Peach Jam

Set out a large, heavy sauce pot or kettle and six 8-oz. jelly glasses.

Wash and sterilize (*page 305*) jelly glasses.

Rinse and plunge into boiling water (to loosen the skins)
12 medium-size (about 3 lbs.) firm, ripe peaches
Plunge peaches into cold water. Gently slip off skins. Cut peaches into halves; remove and discard pits. Finely chop peaches (enough to yield 4 cups chopped peaches). Put peaches into the sauce pot and add
3 cups sugar
2 tablespoons lemon juice
Put sauce pot over medium heat and stir until sugar is dissolved. Increase heat and cook rapidly until clear and thick, stirring frequently to prevent sticking. Length of cooking time will vary with the ripeness and type of peaches. Remove from heat and skim off any foam.

While jam is cooking, melt over simmering water about
¼ lb. paraffin
Immediately fill the drained jelly glasses and cover with paraffin (*page 305*).

About six 8-oz. glasses jam

Cranberry Conserve

MRS. ALBERT MAGHAN, DEERWOOD, MINN.

Set out a large, heavy saucepan and four ½-pt. jars and covers.

Wash and sterilize (*page 305*) jars and covers.

Coarsely chop and set aside
1 cup (about 4 oz.) walnuts
Chop and set aside
1 cup (about 5 oz.) seedless raisins
Rinse and sort
4 cups (1 lb.) cranberries
Put cranberries in saucepan and add
1 cup water
Heat to boiling and cook for 5 min., or until cranberry skins pop.

Force cranberries through a coarse sieve or food mill (enough to yield 2 cups sieved cranberries). Combine the sieved cranberries and chopped raisins in the saucepan and add
2½ cups sugar
⅓ cup orange juice
1 tablespoon grated orange peel (page 5)
Put saucepan over medium heat and stir until sugar is dissolved. Increase heat and cook rapidly for 10 min., stirring frequently to prevent sticking. Remove from heat and add the walnuts, mixing thoroughly. Return to heat and cook 5 min. longer. Remove from heat and skim to remove any foam.

Immediately fill drained jars and seal tightly (*page 305*). *About 2 pints conserve*

▲ Almond-Plum Conserve

A potpourri of fine flavors, this jewel-bright Almond-Plum Conserve may be served with meat or as a spread at breakfast or tea time.

Set out a large, heavy sauce pot or kettle and six 1-pt. jars and covers.

Wash and sterilize (*page 305*) jars and covers.

Blanch (*page 5*), toast (*page 6*), coarsely chop and set aside
1 cup (about 5 oz.) almonds
Rinse, drain, pit and cut into pieces enough plums to yield
8 cups (about 4 lbs.) fresh, firm ripe plums, cut into pieces
Put plums into the sauce pot or kettle and add
5½ cups sugar
3 cups (15 oz.) seedless white raisins
½ teaspoon salt
Set sauce pot aside.

Rinse and remove ends from
1 medium-size orange
1 medium-size lemon
Cut fruit into quarters, discard seeds, and put through the coarse blade of a food chopper. Add to ingredients in the sauce pot and mix together thoroughly.

Put sauce pot over medium heat and stir until sugar is dissolved. Stirring frequently to prevent sticking, continue cooking rapidly about 40 min., or until plums are plump and tender and sirup responds to jelly test (*page 305*).

Remove from heat and add almonds, mixing thoroughly.

Immediately fill drained jars and seal tightly (*page 305*). *About 6 pints conserve*

△ Pineapple-Plum Conserve

Follow ▲ recipe. Thoroughly drain contents of one 9-oz. can **crushed pineapple** (about ¾ cup, drained). Reserve pineapple sirup for use in other food preparation. Add pineapple to the mixture in sauce pot with citrus fruits.

Strawberry Delight

MRS. CHARLES FOX, DETROIT, MICH.

This preserve must stand overnight before completion.

Set out a large, heavy sauce pot or kettle and a large, shallow heat-resistant dish. Three 8-oz. jelly glasses will be needed.

Sort, rinse, drain and hull

4 cups (1 qt.) fresh, ripe strawberries

Put berries into a bowl and add

2 cups boiling water

Set aside for 10 min.

Drain thoroughly; put into sauce pot and add

1½ cups sugar

Set sauce pot over medium heat and gently stir until sugar is dissolved. Increase heat and cook rapidly for 10 min., stirring frequently to prevent sticking. Remove from heat and add

1½ cups sugar

Set sauce pot over medium heat and gently stir until sugar is dissolved. Increase heat and cook rapidly for 15 min., stirring frequently to prevent sticking. Remove from heat and skim off any foam. Pour preserve into shallow dish to cool. Cover and set aside overnight.

The following day, wash and sterilize (*page 305*) jelly glasses.

Melt over simmering water about

¼ lb. paraffin

Stir preserve and immediately fill the drained jelly glasses. Cover with paraffin (*page 305*).

About three 8-oz. glasses preserve

Holiday Treat

MRS. O. P. KNIGHT, GRANTS PASS, ORE.

Three fruits blend their distinctive flavors in this very sweet but refreshing preserve. An interesting treat for holidays or special days, it is an ideal spread for crackers or bread at any time.

Set out a heavy 3-qt. saucepan having a tight-fitting cover, and five ½-pt. jars and covers.

Wash and sterilize (*page 305*) jars and covers.

Drain, reserving sirup, contents of

1 14-oz. can pineapple tidbits (about 1 cup, drained)

Wash, sort and set aside

4 cups (1 lb.) cranberries

Rinse, cut into halves, core, pare and dice enough pears to yield

2 cups (about 3 small) diced pears

Sprinkle evenly over pears ¼ cup of reserved pineapple sirup. (Reserve remaining sirup for use in other food preparation.)

Measure into the saucepan

2 cups sugar
½ cup water

Put the saucepan over medium heat and stir until sugar is dissolved. Bring mixture to boiling, cover and boil 5 min. Uncover; add the

Homemade jellies and preserves **represent an investment of time, money and space. Protect this investment by using quality ingredients and by storing the finished product with care. Use fine granulated sugar and sound, ripe, blemish-free fruit for superior results. Carefully seal glasses or jars with paraffin and cover. Label and date.**

cranberries and cook until cranberry skins pop. Add the diced pears with sirup and the tidbits. Continue cooking until thick, about 20 min. Remove from heat and skim to remove any foam.

Immediately fill drained jars and seal tightly (*page 305*). *About 2½ pints preserve*

Citrus Marmalade

MARTHA McGEE, McGEE'S MILLS, PA.

This marmalade must stand for 3 days before completion.

A large, heavy sauce pot or kettle, a large, shallow heat-resistant dish and twelve 8-oz. jelly glasses will be needed.

The first day, rinse and remove ends from

1 medium-size grapefruit
1 medium-size orange
1 medium-size lemon

Cut the fruit into quarters, discard seeds, and put fruit through fine blade of a food chopper. Measure the chopped fruit and make a note of the amount for future reference.

For *each* cup of chopped fruit, measure

¾ cup water

Combine the chopped fruit and water in a large bowl. Cover and set aside overnight.

The second day, put the fruit and liquid into the sauce pot or kettle and set over high heat. Bring to boiling and cook rapidly for 10 min., stirring frequently to prevent sticking.

Remove from heat and pour into large dish to cool. Cover and set aside overnight.

The third day, wash and sterilize (*page 305*) jelly glasses.

Melt over simmering water about

½ lb. paraffin

Put the fruit into the sauce pot. For *each* cup of raw chopped fruit (as measured on first day) add

4 cups sugar

Put sauce pot over medium heat and stir until sugar is dissolved. Increase heat and cook rapidly, stirring frequently to prevent sticking, until jelly tests done (*page 305*).

Remove from heat and skim off any foam.

Immediately fill the drained jelly glasses and cover with paraffin (*page 305*).

About twelve 8-oz. glasses marmalade

Peach Marmalade

MRS. JAMES C. FAHL, WASHINGTON, D. C.

Set out a large, heavy sauce pot or kettle and three 8-oz. jelly glasses.

Wash and sterilize (*page 305*) jelly glasses.

Rinse, cut off ends and thinly slice (discarding seeds)

1 orange

Set aside.

Rinse and plunge into boiling water (to loosen the skins)

12 medium-size (about 3 lbs.) firm, ripe peaches

Plunge peaches into cold water. Gently slip off skins. Cut the peaches into halves; remove and discard the pits. Coarsely chop peaches (enough to yield 4 cups chopped peaches).

Put peaches and orange into sauce pot with

3 cups sugar

Put sauce pot over medium heat and stir until sugar is dissolved. Increase heat and cook rapidly until clear and thick, stirring frequently to prevent sticking. Length of cooking time will vary with the ripeness and type of peaches.

While marmalade is cooking, melt over simmering water about

¼ lb. paraffin

Remove the marmalade from the heat and skim off any foam.

Immediately fill the drained jelly glasses and cover with paraffin (*page 305*).

About three 8-oz. glasses marmalade

Bread and Butter Pickles I

MRS. E. H. CARLYON, WILLIMANTIC, CONN.

From old New England—A blue-ribbon contender for bread-and-butter-pickle honors.

A large, heavy sauce pot or kettle and three 1-pt. jars and covers will be needed.

Wash thoroughly, drain and cut into ¼-in. slices enough cucumbers to yield

2 qts. (about 16 4- to 5-in.) sliced cucumbers

Thinly slice

2 medium-size onions (*page 6*)

Put the cucumbers and onions into a large bowl and toss with

½ cup coarse salt

Put into a 1-qt. measure for liquids

Ice cubes

Add, bringing water level to the 1-qt. mark

Cold water

Pour the water and cubes over the vegetables. Cover and set aside for 3 hrs.

Wash and sterilize (*page 305*) jars and covers.

Thoroughly drain the vegetables, discarding liquid. Measure into sauce pot or kettle

2 cups sugar
2 cups cider vinegar
2 tablespoons cassia buds
1 tablespoon mustard seed
½ teaspoon turmeric
¼ teaspoon celery seed

Put the sauce pot over medium heat and stir until sugar is dissolved. Increase heat and heat to boiling. Add the drained onions and cucumbers and simmer for 10 min.

Immediately pack the pickles into drained jars and seal tightly (*page 305*).

About 3 pints pickles

Bread and Butter Pickles II

MRS. HERMAN NEBIKER, SR.
CEDAR RAPIDS, IOWA

Another star for the pickle parade comes from the Middle West and merits rave notices from all true pickle fans.

These pickles must stand overnight before their completion.

A large, heavy sauce pot or kettle and four 1-pt. jars and covers will be needed.

Wash thoroughly, drain and cut into ¼-in. slices enough cucumbers to yield

2 qts. (about 16 4- to 5-in.) sliced cucumbers

Put cucumbers into a large bowl and toss with

½ cup coarse salt

Pour over the cucumbers

1 qt. boiling water

Cover and set aside overnight.

The following day, wash and sterilize (*page 305*) jars and covers.

Rinse and coarsely chop enough to yield

2 cups (about 4 medium-size) chopped onion (*page 6*)
2 cups (about 4 medium-size) chopped green pepper (*page 6*)
¾ cup (about 1 large) chopped red pepper

Set aside.

Thoroughly drain cucumbers, discarding liquid. Measure into the large sauce pot or kettle

2 cups cider vinegar
2 cups sugar
1 teaspoon celery seed
1 teaspoon mustard seed
¾ teaspoon turmeric

Put the sauce pot over medium heat and stir until sugar is dissolved. Increase heat and heat to boiling. Add the chopped vegetables and cucumbers and simmer for 5 min.

Immediately pack the pickles into drained jars and seal tightly (*page 305*).

About 4 pints pickles

Candy Pickles

MRS. ELMER P. LEONHARDT
FRANKFORT, IND.

Set out a large, heavy sauce pot or kettle and three 1-pt. jars and covers.

Wash and sterilize (*page 305*) jars and covers.

Wash thoroughly, drain and cut into ¼-in. slices enough cucumbers to yield

2 qts. (about 16 4- to 5-in.) sliced cucumbers

Measure into the large sauce pot or kettle

1½ cups sugar
1 cup cider vinegar
2 tablespoons salt
1 tablespoon mustard seed
1½ teaspoons celery seed
⅛ teaspoon red pepper

Put the sauce pot over medium heat and stir until sugar is dissolved. Increase heat and heat to boiling. Add the cucumbers and simmer for 5 min.

Immediately pack the pickles into drained jars and seal tightly (*page 305*).

About 3 pints pickles

Green Tomato Sweet Pickles

KATE BROOKS, NEW RICHMOND, OHIO

These pickles must stand overnight before completion.

A large, heavy sauce pot or kettle and four 1-pt. jars and covers will be needed.

Rinse, remove stem ends and slice enough green tomatoes to yield

1 gal. (about 7 lbs.) sliced green tomatoes

Measure

1 cup coarse salt

Place one half of the tomatoes in a bowl. Cover with one half of the salt. Add the remaining tomatoes to make a layer. Cover with remaining salt. Cover and set aside overnight.

The following day, wash and sterilize (*page 305*) jars and covers.

Drain tomatoes thoroughly, discarding liquid. Heat to boiling in the sauce pot or kettle, stirring until sugar is dissolved

4 cups cider vinegar
2 cups sugar

Tie together in a spice bag (*page 305*)

4 teaspoons whole cloves
4 teaspoons whole mace
2 3-in. pieces stick cinnamon, broken

Add spice bag to sauce pot. Add the tomatoes and simmer for 10 min.

Immediately pack the pickles into drained jars and cover; seal tightly (*page 305*).

About 4 pints pickles

Spiced Peaches

To obtain a spicier version of these piquant favorites stud each peach with several cloves and add a bit of stick cinnamon to the jar. Here are spiced peaches at their best.

Set out a large, heavy sauce pot or kettle having a cover, and three 1-qt. jars and covers.

Wash and sterilize (*page 305*) jars and covers.

Set out
24 medium-size (about 6 lbs.) firm, ripe peaches
Measure into the sauce pot or kettle
8 cups sugar
2¾ cups cider vinegar
1⅓ cups water
Tie together in a spice bag (*page 305*)
4 3-in. sticks cinnamon
4 teaspoons whole cloves
Add the spice bag and put the sauce pot over medium heat. Stir until sugar is dissolved. Bring mixture to boiling. Cover and boil 5 min. Uncover; cook 5 min. longer. (Enough sirup for three quarts of spiced peaches.)

Meanwhile, rinse and plunge 7 or 8 of the peaches into boiling water to loosen skins. Plunge peaches into cold water. Gently slip off skins. (If desired, cut peaches into halves and remove pits.)

Set out
24 whole cloves
Insert a whole clove into each peach.

Add peaches to hot sirup. Bring to boiling; simmer 10 min., or until peaches are tender.

Quickly drain (*page 305*) one sterilized jar. Pack hot peaches into jar. Cover jar with waxed paper and set aside away from drafts.

Loosen and slip skins from 7 or 8 more peaches and proceed as above. Pack as for first quart. Repeat process for remaining peaches.

Bring sirup to boiling and pour into jars to within ½ in. of top. Seal at once (*page 305*).

About 3 qts. peaches

Cantaloupe Pickles

MRS. ELDEN SAMP, FLANDREAU, S. DAK.

Not as tart as pickles, nor as sweet as preserves—a delightful hybrid flavor.

These pickles must stand overnight before completion.

A large, heavy saucepan, a large heat-resistant dish and three ½-pt. jars and covers will be needed.

Rinse, pare and cut into halves
1 medium-size cantaloupe
Remove and discard seedy center. Cut melon into 1-in. cubes and put into a large bowl.

Mix together until salt is dissolved and pour over the melon cubes
1 qt. water
¼ cup coarse salt
Cover and set aside for 3 hrs.

Drain the melon cubes (discarding liquid).

Measure into a spice bag (*page 305*)
1 tablespoon whole allspice
1 tablespoon whole cloves
1 teaspoon whole mace
1 3-in. piece stick cinnamon, broken
Mix together in saucepan
1 qt. water
4 cups sugar
1 cup white vinegar
Add spice bag to the saucepan and put over medium heat. Stir until sugar is dissolved.

Spiced Peaches: Select only firm, ripe and blemish-free fruit. Wash, handling carefully.

Bring mixture to boiling, reduce heat, cover and boil 10 min. Put cantaloupe in heat-resistant dish. Remove spice bag and pour sirup over the melon. Cool, cover and set the melon mixture aside overnight.

The following day, wash and sterilize (*page 305*) jars and covers.

Drain the melon, reserving the liquid. Put the liquid into the large saucepan and set the pan over high heat. Bring to boiling and cook until sirup is thick. Add the melon and cook rapidly, stirring frequently to prevent sticking, until sirup is thick and melon is clear.

Immediately pack the pickles into drained jars and cover; seal tightly (*page 305*).

About 1½ pints pickles

Watermelon Pickles

MRS. HERMAN NEBIKER, SR.
CEDAR RAPIDS, IOWA

These pickles must stand for 4 days before completion.

Set out a large, heavy sauce pot or kettle and a large, heat-resistant dish. Three 1-pt. jars and covers will be needed.

The first day, set out

1 large, ripe watermelon

Pare and discard outer green rind. Remove pink pulp and set aside for use in other food preparation. Cut enough of the white rind into 1-in. cubes to yield 9 cups watermelon rind. Put rind into sauce pot or kettle and add

6 cups boiling water

Simmer until rind is tender when pierced with a fork. Drain thoroughly and turn into heat-resistant dish.

Combine in a saucepan

4 cups sugar
1 cup white vinegar
¼ teaspoon oil of cinnamon
¼ teaspoon oil of cloves

Put over high heat and bring to boiling, stirring until sugar is dissolved. Pour sirup over rind and set aside to cool. Cover and set aside overnight.

The second day, drain rind, reserving sirup. Heat sirup to boiling. Put rind in the heat-resistant dish and pour sirup over rind. Set aside to cool. Cover and set aside overnight.

The third day, drain rind, reserving sirup. Heat sirup to boiling. Put rind in heat-resistant dish and pour sirup over rind. Set aside to cool. Cover and set aside overnight.

The fourth day, wash and sterilize (*page 305*) jars and covers.

Put rind and sirup in large sauce pot and heat to boiling. If desired, add

1 or 2 drops red or green food coloring

Immediately pack the pickles into drained jars and seal tightly (*page 305*).

About 3 pints pickles

Plunge the peaches first into boiling water and then into cold water to loosen the skins.

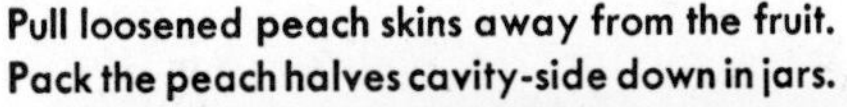

Pull loosened peach skins away from the fruit. Pack the peach halves cavity-side down in jars.

Chili Sauce

CLARK W. CYPHERS, ELNORA, N. Y.

Spicy and full of zest, this Chili Sauce is hot enough to be served with sea-food cocktails. Try it too for a spot of lusty flavor with a roast or with grilled hamburgers.

Set out a large, heavy sauce pot or kettle and three 1-pt. jars and covers.

Rinse

6 lbs. (about 18 medium-size) ripe tomatoes

Taking a few at a time, dip tomatoes into boiling water for several seconds, peel, cut out and discard stem ends. Cut the tomatoes into quarters, discarding the seeds. Coarsely chop the tomatoes (enough to yield 9 cups).

Put through the coarse blade of food chopper and set aside enough to yield

1½ cups (about 3 medium-size) chopped green pepper (*page 6*)
1½ cups (about 3 medium-size) chopped onion (*page 6*)

Finely mince enough for

1 tablespoon hot red pepper

Measure into the large sauce pot or kettle

1½ cups cider vinegar
¾ cup firmly packed brown sugar
1 tablespoon salt

Tie together in a spice bag (*page 305*)

1 teaspoon whole cloves
1 3-in. piece stick cinnamon

Add the spice bag and put the sauce pot over medium heat. Stir until sugar is dissolved.

Bring mixture to boiling. Add the chopped vegetables and cook rapidly until thick, stirring frequently to prevent sticking. Length of cooking time will vary with ripeness of the tomatoes.

While Chili Sauce is cooking, wash and sterilize (*page 305*) jars and covers.

When sauce is thick, skim to remove foam.

Immediately fill drained jars and seal tightly (*page 305*). *About 3 pints Chili Sauce*

Tomato Ketchup

ESTHER C. McCALLISTER, ROCK PORT, ILL.

Set out a large, heavy sauce pot or kettle and three 1-pt. jars and covers.

Rinse

14 lbs. (about 1 peck) firm, ripe tomatoes

Taking a few at a time, dip tomatoes into boiling water for several seconds, peel, cut out and discard stem ends. Cut the tomatoes into quarters, discarding the seeds, and force through coarse sieve or food mill. Measure 4 qts. sieved tomato into sauce pot or kettle.

Tie together in a piece of cheesecloth

2 cups (about 4 medium-size) chopped onion (*page 6*)
½ cup chopped hot red pepper

Put chopped vegetables into sauce pot and add

2 cups sugar
2 cups cider vinegar
1 tablespoon paprika
2 teaspoons salt
1 teaspoon garlic salt

Tie together in a spice bag (*page 305*)

½ teaspoon whole cloves
1 clove garlic (*page 6*)
1 3-in. piece stick cinnamon, broken

Add the spice bag and put the sauce pot over medium heat. Stir until sugar is dissolved. Bring mixture to boiling and cook rapidly until thick (about 1 hr.). Length of cooking time will vary with ripeness of tomatoes.

While ketchup is cooking, wash and sterilize (*page 305*) jars and covers.

When ketchup is thick, skim to remove foam.

Immediately fill drained jars and seal tightly (*page 305*). *About 3 pints ketchup*

Index